Kaplan Publishing are constantly finding new ways to make a difference to yo~~ur studies and our~~ exciting online resources really ~~~~ different to students looking for ~~~~

This book comes with free MyKaplan online resources so that you can study anytime, anywhere. This free online resource is not sold separately and is included in the price of the book.

Having purchased this book, you have access to the following online study materials:

CONTENT	ACCA (including FFA,FAB,FMA)		FIA (excluding FFA,FAB,FMA)	
	Text	Kit	Text	Kit
iPaper version of the book	✓	✓	✓	✓
Interactive electronic version of the book	✓			
Check Your Understanding Test with instant answers	✓			
Material updates	✓	✓	✓	✓
Latest official ACCA exam questions*		✓		
Extra question assistance using the signpost icon*		✓		
Timed questions with an online tutor debrief using the clock icon*		✓		
Interim assessment including questions and answers	✓		✓	
Technical articles	✓	✓	✓	✓

* Excludes F1, F2, F3, FFA, FAB, FMA

How to access your online resources

Kaplan Financial students will already have a MyKaplan account and these extra resources will be available to you online. You do not need to register again, as this process was completed when you enrolled. If you are having problems accessing online materials, please ask your course administrator.

If you are already a registered MyKaplan user go to www.MyKaplan.co.uk and log in. Select the 'add a book' feature and enter the ISBN number of this book and the unique pass key at the bottom of this card. Then click 'finished' or 'add another book'. You may add as many books as you have purchased from this screen.

If you purchased through Kaplan Flexible Learning or via the Kaplan Publishing website you will automatically receive an e-mail invitation to MyKaplan. Please register your details using this email to gain access to your content. If you do not receive the e-mail or book content, please contact Kaplan Flexible Learning.

If you are a new MyKaplan user register at www.MyKaplan.co.uk and click on the link contained in the email we sent you to activate your account. Then select the 'add a book' feature, enter the ISBN number of this book and the unique pass key at the bottom of this card. Then click 'finished' or 'add another book'.

Your Code and Information

This code can only be used once for the registration of one book online. This registration and your online content will expire when the final sittings for the examinations covered by this book have taken place. Please allow one hour from the time you submit your book details for us to process your request.

Please scratch the film to access your MyKaplan code.

Please be aware that this code is case-sensitive and you will need to include the dashes within the passcode, but not when entering the ISBN. For further technical support, please visit www.MyKaplan.co.uk

Paper P4

Advanced Financial Management

EXAM KIT

British Library Cataloguing-in-Publication Data

A catalogue record for this book is available from the British Library.

Published by:

Kaplan Publishing UK

Unit 2 The Business Centre

Molly Millar's Lane

Wokingham

Berkshire

RG41 2QZ

ISBN: 978-1-78415-235-2

© Kaplan Financial Limited, 2015

Printed and bound in Great Britain

Acknowledgements

The past ACCA examination questions are the copyright of the Association of Chartered Certified Accountants. The original answers to the questions from June 1994 onwards were produced by the examiners themselves and have been adapted by Kaplan Publishing.

We are grateful to the Chartered Institute of Management Accountants and the Institute of Chartered Accountants in England and Wales for permission to reproduce past examination questions. The answers have been prepared by Kaplan Publishing.

CONTENTS

Key features in this edition

In addition to providing a wide ranging bank of real past exam questions, we have also included in this edition:

- An analysis of all of the recent examination papers.

- Paper specific information and advice on exam technique.

- Our recommended approach to make your revision for this particular subject as effective as possible.

  This includes step by step guidance on how best to use our Kaplan material (Complete text, pocket notes and exam kit) at this stage in your studies.

- Enhanced tutorial answers packed with specific key answer tips, technical tutorial notes and exam technique tips from our experienced tutors.

- Complementary online resources including full tutor debriefs and question assistance to point you in the right direction when you get stuck.

You will find a wealth of other resources to help you with your studies on the following sites:

www.mykaplan.co.uk

www.accaglobal.com/students/

Quality and accuracy are of the utmost importance to us so if you spot an error in any of our products, please send an email to mykaplanreporting@kaplan.com with full details.

Our Quality Co-ordinator will work with our technical team to verify the error and take action to ensure it is corrected in future editions.

INDEX TO QUESTIONS AND ANSWERS

INTRODUCTION

The majority of the questions within this kit are past ACCA exam questions. The index identifies which sitting the questions were from. An 'A' next to the question in the index means that the past exam question has been adapted in some way, for example some of the past exam questions have been modified to reflect the current format of the exam.

KEY TO THE INDEX

PAPER ENHANCEMENTS

We have added the following enhancements to the answers in this exam kit:

Key answer tips

All answers include key answer tips to help your understanding of each question.

Tutorial note

All answers include more tutorial notes to explain some of the technical points in more detail.

Top tutor tips

For selected questions, we "walk through the answer" giving guidance on how to approach the questions with helpful 'tips from a top tutor', together with technical tutor notes.

These answers are indicated with the "footsteps" icon in the index.

ONLINE ENHANCEMENTS

🕐 *Timed question with Online tutor debrief*

For selected questions, we recommend that they are to be completed in full exam conditions (i.e. properly timed in a closed book environment).

In addition to the examiner's technical answer, enhanced with key answer tips and tutorial notes in this exam kit, online you can find an answer debrief by a top tutor that:

- works through the question in full

- points out how to approach the question

- how to ensure that the easy marks are obtained as quickly as possible, and

- emphasises how to tackle exam questions and exam technique.

These questions are indicated with the "clock" icon in the index.

� *Online question assistance*

Have you ever looked at a question and not known where to start, or got stuck part way through?

For selected questions, we have produced "Online question assistance" offering different levels of guidance, such as:

- ensuring that you understand the question requirements fully, highlighting key terms and the meaning of the verbs used

- how to read the question proactively, with knowledge of the requirements, to identify the topic areas covered

- assessing the detail content of the question body, pointing out key information and explaining why it is important

- help in devising a plan of attack

With this assistance, you should then be able to attempt your answer confident that you know what is expected of you.

These questions are indicated with the "signpost" icon in the index.

Online question enhancements and answer debriefs will be available on MyKaplan at:

www.mykaplan.co.uk

SECTION A-TYPE QUESTIONS

SECTION B-TYPE QUESTIONS

Corporate reconstruction and reorganisation

Treasury and advanced risk management techniques

Economic environment for multinationals

Emerging issues in finance and financial management

KAPLAN PUBLISHING

ANALYSIS OF PAST PAPERS

The table below summarises the key topics that have been tested in recent P4 examinations. The list of topics matches the chapter titles in the Kaplan Complete Text.

Note that the references are to the number of the question in this edition of the exam kit.

TOPIC	Jun 12	Dec 12	Jun 13	Dec 13	Jun 14	Dec 14
The role and responsibility of the financial manager			Q15	Q9	Q22	Q79
Investment appraisal	Q41	Q42			Q43	Q16, Q44
The financing decision	Q31, Q72		Q32			
The dividend decision			Q32			
International operations and international investment appraisal	Q48	Q85		Q9		
International operations - the financing decision and the dividend decision						Q16, Q44
Option pricing	Q14			Q9	Q78	
WACC		Q18	Q15		Q22	
Risk adjusted WACC and APV	Q41	Q18			Q43	
Corporate failure / reconstruction		Q18	Q15	Q57		Q33
An introduction to risk management	Q41	Q42	Q32			Q16, Q44
Hedging foreign exchange risk		Q73	Q76		Q22	
Hedging interest rate risk	Q72			Q77		Q79
Strategic aspects of acquisitions		Q49	Q50	Q51	Q52	Q16
Business valuation	Q14	Q49	Q15, Q50	Q51	Q52	Q16
Topical issues in financial management	Q31, Q48	Q85		Q57		Q79

EXAM TECHNIQUE

- Use the allocated **15 minutes reading and planning time** at the beginning of the exam:
  - read the questions and examination requirements carefully, and
  - begin planning your answers.

  See the Paper Specific Information for advice on how to use this time for this paper.

- **Divide the time** you spend on questions in proportion to the marks on offer:
  - there are 1.8 minutes available per mark in the examination
  - within that, try to allow time at the end of each question to review your answer and address any obvious issues

  Whatever happens, always keep your eye on the clock and **do not over run on any part of any question!**

- Spend the last **five minutes** of the examination:
  - reading through your answers, and
  - **making any additions or corrections**.

- If you **get completely stuck** with a question:
  - leave space in your answer book, and
  - **return to it later.**

- Stick to the question and **tailor your answer** to what you are asked.
  - pay particular attention to the verbs in the question.

- If you do not understand what a question is asking, **state your assumptions**.

  Even if you do not answer in precisely the way the examiner hoped, you should be given some credit, if your assumptions are reasonable.

- You should do everything you can to make things easy for the marker.

  The marker will find it easier to identify the points you have made if your **answers are legible**.

- **Written questions:**

  Your answer should have:
  - a clear structure
  - a brief introduction, a main section and a conclusion.

  Be concise.

  It is better to write a little about a lot of different points than a great deal about one or two points.

- **Computations:**

  It is essential to include all your workings in your answers.

  Many computational questions require the use of a standard format:

  e.g. net present value.

  Be sure you know these formats thoroughly before the exam and use the layouts that you see in the answers given in this book and in model answers.

- **Reports, memos and other documents:**

  Some questions ask you to present your answer in the form of a report, a memo, a letter or other document.

  Make sure that you use the correct format – there could be easy marks to gain here.

PAPER SPECIFIC INFORMATION

THE EXAM

FORMAT OF THE EXAM

		Number of marks
Section A:	1 compulsory question worth 50 marks	50
Section B:	Choice of 2 from 3 questions (25 marks each)	50
		——
		100

Total time allowed: 3 hours, plus 15 minutes for reading and planning

AIM

To apply relevant knowledge, skills and exercise professional judgement as expected of a senior financial executive or advisor, in taking or recommending decisions relating to the financial management of an organisation.

OBJECTIVES

On successful completion of this paper, candidates should be able to:

- explain the role and responsibility of the senior financial executive or advisor in meeting conflicting needs of stakeholders

- evaluate potential investment decisions and assess their financial and strategic consequences, both domestically and internationally

- assess and plan acquisitions and mergers as an alternative growth strategy

- evaluate and advise on alternative corporate re-organisation strategies

- apply and evaluate alternative advanced treasury and risk management techniques

- evaluate the impact of macro economics and recognise the role of international financial institutions in the financial management of multinationals

- identify and assess the potential impact of emerging issues in finance and financial management.

PASS MARK

The pass mark for all ACCA Qualification examination papers is 50%.

READING AND PLANNING TIME

Remember that all three hour paper based examinations have an additional 15 minutes reading and planning time.

ACCA GUIDANCE

ACCA guidance on the use of this time is as follows:

> This additional time is allowed at the beginning of the examination to allow candidates to read the questions and to begin planning their answers before they start to write in their answer books. This time should be used to ensure that all the information and, in particular, the exam requirements are properly read and understood. During this time, candidates may only annotate their question paper. They may not write anything in their answer booklets until told to do so by the invigilator.

KAPLAN GUIDANCE

Since there is a choice of questions in Section B, you must decide which questions to attempt, and in which order.

During the 15 minutes of reading time you should be able to review the questions in Section B and decide which ones are most appealing. All students have different strengths and preferred topics, so it is impossible to give general advice on which questions should be chosen. However, it is worth noting that numerical questions can often be more time consuming than written questions, so you are more likely to over run on numerical questions. Try to choose questions which give a balance between numerical and written elements.

In relation to paper P4, we recommend that you take the following approach with your reading time:

- **Skim through Section B**, assessing the level of difficulty of each question. Try to decide which question looks least appealing and ignore it.

- **Now focus on the other Section B questions** (which, by a process of elimination, you have now decided to attempt). Work out how much time you should spend on each part of the requirements (using the measure of 1.8 minutes per mark). Decide which techniques you will need to attack each of the questions.

- **Turn to Section A**. Skim through the requirements and decide what topics are being tested (e.g. business valuation, NPV).

- **Decide the order** in which you think you will attempt the questions:

  This is a personal choice and you have time on the revision phase to try out different approaches, for example, if you sit mock exams.

  A common approach is to tackle the question you think is the easiest and you are most comfortable with first.

  Others may prefer to tackle the longest question first, or conversely leave it to the last.

  It is usual however that students tackle their least favourite topic and/or the most difficult question in their opinion last. It is sensible to try to attack the preferred questions before attempting the difficult looking ones.

  Whatever your approach, you must make sure that you leave enough time to attempt all questions fully and be very strict with yourself in timing each question.

- **For each question** in turn, read the requirements and then the detail of the question carefully.

  Always read the requirement first as this enables you to **focus on the detail of the question with the specific task in mind**.

  For computational questions:

  Highlight key numbers / information and key words in the question, scribble notes to yourself on the question paper to remember key points in your answer.

  For written questions:

  Take notice of the format required (e.g. letter, memo, notes) and identify the recipient of the answer. You need to do this to judge the level of financial sophistication required in your answer and whether the use of a formal reply or informal bullet points would be satisfactory.

  Plan your beginning, middle and end and the key areas to be addressed and your use of titles and sub-titles to enhance your answer.

  For all questions:

  Spot the easy marks to be gained in a question and parts which can be performed independently of the rest of the question.

  Make sure that you do these parts first when you tackle the question.

  Don't go overboard in terms of planning time on any one question – you need a good measure of the whole paper and a plan for all of the questions at the end of the 20 minutes.

  By covering all questions you can often help yourself as you may find that facts in one question may remind you of things you should put into your answer relating to a different question.

- With your plan of attack in mind, **start answering your chosen question** with your plan to hand, as soon as you are allowed to start.

Always keep your eye on the clock and do not over run on any part of any question!

DETAILED SYLLABUS

The detailed syllabus and study guide written by the ACCA can be found at:

www.accaglobal.com/students/

KAPLAN'S RECOMMENDED REVISION APPROACH

QUESTION PRACTICE IS THE KEY TO SUCCESS

Success in professional examinations relies upon you acquiring a firm grasp of the required knowledge at the tuition phase. In order to be able to do the questions, knowledge is essential.

However, the difference between success and failure often hinges on your exam technique on the day and making the most of the revision phase of your studies.

The **Kaplan complete text** is the starting point, designed to provide the underpinning knowledge to tackle all questions. However, in the revision phase, pouring over text books is not the answer.

Kaplan Online fixed tests help you consolidate your knowledge and understanding and are a useful tool to check whether you can remember key topic areas.

Kaplan pocket notes are designed to help you quickly revise a topic area, however you then need to practise questions. There is a need to progress to full exam standard questions as soon as possible, and to tie your exam technique and technical knowledge together.

The importance of question practice cannot be over-emphasised.

The recommended approach below is designed by expert tutors in the field, in conjunction with their knowledge of the examiner and their recent real exams.

The approach taken for the fundamental papers is to revise by topic area. However, with the professional stage papers, a multi topic approach is required to answer the scenario based questions.

You need to practise as many questions as possible in the time you have left.

OUR AIM

Our aim is to get you to the stage where you can attempt exam standard questions confidently, to time, in a closed book environment, with no supplementary help (i.e. to simulate the real examination experience).

Practising your exam technique on real past examination questions, in timed conditions, is also vitally important for you to assess your progress and identify areas of weakness that may need more attention in the final run up to the examination.

In order to achieve this we recognise that initially you may feel the need to practise some questions with open book help and exceed the required time.

The approach below shows you which questions you should use to build up to coping with exam standard question practice, and references to the sources of information available should you need to revisit a topic area in more detail.

Remember that in the real examination, all you have to do is:

- attempt all questions required by the exam

- only spend the allotted time on each question, and

- get them at least 50% right!

Try to practise this approach on every question you attempt from now to the real exam.

EXAMINER'S COMMENTS

We have included many of the examiner's comments to the examination questions in this kit for you to see the main pitfalls that students fall into with regard to technical content.

However, too many times in the general section of the report, the examiner comments that students had failed due to:

- "misallocation of time"

- "running out of time" and

- showing signs of "spending too much time on an earlier question and clearly rushing the answer to a subsequent question".

Good exam technique is vital.

THE KAPLAN PAPER P4 REVISION PLAN

Stage 1: Assess areas of strengths and weaknesses

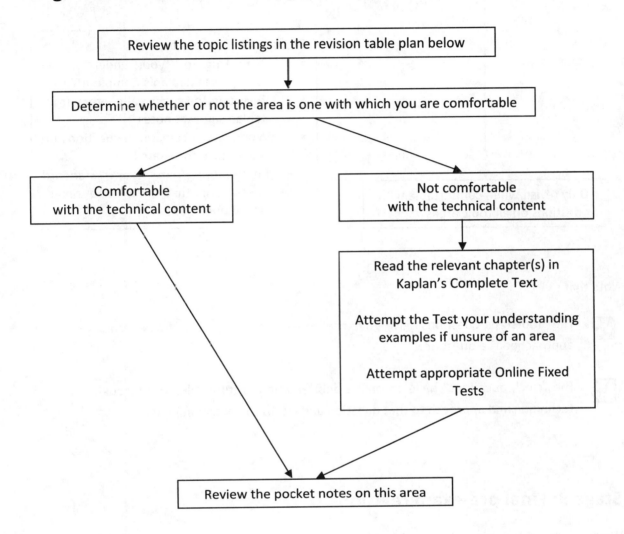

Stage 2: Practise questions

Follow the order of revision of topics as recommended in the revision table plan below and attempt the questions in the order suggested.

Try to avoid referring to text books and notes and the model answer until you have completed your attempt.

Try to answer the question in the allotted time.

Review your attempt with the model answer and assess how much of the answer you achieved in the allocated exam time.

Fill in the self-assessment box below and decide on your best course of action.

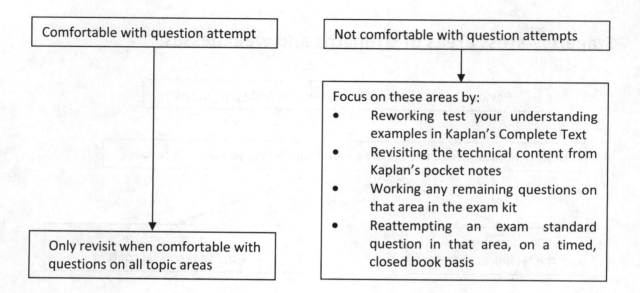

Note that :

The "footsteps questions" give guidance on exam techniques and how you should have approached the question.

The "clock questions" have an online debrief where a tutor talks you through the exam technique and approach to that question and works the question in full.

Stage 3: Final pre-exam revision

We recommend that you **attempt at least one three hour mock examination** containing a set of previously unseen exam standard questions.

It is important that you get a feel for the breadth of coverage of a real exam without advanced knowledge of the topic areas covered – just as you will expect to see on the real exam day.

Ideally this mock should be sat in timed, closed book, real exam conditions and could be a mock examination offered by your tuition provider.

KAPLAN'S DETAILED REVISION PLAN
Module 1: Investment appraisal and WACC

Topic	Complete Text Chapter	Pocket note Chapter	Questions to attempt	Tutor guidance	Date attempted	Self assessment
WACC	8	8	–	Before you can start appraising projects, it is vital to understand how the WACC can be calculated. Notice that several formulae used to derive WACC appear on the formula sheet. Make sure you identify which need to be learned and which are given.		
Investment appraisal	2	2	-	Investment appraisal is very commonly tested. Make sure you understand NPV and MIRR in particular.		
Foreign investment appraisal	5	5	6	Foreign NPV is very similar to "normal" NPV. The parity theories are frequently tested, so learn how to apply the formulae.		
Risk adjusted WACC	9	9	41	Degearing and regearing betas is one of the examiner's favourite topics. The formula is given in the exam, but learn how to apply it.		
APV	9	9	8	APV questions are very common. The key is to remember to discount the investment cash flows at an ungeared cost of equity and the financing cash flows using the risk free rate.		
Module 1 Revision Test			*4, 38, 43*	*Attempt these questions to check your understanding of Module 1 topics.*		

Module 2: Acquisitions and business valuation

Topic	Complete Text Chapter	Pocket note Chapter	Questions to attempt	Tutor guidance	Date attempted	Self assessment
Strategic aspects of acquisitions	14	14	48	Valuation questions tend to contain calculations and discussion. This chapter covers the key discursive aspects.		
Free cash flow analysis	15	15	12, 13	The examiner's favourite method of business valuation is the discounted free cash flow approach, so revise the method from Chapter 15.		
Business valuation	15	15	10	Now cover the other valuation methods. Questions will tend to mix discursive and computational elements, so focus on both aspects.		
Module 2 Revision Test			*16, 50, 51*	*Attempt these questions to check your understanding of Module 1 and 2 topics.*		

KAPLAN PUBLISHING

Module 3: Option pricing, corporate failure and roles / responsibilities of the financial manager

Topic	Complete Text Chapter	Pocket note Chapter	Questions to attempt	Tutor guidance	Date attempted	Self assessment
Option pricing	7	7	58, 36, 40	The Black Scholes formulae are given on the formula sheet, but make sure you can apply them in various circumstances.		
Corporate failure / reconstruction	10	10	56	Following the recent global recession, this is a very topical area, so highly examinable. Learn the indicators of financial distress and the calculation of ratios.		
Roles / responsibilities of the financial manager	1	1	28			
Module 3 Revision Test			*9, 18, 27, 78*	*Attempt these questions to check your understanding of Module 1, 2 and 3 topics.*		

Module 4: Risk management and hedging

Topic	Complete Text Chapter	Pocket note Chapter	Questions to attempt	Tutor guidance	Date attempted	Self assessment
Risk management	11	11	–	Chapter 11 gives a good introduction to risk management topics.		
Hedging – currency risk	12	12	20, 21	Learn the different methods of hedging. The key here is to adapt a systematic approach, laying out your workings carefully so that you don't get muddled.		
Hedging – interest rate risk	13	13	62, 74	As with currency hedging, learn all the methods, and the advantages and disadvantages of using each of them.		
Swaps	12, 13	12, 13	64	Swaps are often overlooked by some students who focus mainly on futures and options. However, they are quite frequently tested – look at Q65 to see how.		
Module 4 Revision Test			**63, 66, 77, 79**	**Attempt these questions to check your understanding of Module 1, 2, 3 and 4 topics.**		

Note that not all of the questions are referred to in the programme above. The remaining questions are available in the kit for extra practice for those who require more questions on some areas.

KAPLAN PUBLISHING

MATHEMATICAL TABLES AND FORMULAE SHEET

Modigliani and Miller Proposition 2 (with tax)

$$k_e = k_e^i + (1 - T)(k_e^i - k_d)\frac{V_d}{V_e}$$

The Capital Asset Pricing Model

$$E(r_i) = R_f + \beta_i(E(r_m) - R_f)$$

The asset beta formula

$$\beta_a = \left[\frac{V_e}{(V_e + V_d(1 - T))}\beta_e\right] + \left[\frac{V_d(1 - T)}{(V_e + V_d(1 - T))}\beta_d\right]$$

The Growth Model

$$P_0 = \frac{D_0(1+g)}{(r_e - g)}$$

Gordon's growth approximation

$$g = br_e$$

The weighted average cost of capital

$$WACC = \left[\frac{V_e}{V_e + V_d}\right]k_e + \left[\frac{V_d}{V_e + V_d}\right]k_d(1 - T)$$

The Fisher formula

$$(1+i) = (1+r)(1+h)$$

Purchasing power parity and interest rate parity

$$S_1 = S_0 \times \frac{(1+h_c)}{(1+h_b)} \qquad F_0 = S_0 \times \frac{(1+i_c)}{(1+i_b)}$$

Modified Internal Rate of Return

$$MIRR = \left[\frac{PV_R}{PV_I}\right]^{\frac{1}{n}} (1 + re) - 1$$

The Black-Scholes option pricing model

$$c = P_a N(d_1) - P_e N(d_2) e^{-rt}$$

Where:

$$d_1 = \frac{\ln(P_a/P_e) + (r + 0.5s^2)t}{s\sqrt{t}}$$

$$d_2 = d_1 - s\sqrt{t}$$

The Put Call Parity relationship

$$p = c - P_a + P_e e^{-rt}$$

MATHEMATICAL TABLES

Standard normal distribution table

	0.00	0.01	0.02	0.03	0.04	0.05	0.06	0.07	0.08	0.09
0.0	.0000	.0040	.0080	.0120	.0159	.0199	.0239	.0279	.0319	.0359
0.1	.0398	.0438	.0478	.0517	.0557	.0596	.0636	.0675	.0714	.0753
0.2	.0793	.0832	.0871	.0910	.0948	.0987	.1026	.1064	.1103	.1141
0.3	.1179	.1217	.1255	.1293	.1331	.1368	.1406	.1443	.1480	.1517
0.4	.1554	.1591	.1628	.1664	.1700	.1736	.1772	.1808	.1844	.1879
0.5	.1915	.1950	.1985	.2019	.2054	.2088	.2123	.2157	.2190	.2224
0.6	.2257	.2291	.2324	.2357	.2389	.2422	.2454	.2486	.2518	.2549
0.7	.2580	.2611	.2642	.2673	.2704	.2734	.2764	.2794	.2823	.2852
0.8	.2881	.2910	.2939	.2967	.2995	.3023	.3051	.3078	.3106	.3133
0.9	.3159	.3186	.3212	.3238	.3264	.3289	.3315	.3340	.3365	.3389
1.0	.3413	.3438	.3461	.3485	.3508	.3531	.3554	.3577	.3599	.3621
1.1	.3643	.3665	.3686	.3708	.3729	.3749	.3770	.3790	.3810	.3830
1.2	.3849	.3869	.3888	.3907	.3925	.3944	.3962	.3980	.3997	.4015
1.3	.4032	.4049	.4066	.4082	.4099	.4115	.4131	.4147	.4162	.4177
1.4	.4192	.4207	.4222	.4236	.4251	.4265	.4279	.4292	.4306	.4319
1.5	.4332	.4345	.4357	.4370	.4382	.4394	.4406	.4418	.4430	.4441
1.6	.4452	.4463	.4474	.4485	.4495	.4505	.4515	.4525	.4535	.4545
1.7	.4554	.4564	.4573	.4582	.4591	.4599	.4608	.4616	.4625	.4633
1.8	.4641	.4649	.4656	.4664	.4671	.4678	.4686	.4693	.4699	.4706
1.9	.4713	.4719	.4726	.4732	.4738	.4744	.4750	.4756	.4762	.4767
2.0	.4772	.4778	.4783	.4788	.4793	.4798	.4803	.4808	.4812	.4817
2.1	.4821	.4826	.4830	.4834	.4838	.4842	.4846	.4850	.4854	.4857
2.2	.4861	.4865	.4868	.4871	.4875	.4878	.4881	.4884	.4887	.4890
2.3	.4893	.4896	.4898	.4901	.4904	.4906	.4909	.4911	.4913	.4916
2.4	.4918	.4920	.4922	.4925	.4927	.4929	.4931	.4932	.4934	.4936
2.5	.4938	.4940	.4941	.4943	.4945	.4946	.4948	.4949	.4951	.4952
2.6	.4953	.4955	.4956	.4957	.4959	.4960	.4961	.4962	.4963	.4964
2.7	.4965	.4966	.4967	.4968	.4969	.4970	.4971	.4972	.4973	.4974
2.8	.4974	.4975	.4976	.4977	.4977	.4978	.4979	.4980	.4980	.4981
2.9	.4981	.4982	.4983	.4983	.4984	.4984	.4985	.4985	.4986	.4986
3.0	.4987	.4987	.4987	.4988	.4988	.4989	.4989	.4989	.4990	.4990

This table can be used to calculate N (d_1), the cumulative normal distribution function needed for the Black-Scholes model of option pricing. If $d_1 > 0$, add 0.5 to the relevant number above. If $d_1 < 0$, subtract the relevant number above from 0.5.

Present value table

Present value of 1, i.e. $(1 + r)^{-n}$

where   r = discount rate

         n = number of periods until payment

Periods (n)	1%	2%	3%	4%	5%	6%	7%	8%	9%	10%
1	0.990	0.980	0.971	0.962	0.952	0.943	0.935	0.926	0.917	0.909
2	0.980	0.961	0.943	0.925	0.907	0.890	0.873	0.857	0.842	0.826
3	0.971	0.942	0.915	0.889	0.864	0.840	0.816	0.794	0.772	0.751
4	0.961	0.924	0.888	0.855	0.823	0.792	0.763	0.735	0.708	0.683
5	0.951	0.906	0.863	0.822	0.784	0.747	0.713	0.681	0.650	0.621
6	0.942	0.888	0.837	0.790	0.746	0.705	0.666	0.630	0.596	0.564
7	0.933	0.871	0.813	0.760	0.711	0.665	0.623	0.583	0.547	0.513
8	0.923	0.853	0.789	0.731	0.677	0.627	0.582	0.540	0.502	0.467
9	0.914	0.837	0.766	0.703	0.645	0.592	0.544	0.500	0.460	0.424
10	0.905	0.820	0.744	0.676	0.614	0.558	0.508	0.463	0.422	0.386
11	0.896	0.804	0.722	0.650	0.585	0.527	0.475	0.429	0.388	0.350
12	0.887	0.788	0.701	0.625	0.557	0.497	0.444	0.397	0.356	0.319
13	0.879	0.773	0.681	0.601	0.530	0.469	0.415	0.368	0.326	0.290
14	0.870	0.758	0.661	0.577	0.505	0.442	0.388	0.340	0.299	0.263
15	0.861	0.743	0.642	0.555	0.481	0.417	0.362	0.315	0.275	0.239

Periods (n)	11%	12%	13%	14%	15%	16%	17%	18%	19%	20%
1	0.901	0.893	0.885	0.877	0.870	0.862	0.855	0.847	0.840	0.833
2	0.812	0.797	0.783	0.769	0.756	0.743	0.731	0.718	0.706	0.694
3	0.731	0.712	0.693	0.675	0.658	0.641	0.624	0.609	0.593	0.579
4	0.659	0.636	0.613	0.592	0.572	0.552	0.534	0.516	0.499	0.482
5	0.593	0.567	0.543	0.519	0.497	0.476	0.456	0.437	0.419	0.402
6	0.535	0.507	0.480	0.456	0.432	0.410	0.390	0.370	0.352	0.335
7	0.482	0.452	0.425	0.400	0.376	0.354	0.333	0.314	0.296	0.279
8	0.434	0.404	0.376	0.351	0.327	0.305	0.285	0.266	0.249	0.233
9	0.391	0.361	0.333	0.308	0.284	0.263	0.243	0.225	0.206	0.194
10	0.352	0.322	0.295	0.270	0.247	0.227	0.208	0.191	0.176	0.162
11	0.317	0.287	0.261	0.237	0.215	0.195	0.178	0.162	0.148	0.135
12	0.286	0.257	0.231	0.208	0.187	0.168	0.152	0.137	0.124	0.112
13	0.258	0.229	0.204	0.182	0.163	0.145	0.130	0.116	0.104	0.933
14	0.232	0.205	0.181	0.160	0.141	0.125	0.111	0.099	0.088	0.078
15	0.209	0.183	0.160	0.140	0.123	0.108	0.095	0.084	0.074	0.065

KAPLAN PUBLISHING

Annuity table

Present value of an annuity of 1, i.e. $\dfrac{1-(1+r)^{-n}}{r}$

where   r = interest rate

           n = number of periods

Periods (n)	1%	2%	3%	4%	5%	6%	7%	8%	9%	10%
1	0.990	0.980	0.971	0.962	0.952	0.943	0.935	0.926	0.917	0.909
2	1.970	1.942	1.913	1.886	1.859	1.833	1.808	.1783	1.759	1.736
3	2.941	2.884	2.829	2.775	2.723	2.673	2.624	2.577	2.531	2.487
4	3.902	3.808	3.717	3.630	3.546	3.465	3.387	3.312	3.240	3.170
5	4.853	4.713	4.580	4.452	4.329	4.212	4.100	3.993	3.890	3.791
6	5.795	5.601	5.417	5.242	5.076	4.917	4.767	4.623	4.486	4.355
7	6.728	6.472	6.230	6.002	5.786	5.582	5.389	5.206	5.033	4.868
8	7.652	7.325	7.020	6.733	6.463	6.210	5.971	5.747	5.535	5.335
9	8.566	8.162	7.786	7.435	7.108	6.802	6.515	6.247	5.995	5.759
10	9.471	8.893	8.530	8.111	7.722	7.360	7.024	6.710	6.418	6.145
11	10.37	9.787	9.253	8.760	8.306	7.887	7.499	7.139	6.805	6.495
12	11.26	10.58	9.954	9.385	8.863	8.384	7.943	7.536	7.161	6.814
13	12.13	11.35	10.63	9.986	9.394	8.853	8.358	7.904	7.487	7.103
14	13.00	12.11	11.30	10.56	9.899	9.295	8.745	8.244	7.786	7.367
15	13.87	12.85	11.94	11.12	10.38	9.712	9.108	8.559	8.061	7.606

Periods (n)	11%	12%	13%	14%	15%	16%	17%	18%	19%	20%
1	0.901	0.893	0.885	0.877	0.870	0.862	0.855	0.847	0.840	0.833
2	1.713	1.690	1.668	1.647	1.626	1.605	1.585	1.566	1.547	1.528
3	2.444	2.402	2.361	2.322	2.283	2.246	2.210	2.174	2.140	2.106
4	3.102	3.037	2.974	2.914	2.855	2.798	2.743	2.690	2.639	2.589
5	3.696	3.605	3.517	3.433	3.352	3.274	3.199	3.127	3.058	2.991
6	4.231	4.111	3.998	3.889	3.784	3.685	3.589	3.496	3.410	3.326
7	4.712	4.564	4.423	4.288	4.160	4.039	3.922	3.812	3.706	3.605
8	5.146	4.968	4.799	4.639	4.487	4.344	4.207	4.078	3.954	3.837
9	5.537	5.328	5.132	4.946	4.772	4.607	4.451	4.303	4.163	4.031
10	5.889	5.650	5.426	5.216	5.019	4.833	4.659	4.494	4.339	4.192
11	6.207	5.938	5.687	5.453	5.234	5.029	4.836	4.656	4.586	4.327
12	6.492	6.194	5.918	5.660	5.421	5.197	4.988	4.793	4.611	4.439
13	6.750	6.424	6.122	5.842	5.583	5.342	5.118	4.910	4.715	4.533
14	6.982	6.628	6.302	6.002	5.724	5.468	5.229	5.008	4.802	4.611
15	7.191	6.811	6.462	6.142	5.847	5.575	5.324	5.092	4.876	4.675

Section 1

PRACTICE QUESTIONS – SECTION A

ROLE AND RESPONSIBILITY TOWARDS STAKEHOLDERS

1 VADENER PLC

Vadener plc, a UK company, has instigated a review of the group's recent performance and potential future strategy. The Board of Directors has publicly stated that it is pleased with the group's performance and proposes to devote resources equally to its three operating divisions. Two of the divisions are in the UK, and focus on construction and leisure respectively, and one is in the USA and manufactures pharmaceuticals.

Recent summarised accounts for the group and data for the individual divisions are shown below:

Statements of profit or loss:

	Group data £ million		
	20X3	20X4	20X5
Revenue	1,210	1,410	1,490
Operating costs	800	870	930
Operating profit	410	540	560
Net interest	40	56	65
Profit before tax	370	484	495
Tax (30%)	111	145	149
Profit after tax	259	339	346
Equity dividends	146	170	185
Retained earnings	113	169	161

Statements of financial position:

Non current assets:			
Tangible assets	1,223	1,280	1,410
Intangible assets	100	250	250
Current assets:			
Inventory	340	410	490
Receivables	378	438	510
Cash	10	15	15
	———	———	———
Total assets	2,051	2,393	2,675
	———	———	———
Shareholders' equity	1,086	1,255	1,406
Long term liabilities	400	410	470
Payables falling due within one year:			
Trade payables	302	401	430
Short term loans	135	170	201
Taxation	55	72	75
Dividends	73	85	93
	———	———	———
	2,051	2,393	2,675
	———	———	———

Note:

The 20X5 amount for shareholders' equity includes a £10 million loss on translation from the US division due to the recent weakness of the $US.

Other group data at year end:	*20X3*	*20X4*	*20X5*
Share price (pence)	1,220	1,417	1,542
Number of issued shares (million)	300	300	300
Equity beta			1.10

The company's share price has increased by an average of 12% per year over the last five years.

Other data at year end:	*20X3*	*20X4*	*20X5*
FT 100 index	3,700	4,600	4,960
PE ratio of similar companies	15:1	14:1	15:1
Risk free rate (%)			5
Market return (%)			12

Divisional data 20X5	*Construction*	*Leisure*	*Pharmaceuticals*
Revenue (£m)	480	560	450
Operating profit	160	220	180
Estimated after tax return (%)	13	16	14

Data for the sector:	*Construction*	*Leisure*	*Pharmaceuticals*
Average asset beta 20X5	0.75	1.10	1.40

Required:

(a) Evaluate and comment on the performance of Vadener plc and each of its divisions. Highlight performance that appears favourable, and any areas of potential concern for the managers of Vadener. Comment upon the likely validity of the company's strategy to devote resources equally to the operating divisions.

All relevant calculations must be shown. Approximately 19 marks are available for calculations, and 9 for discussion.
(28 marks)

Professional marks for format, structure and presentation of the report for part (a).
(4 marks)

(b) Discuss what additional information would be useful in order to more accurately assess the performance of Vadener plc and its divisions.
(7 marks)

(c) Discuss the possible implications for Vadener plc of the £10 million loss on translation, and recommend what action, if any, the company should take as a result of this loss.
(7 marks)

(d) The company has been advised that it can increase income by writing (selling) options. Discuss whether or not this is correct, and provide a reasoned recommendation as to whether or not Vadener plc should adopt this strategy.
(4 marks)

(Total: 50 marks)

ADVANCED INVESTMENT APPRAISAL

2 WURRALL INC

The board of directors of Wurrall Inc has requested the production of a four-year financial plan. The key assumptions behind the plan are:

(i) Historically, sales growth has been 9% per year. Uncertainty about future economic prospects over the next four years from 20X5–8, however, implies that this growth rate will reduce by 1% per year after the financial year 20X5 (e.g. to 8% in 20X6). After four years, growth is expected to remain constant at the 20X8 rate.

(ii) Cash operating costs are estimated to be approximately 68% of sales.

(iii) Tax allowable depreciation for the past few years has been approximately 15% of the net book value of plant and machinery at year end. This is expected to continue for the next few years.

(iv) Inventories, receivables, cash in hand and 'other payables' are assumed to increase in proportion to the increase in sales.

(v) Investment in, and net book value of, plant and machinery is expected to increase in line with sales. No investment is planned in other non-current assets other than a refurbishment of buildings at an estimated cost of $40 million in late 20X7.

(vi) Any change in interest paid as a result of changes in borrowing may be assumed to be effective in the next year. Wurrall plans to meet any changes in financing needs, with the exception of the repayment of the fixed-rate loan, by adjusting its overdraft.

(vii) Wurrall currently pays 7% per annum interest on its short-term borrowing.

(viii) Corporation tax is expected to continue at its present rate over the next four years.

(ix) For the last few years, the company's dividend policy has been to pay a constant percentage of earnings after tax. No changes in this policy are planned.

(x)   Wurrall has borrowed extensively from the banking system, and covenants exist that prevent the company's gearing (book value of total loans to book value of total loans plus equity) exceeding 40% for a period of more than one year.

(xi) The company's managing director has publicly stated that both profits before tax and Wurrall's share price should increase by at least 100% during the next four years.

Summarised financial accounts of Wurrall Inc:

Statement of profit or loss for the year ended March 20X4

	$ (million)
Sales revenue	1,639
Operating costs before depreciation	(1,225)
EBITDA	414
Tax allowable depreciation	(152)
EBIT	262
Net interest payable	(57)
Profit on ordinary activities before tax	205
Tax on ordinary activities (30%)	(62)
Profit after tax	143

Note: Dividends 80

Statement of financial position as at 31 March 20X4

	$ (million)	$ (million)
Non-current assets		
Land and buildings		310
Plant and machinery (net)		1,012
Investments (i)		32
		1,354
Current assets		
Inventory	448	
Receivables	564	
Cash in hand and short-term deposits	20	
		1,032
Total assets		2,386

Equity and liabilities
Called-up share capital (10 cents par)   240
Reserves   864
                                                                            ─────
                                                                            1,104

Non-current liabilities
Borrowings (8% fixed rate) (ii)   580
Current liabilities
Short-term loans and overdrafts   230
Other payables   472
                                                        ─────
                                                                             702
                                                                            ─────
Total equity and liabilities   2,386
                                                                            ─────

(i)   The investments yield negligible interest.

(ii)   Borrowings are scheduled to be repaid at the end of 20X6 and will be refinanced with a similar type of loan in 20X6.

The company's current share price is 210 cents, and its weighted average cost of capital is 11%.

Required:

Prepare a report for the Board of Directors in which you:

(a)   Produce proforma statements of financial position and statements of profit or loss for each of the next four years. Clearly state any assumptions that you make.

(16 marks)

(b)   Critically discuss any problems or implications of the assumptions that are made in each of points (i) to (iv) and point (ix) in the question.   **(8 marks)**

(c)   Using free cash flow analysis, evaluate and discuss whether or not the managing director's claims for the future share price are likely to be achievable. (The operating cash flow element of free cash flow may be estimated by: EBIT(1–T) plus depreciation.)

(10 marks)

(d)   Using financial ratios or other forms of analysis, highlight any potential financial problems for the company during this period. Discuss what actions might be taken with respect to these problems.   **(12 marks)**

Professional marks for format, structure and presentation of the report.   **(4 marks)**

(Total: 50 marks)

3 DARON

Assume that 'now' is December 20X3.

The senior managers of Daron, a company located in a European country, are reviewing the company's medium-term prospects. The company is in a declining industry, and is heavily dependent on a single product. Sales volume is likely to fall for the next few years. A general election will take place in the near future and the managers believe that the future level of inflation will depend upon the result of the election. Inflation is expected to remain at approximately 5% per year if political party A wins the election, or will quickly move to approximately 10% per year if party B wins the election. Opinion polls suggest that there is a 40% chance of party B winning. An increase in the level of inflation is likely to reduce the volume of sales of Daron.

Projected financial data for the next five years, including expected inflation where relevant, are shown below.

Political party A wins, inflation 5% per year

	20X4	20X5	20X6	20X7	20X8
Operating cash flows ($m):					
Sales	28	29	26	22	19
Variable costs	17	18	16	14	12
Fixed costs	3	3	3	3	3
Other financial data:					
Incremental working capital*	–	(1)	(2)	(3)	(3)
Tax allowable depreciation	4	3	3	2	1

Political party B wins, inflation 10% per year

	20X4	20X5	20X6	20X7	20X8
Operating cash flows ($m):					
Sales	30	26	24	20	16
Variable costs	18	16	15	12	11
Fixed costs	3	3	4	4	4
Other financial data:					
Incremental working capital*	1	(2)	(2)	(3)	(3)
Tax allowable depreciation	4	3	3	2	1

*A bracket signifies a decrease in working capital.

Tax allowable depreciation will be negligible after 20X8 in both cases.

Cash flows after year 20X8, excluding tax savings from tax allowable depreciation, are expected to be similar to year 20X8 cash flows for a period of five years, after which substantial new fixed investment would be necessary in order to continue operations.

Working capital will remain approximately constant after the year 20X8.

Corporate taxation is at a rate of 30% per year, and is expected to continue at this rate. Tax may be assumed to be payable in the year that the income arises.

Daron's current ordinary share price is 92 centos (100 centos = $1).

Summarised statement of financial position of Daron Inc as at 31 March 20X3

	$ (million)
Tangible non-current assets	24
Net current assets	12
Total assets less current liabilities	36
Loans and other non-current liabilities	14
Capital and reserves:	
Called-up share capital (25 centos par value)	5
Reserves	17
	36

The company can currently borrow long term from its bank at an interest rate of 10% per year. This is likely to quickly rise to 15.5% per year if the political party B wins the election.

The real risk-free rate (i.e. excluding inflation) is 4% and the real market return is 10%.

Daron's equity beta is estimated to be 1.25. This is not expected to significantly change if inflation increases.

Three alternatives are available to the managers of Daron:

(i)   Recommend the sale of the company now. An informal, unpublicised offer of $20 million for the company's shares has been received from a competitor.

(ii) Continue existing operations, with negligible capital investment for the foreseeable future.

(iii) If the political party A wins the election, diversify operations by buying a going concern in the hotel industry at a cost of $9 million. The purchase would be financed by the issue of 10% convertible debentures. Issue costs are 2% of the gross sum raised. Daron has no previous experience of the hotel industry.

Financial projections of the hotel purchase

	$ (million)				
	20X4	*20X5*	*20X6*	*20X7*	*20X8*
Revenue	9	10	11	12	13
Variable costs	6	6	7	7	8
Fixed costs	2	2	2	2	2
Other financial data:					
Incremental working capital	1	–	–	1	–

Tax allowable depreciation is negligible for the hotel purchase. The after-tax realisable value of the hotel at the end of year 20X8 is expected to be $10 million, including working capital. The systematic risk of operating the hotels is believed to be similar to that of the company's existing operations.

Required:

(a) Using the above data, prepare a report advising the managers of Daron which, if any, of the three alternatives to adopt. Include in your report comment on any weaknesses/limitations of your data analysis. Relevant calculations, including:

(i) estimates of the present values of future cash flows from existing operations, and

(ii) the estimated adjusted present value of diversifying into the hotel industry should form appendices to your report.

The book value and market value of debt may be assumed to be the same. State clearly any other assumptions that you make. (32 marks)

Approximately 20 marks are available for calculations and 12 for discussion.

Professional marks for format, structure and presentation of the report for part (a). (4 marks)

(b) Details of the possible convertible debenture issue for the purchase of the hotel are shown below:

10% $100 convertible debentures 20Y7 (i.e. 14 years from now), issued and redeemable at par. The debentures are convertible into 60 ordinary shares at any date between 1 January 20X9 and 31 December 20Y1. The debentures are callable for conversion by the company subject to the company's ordinary share price exceeding 200 centos between 1 January 20X9 and 31 December 20Y1, and puttable for redemption by the debenture holders if the share price falls below 100 centos between the same dates.

Discuss the implications for Daron if the diversification is financed with convertible debentures with these terms. (8 marks)

(c) The regulation of takeovers varies from country to country. Outline the typical factors that such regulation includes. (6 marks)

(Total: 50 marks)

---

4 SLEEPON HOTELS INC *Walk in the footsteps of a top tutor*

Sleepon Hotels Inc owns a successful chain of hotels. The company is considering diversifying its activities through the construction of a theme park near its capital city. The theme park would have a mixture of family activities and adventure rides. Sleepon has just spent $230,000 on market research into the theme park, and is encouraged by the findings.

The theme park is expected to attract an average of 15,000 visitors per day for at least four years, after which major new investment would be required in order to maintain demand. The price of admission to the theme park is expected to be $18 per adult and $10 per child; 60% of visitors are forecast to be children. In addition to admission revenues, it is expected that the average visitor will spend $8 on food and drinks (of which 30% is profit), and $5 on gifts and souvenirs (of which 40% is profit). The park would open for 360 days per year.

All costs and receipts (excluding maintenance and construction costs and the realisable value) are shown at current prices; the company expects all costs and receipts to rise by 3% per year from current values.

The theme park would cost a total of $400 million and could be constructed and working in one year's time. Half of the $400 million would be payable immediately, and half in one year's time. In addition, working capital of $50 million will be required from the end of year one. The after-tax realisable value of non-current assets is expected to be between $250 million and $300 million after four years of operation.

Maintenance costs (excluding labour) are expected to be $15 million in the first year of operation, increasing by $4 million per year thereafter. Annual insurance costs are $2 million, and the company would apportion $2.5 million per year to the theme park from existing overheads. The theme park would require 1,500 staff costing a total of $40 million per annum (at current prices). Sleepon will use the existing advertising campaigns for its hotels to also advertise the theme park. This will save approximately $2 million per year in advertising expenses.

As Sleepon has no previous experience of theme park management, it has investigated the current risk and financial structure of the closest domestic theme park competitor, Thrillall Inc. Details are summarised below.

Thrillall Inc, summarised statement of financial position

	$ (million)
Non-current assets (net)	1,440
Current assets	570

	2,010

Equity and liabilities	
$1 ordinary shares	400
Reserves	530

	930
Medium- and long-term debt	460
Current liabilities	620

	2,010

Other information:

(i) Sleepon has access to a $450 million Eurodollar loan at 7.5% fixed rate to provide the necessary finance for the theme park.

(ii) $250 million of the investment will attract 25% per year tax allowable depreciation allowances on a reducing balance basis.

(iii) Corporate tax is at a rate of 30%.

(iv) The average stock market return is 10% and the risk-free rate 3.5%.

(v) Sleepon's current weighted average cost of capital is 9%.

(vi) Sleepon's market weighted gearing if the theme park project is undertaken is estimated to be 61.4% equity, 38.6% debt.

(vii) Sleepon's equity beta is 0.70.

(viii) The current share price of Sleepon is 148 cents, and of Thrillall 386 cents.

(ix) Thrillall's medium- and long-term debt comprises long-term bonds with a par value of $100 and current market price of $93.

(x) Thrillall's equity beta is 1.45.

Required:

(a) **Prepare a report analysing whether or not Sleepon should undertake the investment in the theme park. Your report should include a discussion of what other information would be useful to Sleepon in making the investment decision. All relevant calculations must be included in the report or as an appendix to it. State clearly any assumptions that you make.**

Approximately 26 marks are available for calculations and 10 for discussion.

(36 marks)

Professional marks for format, structure and presentation of the report for part (a)

(4 marks)

(b) **Prepare briefing notes for the board of directors discussing issues that might influence the company's capital structure strategy.** **(10 marks)**

(Total: 50 marks)

5   PARTSEA PLC *Walk in the footsteps of a top tutor*

Partsea plc, a UK company, currently exports to a developing country, Hotternia. Hotternia has recently enjoyed a period of sustained economic growth, and inflation has reduced from 60% per year to 10% per year during the last three years. Partsea wishes to expand its sales in Hotternia and is considering either foreign direct investment or a licensing deal with KBD, a large Hotternian company.

Foreign direct investment

Foreign direct investment would involve the purchase of an existing competitor in Hotternia, expansion of its facilities and the introduction of new technologically advanced machinery. A purchase price of 120 million Hotternian dollars ($H) has been agreed for the Hotternian company, in addition to which $H70 million will be needed for expansion of buildings, and $H35 million for working capital. The purchase of the Hotternian company and the working capital outlay would take place immediately, the other cash outflows would occur at the end of year 1. The new machinery will be supplied from the UK parent company at a cost of £4 million, has an expected working life of four years, and will increase the parent company's pre-tax net cash flow in year 1 by £1 million. Tax allowable depreciation is available in Hotternia on the new machinery on a straight line basis at 25% per year from the beginning of year two. The existing Hotternian company has fully depreciated its machinery.

Production and sales is expected to be 1 million units at a price of $H150 per unit in the first year as existing operations continue in the Hotternian company, and 2.5 million units per year for the remainder of Partsea's five-year planning horizon. Sales prices are expected to increase after year 1 in line with Hotternian inflation.

At the end of five years the investment, including working capital, is expected to have a total after tax realisable value of $H150 million.

Variable costs per unit ($H) are expected to be:

	Year 1	Year 2
Labour	35.0	28.6
Materials	33.0	32.0
Distribution	8.0	9.0

Variable costs after year 2 are expected to increase in line with inflation in Hotternia for the relevant year.

Fixed costs in year 1 are expected to be $H23 million, increasing to H$40 million in each of years 2–5.

Semi-finished components for the product will be imported from another of Partsea's subsidiaries in Bottoniland from year 2 onwards at a fixed price of 5 Bottoniland tala (Bt) per unit. 25% of this price represents a profit element to the Bottoniland company.

Licensing

Under a licensing agreement Partsea would permit KBD to manufacture and market its product for an initial period of four years commencing in year 2. Partsea would sell the £4 million new machinery to KBD in year 1, and would also insist on a maintenance contract for the machinery for which it would charge a fixed rate of £500,000 per year. This is double the expected annual cost of maintenance. Partsea would also supply two members of staff to Hotternia to monitor quality control. The cost of these staff (salaries and other expenses) is expected to be £200,000 per year in total at current prices.

KBD would pay Partsea a fee of $H20 per unit for the licence, increasing after year 2 by the rate of inflation in Hotternia. KBD expects to sell 2 million units per year. Partsea would not have a legal presence in Hotternia and would not be liable for Hotternian tax.

Other information:

Exchange rates		$H/£	Bt/£
Spot		15.80	4.2

Forecast inflation rates

Year	UK	Hotternia	Bottoniland
1	2%	10%	5%
2	3%	8%	5%
3	3%	8%	5%
4	3%	8%	5%
5	3%	8%	5%

Corporate taxation is at the rate of 20% per year in Hotternia, and 30% per year in both the UK and Bottoniland. Bilateral tax treaties exist between each pair of countries. Tax is payable in the year that the tax liability arises.

The relevant risk-free rate is 5% and market return 12%. The beta of the proposed foreign direct investment is estimated to be 1.3.

Partsea expects its current exports to Hotternia from the UK to fall by 500,000 units per year, which currently yields a pre-tax net cash flow of £700,000. This would occur with both FDI and licensing.

It is Partsea's policy to remit all available annual cash flows from overseas subsidiaries to the UK.

Required:

Evaluate whether Partsea should expand its sales in Hotternia by using foreign direct investment or licensing. Relevant calculations, and discussion of other information that would assist the investment decision, must be included as part of your evaluation.

State clearly any assumptions that you make. Approximately 31 marks are available for calculations and 9 marks for discussion.

(Total: 40 marks)

Online question assistance

6　BLIPTON INTERNATIONAL　　*Walk in the footsteps of a top tutor*

Timed question with Online tutor debrief

It is now 1 December 20X8. You have been hired as a financial consultant to the Blipton International Entertainment Group which is evaluating a proposal from its hotel division to build a 400 bedroom hotel in the East End of London. This area has developed rapidly over the last 15 years and the prospects have been further enhanced by the announcement that London is to host the 20Y2 Olympics. Blipton is based in Dubai and both reports and accounts for all its transactions in dollars. The current dollar/sterling spot rate is $1.4925/£. The operating costs for the hotel are expected to be £30 per occupied room per day (variable) and a fixed cost of £1.7 million per annum expressed in current prices. The proportion of bedrooms occupied, on the basis of opening for 365 days a year, is expected to be as follows:

Year ended	Occupancy
31 December 20X9	construction
31 December 20Y0	40%
31 December 20Y1	50%
31 December 20Y2	90%
31 December 20Y3	60%
31 December 20Y4	60%

UK inflation is currently projected by the Bank of England as 2.5% per annum and inflation in the United States is 4.8% per annum. These rates are expected to be constant over the term of the project. Blipton's real cost of capital is 4.2%. UK hotel property values within the London area are expected to rise in real terms by 8% per annum.

The construction cost for this hotel is estimated to be £6.2 million and it will be built over the 12 months to 31 December 20X9. As part of the UK's Olympic Development Plan, a 50% first year capital allowance is available for tax purposes on building projects related to the Games. The balance of the capital expenditure can be claimed in equal instalments over the following three years. UK profit tax is 30% and is levied and paid on profits in the year they arise. There is no additional tax liability on remittance to or from Dubai. The company has sufficient UK profits on its other activities to absorb the tax allowable depreciation on this project.

In making investment decisions of this type the company operates the following procedure:

1   All cash flows including construction costs are assumed to arise at the end of the year concerned and are to be projected in nominal (money) terms over the six year period.

2   The residual value of the investment at the end of six years is assumed to be the open market value of the property less a charge for repairs and renewals.

3   The charge for repairs and renewals is expected to be £1.2 million in current prices payable on disposal.

4   The net present value of the project should be based upon a 100% remittance of net cash flows to Dubai and should be calculated in dollars.

5   Average room rates are set at the level required to recover variable cost plus 100%.

Required:

Prepare a report for management to include the following:

(a)   A six year nominal dollar projection of the after tax cash flow for this project distinguishing between cash flows arising from its investment phase and those arising from its return phase.   **(12 marks)**

(b)   An estimate of the project's dollar net present value and the modified internal rate of return.

   Note: you may use the following formula $MIRR = \left[\dfrac{PV_R}{PV_I}\right]^{\frac{1}{n}}(1 + r_e) - 1$

   Where PV_R **is the present value of the return phase of the project,** PV_I **is the present value of the investment phase and** r_e **is the firm's cost of capital.**   **(8 marks)**

(c)   An assessment of the viability of the project with a summary of the relative advantages and disadvantages of the net present value and modified internal rate of return methods in investment appraisal.   **(8 marks)**

   Quality and presentation of the report.   **(2 marks)**

   (Total: 30 marks)

 Calculate your allowed time, allocate the time to the separate parts.

---

7   SEMER

A proposal has been put to the board of directors of Semer that the company should increase its capital gearing to at least 50%, in order to reduce the company's cost of capital and increase its market value.

The managing director of Semer is not convinced by the logic of the proposal, or the accuracy of the calculations, but is unable to explain the reasons for his reservations.

A summary of the proposal and its implications is shown below.

Proposal to increase the capital gearing of Semer

The company's current weighted average cost of capital is estimated to be 10.6%. If the proportion of debt is increased to 50% of total capital, by the repurchase of ordinary shares at their current market value, the cost of capital may be reduced to 9.9%. A reduced cost of capital means that the value of the company will increase which will be welcomed by our shareholders. Calculations supporting the above proposal are shown below:

Existing cost of capital

Cost of equity using the capital asset pricing model:

$4\% + (10.5\% - 4\%)\ 1.2 = 11.8\%$

Cost of debt: 8%

Weighted average cost of capital:

$$11.8\% \times \frac{\$350m}{\$519m} + 8\% \times \frac{\$169m}{\$519m} = 10.56\%$$

Estimated new cost of capital:

$$11.8\% \times \frac{\$259.5m}{\$519m} + 8\% \times \frac{\$259.5m}{\$519m} = 9.90\%$$

Impact on the value of the company:

Current value $\dfrac{\$60m}{0.1056} = \$568$ million

Expected new value $\dfrac{\$60m}{0.099} = \$606$ million

Other information:

(i) Most recent summarised statement of financial position

Semer	$ million
Non current assets (net)	442
Current assets	345
Total assets	787
Issued ordinary shares (50 cents par)	80
Reserves	270
Liabilities falling due after one year:	
Bank loans	119
8% redeemable debenture ($100 par value)	50
Current liabilities	268
Total equity and liabilities	787

(ii) The current price of Semer's ordinary shares is 410 cents.

(iii) The market price of one 8% debenture is $112. The debentures are redeemable in five years.

(iv) The market return is 10.5% and the risk free rate 4.0%.

(v) Semer's equity beta is 1.2.

(vi) Semer currently pays $15 million in dividends.

(vii) The corporate tax rate is 30%.

(viii) The company currently generates a free cash flow of $60 million per year, which is expected to increase by approximately 3% per year.

Required:

(a) **What, if any, are the mistakes in the proposal? Correcting for any mistakes produce revised estimates of the company's *current* cost of capital and *current* value. Brief explanation of the reasons for any revisions should be included.**   **(15 marks)**

(b) **Assuming that the cost of equity and cost of debt do not alter, estimate the effect of the share repurchase on the company's cost of capital and value.**   **(5 marks)**

(c) **Acting as an external consultant to Semer, discuss the validity of the proposed strategy to increase gearing, and explain whether or not the estimates produced in (b) above are likely to be accurate.**   **(10 marks)**

(Total: 30 marks)

8   TRAMONT CO (PILOT 2012)

Tramont Co is a listed company based in the USA and manufactures electronic devices. One of its devices, the X-IT, is produced exclusively for the American market. Tramont Co is considering ceasing the production of the X-IT gradually over a period of four years because it needs the manufacturing facilities used to make the X-IT for other products.

The government of Gamala, a country based in south-east Asia, is keen to develop its manufacturing industry and has offered Tramont Co first rights to produce the X-IT in Gamala and sell it to the USA market for a period of four years. At the end of the four-year period, the full production rights will be sold to a government backed company for Gamalan Rupiahs (GR) 450 million after tax (this amount is not subject to inflationary increases). Tramont Co has to decide whether to continue production of the X-IT in the USA for the next four years or to move the production to Gamala immediately.

Currently each X-IT unit sold makes a unit contribution of $20. This unit contribution is not expected to be subject to any inflationary increase in the next four years. Next year's production and sales estimated at 40,000 units will fall by

20% each year for the following three years. It is anticipated that after four years the production of X-IT will stop. It is expected that the financial impact of the gradual closure over the four years will be cost neutral (the revenue from sale of assets will equal the closure costs). If production is stopped immediately, the excess assets would be sold for $2.3 million and the costs of closure, including redundancy costs of excess labour, would be $1.7 million.

The following information relates to the production of the X-IT moving to Gamala. The Gamalan project will require an initial investment of GR 230 million, to pay for the cost of land and buildings (GR 150 million) and machinery (GR 80 million). The cost of machinery is tax allowable and will be depreciated on a straight line basis over the next four years, at the end of which it will have a negligible value.

Tramont Co will also need GR 40 million for working capital immediately. It is expected that the working capital requirement will increase in line with the annual inflation rate in Gamala. When the project is sold, the working capital will not form part of the sale price and will be released back to Tramont Co.

Production and sales of the device are expected to be 12,000 units in the first year, rising to 22,000 units, 47,000 units and 60,000 units in the next three years respectively.

The following revenues and costs apply to the first year of operation:

- Each unit will be sold for $70

- The variable cost per unit comprising of locally sourced materials and labour will be GR 1,350, and

- In addition to the variable cost above, each unit will require a component bought from Tramont Co for $7, on which Tramont Co makes $4 contribution per unit

- Total fixed costs for the first year will be GR 30 million.

The costs are expected to increase by their countries' respective rates of inflation, but the selling price will remain fixed at $70 per unit for the four-year period.

The annual corporation tax rate in Gamala is 20% and Tramont Co currently pays corporation tax at a rate of 30% per year. Both countries' corporation taxes are payable in the year that the tax liability arises. A bi-lateral tax treaty exists between the USA and Gamala, which permits offset of overseas tax against any US tax liability on overseas earnings. The USA and Gamalan tax authorities allow losses to be carried forward and written off against future profits for taxation purposes.

Tramont Co has decided to finance the project by borrowing the funds required in Gamala. The commercial borrowing rate is 13% but the Gamalan government has offered Tramont Co a 6% subsidised loan for the entire amount of the initial funds required. The Gamalan government has agreed that it will not ask for the loan to be repaid as long as Tramont Co fulfils its contract to undertake the project for the four years. Tramont Co can borrow dollar funds at an interest rate of 5%.

Tramont Co's financing consists of 25 million shares currently trading at $2.40 each and $40 million 7% bonds trading at $1,428 per $1,000. Tramont Co's quoted beta is 1.17. The current risk free rate of return is estimated at 3% and the market risk premium is 6%. Due to the nature of the project, it is estimated that the beta applicable to the project if it is all-equity financed will be 0.4 more than the current all-equity financed beta of Tramont Co. If the Gamalan project is undertaken, the cost of capital applicable to the cash flows in the USA is expected to be 7%.

The spot exchange rate between the dollar and the Gamalan Rupiah is GR 55 per $1. The annual inflation rates are currently 3% in the USA and 9% in Gamala. It can be assumed that these inflation rates will not change for the foreseeable future. All net cash flows arising from the project will be remitted back to Tramont Co at the end of each year.

There are two main political parties in Gamala: the Gamala Liberal (GL) Party and the Gamala Republican (GR) Party. Gamala is currently governed by the GL Party but general elections are due to be held soon. If the GR Party wins the election, it promises to increase taxes of international companies operating in Gamala and review any commercial benefits given to these businesses by the previous government.

Required:

(a) Prepare a report for the Board of Directors (BoD) of Tramont Co that

(i) Evaluates whether or not Tramont Co should undertake the project to produce the X-IT in Gamala and cease its production in the USA immediately. In the evaluation, include all relevant calculations in the form of a financial assessment and explain any assumptions made.

It is suggested that the financial assessment should be based on present value of the operating cash flows from the Gamalan project, discounted by an appropriate all-equity rate, and adjusted by the present value of all other relevant cash flows. **(27 marks)**

(ii) Discusses the potential change in government and other business factors that Tramont Co should consider before making a final decision. **(8 marks)**

Professional marks for format, structure and presentation of the report for part (a). **(4 marks)**

(b) Although not mandatory for external reporting purposes, one of the members of the BoD suggested that adopting a triple bottom line approach when monitoring the X-IT investment after its implementation, would provide a better assessment of how successful it has been.

Discuss how adopting aspects of triple bottom line reporting may provide a better assessment of the success of the X-IT. **(6 marks)**

(c) Another member of the BoD felt that, despite Tramont Co having a wide range of shareholders holding well- diversified portfolios of investments, moving the production of the X-IT to Gamala would result in further risk diversification benefits.

Discuss whether moving the production of the X-IT to Gamala may result in further risk diversification for the shareholders already holding well diversified portfolios. **(5 marks)**

(Total: 50 marks)

9   CHMURA CO (DEC 13)

Since becoming independent just over 20 years ago, the country of Mehgam has adopted protectionist measures which have made it difficult for multinational companies to trade there. However, recently, after discussions with the World Trade Organisation (WTO), it seems likely that Mehgam will reduce its protectionist measures significantly.

Encouraged by these discussions, Chmura Co, a company producing packaged foods, is considering a project to set up a manufacturing base in Mehgam to sell its goods there and in other regional countries nearby. An initial investigation costing $500,000 established that Mehgam had appropriate manufacturing facilities, adequate transport links and a reasonably skilled but cheap work force. The investigation concluded that, if the protectionist measures were reduced, then the demand potential for Chmura Co's products looked promising. It is also felt that an early entry into Mehgam would give Chmura Co an advantage over its competitors for a period of five years, after which the current project will cease, due to the development of new advanced manufacturing processes.

Mehgam's currency, the Peso (MP), is currently trading at MP72 per $1. Setting up the manufacturing base in Mehgam will require an initial investment of MP2,500 million immediately, to cover the cost of land and buildings (MP1,250 million) and machinery (MP1,250 million). Tax allowable depreciation is available on the machinery at an annual rate of 10% on cost on a straight-line basis. A balancing adjustment will be required at the end of year five, when it is expected that the machinery will be sold for MP500 million (after inflation). The market value of the land and buildings in five years' time is estimated to be 80% of the current value. These amounts are inclusive of any tax impact.

Chmura Co will require MP200 million for working capital immediately. It is not expected that any further injections of working capital will be required for the five years. When the project ceases at the end of the fifth year, the working capital will be released back to Chmura Co.

Production of the packaged foods will take place in batches of product mixes. These batches will then be sold to supermarket chains, wholesalers and distributors in Mehgam and its neighbouring countries, who will repackage them to their individual requirements. All sales will be in MP. The estimated average number of batches produced and sold each year is given below:

Year	1	2	3	4	5
Batches produced and sold	10,000	15,000	30,000	26,000	15,000

The current selling price for each batch is estimated to be MP115,200. The costs related to producing and selling each batch are currently estimated to be MP46,500. In addition to these costs, a number of products will need a special packaging material which Chmura Co will send to Mehgam. Currently the cost of the special packaging material is $200 per batch. Training and development costs, related to the production of the batches, are estimated to be 80% of the production and selling costs (excluding the cost of the special packaging) in the first year, before falling to 20% of these costs (excluding the cost of the special packaging) in the second year, and then nil for the remaining years. It is expected that the costs relating to the production and sale of each batch will increase annually by 10% but the selling price and the special packaging costs will only increase by 5% every year.

The current annual corporation tax rate in Mehgam is 25% and Chmura Co pays annual corporation tax at a rate of 20% in the country where it is based. Both countries' taxes are payable in the year that the tax liability arises. A bi-lateral tax treaty exists between the two countries which permits offset of overseas tax against any tax liabilities Chmura Co incurs on overseas earnings.

The risk-adjusted cost of capital applicable to the project on $-based cash flows is 12%, which is considerably higher than the return on short-dated $ treasury bills of 4%. The current rate of inflation in Mehgam is 8%, and in the country where Chmura Co is based, it is 2%. It can be assumed that these inflation rates will not change for the foreseeable future. All net cash flows from the project will be remitted back to Chmura Co at the end of each year.

Chmura Co's finance director is of the opinion that there are many uncertainties surrounding the project and has assessed that the cash flows can vary by a standard deviation of as much as 35% because of these uncertainties.

Recently Bulud Co offered Chmura Co the option to sell the entire project to Bulud Co for $28 million at the start of year three. Chmura Co will make the decision of whether or not to sell the project at the end of year two.

Required:

(a) Discuss the role of the World Trade Organisation (WTO) and the possible benefits and drawbacks to Mehgam of reducing protectionist measures. **(9 marks)**

(b) Prepare an evaluative report for the Board of Directors of Chmura Co which addresses the following parts and recommends an appropriate course of action:

   (i) An estimate of the value of the project before considering Bulud Co's offer. Show all relevant calculations **(14 marks)**

   (ii) An estimate of the value of the project taking into account Bulud Co's offer. Show all relevant calculations **(9 marks)**

   (iii) A discussion of the assumptions made in parts (i) and (ii) above and the additional business risks which Chmura Co should consider before it makes the final decision whether or not to undertake the project. **(14 marks)**

   Professional marks will be awarded in part (b) for the format, structure and presentation of the report. **(4 marks)**

   (Total: 50 marks)

ACQUISITIONS AND MERGERS

10 STANZIAL INC

Stanzial Inc is a listed telecommunications company. The company is considering the purchase of Besserlot Co, an unlisted company that has developed, patented and marketed a secure, medium-range, wireless link to broadband. The wireless link is expected to increase Besserlot's revenue by 25% per year for three years, and by 10% per year thereafter. Besserlot is currently owned 35% by its senior managers, 30% by a venture capital company, 25% by a single shareholder on the board of directors, and 10% by about 100 other private investors.

Summarised accounts for Besserlot for the last two years are shown below:

Statements of profit or loss for the years ended 31 March ($000)

	20X6	20X5
Sales revenue	22,480	20,218
Operating profit before exceptional items	1,302	820
Exceptional items	(2,005)	–
Interest paid (net)	(280)	(228)
Profit before taxation	(983)	592
Taxation	(210)	(178)
Profit after taxation	(1,193)	414
Note: Dividend	200	100

Statements of financial position as at 31 March ($000)

	20X6	*20X5*
Non-current assets (net)		
Tangible assets	5,430	5,048
Goodwill	170	200
Current assets		
Inventory	3,400	2,780
Receivables falling due within one year	2,658	2,462
Receivables falling due after one year	100	50
Cash at bank and in hand	48	48
Total assets	11,806	10,588
Equity and liabilities		
Called-up share capital (25 cents par)	2,000	1,000
Retained profits	3,037	4,430
Other reserves	1,249	335
Total equity	6,286	5,765
Current liabilities – payables	5,520	4,823
	11,806	10,588

Other information relating to Besserlot:

(i) Non-cash expenses, including depreciation, were $820,000 in 20X5–6.

(ii) Corporate taxation is at the rate of 30% per year.

(iii) Capital investment was $1 million in 20X5–6, and is expected to grow at approximately the same rate as revenue.

(iv) Working capital, interest payments and non-cash expenses are expected to increase at the same rate as revenue.

(v) The estimated value of the patent if sold now is $10 million. This has not been included in non-current assets.

(vi) Operating profit is expected to be approximately 8% of revenue in 20X6–7, and to remain at the same percentage in future years.

(vii) Dividends are expected to grow at the same rate as revenue.

(viii) The realisable value of existing inventory is expected to be 70% of its book value.

(ix) The estimated cost of equity of Besserlot is 14%.

Information regarding the industry sector of Besserlot:

(i) The average PE ratio of listed companies of similar size to Besserlot is 30:1.

(ii) Average earnings growth in the industry is 6% per year.

Required:

(a) Estimate the value of Besserlot Co using:

   (i)   Asset based valuation

   (ii) PE ratios

   (iii) Dividend based valuation

   (iv) The present value of expected future cash flows.

   Discuss the potential accuracy of each of the methods used and recommend, with reasons, a value, or range of values that Stanzial might bid for Besserlot.

   State clearly any assumptions that you make.   (27 marks)

   (Approximately 16 marks are available for calculations and 11 marks for discussion.)

(b) Discuss how the shareholder mix of Besserlot and type of payment used might influence the success or failure of the bid.   (8 marks)

(c) Assuming that the bid was successful, discuss other factors that might influence the medium-term financial success of the acquisition.   (5 marks)

   (Total: 40 marks)

11 BURCOLENE *Walk in the footsteps of a top tutor*

Burcolene is a large European-based petrochemical manufacturer, with a wide range of basic bulk chemicals in its product range and with strong markets in Europe and the Pacific region. In recent years, margins have fallen as a result of competition from China and, more importantly, Eastern European countries that have favourable access to the Russian petrochemical industry. However, the company has managed to sustain a 5% growth rate in earnings through aggressive management of its cost base, the management of its risk and careful attention to its value base.

As part of its strategic development, Burcolene is considering a leveraged (debt-financed) acquisition of PetroFrancais, a large petrochemical business that has engaged in a number of high quality alliances with oil drilling and extraction companies in the newly opened Russian Arctic fields. However, the growth of the company has not been particularly strong in recent years, although Burcolene believes that an expected long term growth of 4% per annum is realistic under its current management.

Preliminary discussions with its banks have led Burcolene to the conclusion that an acquisition of 100% of the equity of PetroFrancais, financed via a bond issue, would not have a significant impact upon the company's existing credit rating. The key issues, according to the company's advisors, are the terms of the deal and the likely effect of the acquisition on the company's value and its financial leverage.

Both companies are quoted on an international stock exchange and below are relevant data relating to each company:

Financial data as at 30 November 20X7

	Burcolene	PetroFrancais
Market value of debt in issue ($bn)	3.30	5.80
Market value of equity in issue ($bn)	9.90	6.70
Number of shares in issue (million)	340.00	440.00
Share options outstanding (million)	25.40	–
Exercise price of options ($ per share)	22.00	–
Company tax rate (%)	30.00	25.00
Equity beta	1.85	0.95
Default risk premium	1.6%	3.0%
Net operating profit after tax and net reinvestment ($ million)	450.00	205.00
Current EPS ($ per share)	1.19	0.44

The global equity risk premium is 4.0% and the most appropriate risk free rate derived from the returns on government stock is 3.0%.

Burcolene has a share option scheme as part of its executive remuneration package. In accordance with the accounting standards, the company has expensed its share options at fair value. The share options held by the employees of Burcolene were granted on 1 January 20X4. The vesting date is 30 November 20X9 and the exercise date is 30 November 20Y0. Currently, the company has a 5% attrition rate as members leave the company and, of those remaining at the vesting date, 20% are expected not to have achieved the standard of performance required. Your estimate is that the options have a time value of $7.31.

PetroFrancais operates a defined benefits pension scheme which, at its current actuarial valuation, shows a deficit of $430 million.

You have been appointed to advise the senior management team of Burcolene on the validity of the free cash flow to equity model as a basis for valuing both firms and on the financial implications of this acquisition for Burcolene. Following your initial discussions with management, you decide that the following points are relevant:

1   The free cash flow to all classes of capital invested can be reliably approximated as net operating profit after tax (NOPAT) less net reinvestment.

2   Given the rumours in the market concerning a potential acquisition, the existing market valuations may not fully reflect each company's value.

3   The acquisition would be financed by a new debt issue by Burcolene.

Required:

(a)   Estimate the weighted average cost of capital and the current entity value for each business, taking into account the impact of the share option scheme and the pension fund deficit on the value of each company.   (16 marks)

(b)   Write a report for management, advising them on:

(i)   The validity of the free cash flow model, given the growth rate assumptions made by management for both firms

(ii)   The most appropriate method of deriving a bid price; and

(iii)   The implications of an acquisition such as this for Burcolene's gearing and cost of capital.   (16 marks)

Professional marks for format, structure and presentation of the report for part (b)
(4 marks)

(c)   The managers of Burcolene are also discussing whether or not to set up a foreign subsidiary in a South American country. The government of the country has recently changed, and the country's new leaders have stated that they intend to introduce economic policies to improve the balance of payments. Burcolene is concerned that one of these measures could be to block the remittance of dividends from the South American country to Europe. Burcolene expects to remit about 180 million pesos per year to Europe if the government does not intervene. Blocked funds may be invested internally within the South American country, but the government is likely to control domestic interest rates.

The investment in the South American subsidiary has an expected NPV of $2 million. The peso is expected to devalue by approximately 10% per year relative to the $. Burcolene used a discount rate of 20% per year in the appraisal of its South American capital investment. The current spot exchange rate is 20 pesos/$1.

Required:

(i)   **Assuming that the government blocks the remittance of dividends for a period of three years, estimate the approximate interest rate that would have to exist in the South American country for the proposed investment to remain financially viable. Taxation may be ignored.**   **(8 marks)**

(ii)   **Briefly discuss methods by which Burcolene might try to avoid the block on the remittance of dividends.**   **(6 marks)**

(Total: 50 marks)

12   ANCHORAGE RETAIL COMPANY

Anchorage Retail Company is a large high street and on-line retailer that has lost its position as the premier quality clothes, household goods and food chain in the European market. Five years previously there had been speculation that the company would be a takeover target for any one of a number of private equity firms. However, a newly appointed and flamboyant Chief Executive Officer, John Bear, initiated a major capital reconstruction and a highly aggressive turnaround strategy.

The reaction to that turnaround strategy was an improvement in the company's share price from $3 to $7 per share over the subsequent three years. The private equity firms who had been interested in acquiring the company were deterred for two principal reasons. First John Bear had a reputation for his aggressive style and his history of defending his companies against takeover. Second the share price of Anchorage had reached a record high.

In recent months a belief in the investment community had become widespread that the revival of the company's performance had more to do with the reorganisation of the firm's capital than the success of John Bear's turnaround strategy. John Bear insisted, however, that the improvements in the reported 'bottom line' reflected a sustainable improvement in the performance of the business. However, the recent recession in the European retail market following the 'credit crunch' led to a sharp reduction in Anchorage's share price reinforced by concerns in the financial markets that John Bear has become too dominant in the board of the company.

The most recent accounts for Anchorage Retail, in summary form, are as follows:

Anchorage Retail Company

	20X9 $m	20X8 $m		20X9 $m
Statement of profit or loss			**Summary cash flow statement**	
Sales revenue	9,000	8,500		
Cost of sales	5,500	5,250	Operating cash flow	1,610
Gross profit	3,500	3,250	Less interest	(110)
Less other operating costs	2,250	2,220	Less taxation	(270)
Operating profit	1,250	1,030	Free cash flow before reinvestment	1,230
Finance costs	80	110	Dividend paid	(270)
Profit before tax	1,170	920	CAPEX	(740)
Income tax expense (at 30%)	310	270	Financing	(70)
Profit for the period	860	650	Net cash flow	150

Statement of financial position	20X9 $m	20X8 $m
Assets		
Non-current assets	4,980	4,540
Current assets	1,220	850
Total assets	6,200	5,390
Equity and Liabilities		
Ordinary share capital (25c)	400	425
Share premium	230	200
Capital redemption reserve	2,300	2,300
Other reserves	(6,540)	(6,500)
Retained earnings	5,990	5,400
Dividends payable	(350)	(270)
Total equity	2,030	1,555
Non-current liabilities	1,900	1,865
Current liabilities	2,270	1,970
Total equity and liabilities	6,200	5,390

The management of Polar Finance, a large private equity investment fund, has begun a review following the sale of a substantial part of its investment portfolio. It is now considering Anchorage as a potential target for acquisition. They have contacted you and asked if you would provide a brief report on the financial performance of Anchorage Retail and give an independent view on a bid the company is considering for the business. The suggested bid would be in the form of a cash offer of $3.20 a share which would represent a 60¢ premium on the current share price. Reviewing the fund's existing business portfolio prior to acquisition you estimate that its asset beta is 0.285. Polar Finance has equity funds under management of $1,125 million and a market based gearing ratio (debt as a proportion of total capital employed) of 0.35. This acquisition would be financed from additional cash resources and by additional borrowing of $2.5 billion. It is expected that Anchorage's proportion of the total post-acquisition cash flows will be 20%. Polar Finance does not pay tax on its income.

During your investigations you discover the following:

(1) The equity beta for Anchorage is 0.75. The current risk free rate is 5%. In order to estimate the rate of return on the market using the dividend growth model you note that the current dividend yield on a broadly based market index is 3.1% and the growth in GDP is 4% nominal. The growth of the firms in the index is fairly represented by growth in GDP.

(2) Anchorage has a gearing ratio based upon market capitalisation of 24%. You estimate that its current cost of debt capital is 6.2%. You may assume that Anchorage's cost of finance has been constant over the last twelve months.

You may use year end statement of financial position values when calculating performance ratios.

Required:

Prepare a report for Polar Finance:

(a) **Outlining the principal risks that Polar Finance should consider when assessing an acquisition of this size.** **(6 marks)**

(b) **Summarising the performance of Anchorage in 20X9 compared with 20X8 on the basis of the EVA® for each year and using two other ratios you consider appropriate.** **(12 marks)**

(c) **Estimating the impact of this acquisition upon the required rate of return of equity investors in Polar Finance.** **(6 marks)**

(d) **Evaluating the argument that this company may have been systematically undervalued by the market and therefore a suitable target for acquisition.** **(4 marks)**

Professional marks will be awarded for the appropriateness of the format and presentation of the report and the effectiveness with which its advice is communicated. **(4 marks)**

(Total: 32 marks)

13 PURSUIT CO (JUN 11)

Pursuit Co, a listed company which manufactures electronic components, is interested in acquiring Fodder Co, an unlisted company involved in the development of sophisticated but high risk electronic products. The owners of Fodder Co are a consortium of private equity investors who have been looking for a suitable buyer for their company for some time. Pursuit Co estimates that a payment of the equity value plus a 25% premium would be sufficient to secure the purchase of Fodder Co. Pursuit Co would also pay off any outstanding debt that Fodder Co owed. Pursuit Co wishes to acquire Fodder Co using a combination of debt finance and its cash reserves of $20 million, such that the capital structure of the combined company remains at Pursuit Co's current capital structure level.

Information on Pursuit Co and Fodder Co

Pursuit Co

Pursuit Co has a market debt to equity ratio of 50:50 and an equity beta of 1.18. Currently Pursuit Co has a total firm value (market value of debt and equity combined) of $140 million.

Fodder Co, Statement of profit or loss extracts

Year Ended	31 May 20Y1	31 May 20Y0	31 May 20X9	31 May 20X8
All amounts are in $000				
Sales revenue	16,146	15,229	14,491	13,559
Operating profit (after operating costs and tax allowable depreciation)	5,169	5,074	4,243	4,530
Net interest costs	489	473	462	458
Profit before tax	4,680	4,601	3,781	4,072
Taxation (28%)	1,310	1,288	1,059	1,140
After tax profit	3,370	3,313	2,722	2,932
Dividends	123	115	108	101
Retained earnings	3,247	3,198	2,614	2,831

Fodder Co has a market debt to equity ratio of 10:90 and an estimated equity beta of 1.53. It can be assumed that its tax allowable depreciation is equivalent to the amount of investment needed to maintain current operational levels. However, Fodder Co will require an additional investment in assets of 22c per $1 increase in sales revenue, for the next four years. It is anticipated that Fodder Co will pay interest at 9% on its future borrowings.

For the next four years, Fodder Co's sales revenue will grow at the same average rate as the previous years. After the forecasted four-year period, the growth rate of its free cash flows will be half the initial forecast sales revenue growth rate for the foreseeable future.

Information about the combined company

Following the acquisition, it is expected that the combined company's sales revenue will be $51,952,000 in the first year, and its profit margin on sales will be 30% for the foreseeable future. After the first year the growth rate in sales revenue will be 5.8% per year for the following three years. Following the acquisition, it is expected that the combined company will pay annual interest at 6.4% on future borrowings.

The combined company will require additional investment in assets of $513,000 in the first year and then 18c per $1 increase in sales revenue for the next three years. It is anticipated that after the forecasted four-year period, its free cash flow growth rate will be half the sales revenue growth rate.

It can be assumed that the asset beta of the combined company is the weighted average of the individual companies' asset betas, weighted in proportion of the individual companies' market value.

Other information

The current annual government base rate is 4.5% and the market risk premium is estimated at 6% per year. The relevant annual tax rate applicable to all the companies is 28%.

SGF Co's interest in Pursuit Co

There have been rumours of a potential bid by SGF Co to acquire Pursuit Co. Some financial press reports have suggested that this is because Pursuit Co's share price has fallen recently. SGF Co is in a similar line of business as Pursuit Co and until a couple of years ago, SGF Co was the smaller company. However, a successful performance has resulted in its share price rising, and SGF Co is now the larger company.

The rumours of SGF Co's interest have raised doubts about Pursuit Co's ability to acquire Fodder Co. Although SGF Co has made no formal bid yet, Pursuit Co's board is keen to reduce the possibility of such a bid. The Chief Financial Officer has suggested that the most effective way to reduce the possibility of a takeover would be to distribute the $20 million in its cash reserves to its shareholders in the form of a special dividend. Fodder Co would then be purchased using debt finance. He conceded that this would increase Pursuit Co's gearing level but suggested it may increase the company's share price and make Pursuit Co less appealing to SGF Co.

Required:

Prepare a report to the Board of Directors of Pursuit Co that

(i) **Evaluates whether the acquisition of Fodder Co would be beneficial to Pursuit Co and its shareholders. The free cash flow to firm method should be used to estimate the values of Fodder Co and the combined company assuming that the combined company's capital structure stays the same as that of Pursuit Co's current capital structure. Include all relevant calculations** **(16 marks)**

(ii) **Discusses the limitations of the estimated valuations in part (i) above** **(4 marks)**

(iii) **Estimates the amount of debt finance needed, in addition to the cash reserves, to acquire Fodder Co and concludes whether Pursuit Co's current capital structure can be maintained** **(3 marks)**

(iv) **Explains the implications of a change in the capital structure of the combined company, to the valuation method used in part (i) and how the issue can be resolved** **(4 marks)**

(v) **Assesses whether the Chief Financial Officer's recommendation would provide a suitable defence against a bid from SGF Co and would be a viable option for Pursuit Co.** **(5 marks)**

Professional marks will be awarded in this question for the format, structure and presentation of the report. **(4 marks)**

(Total: 36 marks)

14   NENTE CO (JUN 12)

Nente Co, an unlisted company, designs and develops tools and parts for specialist machinery. The company was formed four years ago by three friends, who own 20% of the equity capital in total, and a consortium of five business angel organisations, who own the remaining 80%, in roughly equal proportions. Nente Co also has a large amount of debt finance in the form of variable rate loans. Initially the amount of annual interest payable on these loans was low and allowed Nente Co to invest internally generated funds to expand its business. Recently though, due to a rapid increase in interest rates, there has been limited scope for future expansion and no new product development.

The Board of Directors, consisting of the three friends and a representative from each business angel organisation, met recently to discuss how to secure the company's future prospects. Two proposals were put forward, as follows:

Proposal 1

To accept a takeover offer from Mije Co, a listed company, which develops and manufactures specialist machinery tools and parts. The takeover offer is for $2.95 cash per share or a share-for-share exchange where two Mije Co shares would be offered for three Nente Co shares. Mije Co would need to get the final approval from its shareholders if either offer is accepted:

Proposal 2

To pursue an opportunity to develop a small prototype product that just breaks even financially, but gives the company exclusive rights to produce a follow-on product within two years.

The meeting concluded without agreement on which proposal to pursue.

After the meeting, Mije Co was consulted about the exclusive rights. Mije Co's directors indicated that they had not considered the rights in their computations and were willing to continue with the takeover offer on the same terms without them.

Currently, Mije Co has 10 million shares in issue and these are trading for $4.80 each. Mije Co's price to earnings (P/E) ratio is 15. It has sufficient cash to pay for Nente Co's equity and a substantial proportion of its debt, and believes that this will enable Nente Co to operate on a P/E level of 15 as well. In addition to this, Mije Co believes that it can find cost-based synergies of $150,000 after tax per year for the foreseeable future. Mije Co's current profit after tax is $3,200,000.

The following financial information relates to Nente Co and to the development of the new product.

Nente Co financial information

Extract from the most recent statement of profit or loss

	$000
Sales revenue	8,780
Profit before interest and tax	1,230
Interest	(455)
Tax	(155)
Profit after tax	620
Dividends	Nil

Extract from the most recent statement of financial position

	$000
Net non-current assets	10,060
Current assets	690
Total Assets	10,750
Share capital (40c per share par value)	960
Reserves	1,400
Non-current liabilities: Variable rate loans	6,500
Current liabilities	1,890
Total liabilities and capital	10,750

In arriving at the profit after tax amount, Nente Co deducted tax allowable depreciation and other non-cash expenses totalling $1,206,000. It requires an annual cash investment of $1,010,000 in non-current assets and working capital to continue its operations.

Nente Co's profits before interest and tax in its first year of operation were $970,000 and have been growing steadily in each of the following three years, to their current level. Nente Co's cash flows grew at the same rate as well, but it is likely that this growth rate will reduce to 25% of the original rate for the foreseeable future.

Nente Co currently pays interest of 7% per year on its loans, which is 380 basis points over the government base rate, and corporation tax of 20% on profits after interest. It is estimated that an overall cost of capital of 11% is reasonable compensation for the risk undertaken on an investment of this nature.

New product development (Proposal 2)

Developing the new follow-on product will require an investment of $2,500,000 initially. The total expected cash flows and present values of the product over its five-year life, with a volatility of 42% standard deviation, are as follows:

Year(s)	Now	1	2	3 to 7 (in total)
Cash flows ($000)	–	–	(2,500)	3,950
Present values ($000)	–	–	(2,029)	2,434

Required:

Prepare a report for the Board of Directors of Nente Co that:

(i) Estimates the current value of a Nente Co share, using the free cash flow to firm methodology (7 marks)

(ii) Estimates the percentage gain in value to a Nente Co share and a Mije Co share under each payment offer (8 marks)

(iii) Estimates the percentage gain in the value of the follow-on product to a Nente Co share, based on its cash flows and on the assumption that the production can be delayed following acquisition of the exclusive rights of production (8 marks)

(iv) Discusses the likely reaction of Nente Co and Mije Co shareholders to the takeover offer, including the assumptions made in the estimates above and how the follow-on product's value can be utilised by Nente Co. (8 marks)

Professional marks will be awarded in this question for the presentation, structure and clarity of the answer. (4 marks)

(Total: 35 marks)

15 MLIMA CO (JUN 13)

Mlima Co is a private company involved in aluminium mining. About eight years ago, the company was bought out by its management and employees through a leveraged buyout (LBO). Due to high metal prices worldwide, the company has been growing successfully since the LBO. However, because the company has significant debt borrowings with strict restrictive covenants and high interest levels, it has had to reject a number of profitable projects. The company has currently two bonds in issue, as follows:

A 16% secured bond with a nominal value of $80m, which is redeemable at par in five years. An early redemption option is available on this bond, giving Mlima Co the option to redeem the bond at par immediately if it wants to; and

A 13% unsecured bond with a nominal value of $40m, which is redeemable at par in ten years.

Mlima Co's Board of Directors (BoD) has been exploring the idea of redeeming both bonds to provide it with more flexibility when making future investment decisions. To do so, the BoD has decided to consider a public listing of the company on a major stock exchange. It is intended that a total of 100 million shares will be issued in the newly-listed company. From the total shares, 20% will be sold to the public, 10% will be offered to the holders of the unsecured bond in exchange for redeeming the bond through an equity-for-debt swap, and the remaining 70% of the equity will remain in the hands of the current owners. The secured bond would be paid out of the funds raised from the listing.

The details of the possible listing and the distribution of equity were published in national newspapers recently. As a result, potential investors suggested that due to the small proportion of shares offered to the public and for other reasons, the shares should be offered at a substantial discount of as much as 20% below the expected share price on the day of the listing.

Mlima Co, financial information

It is expected that after the listing, deployment of new strategies and greater financial flexibility will boost Mlima Co's future sales revenue and, for the next four years, the annual growth rate will be 120% of the previous two years' average growth rate. After the four years, the annual growth rate of the free cash flows to the company will be 3.5%, for the foreseeable future. Operating profit margins are expected to be maintained in the future. Although it can be assumed that the current tax-allowable depreciation is equivalent to the amount of investment needed to maintain the current level of operations, the company will require an additional investment in assets of 30c per $1 increase in sales revenue for the next four years.

Extracts from Mlima Co's past three years' Statement of Profit or Loss

Year ended	31 May 20X3	31 May 20X2	31 May 20X1
	$ million	$ million	$ million
Sales revenue	389.1	366.3	344.7
Operating profit	58.4	54.9	51.7
Net interest costs	17.5	17.7	18.0
Profit before tax	40.9	37.2	33.7
Taxation	10.2	9.3	8.4
Profit after tax	30.7	27.9	25.3

Once listed, Mlima Co will be able to borrow future debt at an interest rate of 7%, which is only 3% higher than the risk-free rate of return. It has no plans to raise any new debt after listing, but any future debt will carry considerably fewer restrictive covenants. However, these plans do not take into consideration the Bahari project (see below).

Bahari Project

Bahari is a small country with agriculture as its main economic activity. A recent geological survey concluded that there may be a rich deposit of copper available to be mined in the north-east of the country. This area is currently occupied by subsistence farmers, who would have to be relocated to other parts of the country. When the results of the survey were announced, some farmers protested that the proposed new farmland where they would be moved to was less fertile and that their communities were being broken up. However, the protesters were intimidated and violently put down by the government, and the state-controlled media stopped reporting about them. Soon afterwards, their protests were ignored and forgotten.

In a meeting between the Bahari government and Mlima Co's BoD, the Bahari government offered Mlima Co exclusive rights to mine the copper. It is expected that there are enough deposits to last at least 15 years. Initial estimates

suggest that the project will generate free cash flows of $4 million in the first year, rising by 100% per year in each of the next two years, and then by 15% in each of the two years after that. The free cash flows are then expected to stabilise at the year-five level for the remaining 10 years.

The cost of the project, payable at the start, is expected to be $150 million, comprising machinery, working capital and the mining rights fee payable to the Bahari government. None of these costs is expected to be recoverable at the end of the project's 15-year life.

The Bahari government has offered Mlima Co a subsidised loan over 15 years for the full $150 million at an interest rate of 3% instead of Mlima Co's normal borrowing rate of 7%. The interest payable is allowable for taxation purposes. It can be assumed that Mlima Co's business risk is not expected to change as a result of undertaking the Bahari project.

At the conclusion of the meeting between the Bahari government and Mlima Co's BoD, the president of Bahari commented that working together would be like old times when he and Mlima Co's chief executive officer (CEO) used to run a business together.

Other Information

Mlima Co's closest competitor is Ziwa Co, a listed company which mines metals worldwide. Mlima Co's directors are of the opinion that after listing Mlima Co's cost of capital should be based on Ziwa Co's ungeared cost of equity. Ziwa Co's cost of capital is estimated at 9.4%, its geared cost of equity is estimated at 16.83% and its pre-tax cost of debt is estimated at 4.76%. These costs are based on a capital structure comprising of 200 million shares, trading at $7 each, and $1,700 million 5% irredeemable bonds, trading at $105 per $100. Both Ziwa Co and Mlima Co pay tax at an annual rate of 25% on their taxable profits.

It can be assumed that all cash flows will be in $ instead of the Bahari currency and therefore Mlima Co does not have to take account of any foreign exchange exposure from this venture.

Required:

(a) Prepare a report for the Board of Directors (BoD) of Mlima Co that:

(i) Explains why Mlima Co's directors are of the opinion that Mlima Co's cost of capital should be based on Ziwa Co's ungeared cost of equity and, showing relevant calculations, estimate an appropriate cost of capital for Mlima Co

(7 marks)

(ii) Estimates Mlima Co's value without undertaking the Bahari project and then with the Bahari project. The valuations should use the free cash flow methodology and the cost of capital calculated in part (i). Include relevant calculations

(14 marks)

(iii) Advises the BoD whether or not the unsecured bond holders are likely to accept the equity-for-debt swap offer. Include relevant calculations

(5 marks)

(iv) Advises the BoD on the listing and the possible share price range, if a total of 100 million shares are issued. The advice should also include:

- A discussion of the assumptions made in estimating the share price range

- In addition to the reasons mentioned in the scenario above, a brief explanation of other possible reasons for changing its status from a private company to a listed one; and

- An assessment of the possible reasons for issuing the share price at a discount for the initial listing

(12 marks)

Professional marks will be awarded in part (a) for the format, structure and presentation of the report.

(4 marks)

(b) Discuss the possible impact on, and response of, Mlima Co to the following ethical issues, with respect to the Bahari project:

(i) The relocation of the farmers; and

(ii) The relationship between the Bahari president and Mlima Co's chief executive officer.

Note: The total marks will be split equally between each part.

(8 marks)

(Total: 50 marks)

16 NAHARA CO AND FUGAE CO (DEC 14)

Nahara Co is a private holding company owned by the government of a wealthy oil-rich country to invest its sovereign funds. Nahara Co has followed a strategy of risk diversification for a number of years by acquiring companies from around the world in many different sectors.

One of Nahara Co's acquisition strategies is to identify and purchase undervalued companies in the airline industry in Europe. A recent acquisition was Fugae Co, a company based in a country which is part of the European Union (EU). Fugae Co repairs and maintains aircraft engines.

A few weeks ago, Nahara Co stated its intention to pursue the acquisition of an airline company based in the same country as Fugae Co. The EU, concerned about this, asked Nahara Co to sell Fugae Co before pursuing any further acquisitions in the airline industry.

Avem Co's acquisition interest in Fugae Co

Avem Co, a UK-based company specialising in producing and servicing business jets, has approached Nahara Co with a proposal to acquire Fugae Co for $1,200 million. Nahara Co expects to receive a premium of at least 30% on the estimated equity value of Fugae Co, if it is sold.

Given below are extracts from the most recent statements of financial position of both Avem Co and Fugae Co.

	Avem Co $ million	Fugae Co $ million
Share capital (50c/share)	800	100
Reserves	3,550	160
Non-current liabilities	2,200	380
Current liabilities	130	30
Total capital and liabilities	6,680	670

Each Avem Co share is currently trading at $7.50, which is a multiple of 7.2 of its free cash flow to equity. Avem Co expects that the total free cash flows to equity of the combined company will increase by $40 million due to synergy benefits. After adding the synergy benefits of $40 million, Avem Co then expects the multiple of the total free cash flow of the combined company to increase to 7.5.

Fugae Co's free cash flow to equity is currently estimated at $76.5 million and it is expected to generate a return on equity of 11%. Over the past few years, Fugae Co has returned 77.3% of its annual free cash flow to equity back to Nahara Co, while retaining the balance for new investments.

Fugae Co's non-current liabilities consist entirely of $100 nominal value bonds which are redeemable in four years at the nominal value, on which the company pays a coupon of 5.4%. The debt is rated at B+ and the credit spread on B+ rated debt is 80 basis points above the risk-free rate of return.

Proposed luxury transport investment project by Fugae Co

In recent years, the country in which Fugae Co is based has been expanding its tourism industry and hopes that this industry will grow significantly in the near future. At present tourists normally travel using public transport and taxis, but there is a growing market for luxury travel. If the tourist industry does expand, then the demand for luxury travel is expected to grow rapidly. Fugae Co is considering entering this market through a four-year project. The project will cease after four years because of increasing competition.

The initial cost of the project is expected to be $42,000,000 and it is expected to generate the following after-tax cash flows over its four-year life:

Year	1	2	3	4
Cash flows ($000s)	3,277.6	16,134.3	36,504.7	35,683.6

The above figures are based on the tourism industry expanding as expected. However, it is estimated that there is a 25% probability that the tourism industry will not grow as expected in the first year. If this happens, then the present value of the project's cash flows will be 50% of the original estimates over its four-year life.

It is also estimated that if the tourism industry grows as expected in the first year, there is still a 20% probability that the expected growth will slow down in the second and subsequent years, and the present value of the project's cash flows would then be 40% of the original estimates in each of these years.

Lumi Co, a leisure travel company, has offered $50 million to buy the project from Fugae Co at the start of the second year. Fugae Co is considering whether having this choice would add to the value of the project.

If Fugae Co is bought by Avem Co after the project has begun, it is thought that the project will not result in any additional synergy benefits and will not generate any additional value for the combined company, above any value the project has already generated for Fugae Co.

Although there is no beta for companies offering luxury forms of travel in the tourist industry, Reka Co, a listed company, offers passenger transportation services on coaches, trains and luxury vehicles. About 15% of its business is in the luxury transport market and Reka Co's equity beta is 1.6. It is estimated that the asset beta of the non-luxury transport industry is 0.80. Reka Co's shares are currently trading at $4.50 per share and its debt is currently trading at $105 per $100. It has 80 million shares in issue and the book value of its debt is $340 million. The debt beta is estimated to be zero.

General information

The corporation tax rate applicable to all companies is 20%. The risk-free rate is estimated to be 4% and the market risk premium is estimated to be 6%.

Required:

(a) **Discuss whether or not Nahara Co's acquisition strategies, of pursuing risk diversification and of purchasing undervalued companies, can be valid.** **(7 marks)**

(b) **Discuss why the European Union (EU) may be concerned about Nahara Co's stated intention and how selling Fugae Co could reduce this concern.** **(4 marks)**

(c) **Prepare a report for the Board of Directors of Avem Co, which:**

   (i) **Estimates the additional value created for Avem Co, if it acquires Fugae Co without considering the luxury transport project** **(10 marks)**

   (ii) **Estimates the additional value of the luxury transport project to Fugae Co, both with and without the offer from Lumi Co** **(18 marks)**

   (iii) **Evaluates the benefit attributable to Avem Co and Fugae Co from combining the two companies with and without the project, and concludes whether or not the acquisition is beneficial. The evaluation should include any assumptions made.** **(7 marks)**

   Professional marks will be awarded in part (c) for the format, structure and presentation of the report. **(4 marks)**

   (Total: 50 marks)

CORPORATE RECONSTRUCTION AND REORGANISATION

11   BBS STORES *Walk in the footsteps of a top tutor*

> ⏱ *Timed question with Online tutor debrief*

BBS Stores, a publicly quoted limited company, is considering unbundling a section of its property portfolio. The company believes that it should use the proceeds to reduce the company's medium-term borrowing and to reinvest the balance in the business (option 1). However, the company's investors have argued strongly that a sale and rental scheme would release substantial cash to investors (option 2). You are a financial consultant and have been given the task of assessing the likely impact of these alternative proposals on the company's financial performance, cost of capital and market value. The company owns all its stores.

BBS Stores' statement of financial position

	As at year end 20X8 $m	As at year end 20X7 $m
ASSETS		
Non-current assets		
Intangible assets	190	160
Property, plant and equipment	4,050	3,600
Other assets	500	530
	4,740	4,290
Current assets	840	1,160
Total assets	5,580	5,450
EQUITY		
Called up share capital – equity	425	420
Retained earnings	1,535	980
Total equity	1,960	1,400
LIABILITIES		
Current liabilities	1,600	2,020
Non-current liabilities		
Medium-term loan notes	1,130	1,130
Other non-financial liabilities	890	900
	2,020	2,030
Total liabilities	3,620	4,050
Total equity and liabilities	5,580	5,450

The company's profitability has improved significantly in recent years and earnings for 20X8 were $670 million (20X7: $540 million).

The company's property, plant and equipment within non-current assets for 20X8 are as follows:

	Land and buildings $m	Fixtures, fittings and equipment $m	Assets under construction $m	Total $m
Year end 20X8				
At revaluation	2,297	4,038	165	6,500
Accumulated depreciation		(2,450)		(2,450)
Net book value	2,297	1,588	165	4,050

The property portfolio was revalued at the year end 20X8. The assets under construction are valued at a market value of $165 million and relate to new building.

In recent years commercial property values have risen in real terms by 4% per annum. Current inflation is 2.5% per annum. Property rentals currently earn an 8% return.

The proposal is that 50% of the property portfolio (land and buildings) and 50% of the assets under construction would be sold to a newly established property holding company called RPH that would issue bonds backed by the assured rental income stream from BBS Stores. BBS Stores would not hold any equity interest in the newly formed company nor would they take any part in its management.

BBS Stores is currently financed by equity in the form of 25c fully paid ordinary shares with a current market value of 400c per share. The capital debt for the company consists of medium-term loan notes of which $360 million are repayable at the end of two years and $770 million are repayable at the end of six years. Both issues of medium term notes carry a floating rate of LIBOR plus 70 basis points. The interest liability on the six year notes has been swapped at a fixed rate of 5.5% in exchange for LIBOR which is also currently 5.5%. The reduction in the firm's gearing implied by option 1 would improve the firm's credit rating and reduce its current credit spread by 30 basis points. The change in gearing resulting from the second option is not expected to have any impact upon the firm's credit rating. There has been no alteration in the rating of the company since the earliest debt was issued.

The BBS Stores equity beta is currently 1.824. A representative portfolio of commercial property companies has an equity beta of 1.25 and an average market gearing (adjusted for tax) of 50%. The risk free rate of return is 5% and the equity risk premium is 3%. The company's current accounting rate of return on new investment is 13% before tax. You may assume that debt betas are zero throughout.

The effective rate of company tax is 35%.

Required:

On the assumption that the property unbundling proceeds, prepare a report for consideration by senior management which should include the following:

(a) A comparative statement showing the impact upon the statement of financial position and on the earnings per share on the assumption that the cash proceeds of the property sale are used:

    (i) To repay the debt, repayable in two years, in full and for reinvestment in non-current assets

    (ii) To repay the debt, repayable in two years, in full and to finance a share repurchase at the current share price with the balance of the proceeds.

                                                        (13 marks)

(b) An estimate of the weighted average cost of capital for the remaining business under both options on the assumption that the share price remains unchanged.

                                                         (10 marks)

(c) An evaluation of the potential impact of each alternative on the market value of the firm (you are not required to calculate a revised market value for the firm).

                                                           (6 marks)

Professional marks will be awarded in this question for the clarity, presentation and persuasiveness of the report.   **(3 marks)**

                                                            (Total: 32 marks)

 Calculate your allowed time, allocate the time to the separate parts.

---

18 COEDEN CO (DEC 12)

Coeden Co is a listed company operating in the hospitality and leisure industry. Coeden Co's board of directors met recently to discuss a new strategy for the business. The proposal put forward was to sell all the hotel properties that Coeden Co owns and rent them back on a long-term rental agreement. Coeden Co would then focus solely on the provision of hotel services at these properties under its popular brand name. The proposal stated that the funds raised from the sale of the hotel properties would be used to pay off 70% of the outstanding non-current liabilities and the remaining funds would be retained for future investments.

The board of directors are of the opinion that reducing the level of debt in Coeden Co will reduce the company's risk and therefore its cost of capital. If the proposal is undertaken and Coeden Co focuses exclusively on the provision of hotel services, it can be assumed that the current market value of equity will remain unchanged after implementing the proposal.

Coeden Co Financial Information

Extract from the most recent Statement of Financial Position

	$000
Non-current assets (re-valued recently)	42,560
Current assets	26,840
Total assets	69,400
Share capital (25c per share par value)	3,250
Reserves	21,780
Non-current liabilities (5.2% redeemable bonds)	42,000
Current liabilities	2,370
Total capital and liabilities	69,400

Coeden Co's latest free cash flow to equity of $2,600,000 was estimated after taking into account taxation, interest and reinvestment in assets to continue with the current level of business. It can be assumed that the annual reinvestment in assets required to continue with the current level of business is equivalent to the annual amount of depreciation. Over the past few years, Coeden Co has consistently used 40% of its free cash flow to equity on new investments while distributing the remaining 60%. The market value of equity calculated on the basis of the free cash flow to equity model provides a reasonable estimate of the current market value of Coeden Co.

The bonds are redeemable at par in three years and pay the coupon on an annual basis. Although the bonds are not traded, it is estimated that Coeden Co's current debt credit rating is BBB but would improve to A+ if the non-current liabilities are reduced by 70%.

Other Information

Coeden Co's current equity beta is 1.1 and it can be assumed that debt beta is 0. The risk free rate is estimated to be 4% and the market risk premium is estimated to be 6%.

There is no beta available for companies offering just hotel services, since most companies own their own buildings. The average asset beta for property companies has been estimated at 0.4. It has been estimated that the hotel services business accounts for approximately 60% of the current value of Coeden Co and the property company business accounts for the remaining 40%.

Coeden Co's corporation tax rate is 20%. The three-year borrowing credit spread on A+ rated bonds is 60 basis points and 90 basis points on BBB rated bonds, over the risk free rate of interest.

Required:

(a)   Calculate, and comment on, Coeden Co's cost of equity and weighted average cost of capital before and after implementing the proposal. Briefly explain any assumptions made.   (20 marks)

(b)   Discuss the validity of the assumption that the market value of equity will remain unchanged after the implementation of the proposal.   (5 marks)

(c)   As an alternative to selling the hotel properties, the board of directors is considering a demerger of the hotel services and a separate property company which would own the hotel properties. The property company would take over 70% of Coeden Co's long-term debt and pay Coeden Co cash for the balance of the property value.

Required:

Explain what a demerger is, and the possible benefits and drawbacks of pursuing the demerger option as opposed to selling the hotel properties.   **(8 marks)**

(Total: 33 marks)

TREASURY AND ADVANCED RISK MANAGEMENT TECHNIQUES

19   SOMAX PLC

Assume that 'now' is June 20X3.

(a)   Somax plc, a UK company, wishes to raise 260 million Swiss francs in floating rate finance for a period of five years.

Required:

Discuss the advantages and disadvantages of raising such funds through:

(i)   **Direct borrowing from a domestic banking system such as the Swiss domestic banking system. (Detailed knowledge of the Swiss banking system is not required.)**

(ii)   **The Euromarket**   **(10 marks)**

(b)   The funds are to be used to establish a new production plant in Switzerland. Somax evaluates its investments using NPV, but is not sure what cost of capital to use in the discounting process.

The company is also proposing to increase its equity finance in the near future for UK expansion, resulting overall in little change in the company's market weighted capital gearing. The summarised financial data for the company before the expansion are shown below:

Statement of profit or loss for the year ending 31 March 20X3

	£ million
Revenue	1,984
Gross profit	432
Profit after tax	81
Dividends	37
Retained earnings	44

Statement of financial position as at 31 March 20X3

	£ million
Non current assets (net)	846
Working capital	350
	1,196
Medium and long-term loans[1]	(210)
	986
Shareholders' funds	
Issued ordinary shares (50 pence par)	225
Reserves	761
	986

[1] Including £75m 14% fixed rate bonds due to mature in five years time and redeemable at £100. The current market price of these bonds is £119.50. Other medium and long-term loans are floating rate UK bank loans at bank base rate plus 1%.

Corporate tax may be assumed to be at the rate of 33% in both the UK and Switzerland.

The company's ordinary shares are currently trading at 376 pence.

Somax's equity beta is estimated to be 1.18. The systematic risk of debt may be assumed to be zero.

The risk free rate is 7.75% and market return 14.5%. Bank base rate is currently 8.25%.

The estimated equity beta of the main Swiss competitor in the same industry as the new proposed plant in Switzerland is 1.5, and the competitor's capital gearing is 35% equity, 65% debt by book values, and 60% equity, 40% debt by market values.

	Exchange rates
Spot	SFr2.3245–2.3300/£1
6 months forward	SFr2.2955–2.3009/£1

Somax can borrow in Swiss francs at a floating rate of between 5.75% and 6% depending upon which form of borrowing is selected (i.e. in the Euromarkets or the Swiss domestic market).

SFr LIBOR is currently 5%.

The interest rate parity theorem may be assumed to hold.

Required:

Estimate the UK sterling cost of capital that Somax should use as the discount rate for its proposed investment in Switzerland.

State clearly any assumptions that you make. **(12 marks)**

(c) Somax's bank has suggested a five year interest rate swap as an alternative to direct SFr borrowing. Somax would issue a five year sterling fixed rate bond, and make the following swap with a Swiss company that is also a client of the bank.

Somax would pay the Swiss company SFr LIBOR + 1% per year.

The Swiss company would pay Somax 9.5% per year.

A 0.2% per year fee would also be payable by each company to the bank. There will be an exchange of principal now, and in five years time, at today's middle spot foreign exchange rate. The Swiss company can borrow fixed rate sterling at 10.5% per annum, and floating rate SFr finance at SFr LIBOR + 1.5%.

Required:

(i) **Estimate the annual interest cost to Somax of issuing a five year sterling fixed rate bond, and calculate whether the suggested swap would be of benefit to both Somax plc and the Swiss company.** **(10 marks)**

(ii) **Excluding cheaper finance, discuss the possible benefits, and the possible risks of such a swap for the two companies and the intermediary bank.** **(8 marks)**

(Total: 40 marks)

20 LAMMER PLC *Walk in the footsteps of a top tutor*

(a) Lammer plc is a UK-based company that regularly trades with companies in the USA. Several large transactions are due in five months' time. These are shown below. The transactions are in '000' units of the currencies shown.

Assume that it is now 1 June and that futures and options contracts mature at the relevant month end.

	Exports to:	Imports from:
Company 1	$490	£150
Company 2	–	$890
Company 3	£110	$750

Exchange rates:	$US/£
Spot	1.9156–1.9210
3 months forward	1.9066–1.9120
1 year forward	1.8901–1.8945

Annual interest rates available to Lammer plc

	Borrowing	Investing
Sterling up to 6 months	5.5%	4.2%
Dollar up to 6 months	4.0%	2.0%

CME $/£ Currency futures (£62,500)

September 1.9045

December 1.8986

CME currency options prices, $/£ options £31,250 (cents per pound)

	CALLS		PUTS	
	Sept	Dec	Sept	Dec
1.8800	4.76	5.95	1.60	2.96
1.9000	3.53	4.70	2.36	4.34
1.9200	2.28	3.56	3.40	6.55

Required:

Prepare a report for the managers of Lammer plc on how the five-month currency risk should be hedged. Include in your report all relevant calculations relating to the alternative types of hedge. **(22 marks)**

16 marks are available for calculations and 6 marks for discussion

Professional marks for format, structure and presentation of the report for part (a) **(4 marks)**

(b) In a typical financial year Lammer plc has net dollar imports of $4.2 million. This is expected to continue for five years.

The company's cost of capital is estimated to be 11% per year. Taxation may be ignored, and cash flows may be assumed to occur at the year end.

Required:

Assuming that there is no change in the physical volume or dollar price of imports, estimate the effect on the expected market value of Lammer plc if the market expects the dollar to strengthen by 3% per year against the pound. **(7 marks)**

(c) **Briefly discuss how Lammer plc might manage the economic exposure of any foreign subsidiaries in the USA.** **(5 marks)**

(Total: 38 marks)

21 CASASOPHIA CO (JUN 11)

Casasophia Co, based in a European country that uses the Euro (€), constructs and maintains advanced energy efficient commercial properties around the world. It has just completed a major project in the USA and is due to receive the final payment of US$20 million in four months.

Casasophia Co is planning to commence a major construction and maintenance project in Mazabia, a small African country, in six months' time. This government-owned project is expected to last for three years during which time Casasophia Co will complete the construction of state-of-the-art energy efficient properties and provide training to a local Mazabian company in maintaining the properties. The carbon-neutral status of the building project has attracted some grant funding from the European Union and these funds will be provided to the Mazabian government in Mazabian Shillings (MShs).

Casasophia Co intends to finance the project using the US$20 million it is due to receive and borrow the rest through a € loan. It is intended that the US$ receipts will be converted into € and invested in short-dated treasury bills until they are required. These funds plus the loan will be converted into MShs on the date required, at the spot rate at that time.

Mazabia's government requires Casasophia Co to deposit the MShs2.64 billion it needs for the project, with Mazabia's central bank, at the commencement of the project. In return, Casasophia Co will receive a fixed sum of MShs1.5 billion after tax, at the end of each year for a period of three years. Neither of these amounts is subject to inflationary increases. The relevant risk adjusted discount rate for the project is assumed to be 12%.

Financial Information

Exchange Rates available to Casasophia

	Per €1	Per €1
Spot	US$1.3585–US$1.3618	MShs116–MShs128
4-month forward	US$1.3588–US$1.3623	Not available

Currency Futures (Contract size €125,000, Quotation: US$ per €1)

2-month expiry	1.3633
5-month expiry	1.3698

Currency Options (Contract size €125,000, Exercise price quotation: US$ per €1, cents per Euro)

	Calls		Puts	
Exercise price	2-month expiry	5-month expiry	2-month expiry	5-month expiry
1.36	2.35	2.80	2.47	2.98
1.38	1.88	2.23	4.23	4.64

Casasophia Co Local Government Base Rate	2.20%
Mazabia Government Base Rate	10.80%
Yield on short-dated Euro Treasury Bills (assume 360-day year)	1.80%

Mazabia's current annual inflation rate is 9.7% and is expected to remain at this level for the next six months. However, after that, there is considerable uncertainty about the future and the annual level of inflation could be anywhere between 5% and 15% for the next few years. The country where Casasophia Co is based is expected to have a stable level of inflation at 1.2% per year for the foreseeable future. A local bank in Mazabia has offered Casasophia Co the opportunity to swap the annual income of MShs1.5 billion receivable in each of the next three years for Euros, at the estimated annual MShs/€ forward rates based on the current government base rates.

Required:

(a) Advise Casasophia Co on, and recommend, an appropriate hedging strategy for the US$ income it is due to receive in four months. Include all relevant calculations.

(15 marks)

(b) Provide a reasoned estimate of the additional amount of loan finance Casasophia Co needs to obtain to undertake the project in Mazabia in six months. (5 marks)

(c) Given that Casasophia Co agrees to the local bank's offer of the swap, calculate the net present value of the project, in six months' time, in €. Discuss whether the swap would be beneficial to Casasophia Co. (10 marks)

(Total: 30 marks)

22 CMC CO (JUN 14)

Cocoa-Mocha-Chai (CMC) Co is a large listed company based in Switzerland and uses Swiss Francs as its currency. It imports tea, coffee and cocoa from countries around the world, and sells its blended products to supermarkets and large retailers worldwide. The company has production facilities located in two European ports where raw materials are brought for processing, and from where finished products are shipped out. All raw material purchases are paid for in US dollars (US$), while all sales are invoiced in Swiss Francs (CHF).

Until recently CMC Co had no intention of hedging its foreign currency exposures, interest rate exposures or commodity price fluctuations, and stated this intent in its annual report. However, after consultations with senior and middle managers, the company's new Board of Directors (BoD) has been reviewing its risk management and operations strategies.

The following two proposals have been put forward by the BoD for further consideration:

Proposal one

Setting up a treasury function to manage the foreign currency and interest rate exposures (but not commodity price fluctuations) using derivative products. The treasury function would be headed by the finance director. The purchasing director, who initiated the idea of having a treasury function, was of the opinion that this would enable her management team to make better decisions. The finance director also supported the idea as he felt this would increase his influence on the BoD and strengthen his case for an increase in his remuneration.

In order to assist in the further consideration of this proposal, the BoD wants you to use the following upcoming foreign currency and interest rate exposures to demonstrate how they would be managed by the treasury function:

(i)   a payment of US$5,060,000 which is due in four months' time; and

(ii)   a four-year CHF60,000,000 loan taken out to part-fund the setting up of four branches (see proposal two below).

Interest will be payable on the loan at a fixed annual rate of 2.2% or a floating annual rate based on the yield curve rate plus 0.40%. The loan's principal amount will be repayable in full at the end of the fourth year.

Proposal two

This proposal suggested setting up four new branches in four different countries. Each branch would have its own production facilities and sales teams. As a consequence of this, one of the two European-based production facilities will be closed. Initial cost-benefit analysis indicated that this would reduce costs related to production, distribution and logistics, as these branches would be closer to the sources of raw materials and also to the customers. The operations and sales directors supported the proposal, as in addition to above, this would enable sales and marketing teams in the branches to respond to any changes in nearby markets more quickly. The branches would be controlled and staffed by the local population in those countries. However, some members of the BoD expressed concern that such a move would create agency issues between CMC Co's central management and the management controlling the branches. They suggested mitigation strategies would need to be established to minimise these issues.

Response from the non-executive directors

When the proposals were put to the non-executive directors, they indicated that they were broadly supportive of the second proposal if the financial benefits outweigh the costs of setting up and running the four branches. However, they felt that they could not support the first proposal, as this would reduce shareholder value because the costs related to undertaking the proposal are likely to outweigh the benefits.

Additional information relating to proposal one

The current spot rate is US$1.0635 per CHF1. The current annual inflation rate in the USA is three times higher than Switzerland.

The following derivative products are available to CMC Co to manage the exposures of the US$ payment and the interest on the loan:

Exchange-traded currency futures

Contract size CHF125,000 price quotation: US$ per CHF1

3-month expiry	1.0647
6-month expiry	1.0659

Exchange-traded currency options

Contract size CHF125,000, exercise price quotation: US$ per CHF1, premium: cents per CHF1.

	Call options		Put options	
Exercise price	3-month expiry	6-month expiry	3-month expiry	6-month expiry
1.06	1.87	2.75	1.41	2.16
1.07	1.34	2.22	1.88	2.63

It can be assumed that futures and option contracts expire at the end of the month and transaction costs related to these can be ignored.

Over-the-counter products

In addition to the exchange-traded products, Pecunia Bank is willing to offer the following over-the-counter derivative products to CMC Co:

(i)   A forward rate between the US$ and the CHF of US$ 1.0677 per CHF1.

(ii) An interest rate swap contract with a counterparty, where the counterparty can borrow at an annual floating rate based on the yield curve rate plus 0.8% or an annual fixed rate of 3.8%. Pecunia Bank would charge a fee of 20 basis points each to act as the intermediary of the swap. Both parties will benefit equally from the swap contract.

Required:

(a)   Advise CMC Co on an appropriate hedging strategy to manage the foreign exchange exposure of the US$ payment in four months' time. Show all relevant calculations, including the number of contracts bought or sold in the exchange-traded derivative markets. **(15 marks)**

(b)   Demonstrate how CMC Co could benefit from the swap offered by Pecunia Bank.
(6 marks)

(c)   As an alternative to paying the principal on the loan as one lump sum at the end of the fourth year, CMC Co could pay off the loan in equal annual amounts over the four years similar to an annuity. In this case, an annual interest rate of 2% would be payable, which is the same as the loan's gross redemption yield (yield to maturity).

Required:

Calculate the modified duration of the loan if it is repaid in equal amounts and explain how duration can be used to measure the sensitivity of the loan to changes in interest rates.   **(7 marks)**

(d)   **Prepare a memorandum for the Board of Directors (BoD) of CMC Co which:**

   (i)   **Discusses proposal one in light of the concerns raised by the non-executive directors; and**   **(9 marks)**

   (ii)   **Discusses the agency issues related to proposal two and how these can be mitigated.**   **(9 marks)**

Professional marks will be awarded in part (d) for the presentation, structure, logical flow and clarity of the memorandum.   **(4 marks)**

(Total: 50 marks)

ECONOMIC ENVIRONMENT FOR MULTINATIONALS

23   AVTO

Avto plc, a UK-based firm, is considering an investment in Terrania, a country with a population of 60 million that has experienced 12 changes of government in the last 10 years. The investment would cost 580 million Terranian francs for machinery and other equipment, and an additional 170 million francs would be necessary for working capital.

Terrania has a well-trained, skilled labour force and good communications infrastructure, but has suffered from a major disease in its main crop, the banana, and the effect of cheaper labour in neighbouring countries.

Terrania is heavily indebted to the IMF and the international banking system, and it is rumoured that the IMF is unwilling to offer further assistance to the Terranian government. The Terranian government has imposed temporary restrictions on the remittance of funds from Terrania on three occasions during the last ten years.

The proposed investment would be in the production of recordable DVD players, which are currently manufactured in the UK, mainly for the European Union market. If the Terranian investment project was undertaken the existing UK factory would either be closed down or downsized. Avto plc hopes to become more competitive by shifting production from the UK.

Additional information:

(i)   UK corporate tax is at the rate of 30% per year, and Terranian corporate tax at the rate of 20% per year, both payable in the year that the tax charge arises. Tax allowable depreciation in Terrania is 25% per year on a reducing balance basis. A bilateral tax treaty exists between Terrania and the UK.

(ii)   The after-tax realisable value of the machinery and other equipment after four years is estimated to be 150 million Terranian francs.

(iii)   £140,000 has recently been spent on a feasibility study into the logistics of the proposed Terranian investment. The study reported favourably on this issue.

(iv)   The Terranian government has offered to allow Avto plc to use an existing factory rent free for a period of four years on condition that Avto employs at least 300 local workers. Avto has estimated that the investment would need 250 local workers. Rental of the factory would normally cost 75 million Terranian francs per year before tax.

(v)   Almost all sales from Terranian production will be to the European Union priced in Euros.

(vi)   Production and sales are expected to be 50,000 units per year. The expected year 1 selling price is 480 Euros per unit.

(vii)   Unit costs throughout year 1 are expected to be:

Labour:	3,800 Terranian (T) francs based upon using 250 workers
Local components:	1,800 T francs
Component from Germany:	30 Euros
Sales and distribution:	400 T francs

(viii)   Fixed costs in year 1 are 50 million T francs.

(ix)   Local costs and the cost of the German component are expected to increase each year in line with Terranian and EU inflation respectively. Due to competition, the selling price (in Euros) is expected to remain constant for at least four years.

(x)   All net cash flows arising from the proposed investment in Terrania would be remitted at the end of each year back to the UK.

(xi)   If the UK factory is closed, Avto will face tax-allowable redundancy and other closure costs of £35 million. Approximately £20 million after tax is expected to be raised from the disposal of land and buildings.

(xii)   If Avto decides to downsize rather than close its UK operations then tax-allowable closure costs will amount to £20 million, and after-tax asset sales to £10 million. Pre-tax net cash flows from the downsized operation are expected to be £4 million per year, at current values. Manufacturing capacity in Terrania would not be large enough to supply the market previously supplied from the UK if downsizing does not occur.

(xiii)   The estimated beta of the Terranian investment is 1.5 and of the existing UK investment is 1.1.

(xiv)   The relevant risk-free rate is 4.5% and market return 11.5%.

(xv)   Money market investment in Terrania is available to Avto, paying a rate of interest equivalent to the Terranian inflation rate.

(xvi) Forecast % inflation levels:

	UK and the EU	Terrania
Year 1	2%	20%
Year 2	3%	15%
Year 3	3%	10%
Year 4	3%	10%
Year 5	3%	10%

(xvii) Spot exchange rates:

Terranian francs/£1	36.85
Terranian francs/Euros	23.32

Required:

(a) **Prepare a financial appraisal of whether or not Avto plc should invest in Terrania and close or downsize its UK factory. State clearly all assumptions that you make.**

(b) **Discuss the wider commercial issues that the company should consider, in addition to the financial appraisal, before making its decision on whether to invest.**

(c) **Estimate the possible impact of blocked remittances in Terrania for the planning horizon of four years, and discuss how Avto might react to blocked remittances.**

28 marks in total are available for calculations, and 12 marks for discussion.

(Total: 40 marks)

24 OBERBERG AG

(a) **Discuss the advantages to a company of establishing an overseas operating subsidiary by either:**

(i) **organic growth, or**

(ii) **acquisition.** (8 marks)

(b) 'Now' is December 20X2.

The Board of Directors of Intergrand plc, a UK-based company, wishes to establish an operating subsidiary in Germany through the acquisition of an existing German company. Intergrand has undertaken research into a number of German quoted companies, and has decided to attempt to purchase Oberberg AG. Initial discussions suggest that the directors of Oberberg AG may be willing to recommend the sale of 100% of the company's equity to Intergrand for a total cash price of €115 million, payable in full on acquisition.

Oberberg has provided the managers of Intergrand with internal management information regarding accounting/cash flow projections for the next four years.

The projections are in money/nominal terms.

	Oberberg AG, financial projections			
	€ (million)			
Year	*20X3*	*20X4*	*20X5*	*20X6*
Sales	38.2	41.2	44.0	49.0
Labour	11.0	12.1	13.0	14.1
Materials	8.3	8.7	9.0	9.4
Overheads	3.2	3.2	3.3	3.4
Interest	2.5	3.0	3.5	3.8
Tax-allowable depreciation	6.3	5.8	5.6	5.2
	31.3	32.8	34.4	35.9
Taxable profit	6.9	8.4	9.6	13.1
Taxation (25%)	1.7	2.1	2.4	3.3
Incremental operating working capital	0.7	0.9	1.0	2.0
Replacement investment	4.2	4.2	4.2	4.2
Investment for expansion	–	–	9.0	–

Oberberg AG, proforma summarised statement of profit or loss for the year ending 31 December 20X2

	€ (million)
Sales revenue	35.8
Operating expenses	21.1
Interest expense	3.4
Depreciation	6.2
	─────
	30.7
	─────
Taxable profit	5.1
Taxation (25%)	1.3
	─────
Profit after tax	3.8
	─────

Oberberg AG summarised statement of financial position as at 31 December 20X2

	€ (million)
Non-current assets	73.2
Current assets	58.1
	131.3
Ordinary shares (€100 par value)	15.0
Reserves	28.0
Medium- and long-term bank loans	30.0
8% Bond 20X9 (par value €1,000)	18.0
Current liabilities	40.3
	131.3

Notes:

(i)   The spot exchange rate between the Euro and pound is €1.625/£1.

(ii)   Inflation is at 4% per year in the UK, and 2% per year in the Eurozone. This differential is expected to continue unless the UK joins the Eurozone.

(iii)   The market return is 11% and the risk-free rate is 4%.

(iv)   Oberberg's equity beta is estimated to be 1.4.

(v)   Oberberg's 8% bond is currently priced at €1,230, and its ordinary share price is €300.

(vi)   Post-merger rationalisation will involve the sale of some non-current assets of Oberberg in 20X3 with an expected after-tax market value of €8 million.

(vii)   Synergies in production and distribution are expected to yield €2 million per annum before tax from 20X4 onwards.

(viii) £175,000 has already been spent researching into possible acquisition targets.

(ix)   The purchase of Oberberg will provide publicity and exposure in Germany for the Intergrand name and brand. This extra publicity is believed to be the equivalent of Intergrand spending €1 million per year on advertising in Germany.

(x)   The weighted average cost of capital of Intergrand is 10%.

(xi)   After-tax cash flows of Oberberg after 20X6 are expected to grow at approximately 2% per year.

(xii)   Oberberg does not plan to issue or redeem any equity or medium- and long-term debt prior to 20X6.

(xiii) After-tax redundancy costs as a result of the acquisition are expected to be €5 million, payable almost immediately.

(xiv)   Operating working capital comprises debtors and stock less creditors (receivables plus inventory less payables). It excludes short-term loans.

(xv)   Current liabilities include negligible amounts of short-term loans.

(xvi) The corporate tax rate in Germany is 25%, and in the UK 30%. A bilateral tax treaty exists between the two countries whereby tax paid in one country may be credited against any tax liability in the other country.

(xvii) If Intergrand acquires Oberberg, existing exports to Germany yielding a pre-tax cash flow of £800,000 per annum will be lost. It is hoped that about half of these exports can be diverted to the French market.

Required:

Intergrand has suggested that Oberberg should be valued based upon the expected present value (to infinity) of the operating free cash flows of Oberberg. These would be discounted at an all-equity rate, and adjusted by the present value of all other relevant cash flows, discounted at an appropriate rate(s).

Acting as a consultant to Intergrand plc, prepare a report evaluating whether or not Intergrand should offer the €115 million required to acquire Oberberg AG. Include in your report discussion of other commercial and business factors that Intergrand should consider prior to making a final decision.

State clearly any other assumptions that you make.   **(32 marks)**

Approximately 22 marks are available for calculations and 10 for discussion.

(Total: 40 marks)

Section 2

PRACTICE QUESTIONS – SECTION B

ROLE AND RESPONSIBILITY TOWARDS STAKEHOLDERS

25   TYR INC

Summarised financial data for TYR Inc is shown below:

TYR Inc

Year	Post-tax earnings ($ million)	Dividends ($ million)	Issued shares (million)	Share price (cents)
20X1	86.2	34.5	180	360
20X2	92.4	36.2	180	410
20X3	99.3	37.6	180	345
20X4	134.1	51.6	240	459
20X5	148.6	53.3	240	448

Year	Stock Market All-share index	Inflation rate
20X1	2895	6%
20X2	3300	5%
20X3	2845	4%
20X4	2610	3%
20X5	2305	3%

TYR's cost of equity is estimated to be 11%.

Required:

(a)   Explain, with supporting numerical evidence, the current dividend policy of TYR Inc, and briefly discuss whether or not this appears to be successful.   **(6 marks)**

(b)   Identify and consider additional information that might assist the managers of TYR in assessing whether the dividend policy has been successful.   **(6 marks)**

(c)   Evaluate whether or not the company's share price at the end of 20X5 was what might have been expected from the Dividend Growth Model. Briefly discuss the validity of your findings.   **(5 marks)**

(d)   Discuss why conflicts of interest might exist between shareholders and bondholders.   **(8 marks)**

(Total: 25 marks)

26   FORTHMATE INC AND HERANDER INC

You have been asked to investigate the dividend policy of two companies, Forthmate Inc and Herander Inc, both of which are based in the USA. Selected financial information on the two companies is shown below.

Forthmate Inc

	Earnings after tax ($000)	Issued ordinary share (m)	Free cash flow to equity ($000)	Dividend per share (cents)
20X1	24,050	100	11,400	4.8
20X2	22,345	100	12,200	4.5
20X3	26,460	100	(3,500)	5.3
20X4	32,450	130	(2,600)	5.0
20X5	35,890	130	9,200	5.5

Herander Inc

	Earnings after tax ($000)	Issued ordinary shares(m)	Free cash flow to equity ($000)	Dividend per share (cents)
20X1	8,250	50	6,100	10.0
20X2	5,920	50	(4,250)	10.0
20X3	9,140	50	10,300	10.3
20X4	10,350	50	4,400	10.5
20X5	8,220	50	3,140	10.5

A colleague has suggested that companies should try to pay dividends that are a constant percentage of a company's free cash flow to equity.

Required:

(a)   **Analyse and contrast the dividend polices of Forthmate Inc and Herander Inc. Include in your analysis estimates of dividends as a percentage of free cash flow, and any other relevant calculations.**

   Discuss possible reasons why the companies' dividend policies differ.   (8 marks)

(b)   **Discuss whether or not a company should pay dividends that are equal to the free cash flow to equity.   (4 marks)**

(c)   In both of the last two years, Herander Inc has had more potential investments with positive NPV than it actually undertook.

Required:

Discuss the implications of your findings in (a) above for the financial strategy of Herander Inc.   (3 marks)

(d)   Forthmate Inc is tendering for an order in Kuwait. The tender conditions state that payment will be made in Kuwait dinars in 18 months from now. The company is unsure as to what price to tender. The marginal cost of producing the goods at that time is estimated to be $350,000 and a 25% mark-up is normal for the company.

Exchange rates

Dinar/$1

Spot 3.2800–3.3000

No forward rate exists for 18 months' time.

	USA	Kuwait
Annual inflation rates	9%	3%
Annual interest rates available to Forthmate Inc:		
Borrowing	14%	9%
Lending	9%	3.5%

Required:

Discuss how Forthmate Inc might protect itself against foreign exchange rate changes for the Kuwait contract, and recommend what tender price should be used. **(10 marks)**

(Total: 25 marks)

27 SATURN SYSTEMS *Walk in the footsteps of a top tutor*

Mr Moon is the CEO of Saturn Systems, a very large listed company in the telecommunications business. The company is in a very strong financial position, having developed rapidly in recent years through a strategy based upon growth by acquisition. Currently, earnings and earnings growth are at all time highs although the company's cash reserves are at a low level following a number of strategic investments in the last financial year. The previous evening Mr Moon gave a speech at a business dinner and during questions made some remarks that Pluto Limited was an attractive company with 'great assets' and that he would be a 'fool' if he did not consider the possibility 'like everyone else' of acquiring the company. Pluto is a long established supplier to Saturn Systems and if acquired would add substantially to the market capitalisation of the business.

Mr Moon's comments were widely reported in the following morning's financial newspapers and, by 10 am, the share price of Pluto had risen 15% in out-of-hours and early trading. The first that you, Saturn's chief financial officer, heard about the issue was when you received an urgent call from Mr Moon's office. You have just completed a background investigation of Pluto, along with three other potential targets instigated at Saturn's last board meeting in May. Following that investigation, you have now commenced a review of the steps required to raise the necessary debt finance for a bid and the procedure you would need to follow in setting up a due diligence investigation of each company.

On arriving at Mr Moon's office you are surprised to see the chairman of the board in attendance. Mr Moon has just put down the telephone and is clearly very agitated. They tell you about the remarks made by Mr Moon the previous evening and that the call just taken was from the Office of the Regulator for Public Companies. The regulator had wanted to know if a bid was to be made and what announcement the company intended to make. They had been very neutral in their response pending your advice but had promised to get back to the regulator within the hour. They knew that if they were forced to admit that a bid was imminent and then withdrew that they would not be able to bid again for another six months. Looking at you they ask as one: 'what do we do now?'

After a short discussion you returned to your office and began to draft a memorandum with a recommendation about how to proceed.

Required:

(a)   Assess the regulatory, financial and ethical issues in this case.   **(15 marks)**

(b)   Propose a course of action that the company should now pursue, including a draft of any announcement that should be made, given that the board of Saturn Systems wishes to hold open the option of making a bid in the near future.   **(5 marks)**

(Total: 20 marks)

28   SOLAR SUPERMARKETS   *Walk in the footsteps of a top tutor*

Solar Supermarkets, a listed company, is reviewing the approach that it should take to remunerating its executive directors and other senior managers. Over the years, the company's share price has performed well although there is now concern that price and cost competition from overseas entrants into the domestic market will have a significant impact on the firm's profitability. As a result, the directors believe that large investment in new technologies and markets will be required over the next five years. Traditionally, management has been rewarded by salary, a generous system of benefits, and a bonus scheme that has taken up to 4% of revenue. The directors are considering introducing a generous share option scheme with a five year vesting period.

There is also a view, expressed by some of the company's principal equity investors, that the company should consider returning cash to them through the sale of its property holdings. The company has over 200 stores nationally and 15 overseas, of which all except five are owned by the company. In the domestic economy, growth in the value of commercial property has averaged 8% per annum in recent years whilst retail growth has remained static at 5.5%. A sale and leaseback, or the flotation of a separate property company that would rent the stores to Solar Supermarkets at commercial rates, are two suggestions that have been made at investor meetings. Either approach, it is suggested, would return value to investors and create a supply of capital for further expansion. There have been press rumours, possibly fed from sources within the investor community, that the company may be a target for a private equity acquisition. However, no formal approach has been made to the company.

The only other area of controversy to emerge about the company which has concerned the directors followed an announcement about the company pension scheme. Although the scheme is well funded the directors took the decision to close the current final salary scheme to new employees and to replace it with a money purchase scheme. Current employees would not be affected.

Required:

Discuss the strategic, financial and ethical issues that this case presents and the merits of the proposed share option and sale and leaseback schemes.

(Total: 20 marks)

29 INTERNATIONAL ENTERPRISES *Walk in the footsteps of a top tutor*

You are the chief financial officer of International Enterprises, a multinational company with interests in Europe and the Far East. You are concerned about certain aspects of the company's financial management. The company has enjoyed a high rate of growth over the last three years as a result of a single product's development. This product has had a big impact in the fast moving mobile communications industry. However, the company does not have any new products in development and is relying on expanding its market share and developing upgraded versions of the current product.

As part of your preparation for the board meeting to discuss the 20X7 draft accounts, you have prepared a projected statement of profit or loss and statement of financial position for the year ending 31 December 20X8. These projections are based upon a number of agreed assumptions taken from the company's strategic plan. As part of the agenda, the board will also consider its dividend target for the forthcoming year.

International Enterprises

Statement of profit or loss for the year ended 31 December

	20X8 (projected) $m	20X7 (draft) $m	20X6 (actual) $m
Revenue	288.1	261.9	220.0
Cost of sales	143.2	132.6	104.0
Gross profit	144.9	129.3	116.0
Less other operating costs	36.1	27.0	24.0
Operating profit	108.8	102.3	92.0
Finance costs	1.8	2.3	2.3
Profit before tax	107.0	100.0	89.7
Income tax expense (at 30%)	32.1	30.0	26.9
Profit for the period	74.9	70.0	62.8

Statement of Financial Position as at 31 December

	20X8 (projected) $m	20X7 (draft) $m	20X6 (actual) $m
Non-current assets (see note)			
Buildings, plant and machinery	168.0	116.0	96.0
Current assets			
Inventories	3.2	3.7	2.3
Receivables	25.6	29.1	19.6
Cash	151.8	155.8	121.7
Total current assets	180.6	188.6	143.6
Total assets	348.6	304.6	239.6

Equity and liabilities

Paid up share capital

Ordinary shares (25c)	25.0	25.0	20.0
Other reserves	12.0	12.0	10.0
Retained earnings	216.9	170.0	120.0
Less dividends payable	0.0	−28.0	−20.0
	216.9	142.0	100.0
Total equity	253.9	179.0	130.0
Current liabilities			
Trade payables	8.8	7.7	6.4
Tax payable	28.5	25.6	23.3
Dividends payable	0.0	28.0	20.0
Interest payable	1.8	2.3	2.3
Total current liabilities	39.1	63.6	52.0
Non-current liabilities			
Loans	35.0	45.0	45.0
Provisions (deferred tax)	20.6	17.0	12.6
Total non-current liabilities	55.6	62.0	57.6
Total liabilities	94.7	125.6	109.6
Total equity and liabilities	348.6	304.6	239.6

Note

	20X8	20X7	20X6
	$m	$m	$m
Non-current assets	280.0	200.0	160.0
Less accumulated depreciation	112.0	84.0	64.0
Net book value of non-current assets	168.0	116.0	96.0

The projected figures assume:

(i) $10 million of the existing loans will be repaid during the year.

(ii)   Capital investment in plant and equipment of $80 million will be undertaken.

The company is quoted on an international stock exchange and its beta value (based upon three years of monthly return data) is 1.40. The current risk free rate is 3% and the equity risk premium is 5%. The current share price is $16.20 and the sector price/earnings ratio is 24. The company's cost of debt capital remains at its current rate of 5%. You may assume that the current cost of equity capital remains unchanged over the term of the projection.

Required:

(a)   Prepare a cash flow forecast for the year ended 31 December 20X8.

Note: the format does not need to comply with accounting standards.   **(7 marks)**

(b)   Draft a brief report for senior management reviewing the potential performance of the business in the year ended 31 December 20X8 if the expectations contained within the strategic plan are fulfilled. You should use the Economic Value Added (EVA™) and any other performance measures you think appropriate.   **(18 marks)**

(Total: 25 marks)

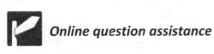 *Online question assistance*

30   KENGAI CO (DEC 11)

The Chairman and the Chief Executive Officer (CEO) of Kengai Co are discussing whether or not the company should adopt a triple bottom line (TBL) reporting system in order to demonstrate Kengai Co's level of sustainable development. Kengai Co's competitors are increasingly adopting TBL reporting and the Chairman feels that it would be beneficial to follow suit. The CEO, on the other hand, feels that pursuing TBL reporting would be expensive and is not necessary.

Required:

(a)   Explain what TBL reporting involves and how it would help demonstrate Kengai Co's sustainable development. Support your explanation by including examples of proxies that can be used to indicate the impact of the factors that would be included in a TBL report.   **(8 marks)**

(b)   Discuss how producing a TBL report may help Kengai Co's management focus on improving the financial position of the company. Illustrate the discussion with examples where appropriate.   **(10 marks)**

(Total: 18 marks)

31   ENNEA CO (JUN 12)

Three proposals were put forward for further consideration after a meeting of the executive directors of Ennea Co to discuss the future investment and financing strategy of the business. Ennea Co is a listed company operating in the haulage and shipping industry.

Proposal 1

To increase the company's level of debt by borrowing a further $20 million and use the funds raised to buy back share capital.

Proposal 2

To increase the company's level of debt by borrowing a further $20 million and use these funds to invest in additional non-current assets in the haulage strategic business unit.

Proposal 3

To sell excess non-current haulage assets with a net book value of $25 million for $27 million and focus on offering more services to the shipping strategic business unit. This business unit will require no additional investment in non-current assets. All the funds raised from the sale of the non-current assets will be used to reduce the company's debt.

Ennea Co financial information

Extracts from the forecast financial position for the coming year

	$m
Non-current assets	282
Current assets	66
Total assets	348

Equity and liabilities

Share capital (40c per share par value)	48
Retained earnings	123
Total equity	171
Non-current liabilities	140
Current liabilities	37
Total liabilities	177
Total liabilities and capital	348

Ennea Co's forecast after tax profit for the coming year is expected to be $26 million and its current share price is $3.20 per share. The non-current liabilities consist solely of a 6% medium term loan redeemable within seven years. The terms of the loan contract stipulates that an increase in borrowing will result in an increase in the coupon payable of 25 basis points on the total amount borrowed, while a reduction in borrowing will lower the coupon payable by 15 basis points on the total amount borrowed.

Ennea Co's effective tax rate is 20%. The company's estimated after tax rate of return on investment is expected to be 15% on any new investment. It is expected that any reduction in investment would suffer the same rate of return.

Required:

(a) Estimate and discuss the impact of each of the three proposals on the forecast statement of financial position, the earnings and earnings per share, and gearing of Ennea Co.   **(20 marks)**

(b) An alternative suggestion to proposal three was made where the non-current assets could be leased to other companies instead of being sold. The lease receipts would then be converted into an asset through securitisation. The proceeds from the sale of the securitised lease receipts asset would be used to reduce the outstanding loan borrowings.

Required:

Explain what the securitisation process would involve and what would be the key barriers to Ennea Co undertaking the process. (5 marks)

(Total: 25 marks)

32 LIMNI CO (JUN 13)

Limni Co is a large company manufacturing hand-held electronic devices such as mobile phones and tablet computers. The company has been growing rapidly over the last few years, but it also has high research and development expenditure. It is involved in a number of projects worldwide, developing new and innovative products and systems in a rapidly changing industry. Due to the nature of the industry, this significant growth in earnings has never been stable, but has depended largely on the success of the new innovations and competitor actions. However, in the last two years it seems that the rapid period of growth is slowing, with fewer products coming to market compared to previous years.

Limni Co has never paid dividends and has financed projects through internally generated funds and with occasional rights issues of new share capital. It currently has insignificant levels of debt. The retained cash reserves have recently grown because of a drop in the level of investment in new projects.

The company has an active treasury division which invests spare funds in traded equities, bonds and other financial instruments; and releases the funds when required for new projects. The division also manages cash flow risk using money and derivative markets. The treasury division is currently considering investing in three companies with the following profit after tax (PAT) and dividend history:

Year	Company Theta		Company Omega		Company Kappa	
	PAT	Dividends	PAT	Dividends	PAT	Dividends
	$000	$000	$000	$000	$000	$000
20X3	57,100	22,840	93,300	60,560	162,400	44,100
20X2	54,400	21,760	90,600	57,680	141,500	34,200
20X1	52,800	21,120	88,000	54,840	108,900	26,300
20X0	48,200	19,280	85,400	52,230	105,700	20,250
20W9	45,500	18,200	82,900	49,740	78,300	15,700

All of the three companies' share capital has remained largely unchanged since 20W9.

Recently, Limni Co's Board of Directors (BoD) came under pressure from the company's larger shareholders to start returning some of the funds, currently retained by the company, back to the shareholders. The BoD thinks that the shareholders have a strong case to ask for repayments. However, it is unsure whether to pay a special, one-off large dividend from its dividend capacity and retained funds, followed by small annual dividend payments; or to undertake a periodic share buyback scheme over the next few years.

Limni Co is due to prepare its statement of profit or loss shortly and estimates that the annual sales revenue will be $600 million, on which its profit before tax is expected to be 23% of sales revenue. It charges depreciation of 25% on a straight-line basis on its non-current assets of $220 million. It estimates that $67 million investment in current and non-current assets was spent during the year. It is due to receive $15 million in dividends from its subsidiary companies, on which annual tax of 20% on average has been paid. Limni Co itself pays annual tax at 26%, and the tax authorities where Limni Co is based charge tax on dividend remittances made by overseas subsidiary companies, but give full credit on tax already paid on those remittances. In order to fund the new policy of returning funds to shareholders, Limni Co's BoD wants to increase the current estimated dividend capacity by 10%, by asking the overseas subsidiary companies for higher repatriations.

Required:

(a)   **Discuss Limni Co's current dividend, financing and risk management policies, and suggest how the decision to return retained funds back to the shareholders will affect these policies.**   **(8 marks)**

(b)   **Evaluate the dividend policies of each of the three companies that Limni Co is considering investing in, and discuss which company Limni Co might select.**

(8 marks)

(c)   **Calculate, and briefly comment on, how much the dividends from overseas companies need to increase by, to increase Limni Co's dividend capacity by 10%.**

(6 marks)

(d)   **Discuss the benefits to Limni Co's shareholders of receiving repayments through a share buyback scheme as opposed to the dividend scheme described above.**

(3 marks)

(Total: 25 marks)

33   KAMALA CO (DEC 14)

Kamala Co, a listed company, manufactures parts and machinery for the construction industry. About five years ago, Kamala Co started to manufacture parts and machinery for hospitals and companies engaged in biomedical research using largely the same manufacturing and processing systems it already had in place. In 2011, a young and ambitious chief executive officer (CEO) took over the running of the company.

With the publication of the latest financial statements for the year to 30 November 2014, the CEO made a brief statement and it includes the following two points:

*   The CEO was very pleased with growth in the financial ratios provided and sales revenue from 2012 to 2014. More pleasing was growth in the share price, which increased even faster than the growth in the market index, suggesting that Kamala Co has been a successful company.

*   The CEO expressed a desire to make Kamala Co the leading manufacturer of parts and machinery for the construction industry by acquiring a major rival manufacturer in 2015, and financing the acquisition through an issue of a new bond and a small rights issue.

An analyst, after examining the recent financial statements and the two points above, was less positive about Kamala Co's future prospects.

Given below are extracts from the recent financial statements, some ratios, and other financial information for Kamala Co.

Year ending 30 November (all amounts in $m)

	2012	2013	2014
Sales revenue	3,760	4,054	5,230
Operating profit	714	819	1,098
Finance costs	97	168	269
Profit before tax	617	651	829
Taxation	154	163	207
Profit for the year	463	488	622
Dividends	139	137	152

Year ending 30 November (all amounts in $m)

	2012	2013	2014
Total non-current assets	3,962	5,507	7,669
Total current assets	980	1,410	1,880
Total non-current and current assets	4,942	6,917	9,549
Equity			
Ordinary shares ($0.25)	750	750	750
Reserves	1,476	1,827	2,297
Total equity	2,226	2,577	3,047
Non-current liabilities			
Bank loans	476	1,176	1,316
Bonds	1,008	1,008	2,218
Total non-current liabilities	1,484	2,184	3,534
Current liabilities			
Trade and other payables	1,232	1,540	2,016
Bank overdraft	–	616	952
Total current liabilities	1,232	2,156	2,968
Total non-current and current liabilities	2,716	4,340	6,502

Kamala Co: By activity

Year ending 30 November (all amounts in $m)

	2012	2013	2014
Sales revenue			
Construction	2,420	2,644	3,660
Hospitals and biomedical	1,340	1,410	1,570
Operating profit			
Construction	460	489	693
Hospitals and biomedical	254	330	405

Ratios: Kamala Co

	2012	2013	2014
Operating profit margin	19.0%	20.2%	21.0%
Dividend cover	3.3	3.6	4.1
Earnings per share	15.4c	16.3c	20.7c
Gearing [(debt/debt + equity)]	40%	46%	54%

Other financial information

	30 November 2012	30 November 2013	30 November 2014
Kamala Co share price ($)	1.69	2.01	2.69
Market index	4,539	5,447	6,550
Industry index	840	1,092	1,422
Industry average PE ratio	9.2:1	12.1:1	15.3:1

	2013 ($m)	2014 ($m)
Depreciation deducted to arrive at the operating profit (equivalent to tax allowable depreciation)	826	1,150
Economic depreciation	990	1,380
Non-cash expenses (excluding depreciation)	150	170

Kamala Co's cost of capital is estimated to be 10%. The company's corporation tax rate is 25%.

Required:

(a) Discuss the advantages and drawbacks of using the economic value added (EVA™) technique to assess a company's performance. **(6 marks)**

(b) Estimate Kamala Co's EVA™ for the years ending 30 November 2013 and 30 November 2014. **(5 marks)**

(c) Evaluate Kamala Co's performance and conclude whether the analyst's opinion or the chief executive officer's opinion has the greater validity. Include any additional ratio and activity trends, and share price analysis, which are deemed to be relevant to the evaluation. **(14 marks)**

(Total: 25 marks)

ADVANCED INVESTMENT APPRAISAL

34 STRAYER INC *Walk in the footsteps of a top tutor*

The managers of Strayer Inc are investigating a potential $25 million investment. The investment would be a diversification away from existing mainstream activities and into the printing industry. $6 million of the investment would be financed by internal funds, $10 million by a rights issue and $9 million by long-term loans. The investment is expected to generate pre-tax net cash flows of approximately $5 million per year, for a period of ten years. The residual value at the end of Year 10 is forecast to be $5 million after tax. As the investment is in an area that the government wishes to develop, a subsidised loan of $4 million out of the total $9 million is available. This will cost 2% below the company's normal cost of long-term debt finance, which is 8%.

Strayer's equity beta is 0.85, and its financial gearing is 60% equity, 40% debt by market value. The average equity beta in the printing industry is 1.2, and average gearing 50% equity, 50% debt by market value. The risk-free rate is 5.5% per annum and the market return 12% per annum. Issue costs are estimated to be 1% for debt financing (excluding the subsidised loan), and 4% for equity financing. These costs are not tax allowable.

The corporate tax rate is 30%.

Required:

(a) **Estimate the Adjusted Present Value (APV) of the proposed investment. (12 marks)**

(b) **Explain the difference between APV and NPV as methods of investment appraisal and comment upon the circumstances under which APV might be a better method of evaluating a capital investment than NPV. (5 marks)**

(c) **Explain the major differences between Islamic finance and other conventional forms of finance such as those being considered by Strayer. Identify, and briefly discuss, two Islamic financial instruments that could be of use to Strayer in the above situation. (8 marks)**

(Total: 25 marks)

35 TAMPEM INC

The financial management team of Tampem Inc is discussing how the company should appraise new investments. There is a difference of opinion between two managers.

Manager A believes that a net present value should be calculated using a suitable WACC as a discount rate. Manager A believes that positive NPV investments are quickly reflected in increases in the company's share price.

Manager B states that NPV is not good enough, as it is only valid in potentially restrictive conditions, and should be replaced by APV (adjusted present value).

Tampem has produced estimates of relevant cash flows and other financial information associated with a new investment. These are shown below:

	$000			
Year	*1*	*2*	*3*	*4*
Investment pre-tax operating cash flows	1,250	1,400	1,600	1,800

Notes:

(i)   The investment will cost $5,400,000 payable immediately, including $600,000 for working capital and $400,000 for issue costs. $300,000 of issue costs is for equity, and $100,000 for debt. Issue costs are not tax allowable.

(ii)   The investment will be financed 50% equity, 50% debt, which is believed to reflect its debt capacity.

(iii)   Expected company gearing after the investment will change to 60% equity, 40% debt by market values.

(iv)   The investment equity beta is 1.5.

(v)   Debt finance for the investment will be an 8% fixed-rate debenture.

(vi)   Tax allowable depreciation allowances are at 25% per year on a reducing-balance basis.

(vii)   The corporate tax rate is 30%. Tax is payable in the year that the taxable cash flow arises.

(viii) The risk-free rate is 4% and the market return 10%.

(ix)   The after-tax realisable value of the investment as a continuing operation is estimated to be $1.5 million (including working capital) at the end of Year 4.

(x)   Working capital may be assumed to be constant during the four years.

Required:

(a)   **Calculate the expected NPV and APV of the proposed investment.**   **(10 marks)**

(b)   **Discuss briefly the validity of the views of the two managers. Use your calculations in (a) to illustrate and support the discussion.**   **(5 marks)**

(c)   **Provide examples of ethical issues that might affect capital investment decisions, and discuss the importance of such issues for strategic financial management.**   **(10 marks)**

          (Total: 25 marks)

36   DIGUNDER

Digunder, a property development company, has gained planning permission for the development of a housing complex at Newtown which will be developed over a three year period. The resulting property sales less building costs have an expected net present value of $4 million at a cost of capital of 10% per annum. Digunder has an option to acquire the land in Newtown, at an agreed price of $24 million, which must be exercised within the next two years. Immediate building of the housing complex would be risky as the project has a volatility attaching to its net present value of 25%.

One source of risk is the potential for development of Newtown as a regional commercial centre for the large number of professional firms leaving the capital, Bigcity, because of high rents and local business taxes. Within the next two years, an announcement by the government will be made about the development of transport links into Newtown from outlying districts including the area where Digunder hold the land option concerned. The risk free rate of interest is 5% per annum.

Required:

(a) Estimate the value of the option to delay the start of the project for two years using the Black and Scholes option pricing model and comment upon your findings. Assume that the government will make its announcement about the potential transport link at the end of the two-year period. **(12 marks)**

(b) On the basis of your valuation of the option to delay, estimate the overall value of the project, giving a concise rationale for the valuation method you have used.

(4 marks)

(c) Describe the limitations of the valuation method you used in (a) above and describe how you would value the option if the government were to make the announcement at ANY time over the next two years. **(4 marks)**

(Total: 20 marks)

37 KENAND CO

(a) Kenand Co has a cash surplus of $1m, which the financial manager is keen to invest in corporate bonds. He has identified two potential investment opportunities, in two different companies which are both rated A by the major credit rating agencies:

Option 1:

AB Co has $100m of bonds already in issue. The bonds carry a coupon rate of 5% per annum, and the financial press is reporting that the bonds have a bid yield of 6.2% per annum. The bonds are redeemable at a 10% premium to nominal value in 4 years.

Option 2:

XY Co is about to issue $50m of 3 year bonds with a coupon rate of 4% per annum. The bonds will be redeemable at par in 3 years. The annual spot yield curve for government bonds is:

1 year 3.54%

2 year 4.01%

3 year 4.70%

4 year 5.60%

Extract from a major credit rating agency's website: Table of spreads (in basis points)

Rating	1 year	2 year	3 year	4 year
AAA	5	18	29	40
AA	16	30	42	50
A	26	39	50	60

Required:

(i) Calculate the theoretical market value of a $100 bond in AB Co, and the theoretical issue price of a $100 bond in XY Co. Calculate how many bonds Kenand Co will be able to buy with its $1m. **(6 marks)**

(ii) Estimate the Macauley duration of the AB Co bonds and the XY Co bonds, and interpret your results. **(8 marks)**

(b)   XY Co (details presented in part (a) above) is keen to hedge against interest rate risk on the new bonds which are being issued. The company treasurer expects interest rates to be flat for the coming year, but he is keen to arrange a Forward Rate Agreement (FRA) which will fix the company's borrowing rate for the following year.

Required:

Calculate the forward rate which the bank will quote for a 12 v 24 FRA.   (3 marks)

(c)   XY Co already has $20m of borrowings in the form of variable rate loans, where the interest rate is based on the given A rated company's yield curve figures. Because of the long-term threat of interest rate rises, the company treasurer has approached the bank to discuss the possibility of entering into a 4 year interest rate swap, whereby XY Co would pay the bank a fixed rate of interest for 4 years, in exchange for receiving a variable rate of return from the bank of the given yield rates less 30 basis points.

Required:

Calculate the fixed rate of interest payable by XY Co to the bank in such a swap arrangement.   (8 marks)

(Total: 25 marks)

38   FUBUKI CO (DEC 10)

Fubuki Co, an unlisted company based in Megaera, has been manufacturing electrical parts used in mobility vehicles for people with disabilities and the elderly, for many years. These parts are exported to various manufacturers worldwide but at present there are no local manufacturers of mobility vehicles in Megaera. Retailers in Megaera normally import mobility vehicles and sell them at an average price of $4,000 each. Fubuki Co wants to manufacture mobility vehicles locally and believes that it can sell vehicles of equivalent quality locally at a discount of 37.5% to the current average retail price.

Although this is a completely new venture for Fubuki Co, it will be in addition to the company's core business. Fubuki Co's directors expect to develop the project for a period of four years and then sell it for $16 million to a private equity firm. Megaera's government has been positive about the venture and has offered Fubuki Co a subsidised loan of up to 80% of the investment funds required, at a rate of 200 basis points below Fubuki Co's borrowing rate. Currently Fubuki Co can borrow at 300 basis points above the five-year government debt yield rate.

A feasibility study commissioned by the directors, at a cost of $250,000, has produced the following information.

1   Initial cost of acquiring suitable premises will be $11 million, and plant and machinery used in the manufacture will cost $3 million. Acquiring the premises and installing the machinery is a quick process and manufacturing can commence almost immediately.

2   It is expected that in the first year 1,300 units will be manufactured and sold. Unit sales will grow by 40% in each of the next two years before falling to an annual growth rate of 5% for the final year. After the first year the selling price per unit is expected to increase by 3% per year.

3   In the first year, it is estimated that the total direct material, labour and variable overheads costs will be $1,200 per unit produced. After the first year, the direct costs are expected to increase by an annual inflation rate of 8%.

4   Annual fixed overhead costs would be $2.5 million of which 60% are centrally allocated overheads. The fixed overhead costs will increase by 5% per year after the first year.

5   Fubuki Co will need to make working capital available of 15% of the anticipated sales revenue for the year, at the beginning of each year. The working capital is expected to be released at the end of the fourth year when the project is sold.

Fubuki Co's tax rate is 25% per year on taxable profits. Tax is payable in the same year as when the profits are earned. Tax allowable depreciation is available on the plant and machinery on a straight-line basis. It is anticipated that the value attributable to the plant and machinery after four years is $400,000 of the price at which the project is sold. No tax allowable depreciation is available on the premises.

Fubuki Co uses 8% as its discount rate for new projects but feels that this rate may not be appropriate for this new type of investment. It intends to raise the full amount of funds through debt finance and take advantage of the government's offer of a subsidised loan. Issue costs are 4% of the gross finance required. It can be assumed that the debt capacity available to the company is equivalent to the actual amount of debt finance raised for the project.

Although no other companies produce mobility vehicles in Megaera, Haizum Co, a listed company, produces electrical-powered vehicles using similar technology to that required for the mobility vehicles. Haizum Co's cost of equity is estimated to be 14% and it pays tax at 28%. Haizum Co has 15 million shares in issue trading at $2.53 each and $40 million bonds trading at $94.88 per $100. The five-year government debt yield is currently estimated at 4.5% and the market risk premium at 4%.

Required:

(a)   **Evaluate, on financial grounds, whether Fubuki Co should proceed with the project.**
                                                                                                              (17 marks)

(b)   **Discuss the appropriateness of the evaluation method used and explain any assumptions made in part (a) above.**   **(8 marks)**

                                                                                                         (Total: 25 marks)

39   INVESTMENT PROJECT REVIEW

You have been conducting a detailed review of an investment project proposed by one of the divisions of your business. Your review has two aims: first to correct the proposal for any errors of principle and second, to recommend a financial measure to replace payback as one of the criteria for acceptability when a project is presented to the company's board of directors for approval. The company's current weighted average cost of capital is 10% per annum.

The initial capital investment is for $150 million followed by $50 million one year later. The post tax cash flows, for this project, in $million, including the estimated tax benefit from tax allowable depreciation, are as follows:

Year	0	1	2	3	4	5	6
Capital investment (plant and machinery):							
First phase	−127.50						
Second phase		−36.88					
Project post tax cash flow ($ millions)			44.00	68.00	60.00	35.00	20.00

Company tax is charged at 30% and is paid/recovered in the year in which the liability is incurred. The company has sufficient profits elsewhere to recover tax allowable depreciation on this project, in full, in the year they are incurred. All the capital investment is eligible for a first year allowance for tax purposes of 50% followed by tax allowable depreciation of 25% per annum on a reducing balance basis.

You notice the following points when conducting your review:

1   An interest charge of 8% per annum on a proposed $50 million loan has been included in the project's post tax cash flow before tax has been calculated.

2   Depreciation for the use of company shared assets of $4 million per annum has been charged in calculating the project post tax cash flow.

3   Activity based allocations of company indirect costs of $8 million have been included in the project's post tax cash flow. However, additional corporate infrastructure costs of $4 million per annum have been ignored which you discover would only be incurred if the project proceeds.

4   It is expected that the capital equipment will be written off and disposed of at the end of year six. The proceeds of the sale of the capital equipment are expected to be $7 million which have been included in the forecast of the project's post tax cash flow. You also notice that an estimate for site clearance of $5 million has not been included nor any tax saving recognised on the unclaimed tax allowable depreciation on the disposal of the capital equipment.

Required:

(a)   **Prepare a corrected project evaluation using the net present value technique supported by a separate assessment of the sensitivity of the project to a $1 million change in the initial capital expenditure.**   **(14 marks)**

(b)   **Estimate the discounted payback period and the duration for this project commenting on the relative advantages and disadvantages of each method.**

(5 marks)

(c)   **Draft a brief report for presentation to the board of directors with a recommendation on the acceptability of this project and on the techniques that the board should consider when reviewing capital investment projects in future.**

(6 marks)

(Total: 25 marks)

40   MMC (JUN 11)

MesmerMagic Co (MMC) is considering whether to undertake the development of a new computer game based on an adventure film due to be released in 22 months. It is expected that the game will be available to buy two months after the film's release, by which time it will be possible to judge the popularity of the film with a high degree of certainty. However, at present, there is considerable uncertainty about whether the film, and therefore the game, is likely to be successful. Although MMC would pay for the exclusive rights to develop and sell the game now, the directors are of the opinion that they should delay the decision to produce and market the game until the film has been released and the game is available for sale.

MMC has forecast the following end of year cash flows for the four-year sales period of the game.

Year	1	2	3	4
Cash flows ($ million)	25	18	10	5

MMC will spend $7 million at the start of each of the next two years to develop the game, the gaming platform, and to pay for the exclusive rights to develop and sell the game. Following this, the company will require $35 million for production, distribution and marketing costs at the start of the four-year sales period of the game.

It can be assumed that all the costs and revenues include inflation. The relevant cost of capital for this project is 11% and the risk free rate is 3˙5%. MMC has estimated the likely volatility of the cash flows at a standard deviation of 30%.

Required:

(a) **Estimate the financial impact of the directors' decision to delay the production and marketing of the game. The Black-Scholes Option Pricing model may be used, where appropriate. All relevant calculations should be shown.** (12 marks)

(b) **Briefly discuss the implications of the answer obtained in part (a) above.** (5 marks)

(Total: 17 marks)

41 TISA CO (JUN 12)

Tisa Co is considering an opportunity to produce an innovative component which, when fitted into motor vehicle engines, will enable them to utilise fuel more efficiently. The component can be manufactured using either process Omega or process Zeta. Although this is an entirely new line of business for Tisa Co, it is of the opinion that developing either process over a period of four years and then selling the productions rights at the end of four years to another company may prove lucrative.

The annual after-tax cash flows for each process are as follows:

Process Omega

Year	0	1	2	3	4
After-tax cash flows ($000)	(3,800)	1,220	1,153	1,386	3,829

Process Zeta

Year	0	1	2	3	4
After-tax cash flows ($000)	(3,800)	643	546	1,055	5,990

Tisa Co has 10 million 50c shares trading at 180c each. Its loans have a current value of $3.6 million and an average after-tax cost of debt of 4.50%. Tisa Co's capital structure is unlikely to change significantly following the investment in either process.

Elfu Co manufactures electronic parts for cars including the production of a component similar to the one being considered by Tisa Co. Elfu Co's equity beta is 1.40, and it is estimated that the equivalent equity beta for its other activities, excluding the component production, is 1.25. Elfu Co has 400 million 25c shares in issue trading at 120c each. Its debt finance consists of variable rate loans redeemable in seven years. The loans paying interest at base rate plus 120 basis points have a current value of $96 million. It can be assumed that 80% of Elfu Co's debt finance and 75% of Elfu Co's equity finance can be attributed to other activities excluding the component production. Both companies pay annual corporation tax at a rate of 25%. The current base rate is 3.5% and the market risk premium is estimated at 5.8%.

Required:

(a) Provide a reasoned estimate of the cost of capital that Tisa Co should use to calculate the net present value of the two processes. Include all relevant calculations. **(8 marks)**

(b) Calculate the internal rate of return (IRR) and the modified internal rate of return (MIRR) for Process Omega. Given that the IRR and MIRR of Process Zeta are 26.6% and 23.3% respectively, recommend which process, if any, Tisa Co should proceed with and explain your recommendation. **(8 marks)**

(c) Elfu Co has estimated an annual standard deviation of $800,000 on one of its other projects, based on a normal distribution of returns. The average annual return on this project is $2,200,000.

Required:

Estimate the project's Value at Risk (VAR) at a 99% confidence level for one year and over the project's life of five years. Explain what is meant by the answers obtained. **(4 marks)**

(Total: 20 marks)

42 ARBORE CO (DEC 12)

Arbore Co is a large listed company with many autonomous departments operating as investment centres. It sets investment limits for each department based on a three-year cycle. Projects selected by departments would have to fall within the investment limits set for each of the three years. All departments would be required to maintain a capital investment monitoring system, and report on their findings annually to Arbore Co's board of directors.

The Durvo department is considering the following five investment projects with three years of initial investment expenditure, followed by several years of positive cash inflows. The department's initial investment expenditure limits are $9,000,000, $6,000,000 and $5,000,000 for years one, two and three respectively. None of the projects can be deferred and all projects can be scaled down but not scaled up.

Investment required at start of year

Project	Year one (Immediately)	Year two	Year three	Project net present value
PDur01	$4,000,000	$1,100,000	$2,400,000	$464,000
PDur02	$800,000	$2,800,000	$3,200,000	$244,000
PDur03	$3,200,000	$3,562,000	$0	$352,000
PDur04	$3,900,000	$0	$200,000	$320,000
PDur05	$2,500,000	$1,200,000	$1,400,000	Not provided

PDur05 project's annual operating cash flows commence at the end of year four and last for a period of 15 years. The project generates annual sales of 300,000 units at a selling price of $14 per unit and incurs total annual relevant costs of $3,230,000. Although the costs and units sold of the project can be predicted with a fair degree of certainty, there is considerable uncertainty about the unit selling price. The department uses a required rate of return of 11% for its projects, and inflation can be ignored.

The Durvo department's managing director is of the opinion that all projects which return a positive net present value should be accepted and does not understand the reason(s) why Arbore Co imposes capital rationing on its departments. Furthermore, she is not sure why maintaining a capital investment monitoring system would be beneficial to the company.

Required:

(a) Calculate the net present value of project PDur05. Calculate and comment on what percentage fall in the selling price would need to occur before the net present value falls to zero. **(6 marks)**

(b) Formulate an appropriate capital rationing model, based on the above investment limits, that maximises the net present value for department Durvo. Finding a solution for the model is not required. **(3 marks)**

(c) Assume the following output is produced when the capital rationing model in part (b) above is solved:

Category 1: Total Final Value

$1,184,409

Category 2: Adjustable Final Values

Project PDur01: 0.958
Project PDur02: 0.407
Project PDur03: 0.732
Project PDur04: 0.000
Project PDur05: 1.000

Category 3:

Constraints Utilised	*Slack*
Year one: $9,000,000	Year one: $0
Year two: $6,000,000	Year two: $0
Year three: $5,000,000	Year three: $0

Required:

Explain the figures produced in each of the three output categories. **(5 marks)**

(d) Provide a brief response to the managing director's opinions by:

(i) Explaining why Arbore Co may want to impose capital rationing on its departments; **(2 marks)**

(ii) Explaining the features of a capital investment monitoring system and discussing the benefits of maintaining such a system. **(4 marks)**

(Total: 20 marks)

43   BURUNG CO (JUN 14)

You have recently commenced working for Burung Co and are reviewing a four-year project which the company is considering for investment. The project is in a business activity which is very different from Burung Co's current line of business.

The following net present value estimate has been made for the project:

All figures are in $ million

Year	0	1	2	34	4
Sales revenue		23.03	36.60	49.07	27.14
Direct project costs		(13.82)	(21.96)	(29.44)	(16.28)
Interest		(1.20)	(1.20)	(1.20)	(1.20)
Profit		8.01	13.44	18.43	9.66
Tax (20%)		(1.60)	(2.69)	(3.69)	(1.93)
Investment/sale	(38.00)				4.00
Cash flows	(38.00)	6.41	10.75	14.74	11.73
Discount factors (7%)	1	0.935	0.873	0.816	0.763
Present values	(38.00)	5.99	9.38	12.03	8.95

Net present value is negative $1.65 million, and therefore the recommendation is that the project should not be accepted.

In calculating the net present value of the project, the following notes were made:

(i)   Since the real cost of capital is used to discount cash flows, neither the sales revenue nor the direct project costs have been inflated. It is estimated that the inflation rate applicable to sales revenue is 8% per year and to the direct project costs is 4% per year.

(ii)   The project will require an initial investment of $38 million. Of this, $16 million relates to plant and machinery, which is expected to be sold for $4 million when the project ceases, after taking any taxation and inflation impact into account.

(iii)   Tax allowable depreciation is available on the plant and machinery at 50% in the first year, followed by 25% per year thereafter on a reducing balance basis. A balancing adjustment is available in the year the plant and machinery is sold. Burung Co pays 20% tax on its annual taxable profits. No tax allowable depreciation is available on the remaining investment assets and they will have a nil value at the end of the project.

(iv)   Burung Co uses either a nominal cost of capital of 11% or a real cost of capital of 7% to discount all projects, given that the rate of inflation has been stable at 4% for a number of years.

(v)   Interest is based on Burung Co's normal borrowing rate of 150 basis points over the 10-year government yield rate.

(vi)   At the beginning of each year, Burung Co will need to provide working capital of 20% of the anticipated sales revenue for the year. Any remaining working capital will be released at the end of the project.

(vii)   Working capital and depreciation have not been taken into account in the net present value calculation above, since depreciation is not a cash flow and all the working capital is returned at the end of the project.

It is anticipated that the project will be financed entirely by debt, 60% of which will be obtained from a subsidised loan scheme run by the government, which lends money at a rate of 100 basis points below the 10-year government debt yield rate of 2.5%. Issue costs related to raising the finance are 2% of the gross finance required. The remaining 40% will be funded from Burung Co's normal borrowing sources. It can be assumed that the debt capacity available to Burung Co is equal to the actual amount of debt finance raised for the project.

Burung Co has identified a company, Lintu Co, which operates in the same line of business as that of the project it is considering. Lintu Co is financed by 40 million shares trading at $3.20 each and $34 million debt trading at $94 per $100. Lintu Co's equity beta is estimated at 1.5. The current yield on government treasury bills is 2% and it is estimated that the market risk premium is 8%. Lintu Co pays tax at an annual rate of 20%.

Both Burung Co and Lintu Co pay tax in the same year as when profits are earned.

Required:

(a) **Calculate the adjusted present value (APV) for the project, correcting any errors made in the net present value estimate above, and conclude whether the project should be accepted or not. Show all relevant calculations.** **(15 marks)**

(b) **Comment on the corrections made to the original net present value estimate and explain the APV approach taken in part (a), including any assumptions made.**

(10 marks)

(Total: 25 marks)

44 RIVIERE CO (DEC 14)

Riviere Co is a small company based in the European Union (EU). It produces high quality frozen food which it exports to a small number of supermarket chains located within the EU as well. The EU is a free trade area for trade between its member countries.

Riviere Co finds it difficult to obtain bank finance and relies on a long-term strategy of using internally generated funds for new investment projects. This constraint means that it cannot accept every profitable project and often has to choose between them.

Riviere Co is currently considering investment in one of two mutually exclusive food production projects: Privi and Drugi. Privi will produce and sell a new range of frozen desserts exclusively within the EU. Drugi will produce and sell a new range of frozen desserts and savoury foods to supermarket chains based in countries outside the EU. Each project will last for five years and the following financial information refers to both projects.

Project Drugi, annual after-tax cash flows expected at the end of each year (€000s)

Year	Current	1	2	3	4	5
Cash flows (€000s)	(11,840)	1,230	1,680	4,350	10,240	2,200

	Privi	Drugi
Net present value	€2,054,000	€2,293,000
Internal rate of return	17.6%	Not provided
Modified internal rate of return	13.4%	Not provided
Value at risk (over the project's life)		
95% confidence level	€1,103,500	Not provided
90% confidence level	€860,000	Not provided

Both projects' net present value has been calculated based on Riviere Co's nominal cost of capital of 10%. It can be assumed that both projects' cash flow returns are normally distributed and the annual standard deviation of project Drugi's present value of after-tax cash flows is estimated to be €400,000. It can also be assumed that all sales are made in € (Euro) and therefore the company is not exposed to any foreign exchange exposure.

Notwithstanding how profitable project Drugi may appear to be, Riviere Co's board of directors is concerned about the possible legal risks if it invests in the project because they have never dealt with companies outside the EU before.

Required:

(a) Discuss the aims of a free trade area, such as the European Union (EU), and the possible benefits to Riviere Co of operating within the EU.   **(5 marks)**

(b) Calculate the figures which have not been provided for project Drugi and recommend which project should be accepted. Provide a justification for the recommendation and explain what the value at risk measures.   **(13 marks)**

(c) Discuss the possible legal risks of investing in project Drugi which Riviere Co may be concerned about and how these may be mitigated.   **(7 marks)**

(Total: 25 marks)

ACQUISITIONS AND MERGERS

45   DOUBLER INC   *Walk in the footsteps of a top tutor*

Doubler Inc is considering a takeover bid for Fader Inc. Doubler's board of directors has issued the following statement: 'Our superior P/E ratio and synergistic effects of the acquisition will lead to a post-acquisition increase in earnings per share and in the combined market value of the companies'.

Summarised financial data for the companies ($ million)

	Doubler	Fader
Sales	48.00	35.30
Profit before tax	6.30	4.10
Tax	(1.89)	(1.23)
Profit after tax	4.41	2.87
Dividends	2.00	1.10

	$ million	
	Doubler	Fader
Non-current assets (net)	28.40	26.50
Current assets	22.64	17.30
Total assets	51.04	43.80

Equity and liabilities

Ordinary shares (10 cents par value)	4.00	3.00
Reserves	21.12	19.20
Medium and long term borrowing	8.60	11.40
Current liabilities	17.32	10.20
	———	———
	51.04	43.80
	———	———

Notes:

(i) After tax savings in cash operating costs of $750,000 per year indefinitely are expected as a result of the acquisition.

(ii) Initial redundancy costs will be $1 million before tax.

(iii) Doubler's cost of capital is 12%.

(iv) Current shares prices are: Doubler 290 cents, Fader 180 cents.

(v) The proposed terms of the takeover are payment of 2 Doubler shares for every 3 Fader shares.

Required:

(a) Calculate the current P/E ratios of Doubler and Fader **(2 marks)**

(b) Estimate the expected post acquisition earnings per share and comment upon the importance of increasing the earnings per share. **(4 marks)**

(c) Estimate the effect on the combined market value as a result of the takeover using:

    (i) P/E based valuation

    (ii) cash flow based valuation.

State clearly any assumptions that you make. **(5 marks)**

(d) Discuss the limitations of your estimates in (c) above. **(3 marks)**

(e) Evaluate the strategic implications of making a hostile bid for a company compared with an aggressive investment programme of organic growth. **(6 marks)**

(f) The regulation of takeovers varies from country to country. Outline the typical factors that such regulation includes. **(5 marks)**

(Total: 25 marks)

 Online question assistance

---

46   MERCURY TRAINING

Mercury Training was established in 1999 and since that time it has developed rapidly. The directors are considering either a flotation or an outright sale of the company.

The company provides training for companies in the computer and telecommunications sectors. It offers a variety of courses ranging from short intensive courses in office software to high level risk management courses using advanced modelling techniques. Mercury employs a number of in-house experts who provide technical materials and other support for the teams that service individual client requirements. In recent years, Mercury has diversified into the financial services sector and now also provides computer simulation systems to companies for valuing acquisitions. This business now accounts for one third of the company's total revenue.

Mercury currently has 10 million, 50c shares in issue. Jupiter is one of the few competitors in Mercury's line of business. However, Jupiter is only involved in the training business. Jupiter is listed on a small company investment market and has an estimated beta of 1.5. Jupiter has 50 million shares in issue with a market price of 580c. The average beta for the financial services sector is 0.9. Average market gearing (debt to total market value) in the financial services sector is estimated at 25%.

Other summary statistics for both companies for the year ended 31 December 20X7 are as follows:

	Mercury	Jupiter
Net assets at book value ($million)	65	45
Earnings per share (c)	100	50
Dividend per share (c)	25	25
Gearing (debt to total market value)	30%	12%
Five year historic earnings growth (annual)	12%	8%

Analysts forecast revenue growth in the training side of Mercury's business to be 6% per annum, but the financial services sector is expected to grow at just 4%.

Background information:

- The equity risk premium is 3.5% and the rate of return on short-dated government stock is 4.5%.

- Both companies can raise debt at 2.5% above the risk free rate.

- Tax on corporate profits is 40%.

Required:

(a)   **Estimate the cost of equity capital and the weighted average cost of capital for Mercury Training. Explain the circumstances where each of the two rates would be used.**   **(10 marks)**

(b)   **Advise the owners of Mercury Training on a range of likely issue prices for the company.**   **(8 marks)**

(c)   **Discuss the advantages and disadvantages, to the directors of Mercury Training, of a public listing versus private equity finance as a means of disposing of their interest in the company.**   **(7 marks)**

(Total: 25 marks)

47 KODIAK COMPANY

Kodiak Company is a small software design business established four years ago. The company is owned by three directors who have relied upon external accounting services in the past. The company has grown quickly and the directors have appointed you as a financial consultant to advise on the value of the business under their ownership.

The directors have limited liability and the bank loan is secured against the general assets of the business. The directors have no outstanding guarantees on the company's debt.

The company's latest statement of profit or loss and the extracted balances from the latest statement of financial position are as follows:

	$000	*Financial Position*	$000
Revenue	5,000	Opening non-current assets	1,200
Cost of Sales	3,000	Additions	66
Gross profit	2,000	Non-current assets (gross)	1,266
Other operating costs	1,877	Accumulated depreciation	367
Operating profit	123	Net book value	899
Interest on loan	74	Net current assets	270
Profit before tax	49	Loan	(990)
Income tax expense	15	Net Assets Employed	179
Profit for the period	34		

During the current year:

(1) Depreciation is charged at 10% per annum on the year end non-current asset balance before accumulated depreciation, and is included in other operating costs in the statement of profit or loss.

(2) The investment in net working capital is expected to increase in line with the growth in gross profit.

(3) Other operating costs consisted of:

	$000
Variable component at 15% of sales	750
Fixed costs	1,000
Depreciation on non-current assets	127

(4) Revenue and variable costs are projected to grow at 9% per annum and fixed costs are projected to grow at 6% per annum.

(5) The company pays interest on its outstanding loan of 7.5% per annum and incurs tax on its profits at 30%, payable in the following year. The company does not pay dividends.

(6) The net current assets reported in the statement of financial position contain $50,000 of cash.

One of your first tasks is to prepare for the directors a forward cash flow projection for three years and to value the firm on the basis of its expected free cash flow to equity. In discussion with them you note the following:

– The company will not dispose of any of its non-current assets but will increase its investment in new non-current assets by 20% per annum. The company's depreciation policy matches the currently available tax allowable depreciation. This straight-line write off policy is not likely to change.

– The directors will not take a dividend for the next three years but will then review the position taking into account the company's sustainable cash flow at that time.

– The level of the loan will be maintained at $990,000 and, on the basis of the forward yield curve, interest rates are not expected to change.

– The directors have set a target rate of return on their equity of 10% per annum which they believe fairly represents the opportunity cost of their invested funds.

Required:

(a) **Prepare a three-year cash flow forecast for the business on the basis described above highlighting the free cash flow to equity in each year.** **(13 marks)**

(b) **Estimate the value of the business based upon the expected free cash flow to equity and a terminal value based upon a sustainable growth rate of 3% per annum thereafter.** **(6 marks)**

(c) **Advise the directors on the assumptions and the uncertainties within your valuation.** **(6 marks)**

(Total: 25 marks)

48 KILENC CO (JUN 12)

Kilenc Co, a large listed company based in the UK, produces pharmaceutical products which are exported around the world. It is reviewing a proposal to set up a subsidiary company to manufacture a range of body and facial creams in Lanosia. These products will be sold to local retailers and to retailers in nearby countries.

Lanosia has a small but growing manufacturing industry in pharmaceutical products, although it remains largely reliant on imports. The Lanosian government has been keen to promote the pharmaceutical manufacturing industry through purchasing local pharmaceutical products, providing government grants and reducing the industry's corporate tax rate. It also imposes large duties on imported pharmaceutical products which compete with the ones produced locally.

Although politically stable, the recent worldwide financial crisis has had a significant negative impact on Lanosia. The country's national debt has grown substantially following a bailout of its banks and it has had to introduce economic measures which are hampering the country's ability to recover from a deep recession. Growth in real wages has been negative over the past three years, the economy has shrunk in the past year and inflation has remained higher than normal during this time.

On the other hand, corporate investment in capital assets, research and development, and education and training, has grown recently and interest rates remain low. This has led some economists to suggest that the economy should start to recover soon. Employment levels remain high in spite of low nominal wage growth.

Lanosian corporate governance regulations stipulate that at least 40% of equity share capital must be held by the local population. In addition at least 50% of members on the Board of Directors, including the Chairman, must be from Lanosia. Kilenc Co wants to finance the subsidiary company using a mixture of debt and equity. It wants to raise additional equity and debt finance in Lanosia in order to minimise exchange rate exposure. The small size of the subsidiary will have minimal impact on Kilenc Co's capital structure. Kilenc Co intends to raise the 40% equity through an initial public offering (IPO) in Lanosia and provide the remaining 60% of the equity funds from its own cash funds.

Required:

(a)   **Discuss the key risks and issues that Kilenc Co should consider when setting up a subsidiary company in Lanosia, and suggest how these may be mitigated.**

(15 marks)

(b)   The directors of Kilenc Co have learnt that a sizeable number of equity trades in Lanosia are conducted using dark pool trading systems.

Required:

Explain what dark pool trading systems are and how Kilenc Co's proposed Initial Public Offering (IPO) may be affected by these. (5 marks)

(Total: 20 marks)

49   SIGRA CO (DEC 12 A)

Sigra Co is a listed company producing confectionary products which it sells around the world. It wants to acquire Dentro Co, an unlisted company producing high quality, luxury chocolates. Sigra Co proposes to pay for the acquisition using one of the following three methods:

Method 1

A cash offer of $5.00 per Dentro Co share; or

Method 2

An offer of three of its shares for two of Dentro Co's shares; or

Method 3

An offer of a 2% coupon bond in exchange for 16 Dentro Co's shares. The bond will be redeemed in three years at its par value of $100.

Extracts from the latest financial statements of both companies are as follows:

	Sigra Co $000	Dentro Co $000
Sales revenue	44,210	4,680
Profit before tax	6,190	780
Taxation	(1,240)	(155)
Profit after tax	4,950	625
Dividends	(2,700)	(275)
Retained earnings for the year	2,250	350
Non-current assets	22,450	3,350
Current assets	3,450	247
Non-current liabilities	9,700	873
Current liabilities	3,600	436
Share capital (40c per share)	4,400	500
Reserves	8,200	1,788

Sigra Co's current share price is $3.60 per share and it has estimated that Dentro Co's price to earnings ratio is 12.5% higher than Sigra Co's current price to earnings ratio. Sigra Co's non-current liabilities include a 6% bond redeemable in three years at par which is currently trading at $104 per $100 par value. Sigra Co estimates that it could achieve synergy savings of 30% of Dentro Co's estimated equity value by eliminating duplicated administrative functions, selling excess non-current assets and through reducing the workforce numbers, if the acquisition were successful.

Required:

(a) **Explain briefly, in general terms, why many acquisitions in the real world are not successful.** **(5 marks)**

(b) **Estimate the percentage gain on a Dentro Co share under each of the above three payment methods. Comment on the answers obtained.** **(16 marks)**

(c) In relation to the acquisition, the board of directors of Sigra Co are considering the following two proposals:

Proposal 1

Once Sigra Co has obtained agreement from a significant majority of the shareholders, it will enforce the remaining minority shareholders to sell their shares.

Proposal 2

Sigra Co will offer an extra 3 cents per share, in addition to the bid price, to 30% of the shareholders of Dentro Co on a first-come, first-serve basis, as an added incentive to make the acquisition proceed more quickly.

Required:

With reference to the key aspects of the global regulatory framework for mergers and acquisitions, briefly discuss the above proposals. **(4 marks)**

(Total: 25 marks)

50   HAV CO (JUN 13)

Hav Co is a publicly listed company involved in the production of highly technical and sophisticated electronic components for complex machinery. It has a number of diverse and popular products, an active research and development department, significant cash reserves and a highly talented management who are very good in getting products to market quickly.

A new industry that Hav Co is looking to venture into is biotechnology, which has been expanding rapidly and there are strong indications that this recent growth is set to continue. However, Hav Co has limited experience in this industry. Therefore it believes that the best and quickest way to expand would be through acquiring a company already operating in this industry sector.

Strand Co is a private company operating in the biotechnology industry and is owned by a consortium of business angels and company managers. The owner-managers are highly skilled scientists who have developed a number of technically complex products, but have found it difficult to commercialise them. They have also been increasingly constrained by the lack of funds to develop their innovative products further.

Discussions have taken place about the possibility of Strand Co being acquired by Hav Co. Strand Co's managers have indicated that the consortium of owners is happy for the negotiations to proceed. If Strand Co is acquired, it is expected that its managers would continue to run the Strand Co part of the larger combined company.

Strand Co is of the opinion that most of its value is in its intangible assets, comprising intellectual capital. Therefore, the premium payable on acquisition should be based on the present value to infinity of the after tax excess earnings the company has generated in the past three years, over the average return on capital employed of the biotechnological industry. However, Hav Co is of the opinion that the premium should be assessed on synergy benefits created by the acquisition and the changes in value, due to the changes in the price-to-earnings (PE) ratio before and after the acquisition.

Given below are extracts of financial information for Hav Co for 20X3 and Strand Co for 20X1, 20X2 and 20X3:

	Hav Co	Strand Co		
Year ended 30 April	20X3	20X3	20X2	20X1
	$ million	$ million	$ million	$ million
Earnings before tax	1,980	397	370	352
Non-current assets	3,965	882	838	801
Current assets	968	210	208	198
Share capital (25c/share)	600	300	300	300
Reserves	2,479	183	166	159
Non-current liabilities	1,500	400	400	400
Current liabilities	354	209	180	140

The current average PE ratio of the biotechnology industry is 16.4 times and it has been estimated that Strand Co's PE ratio is 10% higher than this. However, it is thought that the PE ratio of the combined company would fall to 14.5 times after the acquisition. The annual after tax earnings will increase by $140 million due to synergy benefits resulting from combining the two companies.

Both companies pay tax at 20% per annum and Strand Co's annual cost of capital is estimated at 7%. Hav Co's current share price is $9.24 per share. The biotechnology industry's pre-tax return on capital employed is currently estimated to be 20% per annum.

Hav Co has proposed to pay for the acquisition using one of the following three methods:

(i) A cash offer of $5.72 for each Strand Co share; or

(ii) A cash offer of $1.33 for each Strand Co share plus one Hav Co share for every two Strand Co shares; or

(iii) A cash offer of $1.25 for each Strand Co share plus one $100 3% convertible bond for every $5 nominal value of Strand Co shares. In six years, the bond can be converted into 12 Hav Co shares or redeemed at par.

Required:

(a) **Distinguish between the different types of synergy and discuss possible sources of synergy based on the above scenario.**   **(9 marks)**

(b) **Based on the two different opinions expressed by Hav Co and Strand Co, calculate the maximum acquisition premium payable in each case.**   **(6 marks)**

(c) **Calculate the percentage premium per share that Strand Co's shareholders will receive under each acquisition payment method and justify, with explanations, which payment method would be most acceptable to them.**   **(10 marks)**

(Total: 25 marks)

51   MAKONIS CO (DEC 13)

Makonis Co, a listed company producing motor cars, wants to acquire Nuvola Co, an engineering company involved in producing innovative devices for cars. Makonis Co is keen to incorporate some of Nuvola Co's innovative devices into its cars and thereby boosting sales revenue.

The following financial information is provided for the two companies:

	Makonis Co	*Nuvola Co*
Current share price	$5.80	$2.40
Number of issued shares	210 million	200 million
Equity beta	1.2	1.2
Asset beta	0.9	1.2

It is thought that combining the two companies will result in several benefits. Free cash flows to firm of the combined company will be $216 million in current value terms, but these will increase by an annual growth rate of 5% for the next four years, before reverting to an annual growth rate of 2.25% in perpetuity. In addition to this, combining the companies will result in cash synergy benefits of $20 million per year, for the next four years. These synergy benefits are not subject to any inflationary increase and no synergy benefits will occur after the fourth year. The debt-to-equity ratio of the combined company will be 40:60 in market value terms and it is expected that the combined company's cost of debt will be 4.55%.

The corporation tax rate is 20%, the current risk free rate of return is 2% and the market risk premium is 7%. It can be assumed that the combined company's asset beta is the weighted average of Makonis Co's and Nuvola Co's asset betas, weighted by their current market values.

Makonis Co has offered to acquire Nuvola Co through a mixed offer of one of its shares for two Nuvola Co shares plus a cash payment, such that a 30% premium is paid for the acquisition. Nuvola Co's equity holders feel that a 50% premium would be more acceptable. Makonis Co has sufficient cash reserves if the premium is 30%, but not if it is 50%.

Required:

(a) **Estimate the additional equity value created by combining Nuvola Co and Makonis Co, based on the free cash flows to firm method. Comment on the results obtained and briefly discuss the assumptions made.** **(13 marks)**

(b) **Estimate the impact on Makonis Co's equity holders if the premium paid is increased to 50% from 30%.** **(5 marks)**

(c) **Estimate the additional funds required if a premium of 50% is paid instead of 30% and discuss how this premium could be financed.** **(7 marks)**

(Total: 25 marks)

52 VOGEL CO (JUN 14)

Vogel Co, a listed engineering company, manufactures large scale plant and machinery for industrial companies. Until ten years ago, Vogel Co pursued a strategy of organic growth. Since then, it has followed an aggressive policy of acquiring smaller engineering companies, which it feels have developed new technologies and methods, which could be used in its manufacturing processes. However, it is estimated that only between 30% and 40% of the acquisitions made in the last ten years have successfully increased the company's shareholder value.

Vogel Co is currently considering acquiring Tori Co, an unlisted company, which has three departments. Department A manufactures machinery for industrial companies, Department B produces electrical goods for the retail market, and the smaller Department C operates in the construction industry. Upon acquisition, Department A will become part of Vogel Co, as it contains the new technologies which Vogel Co is seeking, but Departments B and C will be unbundled, with the assets attached to Department C sold and Department B being spun off into a new company called Ndege Co.

Given below are extracts of financial information for the two companies for the year ended 30 April 2014.

	Vogel Co $ million	Tori Co $ million
Sales revenue	790.2	124.6
Profit before depreciation, interest and tax (PBDIT)	244.4	37.4
Interest	13.8	4.3
Depreciation	72.4	10.1
Pre-tax profit	158.2	23.0

	Vogel Co $ million	Tori Co $ million
Non-current assets	723.9	98.2
Current assets	142.6	46.5
7% unsecured bond	–	40.0
Other non-current and current liabilities	212.4	20.2
Share capital (50c/share)	190.0	20.0
Reserves	464.1	64.5

Share of current and non-current assets and profit of Tori Co's three departments:

	Department A	Department B	Department C
Share of current and non-current assets	40%	40%	20%
Share of PBDIT and pre-tax profit	50%	40%	10%

Other information

(i) It is estimated that for Department C, the realisable value of its non-current assets is 100% of their book value, but its current assets' realisable value is only 90% of their book value. The costs related to closing Department C are estimated to be $3 million.

(ii) The funds raised from the disposal of Department C will be used to pay off Tori Co's other non-current and current liabilities.

(iii) The 7% unsecured bond will be taken over by Ndege Co. It can be assumed that the current market value of the bond is equal to its book value.

(iv) At present, around 10% of Department B's PBDIT come from sales made to Department C.

(v) Ndege Co's cost of capital is estimated to be 10%. It is estimated that in the first year of operation Ndege Co's free cash flows to firm will grow by 20%, and then by 5.2% annually thereafter.

(vi) The tax rate applicable to all the companies is 20%, and Ndege Co can claim 10% tax allowable depreciation on its non-current assets. It can be assumed that the amount of tax allowable depreciation is the same as the investment needed to maintain Ndege Co's operations.

(vii) Vogel Co's current share price is $3 per share and it is estimated that Tori Co's price-to-earnings (PE) ratio is 25% higher than Vogel Co's PE ratio. After the acquisition, when Department A becomes part of Vogel Co, it is estimated that Vogel Co's PE ratio will increase by 15%.

(viii) It is estimated that the combined company's annual after-tax earnings will increase by $7 million due to the synergy benefits resulting from combining Vogel Co and Department A.

Required:

(a) Discuss the possible reasons why Vogel Co may have switched its strategy of organic growth to one of growing by acquiring companies. **(4 marks)**

(b) Discuss the possible actions Vogel Co could take to reduce the risk that the acquisition of Tori Co fails to increase shareholder value. **(7 marks)**

(c) Estimate, showing all relevant calculations, the maximum premium Vogel Co could pay to acquire Tori Co, explaining the approach taken and any assumptions made. **(14 marks)**

(Total: 25 marks)

CORPORATE RECONSTRUCTION AND REORGANISATION

53 REFLATOR INC

A division of Reflator Inc has recently experienced severe financial difficulties. The management of the division is keen to undertake a buyout, but in order for the buyout to succeed it needs to attract substantial finance from a venture capital organisation. Reflator Inc is willing to sell the division for $2.1 million, and the managers believe that an additional $1 million of capital would need to be invested in the division to create a viable going concern.

Possible financing sources:

Equity from management $500,000, in 50 cents ordinary shares.

Funds from the venture capital organisation:

Equity $300,000, in 50 cents ordinary shares

Debt: 8.5% fixed-rate loan $2,000,000

9% subordinated loan with warrants attached $300,000.

The warrants are exercisable any time after four years from now at the rate of 100 ordinary shares at the price of 150 cents per share for every $100 of subordinated loan.

The principal on the 8.5% fixed-rate loan is repayable as a bullet payment at the end of eight years. The subordinated loan is repayable by equal annual payments, comprising both interest and principal, over a period of six years.

The division's managers propose to keep dividends to no more than 15% of profits for the first four years.

Independently produced forecasts of earnings before tax and interest after the buyout are shown below:

	$000			
Year	1	2	3	4
EBIT	320	410	500	540

Corporate tax is at the rate of 30% per year.

The managers involved in the buyout have stated that the book value of equity is likely to increase by about 20% per year during the first four years, making the investment very attractive to the venture capital organisation. The venture capital organisation has stated that it is interested in investing, but has doubts about the forecast growth rate of equity value, and would require warrants for 150 shares per $100 of subordinated loan stock rather than 100 shares.

Required:

(a) Briefly discuss the potential advantages of management buyouts.   **(4 marks)**

(b) Discuss the possible problems and pitfalls that might be encountered by the managers involved, both in achieving the buyout and subsequently.   **(5 marks)**

(c) On the basis of the above data, estimate whether or not the book value of equity is likely to grow by 20% per year.   **(7 marks)**

(d) Evaluate the possible implication of the managers agreeing to offer warrants for 150 ordinary shares per $100 of loan stock.   **(3 marks)**

(e) Discuss the advantages and disadvantages of growth by acquisition or merger as compared with organic growth.   **(6 marks)**

(Total: 25 marks)

54 ALASKA SALVAGE

Alaska Salvage is in discussion with potential lenders about financing an ambitious five-year project searching for lost gold in the central Atlantic. The company has had great success in the past with its various salvage operations and is now quoted on the London Alternative Investment Market. The company is currently financed by 120,000 equity shares trading at $85 per share. It needs to borrow $1.6 million and is concerned about the level of the fixed rates being suggested by the lenders. After lengthy discussions the lenders are prepared to offer finance against a mezzanine issue of fixed rate five-year notes with warrants attached. Each $10,000 note, repayable at par, would carry a warrant for 100 equity shares at an exercise price of $90 per share. The estimated volatility of the returns on the company's equity is 20% and the risk free rate of interest is 5%. The company does not pay dividends to its equity investors.

You may assume that the issue of these loan notes will not influence the current value of the firm's equity. The issue will be made at par.

Required:

(a)   **Estimate, using Black-Scholes Option Pricing Model as appropriate, the current value of each warrant to the lender noting the assumptions that you have made in your valuation.**   **(10 marks)**

(b)   **Estimate the coupon rate that would be required by the lenders if they wanted a 13% rate of return on their investment.**   **(4 marks)**

(c)   **Discuss the advantages and disadvantages of issuing mezzanine debt in the situation outlined in the case.**   **(6 marks)**

(Total: 20 marks)

55 PROTEUS CO (DEC 11)

Proteus Co, a large listed company, has a number of subsidiaries in different industries but its main line of business is developing surveillance systems and intruder alarms. It has decided to sell a number of companies that it considers are peripheral to its core activities. One of these subsidiary companies is Tyche Co, a company involved in managing the congestion monitoring and charging systems that have been developed by Proteus Co. Tyche Co is a profitable business and it is anticipated that its revenues and costs will continue to increase at their current rate of 8% per year for the foreseeable future.

Tyche Co's managers and some employees want to buy the company through a leveraged management buy-out. An independent assessment estimates Tyche Co's market value at $81 million if Proteus Co agrees to cancel its current loan to Tyche Co. The managers and employees involved in the buy-out will invest $12 million for 75% of the equity in the company, with another $4 million coming from a venture capitalist for the remaining 25% equity.

Palaemon Bank has agreed to lend the balance of the required funds in the form of a 9% loan. The interest is payable at the end of the year, on the loan amount outstanding at the start of each year. A covenant on the loan states that the following debt-equity ratios should not be exceeded at the end of each year for the next five years:

Year	1	2	3	4	5
Debt / Equity (%)	350%	250%	200%	150%	125%

Shown below is an extract of the latest annual statement of profit or loss for Tyche Co:

	$000
Sales Revenue	60,000
Materials and consumables	12,000
Labour costs	22,000
Other costs	4,000
Allocated overhead charge payable to Proteus Co	14,000
Interest paid	2,000
Taxable Profit	6,000
Taxation	1,500
Retained Earnings	4,500

As part of the management buy-out agreement, it is expected that Proteus Co will provide management services costing $12 million for the first year of the management buy-out, increasing by 8% per year thereafter.

The current tax rate is 25% on profits and it is expected that 25% of the after-tax profits will be payable as dividends every year. The remaining profits will be allocated to reserves. It is expected that Tyche Co will repay $3 million of the outstanding loan at the end of each of the next five years from the cash flows generated from its business activity.

Required:

(a) **Briefly discuss the possible benefits to Proteus Co of disposing Tyche Co through a management buy-out.** **(4 marks)**

(b) **Calculate whether the debt-equity covenant imposed by Palaemon Bank on Tyche Co will be breached over the five-year period.** **(9 marks)**

(c) **Discuss briefly the implications of the results obtained in part (b) and outline two possible actions Tyche Co may take if the covenant is in danger of being breached.**

(5 marks)

(Total: 18 marks)

56 DORIC CO (PILOT 2012)

Doric Co has two manufacturing divisions: parts and fridges. Although the parts division is profitable, the fridges division is not, and as a result its share price has declined to $0.50 per share from a high of $2.83 per share around three years ago. Assume it is now 1 January 20X3.

The board of directors are considering two proposals:

(i) To cease trading and close down the company entirely, or

(ii) To close the fridges division and continue the parts division through a leveraged management buyout. The new company will continue with manufacturing parts only, but will make an additional investment of $50 million in order to grow the parts division after-tax cash flows by 3.5% in perpetuity. The proceeds from the sale of the fridges division will be used to pay the outstanding liabilities. The finance raised from the management buy-out will pay for any remaining liabilities, the funds required for the additional investment, and to purchase the current equity shares at a premium of 20%. The fridges division is twice the size of the parts division in terms of its assets attributable to it.

Extracts from the most recent financial statements:

Financial position as at 31 December 20X3

	$m
Non-Current Assets	110
Current Assets	220
Share capital ($0.40 per share par value)	40
Reserves	10
Liabilities (Non-current and current)	280

Statement of profit or loss for the year ended 31 December 20X2

		$m
Sales revenue:	Parts division	170
	Fridges division	340
Costs prior to depreciation, interest payments and tax:	Parts division	(120)
	Fridges division	(370)
Depreciation, tax and interest		(34)
Loss		(14)

If the entire company's assets are sold, the estimated realisable values of assets are as follows:

	$m
Non-current assets	100
Current assets	110

The following additional information has been provided

Redundancy and other costs will be approximately $54 million if the whole company is closed, and pro rata for individual divisions that are closed. These costs have priority for payment before any other liabilities in case of closure. The taxation effects relating to this may be ignored.

Corporation tax on profits is 20% and it can be assumed that tax is payable in the year incurred. Annual depreciation on non-current assets is 10% and this is the amount of investment needed to maintain the current level of activity. The new company's cost of capital is expected to be 11%.

Required:

(a) Briefly discuss the possible benefits of Doric Co's parts division being divested through a management buy-out. **(4 marks)**

(b) Estimate the return the liability holders and the shareholders would receive in the event that Doric Co is closed and all its assets sold. **(3 marks)**

(c) Estimate the additional amount of finance needed and the value of the new company, if only the assets of fridges division are sold and the parts division is divested through a management buy-out. Briefly discuss whether or not the management buy-out would be beneficial. **(10 marks)**

(d) Doric Co's directors are of the opinion that they could receive a better price if the fridges division is sold as a going concern instead of its assets sold separately. They have been told that they need to consider two aspects when selling a company or part of a company: (i) seeking potential buyers and negotiating the sale price; and, (ii) due diligence.

Discuss the issues that should be taken into consideration with each aspect. **(8 marks)**

(Total: 25 marks)

57 NUBO CO (DEC 13)

Nubo Co has divisions operating in two diverse sectors: production of aircraft parts and supermarkets. Whereas the aircraft parts production division has been growing rapidly, the supermarkets division's growth has been slower. The company is considering selling the supermarkets division and focusing solely on the aircraft parts production division.

Extracts from the Nubo Co's most recent financial statements are as follows:

Year ended 30 November	20X3
	$m
Profit after tax	166
Non-current assets	550
Current assets	122
Non-current liabilities	387
Current liabilities	95

About 70% of Nubo Co's non-current assets and current assets are attributable to the supermarkets division and the remainder to the aircraft parts production division. Each of the two divisions generates roughly half of the total profit after tax. The market value of the two divisions is thought to be equivalent to the price-to-earnings (PE) ratios of the two divisions' industries. The supermarket industry's PE ratio is 7 and the aircraft parts production industry's PE ratio is 12.

Nubo Co can either sell the supermarkets division as a going concern or sell the assets of the supermarkets division separately. If the assets are sold separately, Nubo Co believes that it can sell the non-current assets for 115% of the book value and the current assets for 80% of the book value. The funds raised from the sale of the supermarkets division will be used to pay for all the company's current and non-current liabilities.

Following the sale of the supermarkets division and paying off the liabilities, Nubo Co will raise additional finance for new projects in the form of debt. It will be able to borrow up to a maximum of 100% of the total asset value of the new downsized company.

One of the new projects which Nubo Co is considering is a joint venture with Pilvi Co to produce an innovative type of machinery which will be used in the production of light aircraft and private jets. Both companies will provide the expertise and funding required for the project equally. Representatives from both companies will make up the senior management team and decisions will be made jointly. Legal contracts will be drawn up once profit-sharing and other areas have been discussed by the companies and agreed on.

Pilvi Co has approached Ulap Bank for the finance it requires for the venture, based on Islamic finance principles. Ulap Bank has agreed to consider the request from Pilvi Co, but because the financing requirement will be for a long period of time and because of uncertainties surrounding the project, Ulap Bank wants to provide the finance based on the principles of a Musharaka contract, with Ulap Bank requiring representation on the venture's senior management team. Normally Ulap Bank provides funds based on the principles of a Mudaraba contract, which the bank provides for short-term, low-risk projects, where the responsibility for running a project rests solely with the borrower.

Required:

(a) **Advise Nubo Co whether it should sell the supermarkets division as a going concern or sell the assets separately and estimate the additional cash and debt funds which could be available to the new, downsized company. Show all relevant calculations.**

(7 marks)

(b) An alternative to selling the supermarkets division would be to demerge both the divisions. In this case, all of Nubo Co's liabilities would be taken over by the demerged supermarkets division. Also, either of the demerged companies can borrow up to 100% of their respective total asset values.

Required:

Discuss whether a demerger of the supermarkets division may be more appropriate than a sale. **(6 marks)**

(c) **Discuss why Ulap Bank may want to consider providing the finance based on a Musharaka contract instead of a Mudaraba contract, and the key concerns Nubo Co may have from the arrangement between Pilvi Co and Ulap Bank.** **(12 marks)**

(Total: 25 marks)

TREASURY AND ADVANCED RISK MANAGEMENT TECHNIQUES

58 BLACK-SCHOLES (AVT)

AVT Inc is considering the introduction of an executive share option scheme.

The scheme would be offered to all middle managers of the company. It would replace the existing scheme of performance bonuses linked to the post-tax earnings per share of the company. Such bonuses in the last year ranged between $5,000 and $7,000. If the option scheme is introduced, new options are expected to be offered to the managers each year.

It is proposed for the first year that all middle managers are offered options to purchase 5,000 shares at a price of 500 cents per share, after the options have been held for one year. Assume that the tax authorities allow the exercise of such options after they have been held for one year. If the options are not exercised at that time they will lapse.

The company's shares have just come ex-div and have a current market price of 610 cents. The dividend paid was 25 cents per share, a level that has remained constant for the last three years. Assume that dividends are only paid annually.

The company's share price has experienced a standard deviation of 38% during the last year. The short-term risk-free interest rate is 6% annum.

Required:

(a) **Discuss the relative merits for the company of the existing bonus scheme and the proposed share option scheme.** **(6 marks)**

(b) **Evaluate whether or not the proposed share option scheme is likely to be attractive to middle managers of AVT Inc.** **(11 marks)**

(c) **When told of the scheme one manager stated that he would rather receive put options than call options, as they would be more valuable to him.**

   (1) **Discuss whether or not AVT should agree to offer him put options.**

   (4 marks)

   (2) **Calculate whether or not he is correct in his statement that put options would be more valuable to him.** **(4 marks)**

(Total: 25 marks)

59 UNIGLOW

(a) Discuss how a decrease in the value of each of the determinants of the option price in the Black-Scholes option-pricing model for European options is likely to change the price of a call option. **(8 marks)**

(b) Briefly discuss the meaning and importance of the terms 'delta', 'theta', and 'vega' (also known as kappa or lambda) in option pricing. **(6 marks)**

(c) Assume that your company has invested in 100,000 shares of Uniglow plc, a manufacturer of light bulbs. You are concerned about the recent volatility in Uniglow's share price due to the unpredictable weather in the United Kingdom. You wish to protect your company's investment from a possible fall in Uniglow's share price until winter in three months' time, but do not wish to sell the shares at present. No dividends are due to be paid by Uniglow during the next three months.

Market data:

Uniglow's current share price: 200 pence

Call option exercise price: 220 pence

Time to expiry: 3 months

Interest rate (annual): 6%

Volatility of Uniglow's shares 50% (standard deviation per year)

Assume that option contracts are for the purchase or sale of units of 1,000 shares.

Required:

(i) Devise a delta hedge that is expected to protect the investment against changes in the share price until winter. Delta may be estimated using N(d1). **(9 marks)**

(ii) Comment upon whether or not such a hedge is likely to be totally successful. **(2 marks)**

(Total: 25 marks)

60 MJY PLC

Assume that it is now 31 December. MJY plc is a UK based multinational company that has subsidiaries in two foreign countries. Both subsidiaries trade with other group members and with four third-party companies (company 1–company 4). Projected trade transactions for three months' time are shown below. All currency amounts are in thousands.

Payments (read down) '000'

Receipts (read across) '000'	Co 1	Co 2	Co 3	Co 4	MJY	Subsidiary 1	Subsidiary 2
MJY	$90	£60	€75	–	–	£40	$50
Subsidiary 1	£50	€85	$40	$20	€72	–	€20
Subsidiary 2	£15	–	€52	$30	£55	€35	–
Company 1	–	–	–	–	–	–	–
Company 2	–	–	–	–	$170	–	–
Company 3	–	–	–	–	$120	€50	–
Company 4	–	–	–	–	–	–	€65

Foreign exchange rates	$/£	€/£
Spot	1.7982–1.8010	1.4492–1.4523
3 months forward	1.7835–1.7861	1.4365–1.4390

Currency options. £62,500 contract size. Premium in cents per £

	Calls		Puts	
Strike price	February	May	February	May
1.80	1.96	3.00	3.17	5.34
1.78	2.91	3.84	2.12	4.20

Required:

(a) **Working from the perspective of a group treasurer, devise a hedging strategy for the MJY group, and calculate the expected outcomes of the hedges using forward markets, and, for the dollar exposure only, currency options.** **(15 marks)**

(b) Warren Buffett, the stock market investor, views derivatives as a 'time bomb', but many corporate treasurers clearly perceive them as very useful tools for reducing risk.

Required:

Explain and discuss the reasons for such divergent viewpoints. **(10 marks)**

(Total: 25 marks)

61 COLLAR HEDGE

(a) **Discuss the advantages of hedging with interest rate caps and collars.** **(7 marks)**

(b) Current futures prices suggest that interest rates are expected to fall during the next few months. Troder plc expects to have £400 million available for short-term investment for a period of 5 months commencing late October. The company wishes to protect this short-term investment from a fall in interest rates, but is concerned about the premium levels of interest rate options. It would also like to benefit if interest rates were to increase rather than fall. The company's advisers have suggested the use of a collar option.

LIFFE short sterling options (£500,000), points of 100%

	Calls		Puts	
Strike price	Sept	Dec	Sept	Dec
95250	0.040	0.445	0.040	0.085
95500	0	0.280	0.250	0.170
95750	0	0.165	0.500	0.305

LIBOR is currently 5% and the company can invest short-term at LIBOR minus 25 basis points.

Required:

(i) Assume that it is now early September. The company wishes to receive more than £6,750,000 in interest from its investment after paying any option premium. Illustrate how a collar hedge may be used to achieve this. (NB It is not necessary to estimate the number of contracts for this illustration.)

(10 marks)

(ii) Estimate the maximum interest that could be received with your selected hedge. (3 marks)

(c) Explain the objectives of integrated reporting. (5 marks)

(Total: 25 marks)

62 INTEREST RATE HEDGES *Walk in the footsteps of a top tutor*

Assume that it is now 1 June. Your company expects to receive £7.1 million from a large order in five months' time. This will then be invested in high-quality commercial paper for a period of four months, after that it will be used to pay part of the company's dividend. The company's treasurer wishes to protect the short-term investment from adverse movements in interest rates, by using futures or forward rate agreements (FRAs).

The current yield on high-quality commercial paper is LIBOR + 0.60%.

LIFFE £500,000 three month sterling futures. £12.50 tick size.

September	96.25
December	96.60

Futures contracts mature at the month end. LIBOR is currently 4%.

FRA prices (%)

4 v 5	3.85 – 3.80
4 v 9	3.58 – 3.53
5 v 9	3.50 – 3.45

Required:

(a) Devise a futures hedge to protect the interest yield of the short-term investment, and estimate the expected lock-in interest rate as a result of the hedge. (4 marks)

(b) Ignoring transactions costs, explain whether the futures or FRA hedge would provide the higher expected interest rate from the short-term investment.

(2 marks)

(c) If LIBOR fell by 0.5% during the next five months, show the expected outcomes of each hedge in the cash market, futures market and FRA market as appropriate.

(6 marks)

(d) Explain why the futures market outcome might differ from the outcome in (c) above. (3 marks)

(e) Explain the differences and similarities between an FRA and an interest rate swap.

(5 marks)

(Total: 20 marks)

63 POLYTOT PLC

Assume that it is now 1 July. Polytot plc has received an export order valued at 675 million pesos from a company in Grobbia, a country that has recently been accepted into the World Trade Organisation, but that does not yet have a freely convertible currency.

The Grobbian company only has access to sufficient $US to pay for 60% of the goods, at the official $US exchange rate. The balance would be payable in the local currency, the Grobbian peso, for which there is no official foreign exchange market. Polytot is due to receive payment in four months' time and has been informed that an unofficial market in Grobbian pesos exists in which the peso can be converted into pounds. The exchange rate in this market is 15% worse for Polytot than the 'official' rate of exchange between the peso and the pound.

Exchange rates:

	$/£
Spot	1.5475–1.5510
3 months forward	1.5362–1.5398
1 year forward	1.5140–1.5178
	Grobbian peso/£
Official spot rate	156.30
	Grobbian peso/$
Official spot rate	98.20

Philadelphia SE £/$ options £31,250 (cents per pound)

	CALLS			PUTS		
	Sept	Dec	March	Sept	Dec	March
1.5250	2.95	3.35	3.65	2.00	3.25	4.35
1.5500	1.80	2.25	2.65	3.30	4.60	5.75
1.5750	0.90	1.40	1.80	4.90	6.25	7.35
1.6000	0.25	0.75	1.10	6.75	8.05	9.15

£/$ Currency futures (CME, £62,500)

September	1.5350
December	1.5275

Assume that options and futures contracts mature at the relevant month end.

Required:

(a) Discuss the alternative forms of currency hedge that are available to Polytot plc and calculate the expected revenues, in £ sterling, from the sale to the company in Grobbia as a result of each of these hedges. Provide a reasoned recommendation as to which hedge should be selected. **(19 marks)**

(b) The Grobbian company is willing to undertake a countertrade deal whereby 40% of the cost of the goods is paid for by an exchange of three million kilos of Grobbian strawberries. A major UK supermarket chain has indicated that it would be willing to pay between 50 and 60 pence per kilo for the strawberries.

Discuss the issues that Polytot should consider before deciding whether or not to agree to the countertrade. **(6 marks)**

(Total: 25 marks)

64 ARNBROOK PLC

Arnbrook plc is considering a £50 million three-year interest rate swap. The company wishes to expand and to have use of floating rate funds, but because of its AA credit rating has a comparative advantage over lower-rated companies when borrowing in the domestic fixed-rate market. Arnbrook can borrow fixed rate at 6.25% or floating rate at LIBOR plus 0.75%.

LIBOR is currently 5.25%, but parliamentary elections are due in six months' time and future interest rates are uncertain. A swap could be arranged using a bank as an intermediary. The bank would offset the swap risk with a counterparty BBB-rated company that could borrow fixed rate at 7.25% and floating rate at LIBOR plus 1.25%. The bank would charge a fee of £120,000 per year to each party in the swap. Arnbrook would require 60% of any arbitrage savings (before the payment of fees) from the swap because of its higher credit rating.

Any fees paid to the bank are tax allowable. The corporate tax rate is 30%.

Required:

(a) Discuss the risks that Arnbrook and a participating bank might face when undertaking an interest rate swap. **(3 marks)**

(b) Evaluate whether or not the proposed swap might be beneficial to all parties. **(6 marks)**

(c) If LIBOR was to increase immediately after the forthcoming election to 5.75% and then stay constant for the period of the swap, estimate the present value of the savings from the swap for Arnbrook plc. Interest payments are made semi-annually in arrears. Comment upon whether the swap would have been beneficial to Arnbrook plc.

The money market may be assumed to be an efficient market. **(6 marks)**

(d) Discuss the advantages and disadvantages of arranging a swap through a bank rather than negotiating directly with a counterparty. **(5 marks)**

(e) Explain the nature of a *mudaraba* contract and discuss briefly how this form of Islamic finance could be used to finance the planned expansion. **(5 marks)**

(Total: 25 marks)

65 ASTEROID SYSTEMS *Walk in the footsteps of a top tutor*

Asteroid Systems is a German-based company with a subsidiary in Switzerland. The company's financial manager expects the Swiss business will remit the equivalent of Euros 1.5 million in two months. Her expectations of the future remittance are based upon the current SFr/Euro forward rate. The current spot and forward rates for Swiss francs against the Euro are extracted from the Financial Times and are shown in the table below.

	Closing mid-point	Change on day	Bid/offer spread	Days mid high	low	One month Rate	annual %	Three month Rate	annual %
Switzerland (SFr/€)	1.6242	0.0107	239–244	1.6261	1.6147	1.6223	1.4	1.6176	1.6

In the Euro money market the company can make fixed interest deposits at LIBOR and can borrow at LIBOR plus 20 basis points for terms of greater than one month but up to six months. The company can borrow at fixed rates in the Swiss money market. LIBOR rates, as quoted in the Financial Times, are as follows:

	EUR	CHF
spot	3.56688	2.06000
1 week	3.57300	2.06000
2 week	3.58438	2.07000
1 month	3.60900	2.08000
2 month	3.72538	2.17000
3 month	3.78238	2.20000

The company's financial manager is keen to eliminate transaction risk. However, because of the margin requirements and their impact upon the firm's cash flow, she would prefer not to use exchange traded derivatives. Swiss franc borrowing or lending rates would need to be negotiated with the bank.

Required:

(a) Estimate the lowest acceptable Swiss borrowing or lending rate for a money market hedge maturing in two months. **(10 marks)**

(b) Discuss the relative advantages and disadvantages of the use of a money market hedge compared with using exchange traded derivatives for hedging a foreign exchange exposure. **(6 marks)**

(c) Discuss the extent to which currency hedging can reduce a firm's cost of capital. **(4 marks)**

(Total: 20 marks)

Online question assistance

---

66 **PHOBOS CO** *Walk in the footsteps of a top tutor*

Timed question with Online tutor debrief

Following a collapse in credit confidence in the banking sector globally, there have been high levels of volatility in the financial markets around the world. Phobos Co is a UK listed company and has a borrowing requirement of £30 million arising in two months' time on 1 March and expects to be able to make repayment of the full amount six months from now. The governor of the central bank has suggested that interest rates are now at their peak and could fall over the next quarter. However, the chairman of the Federal Reserve in the United States has suggested that monetary conditions may need to be tightened, which could lead to interest rate rises throughout the major economies. In your judgement there is now an equal likelihood that rates will rise or fall by as much as 100 basis points depending upon economic conditions over the next quarter.

LIBOR is currently 6.00% and Phobos can borrow at a fixed rate of LIBOR plus 50 basis points on the short term money market but the company treasurer would like to keep the maximum borrowing rate at or below 6.6%.

Short term sterling index futures have a contract size of £500,000 and a tick size of £12.50. The open and settlement prices of three month futures contracts are shown below (settlement at the end of the month):

	Open	Settlement
March	93.800	93.880
June	93.870	93.940
September	93.890	93.970

You may assume that basis diminishes to zero at contract maturity at a constant rate over time and that time intervals can be counted in months.

Options on short sterling futures have a contract size of £500,000 and the premiums (shown as an annual percentage) available against a range of exercise prices are as follows:

	Calls			Puts		
Exercise	March	June	September	March	June	September
93750	0.155	0.260	0.320	0.045	0.070	0.100
94000	0.038	0.110	0.175	0.168	0.170	0.205
94250	0.010	0.040	0.080	0.300	0.350	0.360

Required:

(a) **Estimate the effective interest rate cost if the anticipated interest rate exposure is hedged:**

   (i)   **using the sterling interest rate futures; and**

   (ii) **the options on short sterling futures.**   **(14 marks)**

(b) **Outline the benefits and dangers to Phobos of using derivative agreements in the management of interest rate risk.**   **(6 marks)**

(Total: 20 marks)

Calculate your allowed time, allocate the time to the separate parts.

67   MULTIDROP

You are the financial manager of Multidrop (Group) a European based company which has subsidiary businesses in North America, Europe, and Singapore. It also has foreign currency balances outstanding with two non-group companies in the UK and Malaysia. Last year the transaction costs of ad-hoc settlements both within the group and with non-group companies were significant and this year you have reached agreement with the non-group companies to enter into a netting agreement to clear indebtedness with the minimum of currency flows. It has been agreed that Multidrop (Europe) will be the principal in the netting arrangement and that all settlements will be made in Euros at the prevailing spot rate.

The summarised list of year end indebtedness is as follows:

Owed by:	Owed to:	
Multidrop (Europe)	Multidrop (US)	US$6.4 million
Multidrop (Singapore)	Multidrop (Europe)	S$16 million
Alposong (Malaysia)	Multidrop (US)	US$5.4 million
Multidrop (US)	Multidrop (Europe)	€8.2 million
Multidrop (Singapore)	Multidrop (US)	US$5.0 million
Multidrop (Singapore)	Alposong (Malaysia)	Rm25 million
Alposong (Malaysia)	NewRing (UK)	£2.2 million
NewRing (UK)	Multidrop (Singapore)	S$4.0 million
Multidrop (Europe)	Alposong (Malaysia)	Rm8.3 million

Currency cross rates (mid-market) are as follows:

Currency		UK £	US $	Euro	Sing $	Rm
1 UK £	=	1.0000	1.4601	1.0653	2.1956	5.3128
1 US $	=	0.6849	1.0000	0.7296	1.5088	3.6435
1 Euro	=	0.9387	1.3706	1.0000	2.0649	4.9901
1 Sing $	=	0.4555	0.6628	0.4843	1.0000	2.4150
1 Rm	=	0.1882	0.2745	0.2004	0.4141	1.0000

You may assume settlement will be at the mid-market rates quoted.

Required:

(a) Explain why companies should manage their exposure to currency risks. **(5 marks)**

(b) Calculate the inter group and inter-company currency transfers that will be required for settlement by Multidrop (Europe). **(12 marks)**

(c) Discuss the advantages and disadvantages of netting arrangements with both group and non-group companies. **(8 marks)**

(Total: 25 marks)

68 PONDHILLS

(a) Discuss the significance to a multinational company of translation exposure and economic exposure. **(7 marks)**

(b) Pondhills Inc is a US multinational company with subsidiaries in the UK and Africa. The currency of the African country is pegged against the dollar, with a current exchange rate of 246.3 dinars/$US1. In recent months political unrest and an increasing inflation rate has led the finance director of Pondhills to become concerned about a possible devaluation of the dinar. He believes that the dinar could devalue by up to 15% relative to the dollar during the next few months.

Summarised financial data for the African subsidiary, Ponda SA are shown below:

	Million dinars
Revenue	2,300
Non-current assets	510
Current assets	
Cash	86
Receivables	410
Inventory	380
	___
	876
Short-term payables	(296)
Long-term loans	(500)
	___
	590
	___
Shareholders' equity	590
	___

Current exchange rates are:

$US/£1	1.5780
Dinar/$US1	246.3

Notes

(i) All sales from the African subsidiary are denominated in US dollars, and all receivables are therefore payable in dollars.

(ii) 50% of payables are debts owned in sterling to the UK subsidiary by Ponda SA.

(iii) Long-term loans are in dinars from an African bank, at an interest rate of 12% per annum.

(iv) The cost of goods sold and other operating expenses (excluding interest) for Ponda SA are 70% of revenue. 40% of this is payable in dollars or sterling and 60% in dinars.

(v) No significant changes in exchange rates are expected between the dollar and other major currencies.

Required:

(i) Calculate the statement of financial position translation exposure of Pondhills Inc, AND the potential profit or loss on translation of the statement of financial position using the current or closing rate method where all EXPOSED assets and liabilities are translated at the current exchange rate;

(9 marks)

(ii) Calculate the expected impact on the dollar value of Ponda SA's annual cash flow in the first full year after devaluation. The time value of money may be ignored.

(6 marks)

(c) Comment upon whether or not Pondhills Inc should hedge against the exposures estimated in (b)(i) and (b)(ii).

(3 marks)

(Total: 25 marks)

69 CURRENCY SWAPS

(a) **From the perspective of a corporate financial manager, discuss the advantages and potential problems of using currency swaps.** **(10 marks)**

(b) Galeplus plc, a UK-based company, has been invited to purchase and operate a new telecommunications centre in the republic of Perdia. The purchase price is 2,000 million rubbits. The Perdian government has built the centre in order to improve the country's infrastructure, but has currently not got enough funds to pay money owed to the local constructors. Galeplus would purchase the centre for a period of three years, after which it would be sold back to the Perdian government for an agreed price of 4,000 million rubbits. Galeplus would supply three years of technical expertise and training for local staff, for an annual fee of 40 million rubbits, after Perdian taxation. Other after-tax net cash flows from the investment in Perdia are expected to be negligible during the three-year period.

Perdia has only recently become a democracy, and in the last five years has experienced inflation rates of between 25% and 500%. The managers of Galeplus are concerned about the foreign exchange risk of the investment. Perdia has recently adopted economic stability measures suggested by the IMF, and inflation during the next three years is expected to be between 15% per year and 50% per year. Galeplus's bankers have suggested using a currency swap for the purchase price of the factory, with a swap of principal immediately and in three years' time, both swaps at today's spot rate. The bank would charge a fee of 0.75% per year (in sterling) for arranging the swap. Galeplus would take 75% of any net arbitrage benefit from the swap, after deducting bank fees. Relevant borrowing rates are:

	UK	Perdia
Galeplus	6.25%	PIBOR + 2.0%
Perdian counterparty	8.3%	PIBOR + 1.5%

NB PIBOR is the Perdian interbank offered rate, which has tended to be set at approximately the current inflation level. Inflation in the UK is expected to be negligible.

	Exchange rates
Spot	85.4 rubbits/£
3-year forward rate	Not available

Required:

(i) **Estimate the potential annual percentage interest saving that Galeplus might make from using a currency swap relative to borrowing directly in Perdia.** **(6 marks)**

(ii) **Assuming the swap takes place as described, provide a reasoned analysis, including relevant calculations, as to whether or not Galeplus should purchase the communications centre. The relevant risk adjusted discount rate may be assumed to be 15% per year.** **(9 marks)**

(Total: 25 marks)

70   FNDC PLC

Several months ago FNDC plc, a UK television manufacturer, agreed to offer financial support to a major sporting event. The event will take place in seven months' time, but an expenditure of £45 million for temporary facilities will be necessary in five months' time. FNDC has agreed to lend the £45 million, and expects the loan to be repaid at the time of the event. At the time the support was offered, FNDC expected to have sufficient cash to lend the £45 million from its own resources, but new commitments mean that the cash will have to be borrowed. Interest rates have been showing a rising trend, and FNDC wishes to protect itself against further interest rate rises when it takes out the loan. The company is considering using either interest rate futures or options on interest rate futures.

Assume that it is now 1 December and that futures and options contracts mature at the relevant month end.

LIBOR is currently 4%. FNDC can borrow at LIBOR plus 1.25%

Euronext.LIFFE STIR £500,000 three-month sterling futures. Tick size 0.01%, tick value £12.50

December 96.04

March   95.77

June   95.55

Euronext.LIFFE options on three month £500,000 sterling futures. Tick size 0.005%, tick value £6.25. Option premiums are in annual %.

	CALLS			PUTS		
	December	March	June	December	March	June
9400	1.505	1.630	1.670	–	–	–
9450	1.002	1.130	1.170	–	–	–
9500	0.502	0.630	0.685	–	–	0.015
9550	0.252	0.205	0.285	0.060	0.115	0.165
9600	0.002	0.025	0.070	0.200	0.450	0.710

Required:

(a)   **Discuss the relative merits of using short-term interest rate futures and market-traded options on short-term interest rates futures to hedge short-term interest rate risk.**   **(5 marks)**

(b)   **If LIBOR interest rates were to increase by 0.5% or to decrease by 0.5%, estimate the expected outcomes from hedging using:**

   (i)   **an interest rate futures hedge; and**

   (ii)   **options on interest rate futures.**

   Briefly discuss your findings.

   Note: **In the futures hedge, the expected basis at the close-out date should be estimated, but basis risk may be ignored.**   **(15 marks)**

(c)   **Calculate and discuss the outcome of a collar hedge which would limit the maximum interest rate paid by the company to 5.75%, and the minimum to 5.25%. (These interest rates do not include any option premium.)**   **(5 marks)**

                                                                          (Total: 25 marks)

71   LEVANTE CO (DEC 11)

Levante Co has identified a new project for which it will need to increase its long-term borrowings from $250 million to $400 million. This amount will cover a significant proportion of the total cost of the project and the rest of the funds will come from cash held by the company.

The current $250 million borrowing is in the form of a 4% bond which is trading at $98.71 per $100 and is due to be redeemed at par in three years. The issued bond has a credit rating of AA. The new borrowing will also be raised in the form of a traded bond with a par value of $100 per unit. It is anticipated that the new project will generate sufficient cash flows to be able to redeem the new bond at $100 par value per unit in five years. It can be assumed that coupons on both bonds are paid annually.

Both bonds would be ranked equally for payment in the event of default and the directors expect that as a result of the new issue, the credit rating for both bonds will fall to A. The directors are considering the following two alternative options when issuing the new bond:

(i)   Issue the new bond at a fixed coupon of 5% but at a premium or discount, whichever is appropriate to ensure full take up of the bond; or

(ii)   Issue the new bond at a coupon rate where the issue price of the new bond will be $100 per unit and equal to its par value.

The following extracts are provided on the current government bond yield curve and yield spreads for the sector in which Levante Cooperates:

Current Government Bond Yield Curve

Years	1	2	3	4	5
	3.2%	3.7%	4.2%	4.8%	5.0%

Yield spreads (in basis points)

Bond Rating	1 year	2 years	3 years	4 years	5 years
AAA	5	9	14	19	25
AA	16	22	30	40	47
A	65	76	87	100	112
BBB	102	121	142	167	193

Required:

(a)   Calculate the expected percentage fall in the market value of the existing bond if Levante Co's bond credit rating falls from AA to A.   **(3 marks)**

(b)   Advise the directors on the financial implications of choosing each of the two options when issuing the new bond. Support the advice with appropriate calculations.   **(7 marks)**

(c)   Among the criteria used by credit agencies for establishing a company's credit rating are the following: industry risk, earnings protection, financial flexibility and evaluation of the company's management.

Briefly explain each criterion and suggest factors that could be used to assess it.

(8 marks)

(Total: 18 marks)

72 SEMBILAN CO (JUN 12)

Sembilan Co, a listed company, recently issued debt finance to acquire assets in order to increase its activity levels. This debt finance is in the form of a floating rate bond, with a face value of $320 million, redeemable in four years. The bond interest, payable annually, is based on the spot yield curve plus 60 basis points. The next annual payment is due at the end of year one.

Sembilan Co is concerned that the expected rise in interest rates over the coming few years would make it increasingly difficult to pay the interest due. It is therefore proposing to either swap the floating rate interest payment to a fixed rate payment, or to raise new equity capital and use that to pay off the floating rate bond. The new equity capital would either be issued as rights to the existing shareholders or as shares to new shareholders.

Ratus Bank has offered Sembilan Co an interest rate swap, whereby Sembilan Co would pay Ratus Bank interest based on an equivalent fixed annual rate of 3.76¼% in exchange for receiving a variable amount based on the current yield curve rate. Payments and receipts will be made at the end of each year, for the next four years. Ratus Bank will charge an annual fee of 20 basis points if the swap is agreed.

The current annual spot yield curve rates are as follows:

Year	One	Two	Three	Four
Rate	2.5%	3.1%	3.5%	3.8%

The current annual forward rates for years two, three and four are as follows:

Year	Two	Three	Four
Rate	3.7%	4.3%	4.7%

Required:

(a) **Based on the above information, calculate the amounts Sembilan Co expects to pay or receive every year on the swap (excluding the fee of 20 basis points). Explain why the fixed annual rate of interest of 3.76¼% is less than the four-year yield curve rate of 3.8%.** **(6 marks)**

(b) **Demonstrate that Sembilan Co's interest payment liability does not change, after it has undertaken the swap, whether the interest rates increase or decrease.**

(5 marks)

(c) **Discuss the factors that Sembilan Co should consider when deciding whether it should raise equity capital to pay off the floating rate debt.** **(9 marks)**

(Total: 20 marks)

73 LIGNUM CO (DEC 12 A)

Lignum Co, a large listed company, manufactures agricultural machines and equipment for different markets around the world. Although its main manufacturing base is in France and it uses the Euro (€) as its base currency, it also has a few subsidiary companies around the world. Lignum Co's treasury division is considering how to approach the following three cases of foreign exchange exposure that it faces.

Case One

Lignum Co regularly trades with companies based in Zuhait, a small country in South America whose currency is the Zupesos (ZP). It recently sold machinery for ZP140 million, which it is about to deliver to a company based there. It is expecting full payment for the machinery in four months. Although there are no exchange traded derivative products available for the Zupesos, Medes Bank has offered Lignum Co a choice of two over-the-counter derivative products.

The first derivative product is an over-the-counter forward rate determined on the basis of the Zuhait base rate of 8.5% plus 25 basis points and the French base rate of 2.2% less 30 basis points.

Alternatively, with the second derivative product Lignum Co can purchase either Euro call or put options from Medes Bank at an exercise price equivalent to the current spot exchange rate of ZP142 per €1. The option premiums offered are: ZP7 per €1 for the call option or ZP5 per €1 for the put option.

The premium cost is payable in full at the commencement of the option contract. Lignum Co can borrow money at the base rate plus 150 basis points and invest money at the base rate minus 100 basis points in France.

Case Two

Namel Co is Lignum Co's subsidiary company based in Maram, a small country in Asia, whose currency is the Maram Ringit (MR). The current pegged exchange rate between the Maram Ringit and the Euro is MR35 per €1. Due to economic difficulties in Maram over the last couple of years, it is very likely that the Maram Ringit will devalue by 20% imminently. Namel Co is concerned about the impact of the devaluation on its Statement of Financial Position.

Given below is an extract from the current Statement of Financial Position of Namel Co.

	MR '000
Non-current assets	179,574
Current assets	146,622
Total assets	326,196
Share capital and reserves	102,788
Non-current liabilities	132,237
Current liabilities	91,171
Total capital and liabilities	326,196

The current assets consist of inventories, receivables and cash. Receivables account for 40% of the current assets. All the receivables relate to sales made to Lignum Co in Euro. About 70% of the current liabilities consist of payables relating to raw material inventory purchased from Lignum Co and payable in Euro. 80% of the non-current liabilities consist of a Euro loan and the balance are borrowings sourced from financial institutions in Maram.

Case Three

Lignum Co manufactures a range of farming vehicles in France which it sells within the European Union to countries which use the Euro. Over the previous few years, it has found that its sales revenue from these products has been declining and the sales director is of the opinion that this is entirely due to the strength of the Euro. Lignum Co's biggest competitor in these products is based in the USA and US$ rate has changed from almost parity with the Euro three years ago, to the current value of US$1.47 for €1. The agreed opinion is that the US$ will probably continue to depreciate against the Euro, but possibly at a slower rate, for the foreseeable future.

Required:

Prepare a report for Lignum Co's treasury division that:

(i)   Briefly explains the type of currency exposure Lignum Co faces for each of the above cases;   **(3 marks)**

(ii) Recommends which of the two derivative products Lignum Co should use to manage its exposure in case one and advises on alternative hedging strategies that could be used. Show all relevant calculations;   **(9 marks)**

(iii) Computes the gain or loss on Namel Co's Statement of Financial Position, due to the devaluation of the Maram Ringit in case two, and discusses whether and how this exposure should be managed;   **(8 marks)**

(iv) Discusses how the exposure in case three can be managed.   **(3 marks)**

Professional marks will be awarded in this question for the structure and presentation of the report.   **(2 marks)**

(Total: 25 marks)

74   ALECTO CO (PILOT 2012)

Alecto Co, a large listed company based in Europe, is expecting to borrow €22,000,000 in four months' time on 1 May 20X2. It expects to make a full repayment of the borrowed amount nine months from now. Currently there is some uncertainty in the markets, with higher than normal rates of inflation, but an expectation that the inflation level may soon come down. This has led some economists to predict a rise in interest rates and others suggesting an unchanged outlook or maybe even a small fall in interest rates over the next six months.

Although Alecto Co is of the opinion that it is equally likely that interest rates could increase or fall by 0.5% in four months, it wishes to protect itself from interest rate fluctuations by using derivatives. The company can borrow at LIBOR plus 80 basis points and LIBOR is currently 3.3%. The company is considering using interest rate futures, options on interest rate futures or interest rate collars as possible hedging choices.

The following information and quotes from an appropriate exchange are provided on Euro futures and options. Margin requirements may be ignored.

Three month Euro futures, €1,000,000 contract, tick size 0.01% and tick value €25

March 96.27

June 96.16

September 95.90

Options on three month Euro futures, €1,000,000 contract, tick size 0.01% and tick value €25. Option premiums are in annual %.

	Calls		Strike		Puts	
March	*June*	*September*		*March*	*June*	*September*
0.279	0.391	0.446	96.00	0.006	0.163	0.276
0.012	0.090	0.263	96.50	0.196	0.581	0.754

It can be assumed that settlement for both the futures and options contracts is at the end of the month. It can also be assumed that basis diminishes to zero at contract maturity at a constant rate and that time intervals can be counted in months.

Required:

(a) Briefly discuss the main advantage and disadvantage of hedging interest rate risk using an interest rate collar instead of options. **(4 marks)**

(b) Based on the three hedging choices Alecto Co is considering and assuming that the company does not face any basis risk, recommend a hedging strategy for the €22,000,000 loan. Support your recommendation with appropriate comments and relevant calculations in €. **(17 marks)**

(c) Explain what is meant by basis risk and how it would affect the recommendation made in part (b) above. **(4 marks)**

(Total: 25 marks)

75 GNT CO (PILOT 2012)

GNT Co is considering an investment in one of two corporate bonds. Both bonds have a par value of $1,000 and pay coupon interest on an annual basis. The market price of the first bond is $1,079·68. Its coupon rate is 6% and it is due to be redeemed at par in five years. The second bond is about to be issued with a coupon rate of 4% and will also be redeemable at par in five years. Both bonds are expected to have the same gross redemption yields (yields to maturity).

GNT Co considers duration of the bond to be a key factor when making decisions on which bond to invest.

Required:

(a) Estimate the Macaulay duration of the two bonds GNT Co is considering for investment. **(9 marks)**

(b) Discuss how useful duration is as a measure of the sensitivity of a bond price to changes in interest rates. **(8 marks)**

(c) Among the criteria used by credit agencies for establishing a company's credit rating are the following: industry risk, earnings protection, financial flexibility and evaluation of the company's management.

Briefly explain each criterion and suggest factors that could be used to assess it.

(8 marks)

(Total: 25 marks)

76   KENDURI CO (JUN 13)

Kenduri Co is a large multinational company based in the UK with a number of subsidiary companies around the world. Currently, foreign exchange exposure as a result of transactions between Kenduri Co and its subsidiary companies is managed by each company individually. Kenduri Co is considering whether or not to manage the foreign exchange exposure using multilateral netting from the UK, with the Sterling Pound (£) as the base currency. If multilateral netting is undertaken, spot mid-rates would be used.

The following cash flows are due in three months between Kenduri Co and three of its subsidiary companies. The subsidiary companies are Lakama Co, based in the United States (currency US$), Jaia Co, based in Canada (currency CAD) and Gochiso Co, based in Japan (currency JPY).

Owed by	Owed to	Amount
Kenduri Co	Lakama Co	US$ 4.5 million
Kenduri Co	Jaia Co	CAD 1.1 million
Gochiso Co	Jaia Co	CAD 3.2 million
Gochiso Co	Lakama Co	US$ 1.4 million
Jaia Co	Lakama Co	US$ 1.5 million
Jaia Co	Kenduri Co	CAD 3.4 million
Lakama Co	Gochiso Co	JPY 320 million
Lakama Co	Kenduri Co	US$ 2.1 million

Exchange rates available to Kenduri Co

	US$/£1	CAD/£1	JPY/£1
Spot	1.5938–1.5962	1.5690–1.5710	131.91–133.59
3-month forward	1.5996–1.6037	1.5652–1.5678	129.15–131.05

Currency options available to Kenduri Co Contract size £62,500, Exercise price quotation: US$/£1, Premium: cents per £1

	Call Options		Put Options	
Exercise price	3-month expiry	6-month expiry	3-month expiry	6-month expiry
1.60	1.55	2.25	2.08	2.23
1.62	0.98	1.58	3.42	3.73

It can be assumed that option contracts expire at the end of the relevant month

Annual interest rates available to Kenduri Co and subsidiaries

Borrowing rate Investing rate

	Borrowing rate	Investing rate
UK	4.0%	2.8%
United States	4.8%	3.1%
Canada	3.4%	2.1%
Japan	2.2%	0.5%

Required:

(a) Advise Kenduri Co on, and recommend, an appropriate hedging strategy for the US$ cash flows it is due to receive or pay in three months, from Lakama Co. Show all relevant calculations to support the advice given. **(12 marks)**

(b) Calculate, using a tabular format (transactions matrix), the impact of undertaking multilateral netting by Kenduri Co and its three subsidiary companies for the cash flows due in three months. Briefly discuss why some governments allow companies to undertake multilateral netting, while others do not. **(10 marks)**

(c) When examining different currency options and their risk factors, it was noticed that a long call option had a high gamma value. Explain the possible characteristics of a long call option with a high gamma value. **(3 marks)**

(Total: 25 marks)

77 AWAN CO (DEC 13)

Awan Co is expecting to receive $48,000,000 on 1 February 20X4, which will be invested until it is required for a large project on 1 June 20X4. Due to uncertainty in the markets, the company is of the opinion that it is likely that interest rates will fluctuate significantly over the coming months, although it is difficult to predict whether they will increase or decrease.

Awan Co's treasury team want to hedge the company against adverse movements in interest rates using one of the following derivative products:

- Forward rate agreements (FRAs);

- Interest rate futures; or

- Options on interest rate futures.

Awan Co can invest funds at the relevant inter-bank rate less 20 basis points. The current inter-bank rate is 4.09%. However, Awan Co is of the opinion that interest rates could increase or decrease by as much as 0.9% over the coming months.

The following information and quotes are provided from an appropriate exchange on $ futures and options. Margin requirements can be ignored.

Three-month $ futures, $2,000,000 contract size

Prices are quoted in basis points at 100 – annual % yield

December 20X3:   94.80
March 20X4:   94.76
June 20X4:   94.69

Options on three-month $ futures, $2,000,000 contract size, option premiums are in annual %

Calls			Strike	Puts		
December	March	June		December	March	June
0.342	0.432	0.523	94.50	0.090	0.119	0.271
0.097	0.121	0.289	95.00	0.312	0.417	0.520

Voblaka Bank has offered the following FRA rates to Awan Co:

1–7: 4.37%

3–4: 4.78%

3–7: 4.82%

4–7: 4.87%

It can be assumed that settlement for the futures and options contracts is at the end of the month and that basis diminishes to zero at contract maturity at a constant rate, based on monthly time intervals. Assume that it is 1 November 20X3 now and that there is no basis risk.

Required:

(a) **Based on the three hedging choices Awan Co is considering, recommend a hedging strategy for the $48,000,000 investment, if interest rates increase or decrease by 0.9%. Support your answer with appropriate calculations and discussion. (19 marks)**

(b) A member of Awan Co's treasury team has suggested that if option contracts are purchased to hedge against the interest rate movements, then the number of contracts purchased should be determined by a hedge ratio based on the delta value of the option.

Required:

Discuss how the delta value of an option could be used in determining the number of contracts purchased.
(6 marks)

(Total: 25 marks)

78 FAOILEAN CO (JUN 14)

The chief executive officer (CEO) of Faoilean Co has just returned from a discussion at a leading university on the 'application of options to investment decisions and corporate value'. She wants to understand how some of the ideas which were discussed can be applied to decisions made at Faoilean Co. She is still a little unclear about some of the discussion on options and their application, and wants further clarification on the following:

(i) Faoilean Co is involved in the exploration and extraction of oil and gas. Recently there have been indications that there could be significant deposits of oil and gas just off the shores of Ireland. The government of Ireland has invited companies to submit bids for the rights to commence the initial exploration of the area to assess the likelihood and amount of oil and gas deposits, with further extraction rights to follow. Faoilean Co is considering putting in a bid for the rights. The speaker leading the discussion suggested that using options as an investment assessment tool would be particularly useful to Faoilean Co in this respect.

(ii) The speaker further suggested that options were useful in determining the value of equity and default risk, and suggested that this was why companies facing severe financial distress could still have a positive equity value.

(iii) Towards the end of the discussion, the speaker suggested that changes in the values of options can be measured in terms of a number of risk factors known as the 'greeks', such as the 'vega'. The CEO is unclear why option values are affected by so many different risk factors.

Required:

(a) **With regard to (i) above, discuss how Faoilean Co may use the idea of options to help with the investment decision in bidding for the exploration rights, and explain the assumptions made when using the idea of options in making investment decisions.** (11 marks)

(b) **With regard to (ii) above, discuss how options could be useful in determining the value of equity and default risk, and why companies facing severe financial distress still have positive equity values.** (9 marks)

(c) **With regard to (iii) above, explain why changes in option values are determined by numerous different risk factors and what 'vega' determines.** (5 marks)

(Total: 25 marks)

79 KESHI CO (DEC 14)

Keshi Co is a large multinational company with a number of international subsidiary companies. A centralised treasury department manages Keshi Co and its subsidiaries' borrowing requirements, cash surplus investment and financial risk management. Financial risk is normally managed using conventional derivative products such as forwards, futures, options and swaps.

Assume it is 1 December 2014 today and Keshi Co is expecting to borrow $18,000,000 on 1 February 2015 for a period of seven months. It can either borrow the funds at a variable rate of LIBOR plus 40 basis points or a fixed rate of 5.5%. LIBOR is currently 3.8% but Keshi Co feels that this could increase or decrease by 0.5% over the coming months due to increasing uncertainty in the markets.

The treasury department is considering whether or not to hedge the $18,000,000, using either exchange-traded March options or over-the-counter swaps offered by Rozu Bank.

The following information and quotes for $ March options are provided from an appropriate exchange. The options are based on three-month $ futures, $1,000,000 contract size and option premiums are in annual %.

March calls	Strike price	March puts
0.882	95.50	0.662
0.648	96.00	0.902

Option prices are quoted in basis points at 100 minus the annual % yield and settlement of the options contracts is at the end of March 2015. The current basis on the March futures price is 44 points; and it is expected to be 33 points on 1 January 2015, 22 points on 1 February 2015 and 11 points on 1 March 2015.

Rozu Bank has offered Keshi Co a swap on a counterparty variable rate of LIBOR plus 30 basis points or a fixed rate of 4.6%, where Keshi Co receives 70% of any benefits accruing from undertaking the swap, prior to any bank charges. Rozu Bank will charge Keshi Co 10 basis points for the swap.

Keshi Co's chief executive officer believes that a centralised treasury department is necessary in order to increase shareholder value, but Keshi Co's new chief financial officer (CFO) thinks that having decentralised treasury departments operating across the subsidiary companies could be more beneficial. The CFO thinks that this is particularly relevant to the situation which Suisen Co, a company owned by Keshi Co, is facing.

Suisen Co-operates in a country where most companies conduct business activities based on Islamic finance principles. It produces confectionery products including chocolates. It wants to use Salam contracts instead of commodity futures contracts to hedge its exposure to price fluctuations of cocoa. Salam contracts involve a commodity which is sold based on currently agreed prices, quantity and quality. Full payment is received by the seller immediately, for an agreed delivery to be made in the future.

Required:

(a) Based on the two hedging choices Keshi Co is considering, recommend a hedging strategy for the $18,000,000 borrowing. Support your answer with appropriate calculations and discussion. **(15 marks)**

(b) Discuss how a centralised treasury department may increase value for Keshi Co and the possible reasons for decentralising the treasury department. **(6 marks)**

(c) Discuss the key differences between a Salam contract, under Islamic finance principles, and futures contracts. **(4 marks)**

(Total: 25 marks)

ECONOMIC ENVIRONMENT FOR MULTINATIONALS

80   DEPUTY CHIEF FINANCIAL OFFICER 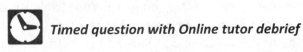 *Walk in the footsteps of a top tutor*

> *Timed question with Online tutor debrief*

You have been appointed as deputy Chief Financial Officer to a large multinational pharmaceutical company with trading interests in 24 countries in sub-Saharan Africa, South America and the Indian sub-continent. Your company also has important trading links with the United States, Malaysia and Singapore. There have been a number of issues arising in the previous six months which have impacted upon the company's business interests.

(i) Following an investigation you discover that commissions were paid to a senior official in one country to ensure that the local drug licensing agency concerned facilitated the acceptance of one of your principal revenue earning drugs for use within its national health service.

(ii) You have discovered that an agent of your firm, aware that the licensing agreement might be forthcoming, purchased several call option contracts on your company's equity.

(iii) A senior member of the firm's treasury team has been taking substantial positions in currency futures in order to protect the risk of loss on the translation of dollar assets into the domestic currency. Over the last 12 months significant profits have been made but the trades do not appear to have been properly authorised. You discover that a long position in 50, $250,000 contracts is currently held but over the last four weeks the dollar has depreciated by 10% and all the signs are that it will depreciate considerably more over the next two months.

(iv)   One drug company has managed to copy a novel drug that you have just released for the treatment of various forms of skin cancer. You have patent protection in the country concerned but your company has not been able to initiate proceedings through the local courts. Contacts with the trade officials at your embassy in the country concerned suggest that the government has made sure that the proceedings have not been allowed to proceed.

The company's chief financial officer has asked you to look into these issues and, with respect to (iv), any World Trade Organisation (WTO) agreements that might be relevant, and to advise her on how the company should proceed in each case.

Required:

Prepare a memorandum advising the Chief Financial Officer on the issues involved and recommending how she should, in each case and in the circumstances, proceed.

(Total: 20 marks)

 Calculate your allowed time, allocate the time to the separate parts.

81   **MOOSE CO**

You are the Chief Financial Officer of Moose Co. Moose Co is a manufacturer of cleaning equipment and has an international market for its products. Your company places a strong emphasis on innovation and design with patent protection across all its product range.

The company has two principal manufacturing centres, one in Europe which has been reduced in size in recent years because of high labour costs and the other in South East Asia. However, Moose Co's development has relied upon ready access to the debt market both in Europe and in South East Asia and the company is planning significant expansion with a new manufacturing and distribution centre in South America. Your company is highly profitable with strong cash flows although in the last two quarters there has been a downturn in sales in all markets as the global recession has begun to take effect.

Since August 20X7, credit conditions have deteriorated across all of the major economies as banks have curtailed their lending following the down rating of US asset-backed securities. In 20X8 and 20X9 many banks recorded significant multibillion dollar losses as they attempted to sell off what had become known as 'toxic debt', leading to a further collapse in their value. In response many banks also attempted to repair their balance sheets by rights and other equity issues.

The founder and executive chairman of the company, Alan Bison, is planning a round of meetings with a number of investment banks in leading financial centres around the world to explore raising a $350 million dollar loan for the new development. It has already been suggested that a loan of this size would need to be syndicated or alternatively raised through a bond issue.

In preparation for those meetings he has asked you to provide him with some briefing notes.

Required:

(a) Given conditions in the global debt market as described above, advise on the likely factors banks will consider in offering a loan of this size. **(7 marks)**

(b) Assess the relative advantages of loan syndication versus a bond issue to Moose Co. **(7 marks)**

(c) Assess the relative advantages and disadvantages of entering into a capital investment of this scale at this stage of the global economic cycle. **(6 marks)**

(Total: 20 marks)

82 LAMRI CO (DEC 10)

Lamri Co (Lamri), a listed company, is expecting sales revenue to grow to $80 million next year, which is an increase of 20% from the current year. The operating profit margin for next year is forecast to be the same as this year at 30% of sales revenue. In addition to these profits, Lamri receives 75% of the after-tax profits from one of its wholly owned foreign subsidiaries – Magnolia Co (Magnolia), as dividends. However, its second wholly owned foreign subsidiary – Strymon Co (Strymon) does not pay dividends.

Lamri is due to pay dividends of $7.5 million shortly and has maintained a steady 8% annual growth rate in dividends over the past few years. The company has grown rapidly in the last few years as a result of investment in key projects and this is likely to continue.

For the coming year it is expected that Lamri will require the following capital investment.

1 An investment equivalent to the amount of depreciation to keep its non-current asset base at the present productive capacity. Lamri charges depreciation of 25% on a straight-line basis on its non-current assets of $15 million. This charge has been included when calculating the operating profit amount.

2 A 25% investment in additional non-current assets for every $1 increase in sales revenue.

3 $4.5 million additional investment in non-current assets for a new project.

Lamri also requires a 15% investment in working capital for every $1 increase in sales revenue.

Strymon produces specialist components solely for Magnolia to assemble into finished goods. Strymon will produce 300,000 specialist components at $12 variable cost per unit and will incur fixed costs of $2.1 million for the coming year. It will then transfer the components to Magnolia at full cost price, where they will be assembled at a cost of $8 per unit and sold for $50 per unit. Magnolia will incur additional fixed costs of $1.5 million in the assembly process.

Tax-Ethic (TE) is a charitable organisation devoted to reducing tax avoidance schemes by companies operating in poor countries around the world. TE has petitioned Lamri's Board of Directors to reconsider Strymon's policy of transferring goods at full cost. TE suggests that the policy could be changed to cost plus 40% mark-up. If Lamri changes Strymon's policy, it is expected that Strymon would be asked to remit 75% of its after-tax profits as dividends to Lamri.

Other Information

1   Lamri's outstanding non-current liabilities of $35 million, on which it pays interest of 8% per year, and its 30 million $1 issued equity capital will not change for the coming year.

2   Lamri's, Magnolia's and Strymon's profits are taxed at 28%, 22% and 42% respectively. A withholding tax of 10% is deducted from any dividends remitted from Strymon.

3   The tax authorities where Lamri is based charge tax on profits made by subsidiary companies but give full credit for tax already paid by overseas subsidiaries.

4   All costs and revenues are in $ equivalent amounts and exchange rate fluctuations can be ignored.

Required:

(a)   Calculate Lamri's dividend capacity for the coming year prior to implementing TE's proposal and after implementing the proposal.   **(14 marks)**

(b)   Comment on the impact of implementing TE's proposal and suggest possible actions Lamri may take as a result.   **(6 marks)**

(Total: 20 marks)

EMERGING ISSUES IN FINANCE AND FINANCIAL MANAGEMENT

83   GOSLO MOTOR CORPORATION

The finance division of GoSlo Motor Corporation has made a number of loans to customers with a current pool value of $200 million. The loans have an average term to maturity of four years. The loans generate a steady income to the business of 10.5% per annum. The company will use 95% of the loan's pool as collateral for a collateralised loan obligation structured as follows:

*   80% of the collateral value to support a tranche of A-rated floating rate loan notes offering investors LIBOR plus 140 basis points.

*   10% of the collateral value to support a tranche of B-rated fixed rate loan notes offering investors 11%.

*   10% of the collateral value to support a tranche as subordinated certificates (unrated).

In order to minimise interest rate risk, the company has decided to enter into a fixed for variable rate swap on the A-rated floating rate notes exchanging LIBOR for 8.5%.

Service charges of $240,000 per annum will be charged for administering the income receivable from the loans. You may ignore prepayment risk.

Required:

(a)   Calculate the expected returns of the investments in each of the three tranches described above. Estimate the sensitivity of the subordinated certificates to a reduction of 1% in the returns generated by the pool.   **(10 marks)**

(b)   Explain the purpose and the methods of credit enhancement that can be employed on a securitisation such as this scheme.   **(4 marks)**

(c)   Discuss the risks inherent to the investors in a scheme such as this.   **(6 marks)**

(Total: 20 marks)

84   JJJ CO

JJJ Co is a large, multinational financial services company which is based in France, in the Eurozone. Its latest accounts showed a revenue of €1,200m and an operating profit of €166m. At the company's Annual General Meeting (AGM) next week, the directors are expecting to face some hostile questioning regarding some of the investments which JJJ Co holds. The company has received several letters and emails from concerned shareholders regarding the following two investments in particular:

- €100m (nominal value) of 5 year, 4.5% coupon French government bonds, and

- €30m (nominal value) of 3 year, 3.5% coupon Belgian government bonds.

The problem is that there has been much press coverage in recent months of the Eurozone debt crisis, and the shareholders are concerned about the possible impact on JJJ Co.

Some extracts from the shareholders' letters and emails are presented below, along with some relevant information from the website of the credit rating agency Standard and Poor's (S&P):

Extracts from the S&P website

'...we have downgraded French government bonds from an AAA rating to an AA+ rating...'

'...the credit rating for Belgian government bonds is being held at AA...'

Spot yield curve (%)

S&P rating	1 year	3 year	5 year
AAA	3.60	3.72	3.95
AA+	3.75	3.89	4.15
AA	3.95	4.11	4.40
AA-	4.33	4.60	4.95

Extracts from shareholders' letters and emails

'...yields on European countries' government bonds are rocketing because of the Eurozone debt crisis and the risk of financial contagion within the Eurozone, yet our interest receipts from our French and Belgian government bonds have not changed since we invested in these bonds...'

'...I am concerned that our Belgian bonds are only paying 3.5% interest, which is less than the rate S&P says they should be paying, and is also less than the rate of 4.5% on the higher rated French government bonds. Surely the riskier bonds should have a higher interest rate...'

'...now that the French government's credit rating has been downgraded, I think we should be demanding that they increase the interest rate from the current 4.5%...'

Required:

Assume that you are an advisor to the directors of JJJ Co. You are required to prepare some briefing notes for the upcoming AGM which deal with the issues raised by the shareholders.

(a)   Discuss the reasons for the existence of the Eurozone debt crisis, and explain briefly what is meant by financial contagion.   **(8 marks)**

(b)   Briefly explain how credit rating agencies (like Standard and Poor's) set credit ratings for corporate and government bonds.   **(5 marks)**

(c)   Explain the likely practical impact on JJJ Co of the decision to downgrade the credit rating on French government bonds. As part of your answer you should address the points regarding interest rates on the French and Belgian government bonds which were made by the shareholders.   **(12 marks)**

(Total: 25 marks)

Note: You are not required to present any calculations in your answer to this question.

85   STROM CO (DEC 12 A)

Assume that it is now December 2012.

Strom Co is a clothing retailer, with stores selling mid-price clothes and clothing accessories throughout Europe. It sells its own-brand items, which are produced by small manufacturers located in Africa, who work solely for Strom Co. The recent European sovereign debt crisis has affected a number of countries in the European Union (EU). Consequently, Strom Co has found trading conditions to be extremely difficult, putting pressure on profits and sales revenue.

The sovereign debt crisis in Europe resulted in countries finding it increasingly difficult and expensive to issue government bonds to raise funds. Two main reasons have been put forward to explain why the crisis took place: firstly, a number of countries continued to borrow excessive funds, because their expenditure exceeded taxation revenues; and secondly, a number of countries allocated significant sums of money to support their banks following the 'credit crunch' and the banking crisis.

In order to prevent countries defaulting on their debt obligations and being downgraded, the countries in the EU and the International Monetary Fund (IMF) established a fund to provide financial support to member states threatened by the risk of default, credit downgrades and excessive borrowing yields. Strict economic conditions known as austerity measures were imposed on these countries in exchange for receiving financial support.

The austerity measures have affected Strom Co negatively, and the years 2011 and 2012 have been particularly bad, with sales revenue declining by 15% and profits by 25% in 2011, and remaining at 2011 levels in 2012. On investigation, Strom Co noted that clothing retailers selling clothes at low prices and at high prices were not affected as badly as Strom Co or other mid-price retailers. Indeed, the retailers selling low-priced clothes had increased their profits, and retailers selling luxury, expensive clothes had maintained their profits over the last two to three years.

In order to improve profitability, Strom Co's board of directors expects to cut costs where possible. A significant fixed cost relates to quality control, which includes monitoring the working conditions of employees of Strom Co's clothing manufacturers, as part of its ethical commitment.

Required:

(a) Explain the role and aims of the International Monetary Fund (IMF) and discuss possible reasons why the austerity measures imposed on European Union (EU) countries might have affected Strom Co negatively. **(10 marks)**

(b) Suggest, giving reasons, why the austerity measures might not have affected clothing retailers at the high and low price range, as much as the mid-price range retailers like Strom Co. **(4 marks)**

(c) Discuss the risks to Strom Co of reducing the costs relating to quality control and how the detrimental impact of such reductions in costs could be decreased.

(6 marks)

(d) Explain what is meant by the term 'money laundering', and explain the steps taken internationally to prevent it. **(5 marks)**

(Total: 25 marks)

86 INTEGRATED REPORTING

TRE plc is a listed high street retailer that sells a range of goods such as food, drink, clothing, electrical goods, CDs, DVS and garden equipment.

At a recent board meeting the topic of Integrated Reporting or <IR> was raised with very mixed views in the discussion.

The Marketing Director argued that <IR> was simply a mixture of the sustainability report and the financial report into a single communication intended mainly for investors. As such it had very little new to offer and was just another compliance requirement.

The Finance Director replied that, in his view, <IR> would give a greater emphasis on the different types of 'capital' within the firm and would assist in more focussed performance management.

Required:

(a) Briefly explain what is meant by an 'Integrated Report' and comment on the views of the Marketing Director. **(5 marks)**

(b) Identify and describe the SIX different types of 'capital' emphasised within the <IR> Framework. **(9 marks)**

(c) Explain FOUR objectives of integrated reporting. **(6 marks)**

(d) Explain how an emphasis on these types of capital could result in more focussed performance management. **(5 marks)**

(Total: 25 marks)

Section 3

ANSWERS TO PRACTICE QUESTIONS – SECTION A

ROLE AND RESPONSIBILITY TOWARDS STAKEHOLDERS

1   VADENER PLC

Key answer tips

Requirement (a) is a standard corporate appraisal. To achieve a good answer ensure that you discuss all ratios calculated and conclude by commenting on the firm's resource allocation plans.

Part (b) is easier if you think of issues as you approach part (a), rather than as a separate exercise.

In part (c) the key issue is that translation losses are unrealised unless the division or asset concerned is sold.

Part (d) covers the problem of using options for speculation rather than hedging.

(a)   Group performance may be analysed by using financial ratios, growth trends and comparative market data. Alternative definitions exist for some ratios, and other ratios are equally valid.

Operating and profitability ratios:

		20X3	20X4	20X5
Return on capital employed:	$\dfrac{EBIT}{Capital\ employed}$	$\dfrac{410}{1,486} = 27.6\%$	$\dfrac{540}{1,665} = 32.4\%$	$\dfrac{560}{1,876} = 29.9\%$
Asset turnover:	$\dfrac{Sales}{Capital\ employed}$	$\dfrac{1,210}{1,486} = 0.81$	$\dfrac{1,410}{1,665} = 0.85$	$\dfrac{1,490}{1,876} = 0.79$
Profit margin:	$\dfrac{EBIT}{Sales}$	$\dfrac{410}{1,210} = 33.9\%$	$\dfrac{540}{1,410} = 38.3\%$	$\dfrac{560}{1,490} = 37.6\%$

Liquidity ratios:

Current ratio:	$\dfrac{\text{Current assets}}{\text{Current liabilities}}$	$\dfrac{728}{565} = 1.29$	$\dfrac{863}{728} = 1.19$	$\dfrac{1,015}{799} = 1.27$
Acid test:	$\dfrac{\text{Current assets - inventory}}{\text{Current liabilities}}$	$\dfrac{388}{565} = 0.69$	$\dfrac{453}{728} = 0.62$	$\dfrac{525}{799} = 0.66$

Market ratios:

Dividend yield:	$\dfrac{\text{Dividend per share}}{\text{Market price}}$	$\dfrac{48.7}{1,220} = 4.0\%$	$\dfrac{56.7}{1,417} = 4.0\%$	$\dfrac{61.7}{1,542} = 4.0\%$
Earnings per share (pence):	$\dfrac{\text{Earnings after tax}}{\text{Number of shares}}$	$\dfrac{259}{300} = 86.3$	$\dfrac{339}{300} = 113.0$	$\dfrac{346}{300} = 115.3$
PE ratio	$\dfrac{\text{Market price}}{\text{Earnings per share}}$	$\dfrac{1,220}{86.3} = 14.1$	$\dfrac{1,417}{113} = 12.5$	$\dfrac{1,542}{115.3} = 13.4$
Gearing:	$\dfrac{\text{Total borrowing}}{\text{Borrowing + equity}}$	$\dfrac{535}{1,621} = 33\%$	$\dfrac{580}{1,835} = 32\%$	$\dfrac{671}{2,077} = 32\%$

It is difficult to reach conclusions about the performance of Vadener without more comparative data from similar companies.

Return on capital at around 30% is dominated by the effect of high profit margins, but the split between divisions is not provided. Asset utilisation is well below 1, which implies relatively inefficient utilisation of assets. Vadener might investigate whether this could be improved.

Liquidity has improved during the last year, and although below some commonly used benchmarks might be satisfactory for the sectors that Vadener is involved with. However, some aspects of working capital require attention. Stock levels have increased from 28% of revenue in 20X3 to 33% in 20X5, and the collection period for debtors has similarly increased from 114 days to 125 days. Creditors have also increased more than proportionately to revenue. Vadener should take action to improve the efficiency of its working capital management.

In contrast operating costs have fallen over the three years from 66% to 62% of revenue, indicating greater efficiency. Gearing appears to be relatively low at around 32%, but comparative data is needed, and interest cover is high at more than eight times in 20X5.

Investors do not appear to be entirely satisfied with group performance. The FT market index has increased by 34% between 20X3 and 20X5, whereas Vadener's share price has only increased by 26%. With an equity beta of 1.1 Vadener's share price would be expected to increase by more than the market index. Vadener's PE ratios are also lower than those of similar companies, suggesting that investors do not value the company's future prospects as highly as those of its competitors.

The required return from Vadener's shares may be estimated using the capital asset pricing model (CAPM).

Required return = 5% + (12% − 5%) 1.1 = 12.7%

An approximation of the actual return from Vadener's shares is the 12% average annual increase in share price plus 4% annual dividend yield, or 16%. The total return is higher than expected for the systematic risk. Given this, Vadener should investigate the reasons why its share price has performed relatively poorly. One possibility is the company's dividend policy.

Dividends have consistently been more than 50% of available after tax earnings, which might not be popular with investors.

Divisional performance

The information on the individual divisions is very sparse. All divisions are profitable, but the return from the pharmaceutical division is relatively low for its systematic risk.

Using CAPM to approximate required returns:

	Required return	Actual return
Construction	5% + (12% − 5%) 0.75 = 10.25%	13%
Leisure	5% + (12% − 5%) 1.1 = 12.7%	16%
Pharmaceuticals	5% + (12% − 5%) 1.40 = 14.8%[1]	14%

[1] It is assumed that the same market parameters are valid for the US based division.

The construction and leisure divisions appear to have greater than expected returns (a positive alpha) and the pharmaceutical division slightly less than expected for the risk of the division. The pharmaceutical division has recently suffered a translation loss due to the weakness of the US dollar, and the potential economic exposure from changes in the value of the dollar should be investigated.

From a financial perspective it would appear that the company should not devote equal resources to the divisions, and should focus its efforts on construction and leisure. However, the future prospects of the sectors are not known, nor the long term strategy of Vadener, which might be to expand international operations in the USA or elsewhere. The strategic use of resources should not be decided on the basis of the limited financial information that is available.

(b) Other information that would be useful includes:

(i) Cash flow forecasts for the group and the individual divisions.

(ii) Full product and market information for each of the divisions.

(iii) Details of recent investments in each of the divisions and the expected impact of such investment on future performance.

(iv) Detailed historic performance data of the divisions over at least three years, and similar data for companies in the relevant sectors.

(v) Competitors and potential growth rates in each of the sectors.

(vi) The economic exposure of the US division

(vii) The future strategic plans of Vadener. Are there any other proposed initiatives?

(viii) How the company's equal resource strategy will be viewed by investors. The company has performed worse than the market in recent years despite having a higher beta than the market.

(c) A translation loss of £10 million is not necessarily a problem for Vadener plc.

Translation exposure, sometimes known as accounting exposure, often does not reflect any real cash flow changes. It is changes in cash flow that, in an efficient market, will impact on the share price and value of a company. For example, a translation loss might in part reflect a lower home currency value of an overseas factory, but the factory will still be the same and will still be producing goods. It is the impact on the home currency cash flows from the continuing operations of the factory that will affect share price.

However, if the market is not efficient, investors might not understand that there are no real cash flow implications from the exposure, and might be worried about the effect of the translation loss on Vadener, and possibly sell their shares. If this is the case Vadener might consider internal hedges to reduce translation exposure. In most cases this would not be recommended, and companies must also be careful that hedges to manage translation exposure do not adversely affect the efficient operations of the business, or be contrary to hedges that are being undertaken to protect against other forms of currency exposure such as transaction exposure.

(d) Income may be increased by writing (selling) options, as the writer of the option receives the option premium.

However, unless the option is hedged, writing options exposes the writer to a theoretically unlimited loss.

Uncovered writing of options is effectively speculating, involves very high risk, and is not normally recommended as a strategy to companies such as Vadener.

ADVANCED INVESTMENT APPRAISAL

2 WURRALL INC

Key answer tips

This is an extremely time-pressured question so a logical approach is vital. Lay out a proforma for all four years before you start, and put figures in for all four years as you go along. For example, when looking at sales revenue, it is quite easy to forecast the figures for all four years at the same time by applying the relevant growth forecast to the number in your calculator.

(a) **Appendix to the report: Proforma accounts**

Proforma statements of profit or loss for the years ended March 20X5–8

	$ million			
	20X5	*20X6*	*20X7*	*20X8*
Sales revenue	1,787	1,929	2,064	2,188
Operating costs before depreciation	(1,215)	(1,312)	(1,404)	(1,488)
EBITDA	572	617	660	700
Tax-allowable depreciation	(165)	(179)	(191)	(203)
EBIT	407	438	469	497
Net interest payable	(63)	(65)	(66)	(70)
Profit on ordinary activities before tax	344	373	403	427
Tax on ordinary activities	(103)	(112)	(121)	(128)
Profit after tax	241	261	282	299
Dividends	135	146	158	167

Proforma statements of financial position 20X5–8

	$ million			
	20X5	*20X6*	*20X7*	*20X8*
Non-current assets				
Land and buildings	310	310	350	350
Plant and machinery (net)	1,103	1,191	1,275	1,351
Investments	32	32	32	32
	1,445	1,533	1,657	1,733
Current assets				
Inventory	488	527	564	598
Receivables	615	664	710	753
Cash in hand and short-term deposits	22	24	25	27
	2,570	2,748	2,956	3,111

Equity and liabilities				
Called-up share capital (10 cents par)	240	240	240	240
Reserves	970	1,085	1,209	1,341
	1,210	1,325	1,449	1,581
Non-current liabilities:				
Borrowings[1]	580	580	580	580
Current liabilities				
Short-term loans and overdrafts (balancing fig)	266	287	332	320
Other payables	514	556	595	630
	2,570	2,748	2,956	3,111

[1]Refinanced with a similar type of loan in 20X6

Tutorial note

This is a fairly straightforward forecast of proforma accounts and should be a good opportunity to score marks. However, ensure that presentation is both clear and appropriate.

(b) **Report to the Board of Directors**

Prepared by A.N. Accountant

Problems with the assumptions

The proforma accounts (see Appendix – part (a)) are based primarily upon the percentage of sales method of forecasting. This provides a simple approach to forecasting, but is based upon assumptions of existing or planned relationships between variables remaining constant, which are highly unlikely. It also does not allow for improvements in efficiency over time.

(i) Accurate forecasts of sales growth are very difficult. Sensitivity or simulation analysis is recommended to investigate the implications of sales differing from the forecast levels. A constant growth rate of 6% forever after four years is most unlikely.

(ii) Cash operating costs are unlikely to increase in direct proportion with sales. The variable elements (wages, materials, distribution costs, etc) could all move at a higher or lower rate than sales, while the fixed elements will not change with the value of sales at all in the short run. If the company becomes more efficient then costs as a proportion of sales should reduce.

(iii) Unless tax-allowable depreciation from new asset purchases exactly offsets the diminishing allowances on older assets, and effect of the increase in assets with sales growth, this relationship is unlikely to be precise. The government might also change the rates of tax-allowable depreciation.

(iv) Assuming a direct relationship between inventories, receivables, cash and other payables to sales could promote inefficiency. Although a strong correlation between such variables exists, there should be no need to increase inventories, receivables and payables in direct proportion to sales.

(v) Paying dividends as a constant percentage of earnings could lead to quite volatile dividend payouts. Most investors are believed to prefer reasonably constant dividends (allowing for inflation) and might not value a company with volatile dividends as highly as one with relatively stable dividends.

(c) **Free cash flow analysis**

Free cash flow will be estimated by EBIT(1–T) plus depreciation less adjustments for changes in working capital and expenditure on non-current assets. (NB other definitions of free cash flow exist)

	$ million			
	20X5	*20X6*	*20X7*	*20X8*
Change in land and buildings	–	–	40	–
Change in plant and machinery	91	88	84	76
Change in working capital	15	27	–	56
Change in assets	106	115	124	132

	$ million			
	20X5	*20X6*	*20X7*	*20X8*
EBIT (1–T)	285	307	328	348
Depreciation	165	179	191	203
Change in assets	(106)	(115)	(124)	(132)
Free cash flow	344	371	395	419

The present value of free cash flow for the company after 20X8 may be estimated by

$$\frac{FCF20X8(1+g)}{WACC-g} \text{ or } \frac{419(1.06)}{0.11-0.06} = 8,883$$

The estimated value of the company at the end of 20X8 is $8,883 million. From this must be deducted the value of any loans in order to find the value accruing to shareholders. From the proforma accounts, loans are expected to total $900 million, leaving a net value of $7,983 million. If the number of issued shares has not changed, the estimated market value per share is $\frac{7,983}{2,400}$ = 333 cents per share, an increase of 58% on the current share price.

Based upon this data, the managing director's claim that the share price will double in four years is not likely to occur. However, the impact of the performance of the economy, and unforeseen significant changes affecting Wurrall Inc mean that such estimates are subject to a considerable margin of error.

(d)   **Ratio analysis**

	20X5	20X6	20X7	20X8
Gearing (%)	41.1	39.6	38.6	36.3
Current ratio	1.44	1.44	1.40	1.45
Quick ratio	0.82	0.82	0.79	0.82
Return on capital employed[1] (%)	22.7	23.0	23.1	23.0
Asset turnover	1.00	1.01	1.02	1.01
EBIT/Sales (%)	22.8	22.7	22.7	22.7
Debtor collection period (days)	126	126	126	126

[1] EBIT/(shareholders equity plus long term debt). Other definitions are possible

Tutorial note

You have a wide choice of ratios in this question. Do not produce a long list of ratios illustrating similar trends. Choose carefully and produce a few key ratios that provide a valuable insight into the business. Equally, there are ratios other than those above that could be used alternatively to provide this insight.

It is difficult to comment upon ratios without comparative data for companies in the same industry. The current gearing level, at 42.3%, breaches the covenant limit of 40%, and it is expected to continue to do so in 20X5. Whether or not this breaches the one-year covenant is not clear, but would need to be investigated by the company and action taken to reduce gearing if the covenant was to be breached for too long a period. The debtor collection period appears high at 126 days. It is unlikely that credit would be given for such a long period, and the company might consider improving its credit control procedures to reduce the collection period. If this is successful it could also reduce the overdraft and help reduce the gearing level.

Another ratio that would need investigating is the asset turnover. At around one this is relatively low. Unless the industry is very capital intensive, management should consider if assets could be utilised more efficiently to improve this ratio, and with it the return on capital employed.

As previously mentioned, managers might also review the company's dividend policy. Paying a constant level of earnings could lead to volatile dividend payments which might not be popular with investors, including financial institutions, that rely upon dividends for part of their annual cash flow.

Wurrall proposes to finance any new capital needs with increases in the overdraft. Overdraft finance is not normally considered to be appropriate for long term financing, and the company should consider longer term borrowing or equity issues for its long-term financing requirements.

3   DARON

Key answer tips

The question clearly states that 12 of the marks for part (a) are for the discussion – make sure you pay sufficient attention to the written aspects as opposed to getting bogged down in the computational aspects of the problem.

(a)   **Report for the managers of Daron**

Offer to purchase the company

Any recommendation regarding the sale of the company to a competitor for $20 million should be made in the best interests of the shareholders. An offer of $20 million is an 8.7% premium over the current share price (which is quite low).

Estimates of the present values of future cash flows from internal data suggest that no matter which party wins the election, the company's value will be in excess of $20 million; $21 million if party B wins, and $30.3 million if party A wins.

However, these estimates are by no means precise. Inaccuracy could exist due to:

(i)   Incorrect inflation estimates.

(ii)   Errors in sales volume and cost projections.

(iii)   Inaccurate discount rate estimates.

(iv)   The assumption of a constant 30% corporate tax rate.

Sensitivity analysis is recommended to analyse the significance of changes in key variables. The cash flow estimates do not incorporate any value for options relating to opportunities that might exist between now and 20Y3 if operations continue. Nor is there data on the expected realisable value of the company in 20Y3 (that is the last year for which cash flow data is available). Even if further investment was not undertaken at that time, the present value of the realisable value of land, buildings and cash flow released from working capital needs to be considered. This would increase the above present-value estimates. On financial grounds the informal offer of $20 million is not high enough to be recommended. Additionally, selling to a competitor might have other implications such as redundancies, closure of part of the existing operations and a detrimental impact on the local community.

Investing in the purchase of a hotel

Appendix 2 shows the financial estimates of the hotel purchase. An APV of $0.56 million suggests that the hotel investment is financially viable. However, this estimate is also subject to many of the possible inaccuracies noted above. The base case NPV is heavily influenced by the realisable value of $10 million in 20X8. Future hotel values could vary substantially from this estimate.

Investment in the hotel industry is a strategic departure from the company's core competence. If the objective is primarily to diversify activities to reduce risk, this may not be in the shareholders' best interest as they can easily achieve diversification of their investment portfolios, through unit trusts or similar investments. As the company is in a declining industry, in the long term diversification may be essential for survival. A medium- to long-term strategic plan should be formulated examining alternative strategies, and alternative investments that may offer better financial returns than the hotel investment, and/or be closer to the company's existing core competence.

Appendix 1

Valuation of business cash flows

Present value estimates:

Political party A wins the election

	$ million					
	20X4	*20X5*	*20X6*	*20X7*	*20X8*	*20X9– Y3*
Sales	28.0	29.0	26.0	22.0	19.0	19.0
Variable costs	17.0	18.0	16.0	14.0	12.0	12.0
Fixed costs	3.0	3.0	3.0	3.0	3.0	3.0
Depreciation	4.0	3.0	3.0	2.0	1.0	–
	24.0	24.0	22.0	19.0	16.0	15.0
Taxable profit	4.0	5.0	4.0	3.0	3.0	4.0
Taxation (30%)	1.2	1.5	1.2	0.9	0.9	1.2
	2.8	3.5	2.8	2.1	2.1	2.8
Add back depreciation	4.0	3.0	3.0	2.0	1.0	–
Working capital	–	1.0	2.0	3.0	3.0	–
Net cash flow	6.8	7.5	7.8	7.1	6.1	2.8
Discount factors at 13%	0.885	0.783	0.693	0.613	0.543	1.910
Present values	6.0	5.9	5.4	4.4	3.3	5.3

Expected total present value, up to year 20Y3 = $30.3 million.

Tutorial note

The discount factor for years 20X9–Y3, which are Years 6–10 (five years) is calculated by taking the cumulative discount factor at 13% for Years 1–5. This (from tables) is 3.517. However, applying this discount factor to the annual cash flows would give a value as at the end of Year 5. To obtain a present value (Year 0 value) we must discount further by the Year 5 factor at 13%, which is 0.54, giving 3.517 × 0.543 = 1.910.

Political party B wins the election

	$ million					
	20X4	*20X5*	*20X6*	*20X7*	*20X8*	*20X9–Y3*
Sales	30.0	26.0	24.0	20.0	16.0	16.0
Variable costs	18.0	16.0	15.0	12.0	11.0	11.0
Fixed costs	3.0	3.0	4.0	4.0	4.0	4.0
Depreciation	4.0	3.0	3.0	2.0	1.0	–
	———	———	———	———	———	———
	25.0	22.0	22.0	18.0	16.0	15.0
	———	———	———	———	———	———
Taxable profit	5.0	4.0	2.0	2.0	0.0	1.0
Taxation (30%)	1.5	1.2	0.6	0.6	–	0.3
	———	———	———	———	———	———
	3.5	2.8	1.4	1.4	0.0	0.7
Add back depreciation	4.0	3.0	3.0	2.0	1.0	–
Working capital	(1.0)	2.0	2.0	3.0	3.0	–
	———	———	———	———	———	———
Net cash flow	6.5	7.8	6.4	6.4	4.0	0.7
Discount factors at 18%	0.847	0.718	0.609	0.516	0.437	1.366
Present values	5.5	5.6	3.9	3.3	1.7	1.0

Expected total present value, up to year 20Y3 = $21 million.

Tutorial note

The discount factor for years 20X9–Y3, is calculated the same way as before, giving 3.127 × 0.437 = 1.366.

Notes

(1)   The use of expected values is not recommended as it does not reflect a situation that is likely to occur in reality.

(2)   **Discount rate, political party A wins**

	$m
Market value of equity 20m shares at 92c =	18.4
Debt	14.0
	———
	32.4
	———

The risk-free rate *including inflation*, given expected inflation of 5% each year, is:

(1.04) (1.05) = 1.092 or 9.2%

The market return including inflation at 5% per annum is:

(1.10) (1.05) = 1.155 or 15.5%

Using CAPM, the cost of equity $K_e = E(r_i) = R_f + \beta_i(E(r_m) - R_f)$

$K_e = 9.2\% + 1.25 (15.5\% - 9.2\%) = 17.075\%$

$$\text{WACC} = 17.075\% \times \frac{18.4}{32.4} + 10\% (1 - 0.3) \frac{14}{32.4}$$

= 12.72% or approximately 13%.

(3) **Discount rate, political party B wins**

The risk-free rate including inflation, given expected inflation of 10% each year, is:

(1.04) (1.10) = 1.144 or 14.4%

The market return including inflation at 10% per annum is:

(1.10) (1.10) = 1.21 or 21%

Using CAPM, the cost of equity $Ke = 14.4\% + 1.25 (21\% - 14.4\%) = 22.65\%$

$$\text{WACC} = 22.65\% \times \frac{18.4}{32.4} + 15.5\% (1 - 0.3) \frac{14}{32.4} = 17.6\% \text{ or approximately } 18\%.$$

Note: This is only a rough estimate of the cost of capital, as the share price is likely to fall with higher inflation, leading to higher gearing and a change in risk for the providers of the debt finance.

Both K_e and K_d could alter because of these factors.

The use of the current share price in both WACC estimates is problematic. In an efficient market this price will reflect the present uncertainty about the forthcoming election. Once this uncertainty is resolved the share price is likely to change, leading to new market weighted gearing levels. Fortunately the investment decision is not highly sensitive to marginal changes in the discount rate.

Appendix 2

Base case NPV

For APV the base case NPV is required, which is estimated from the ungeared cost of equity.

Assuming corporate debt is risk free:

$$\beta_a = \left(\frac{V_e}{(V_e + V_d(1 - T))} \beta_e \right) = 1.25 \times \frac{18.4}{18.4 + 14(1 - 0.3)} = 0.82$$

Ke ungeared = 9.2% + (15.5% − 9.2%) 0.82 = 14.4% or approximately 14%.

A discount rate of 14% has therefore been used to calculate the base case NPV.

Cash flows, possible hotel purchase

	$ million				
	20X4	*20X5*	*20X6*	*20X7*	*20X8*
Revenue	9.0	10.0	11.0	12.0	13.0
Variable costs	6.0	6.0	7.0	7.0	8.0
Fixed costs	2.0	2.0	2.0	2.0	2.0
	8.0	8.0	9.0	9.0	10.0
Taxable profit	1.0	2.0	2.0	3.0	3.0
Taxation (30%)	0.3	0.6	0.6	0.9	0.9
	0.7	1.4	1.4	2.1	2.1
Realisable value					10.0
Working capital	(1.0)	–	–	(1.0)	–
Net cash flows	(0.3)	1.4	1.4	1.1	12.1
Discount factors at 14%	0.877	0.769	0.675	0.592	0.519
Present values	(0.3)	1.1	0.9	0.7	6.3

Base case NPV = ($9.0)m + $8.7m = $(0.3)m

Financing side effects for the five-year period:

Including issue costs, the gross sum of finance to be raised will be $\dfrac{9m}{0.98}$ = $9,184,000.

Issue costs are therefore $184,000.

Interest is at 10%, so this will give **annual tax savings** of:

$9.18m × 10% × 30% = $275,520 per year.

Discounted at 10%, this gives a present value of 3.791 × $275,520 = $1,044,000

Note: This assumes that an extra $9.184 million debt capacity is created by the hotel investment. If less debt capacity is created, the present value of the tax shield attributable to the investment will be reduced.

The 10% coupon is assumed to reflect correctly the risk of the convertible, and is used as the discount rate for the tax savings.

The estimated APV is the base case NPV plus the financing side effects.

	$m
Base case NPV	(0.30)
Issue costs	(0.18)
PV of tax saving	1.04
APV	0.56

(b)   Daron's current gearing, measured by the *book value* of medium and long term loans to the *book value* of equity is: 14/22 or 63.6%

No information is provided about short-term loans which would increase this gearing figure further. A $9 million convertible debenture issue would initially increase gearing to 23/22 = 104.5%.

Such a high level of gearing involves 'high' financial risk, especially for a company in a declining industry. The coupon rate of 10%, or $918,400 interest per year would have to be paid for five years or more. Convertible debentures normally carry lower coupon rates than straight debt. Daron can borrow long term from its bank at 10% per year, and the 10% coupon on the convertible appears to be expensive. However, this could be explained by the market seeking a relatively high return because of the size of the loan.

If conversion takes place the gearing level will fall, but this is will not occur for at least five years. At the $100 issue price the effective conversion price is $100/60 or 167 centos per share

This represents an average share price increase of 12.7% per year over five years, which is possible if market prices in general increase, but is by no means guaranteed.

The existence of the call and put options has potentially significant implications for Daron plc. The call option allows the company to limit the potential gains made by debenture holders. If the share price reaches 200 centos between 1 January 20X9 and 31 December 20Y1 the company can force the debenture holders to convert, giving maximum capital gains on conversion of 33 centos per share (relative to the $100 issue price). This is a small gain and may not be popular with investors. If the share price falls below 100 centos between the same dates, the debenture holders can ask the company to redeem the debentures at par, forcing the company to find $9 million for repayment of the debentures. If the market price of the shares has only moved by a maximum of eight centos over five years, the company might experience difficulty refinancing the $9 million, leading to severe problems in finding the cash for redemption.

(c)   The regulation of takeovers usually includes the following factors:

- At the most important time in the company's life – when it is subject to a takeover bid – its directors should act in the best interest of their shareholders, and should disregard their personal interests.

- All shareholders must be treated equally

- Shareholders must be given all the relevant information to make an informed judgement.

- The board of the target company must not take action without the approval of shareholders, which could result in the offer being defeated.

- All information supplied to shareholders must be prepared to the highest standards of care and accuracy.

- The assumptions on which profit forecasts are based and the accounting polices used should be examined and reported on by accountants.

- An independent valuer should support valuations of assets

4   SLEEPON HOTELS INC *Walk in the footsteps of a top tutor*

Walkthrough question – key answer tips

This is an excellent investment appraisal question, which covers all the examiner's favourite tricks in this syllabus area. It also contains a fully written part (b), which comprises little more than bookwork, so should yield plenty of easy marks.

A clear answer layout and systematic approach that gets the easier numerical marks first will help tremendously.

Also, it is important to note that the question contains 10 marks for discussion points in part (a), specifically for "...a discussion of what other information would be useful..." and for stating assumptions (stated in the requirement). As you go through the numbers, keep thinking about these written elements at the same time, and jot ideas down as you go along, to save you having to rush things at the end.

Calculations: The main tricks to look out for in the calculations are:

- You need to calculate a cost of capital that reflects the risks and finance of the project – the existing WACC of the company is no use. You need to de-gear and re-gear the beta of Thrillall.

- You need to make assumptions about the timing of asset purchases, as this will affect the timing of tax allowable depreciation.

- Only $250 million of the investment will attract tax allowable depreciation – this is assumed to be split equally between the two payments.

- Be careful identifying relevant cash flows, particularly with respect to interest, overheads and the 'savings' in advertising costs.

- Incorporating inflation – most (but not all!) figures are in current terms. The question is not clear regarding the working capital as strictly speaking the outflow at t=1 is not a cost. The examiner's answer inflates the working capital requirement and hence has annual increments.

- Ensure all working capital is released at the end of the project.

- Use a worst-case estimate for the realisable value of assets.

If you set up your pro forma answer neatly and slot in numbers as you calculate them, it doesn't really matter if you don't complete the full question in the time available, you will still score plenty of method marks for the work you have done.

Make sure you leave time for the easier part (b), and structure your answer to part (a) professionally to ensure you pick up the 4 professional skills marks.

(a)   **Report on the proposed theme park investment**

The decision to invest in a major project must be evaluated using both financial and non-financial information. From a financial perspective the estimated net present value of the investment will provide an indicator of whether or not the project will create wealth. Non-financial considerations will include the strategic fit of the investment with the company and its future plans.

Financial evaluation

Cash flow forecasts ($ million)

Year	0	1	2	3	4	5	6
Cash receipts:							
Adult admission			41.25	42.49	43.76	45.07	
Child admission			34.37	35.40	36.47	37.56	
Food (incremental cash flow)			13.75	14.16	14.59	15.02	
Gifts (incremental cash flow)			11.46	11.80	12.16	12.52	
Total receipts			100.83	103.85	106.98	110.17	
Expenses:							
Labour			42.44	43.70	45.02	46.37	
Maintenance			15.00	19.00	23.00	27.00	
Insurance			2.12	2.19	2.25	2.32	
Tax allowable depreciation			62.50	46.88	35.16	26.37	
Total expenses			122.06	111.77	105.43	102.06	
Taxable			(21.23)	(7.92)	1.55	8.11	
Taxation (30%)			6.37	2.38	(0.47)	(2.43)	
			(14.86)	(5.54)	1.08	5.68	
Add back tax allowable depreciation			62.50	46.88	35.16	26.37	
Initial cost	(200)	(200)					
Realisable value						250.00	
Working capital		(51.5)	(1.55)	(1.59)	(1.64)	(1.69)	57.97
Net cash flow	(200)	(251.50)	46.09	39.75	34.60	280.36	57.97
Discount factors (11%)		0.901	0.812	0.731	0.659	0.593	0.535
Present values	(200)	(226.60)	37.43	29.06	22.80	166.25	31.01

The estimated net present value is ($140.05 million).

Even if the higher realisable value estimate is used, the expected net present value is still significantly negative.

Notes:

(i) Receipts Year 2

Adult admission $(6,000) (360) (18) (1.03)^2$ = 41.25 million

Child admission $(9,000) (360) (10) (1.03)^2$ = 34.37 million

Food $(15,000) (360) (8) (0.3) (1.03)^2$ = 13.75 million

Gifts $(15,000) (360) (5) (0.4) (1.03)^2$ = 11.46 million

(ii) Tax allowable depreciation:

It is assumed that allowances are available with a one-year lag.

Year	Written down value	Tax allowable depreciation (25%)	Year available
0 + 1	250	62.50	2
2	187.50	46.88	3
3	140.62	35.16	4
4	105.47	26.37	5

No balancing allowances or charges have been estimated as the Year 5 realisable value of non-current assets has been estimated on an after-tax basis.

As the hotel business is successful, it is assumed that allowances may be used as soon as they are available against other taxable cash flows of Sleepon.

(iii) Interest is not a relevant cash flow. All financing costs are included in the discount rate.

(iv) The market research is a sunk cost.

(v) Apportioned overhead is not a relevant cash flow.

(vi) Although the company will save money by advertising in its existing hotels, this is not a change in cash flow as a result of the project and is not included in cash flows. (In effect the benefit from the savings is present as there is no cash outflow for advertising.)

(vii) Discount rate

The current weighted average cost of capital should not be used. The discount rate should reflect the risk of the investment being undertaken; theme parks are likely to have very different risks to hotels. The cost of capital will be estimated using the risk (beta) of Thrillall, as Thrillall operates in the theme park sector.

The market weighted capital gearing of Thrillall is:

Equity 400 × 3.86 = $1,544 m (78.3%)

Debt 460 × 0.93   = $428 m (21.7%)

As the gearing of Thrillall is much less than that of Sleepon, the beta used to estimate the relevant cost of equity will need to be adjusted to reflect this difference in gearing.

Assuming corporate debt is virtually risk free:

Ungearing Thrillall's equity beta:

$$\beta_a = \left(\frac{V_e}{(V_e + V_d(1-T))} \beta_e \right) = 1.45 \times \frac{1,544}{1,544 + 428(1-0.3)} = 1.214$$

Regearing to take into account the gearing of Sleepon:

$$\beta_e = \beta_a \times \frac{V_e + V_d(1-T)}{V_e} = 1.214 \times \frac{61.4 + 38.6(1-0.3)}{61.4} = 1.748$$

The cost of equity may be estimated using the capital asset pricing model.

$$E(r_i) = R_f + \beta(E(r_m) - R_f)$$

Ke = 3.5% + 1.748 (10% – 3.5%) = 14.86%

Kd is 7.5%, the cost of the new debt used for the project.

The weighted average cost of capital relevant to the new investment is estimated to be:

14.86% (0.614) + 7.5% (1 – 0.3) (0.386) = 11.15%

11% will be used as the discount rate for the investment.

Other relevant information

The financial projections used in the estimated net present value are the subject of considerable inaccuracy. It would be useful to know:

(i)   The accuracy of estimates of attendance levels and spending in the theme park.

(ii)   The accuracy of price and cost changes.

(iii)   Whether or not tax rates are subject to change.

(iv)   The accuracy of the estimate of realisable value in Year 4.

(v)   The accuracy of the discount rate estimate. The activities of Thrillall are not likely to be of exactly the same risk as the theme park project.

For a major investment it is unwise to rely on a single estimate of expected net present value. Sensitivity analysis or simulation analysis should be used in order to ascertain the impact on the expected NPV of changes in attendance and other key cash flows. It would be better to undertake simulation analysis, based upon different possible attendance levels, costs, risk, tax rates, etc, in order to estimate a range of possible net present values, rather than use a single point value.

A crucial question is what happens to cash flows beyond the company's four-year planning horizon. The Year 5 realisable values are asset values, not the value of the theme park as a going concern. The value as a going concern could be very different from the asset values, and have a major influence on the investment decision.

Will the theme park investment lead to future opportunities/investments (real options), for example in other theme parks or leisure activities? If so, the value of such options should be estimated, and should form part of the investment decision.

Strategic and other issues

The strategic importance of the venture to Sleepon must also be investigated, as this may heavily influence the final decision. Sleepon currently runs a successful hotel chain. It might be better to keep to its core competence in hotels rather than diversify into another sector. If new investments are sought, are there better opportunities within the hotel sector?

Any final decision must encompass all relevant non-financial factors of which little detail has been provided. Sleepon must be satisfied that it can recruit an appropriately skilled labour force for the theme park, and should thoroughly investigate the competition in the theme park sector, and the likely reaction of competitors if it enters this new market.

(b)   **Briefing notes on capital structure strategy**

From a corporate perspective there are two vital questions:

Can the value of a company, and hence shareholder wealth, be increased by varying the capital structure?

What effect will capital structure have on risk?

If value can be created by a sensible choice of capital structure, then companies should try to achieve an optimal, or almost optimal, capital mix, as long as this mix does not have detrimental effects on other aspects of the company's activities.

Evidence on the importance of capital structure to a company's value is not conclusive. There is general agreement that, as long as a company is in a tax-paying position, the use of debt can reduce the overall cost of capital due to the interest on debt being a tax-allowable expense in almost all countries. This was suggested by two Nobel prize-winning economists, Miller and Modigliani. However, high levels of debt also bring problems, and companies with very high gearing are susceptible to various forms of risk, sometimes known as the costs of financial distress. This might include the loss of cash flows because customers and suppliers are worried about the financial stability and viability of the company and move business elsewhere or impose less-favourable trading terms, or even extra costs that would exist (payments to receivers, etc) if the company was to go out of business.

A common perception about capital structure is that as capital gearing is increased, the weighted average cost of capital falls at first. However, beyond a certain level of gearing the risk to both providers of debt and equity finance increases, and the return demanded by them to compensate for this risk also increases, leading to an increase in the weighted average cost of capital. There is a trade-off between the value created by additional tax relief on debt and the costs of financial distress. Overall, there is therefore an optimal capital structure, which will vary between companies and will depend upon factors such as the nature of the company's activities, realisable value of assets, business risk, etc. According to the theory, companies with many tangible assets should have relatively high gearing, companies with high growth, or that are heavily dependent on R & D or advertising would have relatively low gearing.

The impact of personal taxation on the capital structure decision is less clear, although investors are undoubtedly interested in after-tax returns. If personal tax treatment differs on different types of capital, then investors may have a preference for the most tax-efficient type of capital.

Not all companies behave as if there is an optimal capital structure, and on average, in countries such as the UK and USA, the average capital gearing is lower than might be expected if companies were trying to achieve an optimal structure. It must, however, be remembered that moving from one capital structure to another cannot take place overnight. The cost of debt, via interest rates, and the cost of equity, can change quite quickly. It is no surprise that companies do not appear to be at an optimal level.

Where no optimal level appears to be sought by a company, there are several suggested strategies with respect to capital structure. Among the most popular is the pecking order theory, which is based upon information asymmetry, the fact that managers have better information about their company than the company's shareholders. This leads to a company preferring internal finance to external finance, and only using external finance in order to undertake wealth-creating (positive NPV) investments. Companies use the safest sources of finance first.

(1)   Internal funds (including selling marketable securities)

(2)   Debt

(3)   Equity

The amount of external finance used depends upon the amount of investment compared with the amount of internal funds, and the resultant capital structure reflects the relative balance of investment and available internal funds.

Another view is that capital structure is strongly influenced by managerial behaviour. There are potential conflicts of objectives between owners and managers (agency problems). Capital structure will be influenced by senior managers' personal objectives, attitudes to risk, compensation schemes and availability of alternative employment. A risk-averse manager seeking security may use relatively little debt. Free cash flow (cash flow available after replacement investment) is sometimes perceived to be used by managers for unwise acquisitions/investments that satisfy their personal objectives, rather than returning it to shareholders. Many such managerial/agency aspects may influence capital structure, and this does not give clear guidance as to capital structure strategy.

No matter what the conclusion about the impact of capital structure on cash flows, it is likely that some financing packages may be more highly regarded by investors than others. For example, securities designed to meet the needs of certain types of investor (zero coupon bonds, etc), securities that are more liquid, securities with lower transactions costs, and securities that reduce conflict between parties concerned with the company, especially shareholders, managers and the providers of debt.

Conclusion

It is likely that the choice of capital structure can directly affect cash flows and shareholder wealth, but too high a level of gearing will increase risk. The impact on cash flows and corporate value of the capital structure decision is far less than the impact of capital investment decisions.

5 PARTSEA PLC *Walk in the footsteps of a top tutor*

> **Key answer tips**
>
> Note that the requirement comprises three parts: relevant calculations, a discussion of other information, and stating assumptions. Make sure that you leave time to address all three parts.

The proposals will be evaluated using the NPV of relevant cash flows to the UK.

Forecast exchange rates using purchasing power parity:	$H/£	Bt/£	$H/Bt
Spot	15.80	4.20	3.76
Year 1	17.04	4.32	3.94
Year 2	17.87	4.41	4.05
Year 3	18.73	4.49	4.17
Year 4	19.64	4.58	4.29
Year 5	20.60	4.67	4.41

Expected cash flows from foreign direct investment

$H million

Year	0	1	2	3	4	5
Sales		150	405	437	472	510
Variable costs		76	174	188	203	219
Fixed costs		23	40	40	40	40
Component (2.5m × 5Bt × X rate)			51	52	54	55
Depreciation			17	17	17	17
Total expenses		99	282	297	314	331
Taxable		51	123	140	158	179
Taxation (20%)		(10)	(25)	(28)	(32)	(36)
		41	98	112	126	143
Add back depreciation			17	17	17	17
Initial cost	(120)					
Land and buildings		(70)				
New machinery		(68)				
Working capital	(35)	(4)	(3)	(3)	(4)	(4)
Realisable value						150
Remittable cash flow	(155)	(101)	112	126	139	306

£ million

Year	0	1	2	3	4	5
Remittable from H	(9.81)	(5.93)	6.27	6.73	7.08	14.85
Extra tax (10%)		(0.30)	(0.69)	(0.75)	(0.80)	(0.87)
Remittable from B [4]			0.50	0.49	0.48	0.47
Incremental cash flow from machinery		1.00				
Tax on profit (30%)		(0.30)				
Lost exports (after tax) [2]		(0.50)	(0.51)	(0.53)	(0.55)	(0.56)
Net cash flow	(9.81)	(6.03)	5.57	5.94	6.21	13.89
DF (14%) [3]		0.877	0.769	0.675	0.592	0.519
Present values	(9.81)	(5.29)	4.28	4.01	3.68	7.21

The expected net present value is £4,080,000

Notes:

[1] The extra after tax cash flow earned by the subsidiary in Bottoniland is an incremental cash flow to the group as a result of the investment. The data is shown in £ after tax for the relevant year.

[2] Lost exports are assumed to increase with UK inflation. It might be argued that such losses would continue beyond five years and have a more detrimental effect on cash flows.

[3] Using CAPM, the discount rate is 5% + (12% − 5%) × 1.3 = 14.1%. 14% will be used.

[4] 25% of component cost, translated into $H and then stated after tax

(e.g. for year 2: 2.5 million × 5 Bt × 4.05 × 25% × (1-0.30)/17.87 = 0.50)

Working capital requirements in Hotternia are assumed to increase at the rate of inflation in Hotternia.

Licensing

		£ million			
Year	1	2	3	4	5
Receipts from fees $H		40.00	43.20	46.66	50.39
Receipts from fees £		2.24	2.31	2.38	2.45
Incremental cash flow from maintenance		0.25	0.25	0.25	0.25
Incremental cash flow from machinery	1.00				
Staff costs		(0.21)	(0.22)	(0.22)	(0.23)
Taxable	1.00	2.28	2.34	2.41	2.47
Tax at 30%	(0.30)	(0.68)	(0.70)	(0.72)	(0.74)
	0.70	1.60	1.64	1.69	1.73
Lost exports (after tax)[5]		(0.51)	(0.53)	(0.55)	(0.56)
Net cash flows	0.70	1.09	1.11	1.14	1.17
Discount factors (14%)	0.877	0.769	0.675	0.592	0.519
Present values	0.61	0.84	0.75	0.67	0.61

The expected net present value from licensing is £3,480,000.

[5] With licensing, no exports are lost in year 1.

The financial analysis suggests that foreign direct investment is the better choice, as it results in a higher expected NPV.

Other information that might influence the decision includes:

(i)   Are there strategic reasons for preferring a specific method of market entry?

(ii) What happens after five years? Would the licence be renewed? Do real options exist for each alternative and if so what is their expected net present value?

(iii) How accurate are the cash flow projections? Simulation analysis or sensitivity analysis would be useful.

(iv) How reliable is KBD? Could quality be maintained and is there the risk of technology transfer?

(v)   What are the risks of the investments? What are the political and other non-financial risks associated with FDI and licensing? FDI normally involves much more risk than licensing.

(vi) Does the discount rate of 14% correctly reflect the risk? Licensing should probably be discounted at a lower rate if it is less risky.

(vii) Is the FDI realisable value estimated using an asset basis or going concern basis? A going concern valuation could be much higher than an asset based valuation.

6   BLIPTON INTERNATIONAL   *Walk in the footsteps of a top tutor*

> **Key answer tips**
>
> This is a good example of an advanced investment appraisal question. A neat and systematic layout for the NPV part of the question is critical to ensure you pick up all the marks you deserve.
>
> Note that there are plenty of easy marks to be gained even if you struggle to understand all the numbers: part (c) is independent of the numbers, and there are 2 marks available for presenting a professional report.

Management Report: Blipton International Entertainment Group

400 bed Olympic Hotel, London

Completion: 31 December 20X9

(a)   **Projection of $value cash flows for both the project investment and the project return.**

In projecting the cash flow for this project we have created a forecast of the capital requirement, the six year operating cash flow and the residual value of the property net of repairs and renewals at the end of the project. On the basis of the specified occupancy rates and a target nightly rental of £60 we have projected the revenues for the hotel and the expected costs. These are projected at current prices to give a real cash flow before conversion to nominal at the UK rate of inflation. Tax is calculated both in terms of the offset available against the construction costs but also at 30% of the operating surplus from the project.

Finally, using purchasing power parity, future spot rates are estimated. The rate specified is indirect with respect to the dollar and declines as sterling strengthens.

We have separated the calculation of the present value of the investment phase from that of the return phase as follows:

> **Tutorial note**
>
> *This answer assumes that the benefit of the tax allowable depreciation will be recovered irrespective of the success of the operating phase of the project. They are therefore treated as a credit to the investment phase. Students who treated them as part of the recovery phase would not have been penalised.*

Investment phase (values in £)	01 Jan 20X9	31 Dec 20X9	31 Dec 20Y0	31 Dec 20Y1	31 Dec 20Y2	31 Dec 20Y3	31 Dec 20Y4
Nominal project cash flow		−6,200,000					
TAD (tax saving)		930,000	310,000	310,000	310,000		
Nominal project cash flow after tax (investment phase)		−5,270,000	310,000	310,000	310,000		
Rate of exchange	0.6700	0.6552	0.6409	0.6268	0.6130	0.5996	0.5864
$ value of investment phase		−8,043,346	483,695	494,576	505,710	0	0
Return phase (value in £)							
Occupancy rate	0	0.4	0.5	0.9	0.6	0.6	
Terminal value of property							8,915,309
Rooms let (400 × occ. Rate × 365)		58,400	73,000	131,400	87,600	87,600	
Revenue (rooms let × £60)		3,504,000	4,380,000	7,884,000	5,256,000	5,256,000	
Variable operating costs (rooms let × £30)		−1,752,000	−2,190,000	−3,942,000	−2,628,000	−2,628,000	
Fixed costs		−1,700,000	−1,700,000	−1,700,000	−1,700,000	−1,700,000	
Project operating cash flow (real)		52,000	490,000	2,242,000	928,000	928,000	
Project operating cash flow (nominal)		54,633	527,676	2,474,749	1,049,947	1,076,195	
Tax on operating cash flows (at 30%)		−16,390	−158,303	−742,425	−314,984	−322,859	
Nominal project cash flow after tax (return phase)		38,243	369,373	1,732,324	734,963	9,668,646	
Rate of exchange	0.6700	0.6552	0.6409	0.6268	0.6130	0.5996	0.5864
$ value of return phase		59,670	589,300	2,825,977	1,225,755	16,488,141	

Tutorial note

The terminal value of the property is the figure which most students struggle with. The value of £8,915,309 has been calculated as the difference between:

– the forecast open market value, being £6.2m × (1.08 × 1.025)^5 = £10,306,941

– the charge for repairs and renewals, being £1.2m × 1.025^6 = £1,391,632

(b)   **Project evaluation**

Net present value

Given that the Dubai rate of inflation is 4.8% per annum and the company's real cost of capital is 4.2% per annum the nominal cost of capital is estimated using the Fisher formula:

$i_{nom} = (1 + inf)(1 + i_{real}) - 1$

$i_{nom} = (1.048)(1.042) - 1 = 9.2016\%$

Discounting the project cash flows (investment plus return) at this nominal cost of capital gives a project net present value as follows:

	01 Jan 20X9	31 Dec 20X9	31 Dec 20Y0	31 Dec 20Y1	31 Dec 20Y2	31 Dec 20Y3	31 Dec 20Y4
Nominal project cash flow (investment plus return)		−8,043,346	543,365	1,083,876	3,331,687	1,225,755	16,488,141
Nominal cost of capital (Dubai)	0.092016						
Discounted cash flow	0	−7,365,593	455,653	832,324	2,342,870	789,330	9,722,942
Net present value	6,777,525						

A net present value of $6,777,525 strongly suggests that this project is viable and will add to shareholder value.

Modified internal rate of return

The modified internal rate of return can be estimated by calculating the internal rate of return of the sum of the return cash flows compounded at the cost of capital to give a year six terminal value. The discount rate which equates the present value of this terminal value of return cash flows with the present value of the investment cash flows is the modified internal rate of return.

$$MIRR = \left(\frac{PV_R}{PV_1}\right)^{\frac{1}{n}}(1 + r_e) - 1$$

Where PV_R is the present value of the return phase of the project, PV_I is the present value of the investment phase and r_e is the firm's cost of capital.

	01 Jan 20X9	31 Dec 20X9	31 Dec 20Y0	31 Dec 20Y1	31 Dec 20Y2	31 Dec 20Y3	31 Dec 20Y4
Modified internal rate of return							
Present value of return phase	13,002,093		50,038	452,532	1,987,251	789,330	9,722,942
Present value of investment phase	−6,224,568	−7,365,593	405,514	379,792	355,619		
Present value per $ investment	2.0888						
Sixth root of present value of PV_R/PV_1	1.1306						
MIRR	23.47%						

The calculation of the MIRR is as follows:

$$MIRR = \left(\frac{13,002,093}{6,224,568}\right)^{\frac{1}{6}}(1.092016) - 1 = 23.47\%$$

(c)   **Recommendation and discussion of method**

I have examined the project plan for the proposed project and referring to the appendices (see above) report that this project is expected to deliver an increase in shareholder value of $6.78 million, at the firm's current cost of finance. I have estimated the increase in shareholder value using the net present value (NPV) method. Net present value focuses on the current equivalent monetary value associated with capital expenditure leading to future cash flows arising from investment. The conversion to present value is achieved by discounting the future cash flows at the firm's cost of capital – a rate designed to reflect the scarcity of capital finance, inflation and risk.

Although the net present value technique is subject to a number of assumptions about the perfection and efficiency of the capital market it does generate an absolute measure of increase in shareholder value and as such avoids scale and other effects associated with percentage performance measures. Given the magnitude of the net present value of the project it is safe to assume that it is value-adding assuming that the underlying cash projections can be relied upon.

However, in certain circumstances it can be useful to have a 'headroom' percentage which reliably measures the rate of return on an investment such as this. In this case the modified internal rate of return of 23.47% is 14.26% greater than the firm's cost of capital. MIRR measures the economic yield of the investment (i.e. the discount rate which delivers a zero net present value) under the assumption that any cash surpluses are reinvested at the firm's current cost of capital. The standard IRR assumes that reinvestment will occur at the IRR which may not, in practice, be achievable.

Although MIRR, like IRR, cannot replace net present value as the principle evaluation technique it does give a measure of the maximum cost of finance that the firm could sustain and allow the project to remain worthwhile. For this reason it gives a useful insight into the margin of error, or room for negotiation, when considering the financing of particular investment projects.

	ACCA marking scheme	
		Marks
(a)	Identification of construction cost and estimation of terminal value	1
	Estimation of the number of room/nights let	2
	Projection of real cash flow on the return phase	2
	Conversion to nominal using the UK inflation rate	2
	Estimation of investment phase including the savings attaching to tax allowable depreciation	2
	Tax charge and capital gain	1
	Conversion to dollars	2
		———
	Total	12
(b)	Calculation of the nominal $ rate of discount using the Fisher formula	2
	Calculation of the net present value	2
	Calculation of the MIRR	4
		———
		8
(c)	NPV as absolute as opposed to relative measure of increase in shareholder value	1
	Problems with underlying assumptions of the NPV model (efficiency arguments)	2
	Weaknesses of return measures	2
	Advantage of MIRR to IRR (reinvestment rate and single root arguments)	2
	MIRR gives headroom in cost of finance negotiations	1
		———
		8
(d)	Professional marks	2
		———
Total		**30**
		———

7   SEMER

> **Key answer tips**
>
> Part (a) is tricky as it is easy to accept the mistakes when presented with them. The best approach is to plan your own calculations first and then assess the ones given.
>
> In part (b) there is no need to calculate the change in the cost of equity to reflect the higher gearing. This part is tricky enough already, particularly when calculating the new level of dividends, the revised free cash flow and hence be able to estimate market value.
>
> Part (c) should be a fairly routine discussion of the impact of higher gearing but make sure you also discuss the accuracy of the estimates produced in part (b)

(a)   Revised estimates of the current cost of capital and value

The cost of equity has been correctly estimated using the capital asset pricing model to be 11.8%.

The cost of debt should be the current cost of debt, not the historic cost of debt of 8% when the debenture was issued. It should also be estimated on an after tax basis as interest on debt is a tax allowable expense.

The current cost of debt may be estimated from the redemption yield of the existing debenture. The debenture matures in five year's time. The redemption yield may be estimated by solving the following equation for kd.

$$112 = \frac{8(1-0.3)}{1+kd} + \frac{8(1-0.3)}{(1+kd)^2} \dots\dots + \frac{8(1-0.3)}{(1+kd)^5} + \frac{100}{(1+kd)^5}$$

By trial and error:

At 5% interest:

PV annuity 5.6 × 4.329	=	24.24
PV 100 × 0.784	=	78.40
		102.64

At 3% interest:

PV annuity 5.6 × 4.580	=	25.65
PV 100 × 0.863	=	86.30
		111.95

The after tax cost of debt is approximately 3%

The weighted average cost of capital (WACC) should be estimated using the market values of equity and debt, not book values.

The market value of equity is 160 million × 410 cents = $656m

The market value of debt is $119m + ($50m × 1.12) = $175m

$$WACC = 11.8\% \times \frac{656}{831} + 3\% \times \frac{175}{831} = 9.95\%$$

As free cash flow is expected to grow by 3% per year, the present value of the company's free cash flows may be estimated by using the equation for a growth perpetuity:

$$PV = \frac{FCF(1+g)}{WACC-g} \text{ or } \frac{60(1.03)}{0.0995-0.03} = \$889 \text{ million}$$

(b) Estimated new cost of capital:

If equity is repurchased such that the gearing becomes 50% equity, 50% debt, the new estimated weighted average cost of capital is:

$$11.8\% \times \frac{415.5}{831} + 3\% \times \frac{415.5}{831} = 7.40\%$$

Impact on the value of the company:

The free cash flow to the company will not change when equity is replaced by debt.

Expected new value

$$\frac{60(1.03)}{0.074-0.03} = \$1,404.5 \text{ million}$$

This is a very large potential increase in value.

(c) **Report on the proposed adjustment of gearing through the repurchase of ordinary shares**

The effect of capital structure on the value of a company is not fully understood.

Increasing the proportion of debt in the capital structure may reduce the overall cost of capital due to the interest on debt being a tax allowable expense. Even if a company is in a non-tax paying position, mixing additional low cost debt with relatively expensive equity might reduce the weighted average cost of capital. In such circumstances the proposed strategy to increase gearing would have some validity. However, increasing gearing can also bring problems. Risk to investors, and therefore the required returns on equity and debt, will increase as gearing increases. Very high levels of gearing might lead to direct and indirect bankruptcy costs, with a detrimental effect on cash flow and corporate value. Any benefits from increasing the proportion of debt in the capital structure will be to some extent offset as a result of increased risk with high gearing.

The revised estimates of the effect on the cost of capital and value of Semer are not likely to be accurate. Reasons for this include:

(i) The company will not be able to repurchase the necessary shares at their current market value. Approximately $240 million value of equity would need to be repurchased, or more than one third of the existing market value of equity. As repurchases take place it is likely that the share price will significantly increase.

(ii)   The cost of debt is unlikely to remain constant. As more debt is issued lenders will demand a higher interest rate to compensate for the extra risk resulting from higher gearing levels. The cost of equity will also increase with higher gearing. These effects will increase the weighted average cost of capital to a higher level than that estimated.

(iii)   The precise market values of debt and equity after the repurchase are unknown, and again will reflect the market attitude to the new risk of the higher gearing.

The value of the company is likely to be much lower than that estimated, as the weighted average cost of capital is likely to be underestimated.

8   TRAMONT CO (PILOT 2012)

Key answer tips

This was the first 50 mark question published by the examiner when the format of the exam changed. It is important to note that the examiner's 50 mark questions are always split into several different parts, so don't allow yourself to get bogged down in any one part. The key to success is to attempt the easier parts of the question first and to leave sufficient time to attempt all parts of the question.

REPORT TO THE BOARD OF DIRECTORS, TRAMONT CO

EVALUATION OF WHETHER THE PRODUCTION OF X-IT SHOULD MOVE TO GAMALA

This report evaluates the possibility of moving the production of the X-IT to Gamala from the USA. Following the initial evaluation the report discusses the key assumptions made, the possible impact of a change in the government in Gamala after the elections due to take place shortly and other business factors that should be considered before a final decision is made.

Initially a base case net present value calculation is conducted to assess the impact of the production in Gamala. This is then adjusted to show the impact of cash flows in the USA as a result of the move, the immediate impact of ceasing production and the impact of the subsidy and the tax shield benefits from the loan borrowing.

Based on the calculations presented in the appendix, the move will result in a positive adjusted present value of just over $2.4 million. On this basis, the initial recommendation is that the production of X-IT should cease in the USA and the production moved to Gamala instead.

Assumptions

It is assumed that the borrowing rate of 5% is used to calculate the benefits from the tax shield. It could be argued that the risk free rate of 3% could be used as the discount rate instead of 5% to calculate the present value of benefits from the tax shields and the subsidies.

In adjusted present value calculations, the tax shield benefit is normally related to the debt capacity of the investment, not the actual amount of debt finance used. Since this is not given, it is assumed that the increase in debt capacity is equal to the debt finance used.

It has been assumed that many of the input variables, such as for example the tax and tax allowable depreciation rates, the various costs and prices, units produced and sold, the rate of inflation and the prediction of future exchange rates based on the purchasing power parity, are accurate and will change as stated over the four-year period of the project. In reality any of these estimates could be subject to change to a greater or lesser degree and it would appropriate for Tramont Co to conduct uncertainty assessments like sensitivity analysis to assess the impact of the changes to the initial predictions.

Government Change

From the facts of the case it would seem that a change of government could have a significant impact on whether or not the project is beneficial to Tramont Co. The threat to raise taxes may not be too significant as the tax rates would need to increase to more than 30% before Tramont Co would lose money. However, the threat by the opposition party to review 'commercial benefits' may be more significant.

Just over 40% of the present value comes from the tax shield and subsidy benefits. If these were reneged then Tramont Co would lose a significant of the value attached to the project. Also the new government may not allow remittances every year, as is assumed in part (i). However this may not be significant since the largest present value amount comes from the final year of operation.

Other Business Factors

Tramont Co should consider the possibility of becoming established in Gamala, and this may lead to follow-on projects. The real options linked to this should be included in the analysis.

Tramont Co's overall corporate strategy should be considered. Does the project fit within this strategy? Even if the decision is made to close the operation in the USA, there may be other alternatives and these need to be assessed.

The amount of experience Tramont Co has in international ventures needs to be considered. For example, will it be able to match its systems to the Gamalan culture? It will need to develop strategies to deal with cultural differences. This may include additional costs such as training which may not have been taken into account.

Tramont Co needs to consider if the project can be delayed at all. From part (i), it can be seen that a large proportion of the opportunity cost relates to lost contribution in years 1 and 2. A delay in the commencement of the project may increase the overall value of the project.

Tramont Co needs to consider the impact on its reputation due to possible redundancies. Since the production of X-IT is probably going to be stopped in any case, Tramont Co needs to communicate its strategy to the employees and possibly other stakeholders clearly so as to retain its reputation. This may make the need to consider alternatives even more important.

Conclusion

Following from a detailed sensitivity analysis, analysis of a possible change in the government and an evaluation of the financial benefits accruing from the other business factors discussed above, the BoD can make a decision of whether to move the production to Gamala or not. This initial evaluation suggests that moving the production of the X-IT to Gamala would be beneficial.

Appendix

Gamalan Project Operating Cash Flows

(All amounts in GR/$000's)

Year	Now	1	2	3	4
Sales revenue (w2)		48,888	94,849	214,442	289,716
Local variable costs (w3)		(16,200)	(32,373)	(75,385)	(104,897)
Imported component (w4)		(4,889)	(9,769)	(22,750)	(31,658)
Fixed costs		(30,000)	(32,700)	(35,643)	(38,851)
Profits before tax		(2,201)	20,007	80,664	114,310
Taxation (w5)		0	0	(7,694)	(18,862)
Investment	(230,000)				450,000
Working capital	(40,000)	(3,600)	(3,924)	(4,277)	51,801
Cash flows (GR)	(270,000)	(5,801)	16,083	68,693	597,249
Exchange rate (w1)	55.00	58.20	61.59	65.18	68.98
Cash flows ($)	(4,909)	(100)	261	1,054	8,658
Discount factor for 9.6% (w6)		0.912	0.832	0.760	0.693
(Full credit given if 10% is used as the discount rate)					
Present values ($)	(4,909)	(91)	217	801	6,000

Net present value (NPV) of the cash flows from the project is approx. $2,018,000.

Adjusted present value (APV)	$000
NPV of cash flows	2,018
Additional USA tax	
Opportunity cost (revenues foregone from current operations)	
Additional contribution from component exported to project (net of tax) (w7)	(1,237)
Closure revenues and costs ($2,300,000 – $1,700,000)	600
Tax shield	
Benefit of subsidy (w8)	1,033
Total APV	2,414

Workings

(1) **Exchange rates**

Year	1	2	3	4
GR/$1	55 × 1.09/1.03 = 58.20	58.20 × 1.09/ 1.03 = 61.59	61.59 × 1.09/ 1.03 = 65.18	65.18 × 1.09/ 1.03 = 68.98

(2) **Sales revenue** (GR 000's)

Year	1	2	3	4
Price × units × exchange rate	70 × 12,000 × 58.20 = 48,888	70 × 22,000 × 61.59 = 94,849	70 × 47,000 × 65.18 = 214,442	70 × 60,000 × 68.98 = 289,716

(3) **Local variable costs** (GR 000's)

Year	1	2	3	4
Cost × units × inflation after yr 1	1,350 × 12,000 = 16,200	1,350 × 22,000 × 1.09 = 32,373	1,350 × 47,000 × 1.09^2 = 75,385	1,350 × 60,000 × 1.09^3 = 104,897

(4) **Imported component** (GR 000's)

Year	1	2	3	4
Price × units × inflation after year 1 × exchange rate	7 × 12,000 × 58.20 = 4,889	7 × 22,000 × 1.03 × 61.59 = 9,769	7 × 47,000 × 1.03^2 × 65.18 = 22,750	70 × 60,000 × 1.03^3 × 68.98 = 31,658

(5) **Taxation**

Year	1	2	3	4
Profits before tax	(2,201)	20,007	80,664	114,310
Tax allowable depreciation	(20,000)	(20,000)	(20,000)	(20,000)
Profit/(loss) after depreciation	(22,201)	7	60,664	94,310
Taxable profits	0	0	38,470	94,310
Taxation (20%)	0	0	(7,694)	(18,862)

(6) **Gamala project all-equity financed discount**

Tramont Co equity beta = 1.17

MVe = $2.40 × 25m shares = $60m

MVd = $40m × $1,428/$1,000 = $57.12m

Tramont Co asset beta (assuming debt is rate risk free)

1.17 × 60m/(60m + 57.12m × 0.7) = 0.70

Project asset beta = 0.70 + 0.40 = 1.10

Project all-equity financed discount rate = 3% + 6% × 1.1 = 9.6%

(7) **Additional tax, additional contribution and opportunity cost** ($000's)

Year	1	2	3	4
Additional tax				
Taxable profits × 1/exchange rate × 10%	0	0	38,470 × 1/65·18 × 10% = (59)	94,310 × 1/68·98 × 10% = (137)
Opportunity cost				
Units × contribution × (1 – tax)	40 × $20 × 0.7 = (560)	32 × $20 × 0.7 = (448)	25.6 × $20 × 0.7 = (358)	20.48 × $20 × 0.7 = (287)
Additional Contribution				
Units × contribution × inflation × (1 – tax)	12 × $4 × 0.7 = 34	22 × $4 × 1.03 × 0.7 = 63	47 × $4 × 1.032 × 0.7= 140	60 × $4 × 1.033 × 0.7 = 184
Total cash flows	(526)	(385)	(277)	(240)
PV of cash flows				
Discount at 7%	(492)	(336)	(226)	(183)

NPV is approx. $(1,237,000)

(8) **Tax shield and subsidy benefits** ($/GR 000's)

Year	1	2	3	4
Interest × loan × tax rate	6% × 270m × 20% = 3,240	3,240	3,240	3,240
Annual subsidy benefit (GR)				
Interest gain × loan × (1 – tax rate)	7% × 270m × 0.8 = 15,120	15,120	15,120	15,120
Total tax shield + subsidy benefits (GR)	18,360	18,360	18,360	18,360
Exchange rate (GR/$1)	58.20	61.59	65.18	68.98
Cash flows ($)	**315**	**298**	**282**	**266**
PV of cash flows				
Discount at 5%	**300**	**270**	**244**	**219**

NPV of tax shield and subsidy benefit is approx. $1,033,000

(b)   A triple bottom line (TBL) report provides a quantitative summary of performance in terms of economic or financial impact, impact on the environment and impact on social performance. TBL provides the measurement tool to assess a corporation's or project's performance against its objectives.

The principle of TBL reporting is that true performance should be measured in terms of a balance between economic (profits), environmental (planet) and social (people) factors; with no one factor growing at the expense of the others. The contention is that a corporation that accommodates the pressures of all the three factors in its strategic investment decisions will enhance shareholder value, as long as the benefits that accrue from producing such a report exceeds the costs of producing it.

For example, in the case of the X-IT, reporting on the impact of moving the production to Gamala, in terms of the impact on the employees and environment in the USA and in Gamala will highlight Tramont Co as a good corporate citizen, and thereby increase its reputation and enable it to attract and retain high performing, high calibre employees. It can also judge the impact on the other business factors mentioned in the report above.

(Note: credit will be given for alternative relevant answers)

(c)   Portfolio theory suggests that shareholders holding well-diversified portfolios will have diversified away unsystematic or company specific risk, and will only face risk systematic risk, i.e. risk that cannot be diversified away. Therefore a company cannot reduce risk further by undertaking diversification within the same system or market. However, further risk reduction may occur if the diversification is undertaken by the company, on behalf of the shareholders, into a system or market where they themselves do not invest. Some studies indicate that even shareholders holding well-diversified portfolios may benefit from risk diversification where companies invest in emerging markets.

In the case of Tramont Co and the X-IT, it is not clear whether diversification benefits will result in the investment in Gamala. The benefits are dependent on the size of the investment, and on the nature of the business operations undertaken in Gamala by Tramont Co. And whether these operations mirror an investment in a significantly different system or market. If the investment is large, the operations are similar to undertaking a Gamalan company. Tramont Co's shareholders who do not hold similar companies' shares in their portfolios may then gain risk diversification benefits from the Gamalan investment.

9   CHMURA CO (DEC 13)

Key answer tips

Investment appraisal and option pricing are very commonly tested syllabus areas. Note that in this question there were lots of easy discussion marks (e.g. assumptions, role of WTO) as well as the many complex calculations. In order to guarantee success, you must attempt all parts of the question, both calculations and discussion.

(a)   The World Trade Organisation (WTO) was set up to continue to implement the General Agreement on Tariffs and Trace (GATT), and its main aims are to reduce the barriers to international trade. It does this by seeking to prevent protectionist measures such as tariffs, quotas and other import restrictions. It also acts as a forum for negotiation and offering settlement processes to resolve disputes between countries.

The WTO encourages free trade by applying the most favoured nation principle between its members, where reduction in tariffs offered to one country by another should be offered to all members.

Whereas the WTO has had notable success, some protectionist measures between groups of countries are nevertheless allowed and some protectionist measures, especially non-tariff based ones, have been harder to identify and control.

Mehgam could benefit from reducing protectionist measures because its actions would make other nations reduce their protectionist measures against it. Normally countries retaliate against each other when they impose protectionist measures. A reduction in these may allow Mehgam to benefit from increased trade and economic growth. Such a policy may also allow Mehgam to specialise and gain competitive advantage in certain products and serv ces, and compete more effectively globally. Its actions may also gain political capital and more influence worldwide.

Possible drawbacks of reducing protectionist policies mainly revolve around the need to protect certain industries. It may be that these industries are developing and in time would be competitive on a global scale. However, inaction to protect them now would damage their development irreparably. Protection could also be given to old, declining industries, which, if not protected, would fail too quickly due to international competition, and would create large scale unemployment making such inaction politically unacceptable. Certain protectionist policies are designed to prevent 'dumping' of goods at a very cheap price, which hurt local producers.

(**Note:** Credit will be given for alternative relevant discussion)

(b)   **Report to the Board of Directors (BoD), Chmura Co**

This report recommends whether or not Chmura Co should invest in a food packaging project in Mehgam, following Mehgam reducing its protectionist measures. It initially considers the value of the project without taking into account the offer made by Bulud Co to purchase the project after two years. Following this, Bulud Co's offer is considered. The report concludes by recommending a course of action for the BoD to consider further.

Estimated value of the Mehgam project and initial recommendation

The initial net present value of the project is negative at approximately $(451,000) [see Appendix 1]. This would suggest that Chmura Co should not undertake the project.

Bulud Co's offer is considered to be a real option for Mehgam Co. Since it is an offer to sell the project as an abandonment option, a put option value is calculated based on the finance director's assessment of the standard deviation and using the Black-Scholes option pricing (BSOP) model. The value of the put option is added to the initial net present value of the project without the option, to give the value of the project. Although Chmura Co will not actually obtain any immediate cash flow from Bulud Co's offer, the real option computation indicates that the project is worth pursuing because the volatility may result in increases in future cash flows.

After taking account of Bulud Co's offer and the finance director's assessment, the net present value of the project is positive at approximately $2,993,000 [see Appendix 2]. This would suggest that Chmura Co should undertake the project.

Assumptions

It is assumed that all the figures relating to variables such as revenues, costs, taxation, initial investments and their recovery, inflation figures and cost of capital are accurate. There is considerable uncertainty surrounding the accuracy of these, and in addition to the assessments of value conducted in appendices one and two, sensitivity analysis and scenario analysis are probably needed to assess the impact of these uncertainties.

It is assumed that future exchange rates will reflect the differential in inflation rates between the two countries. It is, however, unlikely that exchange rates will move fully in line with the inflation rate differentials.

It is assumed that the value of the land and buildings at the end of the project is a relevant cost, as it is equivalent to an opportunity benefit, even if the land and buildings are retained by Chmura Co.

It is assumed that Chmura Co will be given and will utilise the full benefit of the bi-lateral tax treaty and therefore will not pay any additional tax in the country where it is based.

It is assumed that the short-dated $ treasury bills are equivalent to the risk-free rate of return required for the BSOP model.

And it is assumed that the finance director's assessment of the 35% standard deviation of cash flows is accurate.

It is assumed that Bulud Co will fulfil its offer to buy the project in two years' time and there is no uncertainty surrounding this. Chmura Co may want to consider making the offer more binding through a legal contract.

The BSOP model makes several assumptions such as perfect markets, constant interest rates and lognormal distribution of asset prices. It also assumes that volatility can be assessed and stays constant throughout the life of the project, and that the underlying asset can be traded. Neither of these assumptions would necessarily apply to real options. Therefore the BoD needs to treat the value obtained as indicative rather than definitive.

Additional business risks

Before taking the final decision on whether or not to proceed with the project, Chmura Co needs to take into consideration additional risks, including business risks, and where possible mitigate these as much as possible. The main business risks are as follows:

Investing in Mehgam may result in political risks. For example, the current government may be unstable and if there is a change of government, the new government may impose restrictions, such as limiting the amount of remittances which can be made to the parent company. Chmura Co needs to assess the likelihood of such restrictions being imposed in the future and consider alternative ways of limiting the negative impact of such restrictions.

Chmura Co will want to gain assurance that the countries to which it will sell the packaged food batches remain economically stable and that the physical infrastructure such as railways, roads and shipping channels are maintained in good repair. Chmura Co will want to ensure that it will be able to export the special packaging material into Mehgam. Finally, it will need to assess the likelihood of substantial protectionist measures being lifted and not re-imposed in the future.

As much as possible, Chmura Co will want to ensure that fiscal risks such as imposition of new taxes and limits on expenses allowable for taxation purposes do not change. Currently, the taxes paid in Mehgam are higher than in Chmura Co's host country, and even though the bi-lateral tax treaty exists between the countries, Chmura Co will be keen to ensure that the tax rate does not change disadvantageously.

Chmura Co will also want to protect itself, as much as possible, against adverse changes in regulations. It will want to form the best business structure, such as a subsidiary company, joint venture or branch, to undertake the project. Also, it will want to familiarise itself on regulations such as employee health and safety law, employment law and any legal restrictions around land ownership.

Risks related to the differences in cultures between the host country, Mehgam, and the countries where the batches will be exported to would be a major concern to Chmura Co. For example, the product mix in the batches which are suitable for the home market may not be suitable for Mehgam or where the batches are exported. It may contain foods which would not be saleable in different countries and therefore standard batches may not be acceptable to the customers. Chmura Co will also need to consider the cultural differences and needs of employees and suppliers.

The risk of the loss of reputation through operational errors would need to be assessed and mitigated. For example, in setting up sound internal controls, segregation of duties is necessary. However, personal relationships between employees in Mehgam may mean that what would be acceptable in another country may not be satisfactory in Mehgam. Other areas where Chmura Co will need to focus on are the quality control procedures to ensure that the quality of the food batches is similar to the quality in the host country.

Recommendation

With Bulud Co's offer, it is recommended that the BoD proceed with the project, as long as the BoD is satisfied that the offer is reliable, the sensitivity analysis/scenario analysis indicates that any negative impact of uncertainty is acceptable and the business risks have been considered and mitigated as much as possible.

If Bulud Co's offer is not considered, then the project gives a marginal negative net present value, although the results of the sensitivity analysis need to be considered. It is recommended that, if only these results are taken into consideration, the BoD should not proceed with the project. However, this decision is marginal and there may be other valid reasons for progressing with the project such as possibilities of follow-on projects in Mehgam.

Report compiled by:

Date:

APPENDICES

Appendix 1: Estimated value of the Mehgam project excluding the Bulud Co offer

(Cash flows in MP, millions)

Year	1	2	3	4	5
Sales revenue (w2)	1,209.6	1,905.1	4,000.8	3,640.7	2,205.4
Production and selling costs (w3)	(511.5)	(844.0)	(1,856.7)	(1,770.1)	(1,123.3)
Special packaging costs (w4)	(160.1)	(267.0)	(593.7)	(572.0)	(366.9)
Training and development costs	(409.2)	(168.8)	0	0	0
Tax allowable depreciation	(125)	(125)	(125)	(125)	(125)
Balancing allowance					(125)
Taxable profits/(loss)	3.8	500.3	1,425.4	1,173.6	465.2
Taxation (25%)	(1.0)	(125.1)	(356.4)	(293.4)	(116.3)
Add back depreciation	125	125	125	125	250
Cash flows (MP, millions)	127.8	500.2	1,194.0	1,005.2	598.9

(All amounts in $, 000s)

Year	1	2	3	4	5
Exchange rate (w1)	76.24	80.72	85.47	90.50	95.82
Cash flows ($ 000s)	1,676.3	6,196.7	13,969.8	11,107.2	6,250.3
Discount factor for 12%	0.893	0.797	0.712	0.636	0.567
Present values ($ 000s)	1,496.9	4,938.8	9,946.5	7,064.2	3,543.9

Present value of cash flows approx. = $26,990,000

PV of value of land, buildings and machinery in year 5 = (80% × MP1,250m + MP500m)/95.82 × 0.567 approx. = $8,876,000

PV of working capital = MP200m/95.82 × 0.567 approx. = $1,183,000

Cost of initial investment in $ = (MP2,500 million + MP200 million)/72 = $37,500,000

NPV of project = $26,990,000 + $8,876,000 + $1,183,000 − $37,500,000 = $(451,000)

Workings

(1) **Exchange rates**

Year	1	2	3	4	5
MP/$1	72 × 1.08/1.02 = 76.24	76.24 × 1.08/1.02 = 80.72	80.72 × 1.08/1.02 = 85.47	85.47 × 1.08/1.02 = 90.50	90.50 × 1.08/1.02 = 95.82

(2) **Sales revenue (MP million)**

Year	1	2	3	4	5
	10,000 × 115,200 × 1.05 = 1,209.6	15,000 × 115,200 × 1.05^2 = 1,905.1	30,000 × 115,200 × 1.05^3 = 4,000.8	26,000 × 115,200 × 1.05^4 = 3,640.7	15,000 × 115,200 × 1.05^5 = 2,205.4

(3) **Production and selling (MP million)**

Year	1	2	3	4	5
	10,000 × 46,500 × 1.1 = 511.5	15,000 × 46,500 × 1.1^2 = 844.0	30,000 × 46,500 × 1.1^3 = 1,856.7	26,000 × 46,500 × 1.1^4 = 1,770.1	15,000 × 46,500 × 1.1^5 = 1,123.3

(4) **Special packaging (MP million)**

Year	1	2	3	4	5
	10,000 × 200 × 76.24 × 1.05 = 160.1	15,000 × 200 × 80.72 × 1.05^2 = 267.0	30,000 × 200 × 85.47 × 1.05^3 = 593.7	26,000 × 200 × 90.50 × 1.05^4 = 572.0	15,000 × 200 × 95.82 × 1.05^5 = 366.9

Appendix 2: Estimated value of the Mehgam project including the Bulud Co offer

Present value of underlying asset (Pa) = $30,613,600 (approximately)

(This is the sum of the present values of the cash flows foregone in years 3, 4 and 5)

Price offered by Bulud Co (Pe) = $28,000,000

Risk free rate of interest (r) = 4% (assume government treasury bills are valid approximation of the risk free rate of return) Volatility of underlying asset (s) = 35%

Time to expiry of option (t) = 2 years

d_1 = [ln(30,613.6/28,000) + (0.04 + 0.5 × 0.35^2) × 2]/[0.35 × $2^{1/2}$] = 0.589

d_2 = 0.589 – 0.35 × $2^{1/2}$ = 0.094

$N(d_1)$ = 0.5 + 0.2220 = 0.7220

$N(d_2)$ = 0.5 + 0.0375 = 0.5375

Call value = $30,613,600 × 0.7220 – $28,000,000 × 0.5375 × $e^{-0.04 \times 2}$ = approx. $8,210,000

Put value = $8,210,000 – $30,613,600 + $28,000,000 × $e^{-0.04}$ × 2 = approx. $3,444,000

Net present value of the project with put option = $3,444,000 – $451,000 = approx. $2,993,000

(**Note:** Credit will be given for relevant discussion and recommendation)

			Marks
(a)		Role of the World Trade Organisation	4–5
		Benefits of reducing protectionist measures	2–3
		Drawbacks of reducing protectionist measures	2–3
		Maximum	9
(b)	**(i)**	Future exchange rates predicted on inflation rate differential	1
		Sales revenue	1
		Production and selling costs	1
		Special packaging costs	2
		Training and development costs	1
		Correct treatment of tax and tax allowable depreciation	2
		Years 1 to 5 cash flows in $ and present values of cash flows	2
		Ignoring initial investigation cost and additional taxation in Chmura Co host country	1
		Correct treatment of land, buildings, machinery and working capital	2
		Net present value of the project	1
		Maximum	14
	(ii)	Inputting correct values for the variables	2
		Calculation of d1 and d2	2
		Establishing N(d1) and N(d2)	2
		Call value	1
		Put value	1
		Value of the project	1
			9
	(iii)	Estimated value and initial recommendation	2–3
		Up to 2 marks per assumption discussed	5–6
		Up to 2 marks per additional business risk discussed	5–6
		Overarching recommendation(s)	1–2
		Maximum	14
		Professional marks	
		Report format	1
		Structure and presentation of the report	3
		Maximum	4
Total			50

ACCA marking scheme

ACQUISITIONS AND MERGERS

10 STANZIAL INC

Key answer tips

This is a very good question on business valuation, one of the most important syllabus topics.

Notice that in part (a) you are expected to calculate the value using four different valuation methods, but also to comment on the methods and state your assumptions. Unless you attempt all these different elements, you'll struggle to score a pass mark here.

(a)   The valuation of private companies involves considerable subjectivity. Many alternative solutions to the one presented below are possible and equally valid.

As Stanzial is considering the purchase of Besserlot, this will involve gaining ownership through the purchase of Stanzial's shares, hence an equity valuation is required.

Before undertaking any valuations it is advisable to recalculate the earnings for 20X6 without the exceptional item. It is assumed that this is a one-off expense, which was not fully tax allowable.

The revised statement of profit or loss is:

	20X6 $000
Sales revenue	22,480
Operating profit before exceptional items	1,302
Interest paid (net)	280
Profit before taxation	1,022
Taxation (30%)	307
Profit after tax	715
Dividend	200
Change in equity	515

Asset-based valuation

An asset valuation might be regarded as the absolute minimum value of the company. Asset-based valuations are most useful when the company is being liquidated and the assets disposed of. In an acquisition, where the company is a going concern, asset-based values do not fully value future cash flows, or items such as the value of human capital, market position, etc.

Asset values may be estimated using book values, which are of little use, replacement cost values, or disposal values. The information provided does not permit a full disposal value, although some adjustments to book value are possible. In this case an asset valuation might be:

	$000
Net assets	6,286
Patent	10,000
Inventory adjustment	(1,020)
	15,266 or $15,266,000

This value is not likely to be accurate as it assumes the economic value of non-current assets is the same as the book value, which is very unlikely. The same argument may also be related to current assets and liabilities other than inventory.

P/E ratios

P/E ratios of competitors are sometimes used in order to value unlisted companies. This is problematic as the characteristics of all companies differ, and a P/E ratio valid for one company might not be relevant to another.

There is also a question of whether or not the P/E ratio should be adjusted downwards for an unlisted company, and how different expected growth rates should be allowed for.

Expected earnings growth for Besserlot is much higher than the average for the industry, especially during this next three years. In view of this it might be reasonable to apply a P/E ratio of at least the industry average when attempting to value Besserlot.

The after-tax earnings of Besserlot, based upon the revised statement of profit or loss, are:

$$1,022 - 307 = 715$$

Using a P/E ratio of 30:1, this gives an estimated value of $715 \times 30 = \$21,450,000$.

This is a very subjective estimate, and it might be wise to use a range of P/E ratio values, for example from 25:1 to 35:1, which would result in a range of values from $17,875,000 to $25,025,000.

It could also be argued that the value should be based upon the anticipated next earnings rather than the past earnings several months ago.

This is estimated to be:

	20X7
	$000
Sales revenue	28,100
Operating profit before exceptional items	2,248
Interest paid (net)	350
Profit before taxation	1,898
Taxation	569
	1,329

1,329 × 30 gives a much higher estimate of $39,870,000

PE-based valuation might also be criticised as it is based upon profits rather than cash flows.

Dividend-based valuation

Dividend-based valuation assumes that the value of the company may be estimated from the present value of future dividends paid. In this case the expected dividend growth rates are different during the next three years and the subsequent period.

The estimated dividend valuation is:

Year	1	2	3	After Year 3	
Expected dividend				$\dfrac{391\,(1.1)}{0.14 - 0.10}$	Using $P_o = \dfrac{D_o(1+g)}{(r_e - g)}$
	250	313	391		
Discount factors (14%)	0.877	0.769	0.675	0.675	
Present values	219	241	264	7,258	

The estimated value is $7,982,000.

This is a rather low estimated value and might be the result of Besserlot having a relatively low dividend payout ratio, and no value being available for a final liquidating dividend.

The present value of expected future cash flows

The present value of future cash flows will be estimated using the expected free cash flow to equity. In theory, this is probably the best valuation method, but in reality it is impossible for an acquiring company to make accurate estimates of these cash flows. The data below relies upon many assumptions about future growth rates and relationships between variables.

	20X7	20X8	20X9	After 20X9
Sales revenue	28,100	35,125	43,906	
Operating profit	2,248	2,810	3,512	
Interest paid (net)	350	438	547	
Profit before taxation	1,898	2,372	2,965	
Taxation	569	712	890	
	1,329	1,660	2,075	
Add back non-cash expenses	1,025	1,281	1,602	
Less increase in working capital	(172)	(214)	(268)	
Less capital investment	(1,250)	(1,562)	(1,953)	
Free cash flow to equity	932	1,165	1,456	40,040
Discount factors (14%)	0.877	0.769	0.675	0.675
Present values	817	896	983	27,027

The estimated present value of free cash flows to equity is $29,723,000

Note:

Free cash flow after 20X9 is estimated by $\dfrac{1.456\,(1.1)}{0.14 - 0.10} = 40,040$

This valuation also ignores any real options that arise as a result of the acquisition.

Recommended valuation

It is impossible to produce an accurate valuation. The valuation using the dividend growth model is out of line with all others and will be ignored.

On the basis of this data, the minimum value should be the adjusted asset value, a little over $15,000,000, and the maximum approximately $30,000,000.

All of the above valuations may be criticised as they are based upon the value of Besserlot as a separate entity, not the valuation as part of Stanzial Inc. There might be synergies, such as economies of scale, savings in duplicated facilities, processes, etc, as a result of the purchase, which would increase the above estimates.

(b)   The success of the purchase would depend upon enticing the existing shareholders to sell their shares. The most important shareholders are the senior managers, the venture capital company, and the single shareholder holding 25% of the shares. If any two of these types of shareholder can be persuaded to sell, Stanzial can gain control of Besserlot.

If the shareholders of a private company do not want to sell, there is little Stanzial can do. However, most shareholders will sell if the price or other conditions are attractive enough.

The venture capital company will probably have invested in Besserlot with a view to making a large capital gain, possibly if Besserlot was itself to seek a listing on a stock market. Stanzial will have to offer a sum large enough to satisfy the venture capital company relative to possible alternatives such as the listing.

Similarly, the managers and major shareholder would need to be satisfied. In the case of the managers it might also be necessary to provide some guarantee that they would continue to have managerial positions with attractive contracts within Stanzial, and the large single shareholder might insist on continued representation on the Board of Directors.

The nature of payment might also be important. The managers and single investor could be liable to immediate capital gains tax if payment was to be made in cash. They might have a preference for shares in Stanzial. The venture capital company might prefer cash rather than maintain an equity stake in a different company.

(c)   Factors that might influence the medium-term success of the acquisition include:

(i)   The thoroughness of the planning of the acquisition. This would include establishing key reporting relationships and control of key factors.

(ii)   Corporate objectives and plans should be harmonised. Effective integration will require mutual respect for the different cultures and systems of the two companies.

(iii)   Human resource issues are important, such as how any redundancies are dealt with, and the role of the managers of the acquired company in the new organisation.

(iv)   Effective post-acquisition audit. Monitoring of whether or not the post-acquisition performance is as expected, and implementation of any necessary action to remedy problems and under-performance.

(v)   The reaction of competitors; in particular, can they produce alternative wireless links that would adversely affect Stanzial's market share?

(vi)   Maintenance of the pension rights of existing employees post-acquisition.

11   BURCOLENE   *Walk in the footsteps of a top tutor*

Walkthrough question – key answer tips

During your 15 minutes of reading time in the exam, you should aim to identify which part of the syllabus is being tested by each question.

This question is a 50-mark compulsory question which focuses on business valuation and a foreign investment.

Part (a) is 16 marks of calculations and Part (b) is fully written for 16 marks. In questions like this, you should be looking at Part (b) to establish to what extent it relies on the calculations in Part (a). In many questions, there are easy marks available in Part (b) even if you have struggled to make much headway with the numbers in Part (a). This is one such question – most of the marks in Part (b) are totally unrelated to the specific calculations in Part (a), so you must leave plenty of time to attempt Part (b).

Note also that part (c) is totally unrelated to either part (a) or part (b). This means that you can start this question with whichever is your preferred part.

Part (a) calculations:

First, you are asked to derive a weighted average cost of capital (WACC) for each business. Don't panic when you see lots of financial information quoted in the question. On the formula sheet you are given a formula for WACC which contains 4 inputs – the cost of equity and the market value of equity, and the cost of debt and the market value of debt. Write the formula down first and then pick out the relevant figures from the mass of information provided. Even if you don't manage to pick out all the figures correctly, you will score method marks for your approach.

Next, you are asked to estimate the value of each of the businesses. Typically, you are not told which business valuation method to use, but you must pick up on the clues scattered around in the question. For example, in this question you are not given any P/E ratio information so don't start trying to present a P/E based valuation. However, you are asked to compute a WACC, and then to comment on the Free Cash Flow method in Part (b), so you should try to use the WACC to discount Free Cash Flows here.

You are asked to take account of the impact of the share option scheme and pension fund deficit, which may be something you've not encountered before. Don't panic when you come across requirements like this. You'll see from the model answer that these two issues only come in AFTER the standard calculations have been presented.

If you're not sure how to deal with unusual points like these, the best advice is to ignore them and make sure you get the basic marks first. In this question's marking key, it shows that you could have scored 11 of the 16 marks before starting to worry about these two unusual issues.

> Part (b) written elements:
>
> Leave plenty of time to attempt Part (b). There are plenty of easy marks here.
>
> Present your answer neatly and professionally to ensure you pick up the 4 professional marks on offer.
>
> Use subheadings to show the examiner that you have addressed all three parts of the requirement specifically.
>
> Part (c) foreign subsidiary:
>
> The calculations in part (i) are tricky. However, even if you are not particularly mathematically gifted, a trial and error approach can be used successfully. Part (ii) is much easier though, so leave enough time to attempt it fully.

(a) The first step in the valuation is to calculate each company's weighted average cost of capital. The cost of capital is calculated post tax and using the relevant market values to calculate the market gearing ratio.

	Burcolene	PetroFrancais
Cost of equity (using the CAPM, 3% risk free and 4% equity risk premium)	$= 0.03 + 1.85 \times 0.04$ $= 0.104$	$= 0.03 + 0.95 \times 0.04$ $= 0.068$
Market gearing	$= 3.3/(3.3 + 9.9) = 0.25$	$5.8/(5.8 + 6.7) = 0.464$
Cost of debt	$= 0.03 + 0.016 = 0.046$	$= 0.03 + 0.03 = 0.06$
WACC	$= (0.75 \times .104) + (0.25 \times 0.046 \times 0.7) = 0.0861$	$= (0.536 \times .068) + (0.464 \times .06 \times 0.75) = 0.0573$

Examiner's note: There may be rounding differences.

The core valuation formula is:

$$V_0 = \frac{FCF_1}{WACC - g}$$

As free cash flow is NOPAT − net reinvestment then:

$$V_0 = \frac{FCF_1}{WACC - g} = \frac{(NOPAT - net\ reinvestment)_1}{WACC - g}$$

The figures quoted are for NOPAT − reinvestment for the current year. For the two companies the value before either pension or share option scheme adjustments is therefore (in $):

$$V_B = \frac{450 \times (1.05)}{0.08606 - 0.05} = \$13.107\ bn$$

and

$$V_P = \frac{205 \times (1.04)}{0.0573 - 0.04} = \$12.303\ bn$$

However, both company values will need to be reduced by the relevant charge for the outstanding options and the pension deficit. Using the fair value approach the value of each option outstanding is given by:

Option value = intrinsic value + time value

Option value = (actual price − exercise price) + time value

Option value = 29.12 − 22.00 + 7.31 = $14.43

(the actual price is given by the total value of equity $9.9 billion/340 million = $29.12 per share)

The number of options likely to be exercised:

options = 25.4m × (1 –0.05)^3 × 0.8 = 17.42 million

Which gives a value of options outstanding = $251.4m

And an estimated market valuation of Burcolene of:

V_B = $13.107 bn – $251.35m = $12.855 bn

The value of PetroFrancais is much more straightforward being:

V_P = $12.303 bn – $430m = $11.873 bn

(b) **Burcolene**

Report to management

Subject: Valuation and Financial Implications of an Acquisition of PetroFrancais

This is potentially a type three acquisition where both the firm's exposure to business risk and financial risk change. As a consequence the value of the combined entity will depend upon the post acquisition values of the component cash streams: (i) the cash flow from the existing business; (ii) the cash flow from the acquired business and (iii) any synergistic cash flows less the cost of acquisition. However, estimating the value of these cash flows relies upon an estimate of the post acquisition required rate of return – which cannot be estimated until we know the value of the component cash flows. This problem requires an iterative solution and which can be solved using a spreadsheet package.

Validity of the Free Cash Flow to Equity Model

Our estimates of the value using NOPAT as a proxy for free cash flow produces values that are reasonably close to the current market valuation of both companies. The models value Burcolene at $12.855 billion and PetroFrancais at $11.873 billion compared with current market valuations of $13.1 billion and $12.5 billion respectively. The estimation error is 1.9% and 5.3% respectively. Although minor the differences can be explained by any of the following:

- The model used may mis-specify the market valuation process. In either case NOPAT may not be a sufficiently close approximation to each firm's free cash flow.

- The underpinning models in the cost of capital calculations may not be valid. The capital asset pricing model, for examples, does not capture fully all the risk elements that are priced in competitive markets.

- The estimates of growth may be overoptimistic (both valuations are highly sensitive to variation in the implied level of growth).

- The markets may have reacted positively to rumours of an acquisition.

- The capital markets may be inefficient.

However, on the basis of this preliminary analysis, the low levels of modelling error suggest that the NOPAT based model should form the basis for valuing a combined business.

Deriving a bid price:

In preparation of an offer, a due diligence process should, as part of its brief, consider the likely growth of each cash stream within the context of the combined business and the variability associated with the future growth rates of each cash stream. This information could then be used to estimate the firm's future cash flows (i) to (iii) above using a cost of capital derived from the current required rates of return and market values. An iterative procedure can then be employed to bring the derived values into agreement with those used to estimate the firm's cost of capital. This valuation less the cost of acquisition and the firm's current debt gives the post acquisition equity value. The maximum price that should be paid for PetroFrancais is that which leaves the equity value of Burcolene unchanged. This estimation process whilst procedurally complex does reinforce a key point with type III acquisitions that the sum of the equity valuation of both parties is not a good indication of the value of the combined business.

Providing the management of Burcolene can come to a reliable valuation of the combined business then, providing they remain within the bid-price parameters, the acquisition should increase shareholder value. Good valuation methods should capture the benefits and the consequential costs of combined operation. It is important that management recognises this point and do not double count strategic opportunities when negotiating a bid price. In this case, improving equity value for the Burcolene investors depends upon a number of factors. A simulation of the most important parameters in the valuation model: forward growth, the cost of equity, default premiums and the cost of debt should allow Burcolene to estimate the likely equity value at risk given any chosen bid price. A simulation would also provide an estimate of the probability of a loss of equity value for Burcolene's investors at the chosen bid price.

Implications for gearing and cost of capital:

Financing an acquisition of this magnitude through debt will raise the book gearing of the business although its impact upon the market gearing of the firm is less easy to predict. Much depends on the magnitude of any surplus shareholder value generated by the combination and how it is distributed. An acquisition such as this will increase market gearing if the benefits accrue to the target shareholders. The reverse may occur if the bulk of the acquisition value accrues to the Burcolene investors. Similarly the impact upon the firm's overall cost of capital, the impact of the tax shield and the exposure to default risk again all depend upon the agreed bid price and the distribution of acquisition value between the two groups of investors.

(c)   (i)   The presumption in this question is that if dividend payments out of the country are blocked for three years, the peso income will be invested locally to earn interest, and at the end of the three years, the pesos plus interest will be converted into $ at the spot rate and remitted to Europe.

If there are no blocked funds, the present value in $ expected from dividend remittances is:

Year	1	2	3
Peso remittance (million pesos)	180	180	180
Exchange rate	22/$1	24.2/$1	26.62/$1
$ million	8.182	7.438	6.762
Discount factors (at 20%)	0.833	694	0.579
Present values ($ million)	6.816	5.162	3.915

Total present value is $15.893 million.

If the investment is no longer to be financially viable, the NPV of the investment would have to fall by at least $2 million (its expected NPV), or the present value of cash flows from remittances would have to fall to less than $13.893 million.

If dividend remittances are blocked, and peso income is invested at x%, the cash flows will be as follows.

Year	Income	Interest rate	Income plus interest, end of Year 3
	million pesos		million pesos
1	180	×	$180 (1 + x)^2$
2	180	×	$180 (1 + x)$
3	180	×	180

The interest rate that will yield at least $13.893 million may be estimated by solving for x, where × is the interest rate in decimal format:

$$\frac{0.579(180(1+x)^2 + 180(1+x) + 180)}{26.62} = \$13.893 \text{ million}$$

This may be solved using mathematical formulae, but can be estimated by trial and error.

If x = 0.15

$$\frac{0.579(180(1.15)^2 + 180(1.15) + 180)}{26.62} = \$13.595 \text{ million}$$

15% is too low

If x = 0.18

$$\frac{0.579(180(1.18)^2 + 180(1.18) + 180)}{26.62} = \$13.986 \text{ million}$$

At an 18% interest rate the investment will just remain financially viable.

(ii) Blocked remittances might be avoided by means of:

(i) Increasing transfer prices paid by the foreign subsidiary to the parent company.

(ii) Lending the equivalent of the dividend to the parent company.

(iii) Making payments to the parent company in the form of royalties, payment for patents, or management fees.

(iv) Charging the subsidiary additional head office overhead.

(v) Parallel loans, whereby the subsidiary of Burcolene in the South American country lends cash to the subsidiary of another company requiring funds in the South American country. In return Burcolene would receive the loan of an equivalent amount of cash in Europe from the other subsidiary's parent company.

The government of the South American country might try to prevent many of these measures being used.

12   ANCHORAGE RETAIL COMPANY

Key answer tips

EVA® is commonly used to assess the performance of a business. An increasing level of EVA® is taken as a positive sign.

When considering which other methods to use for performance appraisal in part (b), make sure that you use some ratios which enable you to broaden out your discussion e.g. perhaps use one ratio which focuses on profitability issues and another which focuses on liquidity.

To Polar Finance

Report on Anchorage Retail Limited

Following your terms of reference we report as follows:

(a)   There are many risks in acquisitions which have both a high likelihood of occurring and potentially a significant impact upon your business if they do occur. The principal risks to which Polar Finance might be exposed in an acquisition of this type are as follows:

   (1)   Disclosure risk: in making an acquisition of this type it is important to ensure that the information upon which the acquisition is made is reliable and fairly represents the potential earning power, financial position and cash generation of the business. As part of a due diligence exercise it would be necessary to ensure that the financial accounts have not been unduly manipulated to give a more attractive view of the business than the underlying reality would support. To this end it is important to ensure that the statement of profit or loss can be supported by the reported cash flow. In addition to this all other company documents should, in due course, be scrutinised as part of a full due diligence exercise.

   (2)   Valuation risk: a substantial acquisition has the potential to alter the risk of the acquirer either because of an alteration in the fund's exposure to financial risk or in its exposure to market risk. Ultimately the value of Polar Finance to its equity investors depends upon the potential returns it offers to them and the risk of those returns. A substantial acquisition of this type can impact upon the perceived risk attaching to the equity which investors have already subscribed and hence the value they place upon the fund. As a consequence the post acquisition value of Polar Finance may not be a simple sum of the fund's current value and the existing equity valuation of Anchorage Retail.

   (3)   Regulatory risk: an acquisition of the size proposed may raise concern with the government or with other regulatory agencies if it is seen to be against the public interest. As Polar Finance is not another retail company then the acquisition is unlikely to be seen as against the public interest on competition grounds. However, concern has been raised in a number of jurisdictions about the lack of accountability of private equity funds and given the reputation of Anchorage Retail this acquisition may result in adverse regulatory scrutiny and pressure.

Each of these risks would need to be explicitly considered as part of your due diligence investigation to ensure that they are either mitigated or avoided. Credit may be given for alternative, relevant risks.

(b) In examining the reported return we have considered the following measures

Tutorial note

Only two measures are required as well as EVA. Note that other sensible measures which are not shown in this model answer would also have been acceptable, for example balance sheet gearing, interest cover, and/or other profitability ratios.

Return on capital employed which can be measured as either net operating profit before tax or net operating profit after tax (NOPAT) as a percentage of capital employed.

Economic Value Added which is the difference in a firm's reported return on capital employed and its weighted average cost of capital. EVA measures that rate of value creation within a business reflecting the degree of economic 'super normal profit' or, in other terms, the residual income of the business. EVA return is also reported as the difference between return on capital employed and the weighted average cost of capital for the business.

Return on fixed capital employed which in comparison with return on capital employed indicates the return advantage associated with the company's management of its working capital.

Return on equity which measures the rate of return earned on the total equity funds employed.

Each of the above return measures is presented using the year end figures (although mid-year averages for capital employed are more appropriate in each case). Credit may be given for alternative, relevant suggestions and calculations.

Return on Capital Employed

Return on capital employed focuses attention upon the return generated by all classes of asset. Its measurement in post tax form as NOPAT/(Equity + Debt) gives a measure of the return excluding the benefit of the tax shield on debt. Alternatives, not given here, are (i) to measure the gross return using net operating profit before tax or (ii) the distributable profit plus interest payable. ROCE, using our preferred method and year end capital figures is:

ROCE (20X9) = $1,250 \times (1 - 30\%)/(2,030 + 1,900) = 22.26\%$

ROCE (20X8) = $1,030 \times (1 - 30\%)/(1,555 + 1,865) = 21.08\%$

ROCE has shown a modest improvement but a further investigation of the accounting information would be required to establish whether the improvement is a genuine improvement in the underlying performance of the business. A thorough accounting investigation as part of a due diligence exercise should answer the question as to whether the ROCE measure can be trusted.

Marginal ROCE

Marginal ratios can be calculated for one or all of the return ratios. They measure the return generated by the latest capital reinvested within the business. Marginal return on capital employed measures the return generated on capital introduced or reinvested over the last period of account. It is measured as:

$$\Delta ROCE \frac{\Delta NOPAT}{\Delta CE} = \frac{(1,250 - 1,030) \times 0.7}{3,930 - 3,420} = 30.20\%$$

Movements in this ratio year-on-year give a clearer indication of the improvement or deterioration in the company's performance. In the case of Anchorage, the performance on new capital is considerably better than that on the accumulated capital employed in the business.

Economic Value Added and Economic Value Added Return

EVA is derived from the difference between accounting return on capital employed and the weighted average cost of capital:

EVA% = ROCE – WACC

Where ROCE is measured as net operating profit after tax (NOPAT) over total capital employed.

In absolute terms EVA can be expressed as a financial surplus by multiplying throughout by the denominator of the ROCE ratio:

EVA = NOPAT – WACC × Capital Employed

Proponents of the EVA measure offer a variety of procedures for 'cleaning' the NOPAT and capital employed figures to increase their economic significance and to reduce distortion through accounting manipulation. Insufficient detail is available at this stage to make any such adjustments. The calculation of the weighted average cost of capital is shown in Annex 1 to this report.

On the stated assumptions and on the basis that WACC has not changed EVA, and the percentage EVA return, for the two years of account is as follows:

EVA (20X9) = 1,250 × (1 – 30%) – 6.12% × (2,030 + 1,900) = $634 million (16.14%)

EVA (20X8) = 1,030 × (1 – 30%) – 6.12% × (1,555 + 1,865) = $512 million (14.96%)

This suggests that there has been a significant improvement in EVA for the business over the two years both in absolute terms and in terms of EVA return. As with ROCE, reliance should only be placed on these figures once a full accounting investigation has been conducted.

Return on equity

This ratio measures in both its absolute and marginal form the return exclusively for the equity investor within the business:

ROE (20X9) = 860/2,030 = 42.36%

ROE (20X8) = 650/1,555 = 41.80%

As with ROCE this return measure has shown a modest improvement over the year.

Return on Fixed Capital Employed

This measure reflects the return on the capital employed in investment in non-current assets. When compared with ROCE it indicates the return leverage through the firm's working capital policy.

ROFCE (20X9) = 1,250 × (1 – 30%)/4,980 = 17.57%

ROFCE (20X8) = 1,030 × (1 – 30%)/4,540 = 15.88%

If the current asset ratio of a company is one then ROFCE and ROCE should be identical. If the CAR is greater than one, capital on the form of owner's equity and long-term liabilities is being diverted into financing working as opposed to fixed capital employed in the business and vice versa. The comparison of ROFCE with ROCE for Anchorage suggests that, on the basis of the accumulated capital of the business, the company is leveraging additional return through its working capital management policy.

(c) The impact upon the equity cost of capital of this acquisition is an approximation at this stage, pending a more intensive valuation exercise focusing on the impact it would have upon the equity valuation of the fund overall. Unravelling the gearing effect upon the betas of both Anchorage and Polar finance we estimate that the asset beta of each is as follows (assuming that debt beta is zero):

Where there is no tax benefit attaching to debt:

$$\beta_a = \beta_e \left[\frac{V_e}{V_e + V_d} \right]$$

Where there is a tax benefit attaching to debt

$$\beta_a = \beta_e \left[\frac{V_e}{V_e + V_d(1-T)} \right]$$

Note that Polar Finance does not pay tax on its income and thus there is no benefit attributable to the tax shield on debt. In this case the market value of debt will not be tax adjusted. However, with Anchorage this is not the case as the current equity beta will reflect a tax shield on its debt.

Before the acquisition

Asset beta:

Polar asset beta = 0.285 (given)

Gearing:

Polar debt before acquisition is 85%, therefore equity is 15% and $1.125bn. Therefore, debt is $1.125/0.15 × 0.85 = $6.375bn.

Equity beta:

Equity beta of Polar before acquisition = 0.285 × (6.375 + 1.125)/1.125 = 1.9

Application of CAPM:

Required rate of return of equity investors before acquisition =

Cost of equity = 5% + 1.9 × 2.224% (see Annex 1) = 9.23%

After the acquisition:

Asset beta:

Anchorage asset beta can be calculated as follows:

Anchorage equity beta = 0.75

Anchorage debt proportion = 24%

Therefore equity proportion = 76%

1 – tax rate = 1 – 0.3 = 0.7

Anchorage asset beta = 0.75 × 76/(76 + 24 × 0.7) = 0.614

So, asset beta of combined entity (Polar + Anchorage) = 0.8 × 0.285 + 0.2 × 0.614 = 0.351

(this is based on the information that if Anchorage's proportion of cash flows is 20%, then Polar's cash flows without Anchorage would be 80%).

Gearing:

Level of debt after acquisition is $6.375bn + $2.5bn = $8.875bn.

Equity beta:

Equity beta of the combined entity = 0.351 × (8.875 + 1.125)/1.125 = 3.12

Application of CAPM:

Required rate of return of equity investors after acquisition =

Cost of equity = 5% + 3.12 × 2.224% = 11.94%

Hence Polar's shareholders will require an increase of 2.71% return (=11.94% – 9.23%) as a result of the acquisition.

(d)   The view that Anchorage Retail has been undervalued by the market implies that the market is inefficient in pricing the equity of firms of this size. The evidence from tests of the efficient market hypothesis suggests that this is unlikely and given the number of investors involved in an active market for a company of this type we should not assume that, on average, they have mispriced this business. It maybe that investors have irrational as well as rational expectations about this company but we would expect that in the aggregate the irrational component would be unsystematic with respect to the underlying value of the business and thus diversified away in the pricing process.

Assuming that the market has priced in zero growth for Anchorage, capitalising the current dividend payments of $270 million at an equity cost of 6.668% suggests an equity market capitalisation of $4.049bn. The current share price of $2.6 per share, with 1.6 bn shares in issue implies an equity value of $4.16 bn which suggests that the market expects little growth in the business over the longer term. This probably reflects both perceptions of weakness in Anchorage Retail and in its ability to compete in a weakening market. Given what the price reveals about expectations, it is likely that a bid of $3.20 would be attractive to Anchorage shareholders. Whether it is an attractive purchase for Polar depends on how Polar's management deploy their strategies to improve Anchorage's performance.

Annex 1– weighted average cost of capital

Estimation of the Weighted Average Cost of Capital (WACC) for Anchorage Retail

To estimate the cost of equity capital for the company we first measure the expected return on the market using the rearranged dividend valuation model on the broadly based market index:

$$r_e = \frac{D_0}{P_0}(1+g) + g$$

$$r_e = 3.1\% \times (1.04) + 4\% = 7.224\%$$

Given the market index should have a beta of 1 and with a risk-free rate of interest of 5% this suggests that the rate of return expected on the market is 7.224% and the equity risk premium is 2.224%

Putting this result into the Capital Asset Pricing Model:

$$r_e = R_F + \beta_i(r_m - R_F)$$

$$r_e = 5\% + 0.75 \times 2.224\% = 6.668\%$$

This gives a weighted average cost of capital as follows:

$$WACC = 76\% \times 6.668\% + 24\% \cdot 6.2\% \times (1 - 30\%) = 6.12\%$$

ACCA marking scheme		Marks
Note candidates may answer this question in a variety of ways and in different order to that set.		
(a) Identification of principal risks (2 each to a maximum of 6) Disclosure, Valuation, Regulatory, Other		
	Maximum	6.0
(b) Calculation of the equity risk premium and return on equity		2.0
Estimation of the WACC		1.0
Calculation of the EVA for each year		3.0
Other performance ratios and associated commentary – up to:		6.0
	Maximum	12.0
(c) Ungearing the component betas		1.0
Calculation of the combined beta		2.0
Estimation of impact upon required equity rate of return		3.0
	Maximum	6.0
(d) Undervaluation and the implication of inefficiency		2.0
Review of current price and whether the acquisition may be attractive		2.0
	Maximum	4.0
(e) Professional marks		4.0
	Maximum	4.0
Total		**32**

13   PURSUIT CO (JUN 11)

Key answer tips

Business valuation, especially using free cash flows, is very commonly tested. Lay out your forecast free cash flows neatly, and leave time to also attempt all the discussion parts of the question.

(i)   The calculations and estimations for part (i) are given in the appendix. To assess whether or not the acquisition would be beneficial to Pursuit's shareholders, the additional synergy benefits after the acquisition has been paid for need to be ascertained.

The estimated synergy benefit from the acquisition is approximately $9,074,000 (see appendix), which is the post-acquisition value of the combined company less the values of the individual companies. However, once Fodder Co's debt obligations and the equity shareholders have been paid, the benefit to Pursuit Co's shareholders reduces to approximately $52,000 (see appendix), which is minimal. Even a small change in the variables and assumptions could negate it. It is therefore doubtful that the shareholders would view the acquisition as beneficial to themselves or the company.

(ii)   The limitations of the estimates stem from the fact that although the model used is theoretically sound, it is difficult to apply it in practice for the following reasons.

The calculations in part (i) are based on a number of assumptions such as the growth rate in the next four years, the perpetual growth rate after the four years, additional investment in assets, stable tax rates, discount rates and profit margins, assumption that debt is risk free when computing the asset beta. All these assumptions would be subject to varying margins of error.

It may be difficult for Pursuit Co to assess the variables of the combined company to any degree of accuracy, and therefore the synergy benefits may be hard to predict.

No information is provided about the pre-acquisition and post-acquisition costs.

Although it may be possible to estimate the equity beta of Pursuit Co, being a listed company, to a high level of accuracy, estimating Fodder Co's equity beta may be more problematic, because it is a private company.

Given the above, it is probably more accurate to present a range of possible values for the combined company depending on different scenarios and the likelihood of their occurrence, before a decision is made.

(iii)   The current value of Pursuit Co is $140,000,000, of which the market value of equity and debt are $70,000,000 each. The value of the combined company before paying Fodder Co shareholders is approximately $189,169,000, and if the capital structure is maintained, the market values of debt and equity will be approximately $94,584,500 each. This is an increase of approximately $24,584,500 in the debt capacity.

The amount payable for Fodder Co's debt obligations and to the shareholders including the premium is approximately $49,116,500 [4,009 + 36,086 × 1.25]. If $24,584,500 is paid using the extra debt capacity and $20,000,000 using cash reserves, an additional amount of approximately $4,532,000 will need to be raised. Hence, if only debt finance and cash reserves are used, the capital structure cannot be maintained.

(iv) If Pursuit Co aims to acquire Fodder Co using debt finance and cash reserves, then the capital structure of the combined company will change. It will also change if they adopt the Chief Financial Officer's recommendation and acquire Fodder Co using only debt finance.

Both these options will cause the cost of capital of the combined company to change. This in turn will cause the value of the company to change. This will cause the proportion of market value of equity to market value of debt to change, and thus change the cost of capital. Therefore the changes in the market value of the company and the cost of capital are interrelated.

To resolve this problem, an iterative procedure needs to be adopted where the beta and the cost of capital are recalculated to take account of the changes in the capital structure, and then the company is re-valued. This procedure is repeated until the assumed capital structure is closely aligned to the capital structure that has been re-calculated. This process is normally done using a spreadsheet package such as Excel. This method is used when both the business risk and the financial risk of the acquiring company change as a result of an acquisition (referred to as a type III acquisition).

Alternatively an adjusted present value approach may be undertaken.

(v) The Chief Financial Officer's suggestion appears to be a disposal of 'crown jewels'. Without the cash reserves, Pursuit Co may become less valuable to SGF Co. Also, the reason for the depressed share price may be because Pursuit Co's shareholders do not agree with the policy to retain large cash reserves. Therefore returning the cash reserves to the shareholders may lead to an increase in the share price and make a bid from SGF Co more unlikely. This would not initially contravene the regulatory framework as no formal bid has been made. However, Pursuit Co must investigate further whether the reason for a possible bid from SGF Co might be to gain access to the large amount of cash or it might have other reasons. Pursuit Co should also try to establish whether remitting the cash to the shareholders would be viewed positively by them.

Whether this is a viable option for Pursuit Co depends on the bid for Fodder Co. In part (iii) it was established that more than the expected debt finance would be needed even if the cash reserves are used to pay for some of the acquisition cost. If the cash is remitted, a further $20,000,000 would be needed, and if this was all raised by debt finance then a significant proportion of the value of the combined company would be debt financed. The increased gearing may have significant implications on Pursuit Co's future investment plans and may result in increased restrictive covenants. Ultimately gearing might have to increase to such a level that this method of financing might not be possible. Pursuit Co should investigate the full implications further and assess whether the acquisition is worthwhile given the marginal value it provides for the shareholders (see part (i)).

Tutorial note

Up to 4 professional marks are available for the presentation of the answer, which should be in a report style.

APPENDIX

Part (i)

Interest is ignored as its impact is included in the companies' discount rates

Fodder cost of capital

Ke = 4.5% + 1.53 × 6% = 13.68%

Cost of capital = 13.68% × 0.9 + 9% × (1 − 0.28) × 0.1 = 12.96% assume 13%

Fodder

Sales revenue growth rate = (16,146/13,559)1/3 − 1 × 100% = 5.99% assume 6%
Operating profit margin = approx. 32% of sales revenue

Fodder Co cash flow and value computation ($000)

Year	1	2	3	4
Sales revenue	17,115	18,142	19,231	20,385
Operating profit	5,477	5,805	6,154	6,523
Less tax (28%)	(1,534)	(1,625)	(1,723)	(1,826)
Less additional investment (22c/$1 of sales revenue increase)	(213)	(226)	(240)	(254)
Free cash flows	3,730	3,954	4,191	4,443
PV (13%)	3,301	3,097	2,905	2,725

	$(000)
PV (first 4 years)	12,028
PV (after 4 years) [4,443 × 1.03/(0.13 − 0.03)] × 1.13^{-4}	28,067
Firm value	40,095

Combined Company: Cost of capital calculation

Asset beta (Pursuit Co) = 1.18 × 0.5/(0.5 + 0.5 × 0.72) = 0.686

Asset beta (Fodder Co) = 1.53 × 0.9/(0.9 + 0.1 × 0.72) = 1.417

Asset beta of combined co. = (0.686 × 140,000 + 1.417 × 40,095)/(140,000 + 40,095) = 0.849

Equity beta of combined company = 0.849 × (0.5 + 0.5 × 0.72)/0.5 = 1.46

Ke = 4.5% + 1.46 × 6% = 13.26%

Cost of capital = 13.26% × 0.5 + 6.4% × 0.5 × 0.72 = 8.93%, assume 9%

Combined Co cash flow and value computation ($000)

Sales revenue growth rate = 5.8%, operating profit margin = 30% of sales revenue

Year	1	2	3	4
Sales revenue	51,952	54,965	58,153	61,526
Operating profit	15,586	16,490	17,446	18,458
Less tax (28%)	(4,364)	(4,617)	(4,885)	(5,168)
Less additional investment (18c/$1 of sales revenue increase)	(513)	(542)	(574)	(607)
Free cash flows	10,709	11,331	11,987	12,683
PV (9%)	9,825	9,537	9,256	8,985

	$(000)
PV (first 4 years)	37,603
PV (after 4 years) $[12,683 \times 1.029/(0.09 - 0.029)] \times 1.09^{-4}$	151,566
Firm value	189,169

Synergy benefits = 189,169,000 – (140,000,000 + 40,095,000) = $9,074,000

Estimated premium required to acquire Fodder Co = 0.25 × 36,086,000 = $9,022,000

Net benefit to Pursuit Co shareholders = $52,000

ACCA marking scheme		Marks
(i)	Ignore interest in calculations	1
	Estimate of cost of capital of Fodder Co	1
	Estimates of growth rates and profit margins for Fodder Co	2
	Estimate of intrinsic value of Fodder Co	3
	Equity beta of combined co	3
	Cost of capital of combined company	1
	Estimate of value of combined company	3
	Synergy benefits, value to Pursuit Co shareholders and conclusion	2–3
	Maximum	16
(ii)	1 to 2 marks per each point discussed	
	Credit will be given for alternative, relevant points	
	Maximum	4
(iii)	Estimate of the increase in debt capacity after acquisition	1
	Estimate of the funds required to acquire Fodder Co	1
	Conclusion	1
	Maximum	3
(iv)	Explanation of the problem of the changing capital structure	2
	Explanation of the resolution of the problem using the iterative process	2
	Maximum	4
(v)	Assessment of suitable defence	2–3
	Assessment of viability	2–3
	Credit will be given for alternative, relevant points	
	Maximum	5
	Professional Marks	
	Report format	1
	Layout, presentation and structure	3
	Maximum	4
Total		36

14   NENTE CO (JUN 12)

Key answer tips

Always make sure that you use a report format in the Section A question. Presenting your answer professionally will enable you to score 4 "professional marks" – the easiest marks on the whole paper.

REPORT TO THE BOARD OF DIRECTORS, NENTE CO

IMPACT OF THE TAKEOVER PROPOSAL FROM MIJE CO AND PRODUCTION RIGHTS OF THE FOLLOW-ON PRODUCT

The report considers the value of the takeover to Nente Co and Mije Co shareholders based on a cash offer and on a share-for-share offer. It discusses the possible reaction of each group of shareholders to the two offers and how best to utilise the follow-on product opportunity. The significant assumptions made in compiling the report are also explained.

The appendices to the report show the detailed calculations in estimating the equity value of Nente Co, the value to Nente Co and Mije Co shareholders of acquiring Nente Co by cash and by a share-for-share exchange, and the value to Nente Co of the exclusive rights to the follow-on product. The results of the calculation are summarised below:

Estimated price of a Nente Co share before the takeover offer and follow-on product is

£2.90/share (appendix i)

Estimated increase in share price	Nente Co	Mije Co
Cash offer (appendix ii)	1.7%	9.4%
Share-for-share offer (appendix ii)	17.9%	6.9%

Estimate of the value per share of the follow-on product to Nente Co is

8.7% (appendix iii)

It is unlikely that Nente Co shareholders would accept the cash offer because it is little more than the estimated price of a Nente Co share before the takeover offer. However, the share-for-share offer gives a larger increase in value of a share of 17.9%. Given that the normal premium on acquisitions ranges from 20% to 40%, this is closer to what Nente Co shareholders would find acceptable. It is also greater than the additional value from the follow-on product. Therefore, based on the financial figures, Nente Co's shareholders would find the offer of a takeover on a share-for-share exchange basis the most attractive option. The other options considered here yield lower expected percentage increase in share price.

Mije Co shareholders would prefer the cash offer so that they can maximise the price of their shares and also not dilute their shareholding, but they would probably accept either option because the price of their shares increases. However, Mije Co shareholders would probably assess whether or not to accept the acquisition proposal by comparing it with other opportunities that the company has available to it and whether this is the best way to utilise its spare cash flows.

The calculations and analysis in each case is made on a number of assumptions. For example, in order to calculate the estimated price of a Nente Co share, the free cash flow valuation model is used. For this, the growth rate, the cost of capital and effective time period when the growth rate will occur (perpetuity in this instance) are all estimates or based on assumptions. For the takeover offer, the synergy savings and P/E ratio value are both assumptions. For the value of the follow-on product and the related option, the option variables are estimates and it is assumed that they would not change during the period before the decision. The value of the option is based on the possibility that the option will only be exercised at the end of the two years, although it seems that the decision can be made any time within the two years.

The follow-on product is initially treated separately from the takeover, but Nente Co may ask Mije Co to take the value of the follow-on product into consideration in its offer. The value of the rights that allow Nente Co to delay making a decision are themselves worth $603,592 (appendix iii) and add just over 25c or 8.7% to the value of a Nente Co share. If Mije Co can be convinced to increase their offer to match this or the rights could be sold before the takeover, then the return for Nente Co's shareholders would be much higher at 26.6% (17.9% + 8.7%).

In conclusion, the most favourable outcome for Nente Co shareholders would be to accept the share-for-share offer, and try to convince Mije Co to take the value of the follow-on product into consideration. Prior to accepting the offer Nente Co shareholders would need to be assured of the accuracy of the results produced by the computations in the appendices.

Report compiled by: XXX

Date: XXX

(Note: credit will be given for alternative relevant discussion and suggestions)

APPENDICES

Appendix i: Estimate of Nente Co Equity Value Based on Free Cash Flows

Company value = Free cash flows (FCF) × (1 + growth rate (g))/(cost of capital (k) − g)

k = 11%

Past g = (latest profit before interest and tax (PBIT)/earliest PBIT)$^{1/\text{no. of years of growth}}$ − 1

Past g = $(1,230/970)^{1/3}$ − 1 = 0·0824

Future g = ¼ × 0·0824 = 0·0206

FCF Calculation

FCF = PBIT + non cash flows − cash investment − tax

FCF = $1,230,000 + $1,206,000 − $1,010,000 − ($1,230,000 × 20%) = $1,180,000

Company value = $1,180,000 × 1.0206/(0.11 − 0.0206) = $13,471,000

Equity value = $13,471,000 − $6,500,000 = $6,971,000

Per share = $6,971,000/2,400,000 shares = $2.90

Appendix ii: Estimated Returns to Nente Co and Mije Co Shareholders

Cash Offer

Gain in value to a Nente Co share = ($2.95 – $2.90)/$2.90 = 1.7%

Additional earnings after acquisition = $620,000 + $150,000 = $770,000

Additional EPS created from acquisition = $770,000/10,000,000 = 7.7c/share

Increase in share price based on P/E of 15 = 7.7c × 15 = $1.16

Additional value created = $1.16 × 10,000,000 =	$11,600,000
Less: paid for Nente Co acquisition = ($2.95 × 2,400,000 shares)	$(7,080,000)
Value added for Mije shareholders =	$4,520,000
Gain in value to a Mije Co share = $4,520,000/10,000,000 =	45.2c
or 45.2c/480c =	9.4%

Share-for-share Offer

Earnings combined company = $620,000 + $150,000 + $3,200,000 = $3,970,000

Shares in combined company = 10,000,000 + 2,400,000 × 2/3 = 11,600,000

EPS = 34.2c/share [$3,970,000/11,600,000]

Expected share price = 34.2c × 15 = 513c or $5.13/share

Three Nente Co shares = $2.90 × 3 = $8.70

Gain in value to a Mije Co share = ($5.13 – $4.80)/$4.80	= 6.9%
Gain in value to a Nente Co share = ($10.26 – $8.70)/$8.70	= 17.9%

Appendix iii: Increase in Value of Follow-On Product

Present value of the positive cash flows	= $2,434,000
Present value of the cash outflow	= $(2,029,000)
Net present value of the new product	= $405,000

Based on conventional NPV, without considering the value of the option to delay the decision, the project would increase the value of the company by $405,000.

Considering the value of the option to delay the decision

Price of asset (PV of future positive cash flows)	= $2,434,000
Exercise price (initial cost of project, not discounted)	= $2,500,000
Time to expiry of option	= 2 years
Risk free rate (estimate)	= 3.2%
Volatility	= 42%

$d_1 = [\ln(2,434/2,500) + (0.032 + 0.5 \times 0.42^2) \times 2]/(0.42 \times 2^{1/2}) = 0.359$

$d_2 = 0.359 - (0.42 \times 2^{1/2}) = -0.235$

$N(d1) = 0.5 + (0.1368 + 0.9 \times (0.1406 - 0.1368)) = 0.6402$

$N(d2) = 0.5 - (0.0910 + 0.5 \times (0.0948 - 0.0910)) = 0.4071$

Value of option to delay the decision = $2,434,000 \times 0.6402 - 2,500,000 \times 0.4071 \times e^{-(0.032 \times 2)}$
= $1,558,247 – $954,655 = $603,592

The project increases the value of the company by $603,592 or 25.1c per share ($603,592/2,400,000 shares). In percentage terms this is an increase of about 8.7% (25.1c/290c).

ACCA marking scheme		
		Marks
Appendix i		
Based on PBIT, calculation of the growth rate		2
Calculation of free cash flows		2
Calculation of company value, equity value and value of each share		3
		—
	Maximum	7
		—
Appendix ii		
Cash offer		
Additional value created for Mije Co shareholders		3
Value created per share for Nente Co shareholders		1
Share-for-share offer		
Expected share price for the combined company		2
Value created for Nente Co share		1
Value created for Mije Co share		1
		—
	Maximum	8
		—
Appendix iii		
PV of underlying asset		1
Value of exercise price		1
N(d1)		2
N(d2)		2
Value of call		1
Value added to Nente Co share		1
		—
	Maximum	8
		—
Discussion		
Nente Co shareholders		2–3
Mije Co shareholders		1–2
Assumptions made		2–3
Use of value of follow-on product		2–3
		—
	Maximum	8
		—
Professional Marks		
Report format		1
Structure and presentation of the report		3
		—
	Maximum	4
		—
Total		**35**
		—

15   MLIMA CO (JUN 13)

Key answer tips

Notice that part (b) of this question is totally independent of part (a). Feel free to attempt part (b) first if you feel that it is easier than part (a).

(a)   **Report to the Board of Directors, Mlima Co Initial public listing: price range and implications**

This report considers a range of values of Mlima Co and possible share price, based on 100 million issued shares in preparation of the initial public listing. The assumptions made in determining the value range and the likelihood of the unsecured bond holders accepting the 10% equity-for-debt swap offer are discussed. Alternative reasons for the listing and reasons for issuing the share at a discount are evaluated.

Mlima Co cost of capital explanation

Ziwa Co's ungeared cost of equity represents the return Ziwa Co's shareholders would require if Ziwa Co was financed entirely by equity and had no debt. The return would compensate them for the business risk undertaken by the company.

This required rate of return would compensate Mlima Co's shareholders as well because, since both companies are in the same industry, they face the same business risk. This rate is then used as Mlima Co's cost of capital because of the assumption that Mlima Co will not issue any debt and faces no financial risk. Therefore its cost of equity (ungeared) is its cost of capital.

Mlima Co Estimated Value

Based on a cost of capital of 11% (appendix 1), the value of Mlima Co is estimated at $564.3m (appendix 2), prior to considering the impact of the Bahari project. The value of the Bahari project, without taking into account the benefits of the tax shield and the subsidies, does not exceed the initial investment. With the benefits of the tax shield and subsidies, it is estimated that the project will generate a positive net present value of $21.5m (appendix 3). Taking the Bahari project into account gives a value for Mlima Co at just under $586m.

Possible share price (100m shares)	Without the Bahari project	With the Bahari project
At full value	$5.64/share	$5.86/share
With 20% discount	$4.51/share	$4.69/share

Unsecured bond holders (equity-for-debt swap)

The current value of the unsecured bond is estimated at $56.8m (appendix 4) and if the unsecured bond holders are to be offered a 10% equity stake in Mlima Co post-listing, then only the share price at $5.86 would be acceptable to them. If the listing is made at the lowest price of $4.51/share, then they would need to be offered around a 12.6% equity stake ($56.8m/$4.51 = 12.594m).

The value of the bond is based on a flat yield curve (or yield to maturity) of 7%, which is the rate at which Mlima Co can borrow funds and therefore its current yield. A more accurate method would be to assess the yield curve based on future risk-free rates and credit spreads for the company.

Assumptions

The main assumptions made are around the accuracy of the information used in estimating the values of the company and the project. For example, the value of the company is based on assumptions of future growth rates, profit margins, future tax rates and capital investment. The basis for estimating the future growth rates and profit margins on past performance may not be accurate. With the Bahari project, for example, projections of future cash flows are made for 15 years and the variability of these has been estimated. Again, the reasonableness of these estimates needs to be assessed. Are they, for example, based on past experience and/or have professional experts judged the values?

The cost of capital is estimated based on a competitor's ungeared cost of equity, on the basis that Mlima Co is in a similar line of business and therefore faces similar business risk. The financial risk element has been removed since it has been stated that Mlima Co is not looking to raise extra debt finance. However, it is possible that the business risks faced by Mlima Co and that faced by Ziwa Co, the competitor, are not the same. Accepting the Bahari project would also change the risk profile of Mlima Co and therefore its discount rate.

The values are based on the Bahari government fulfilling the subsidised loan concession it has offered. Mlima Co needs to consider the likelihood of this concession continuing for the entire 15 years and whether a change of government may jeopardise the agreement. The political and other risks need to be assessed and their impact assessed.

It has been assumed that the underwriting and other costs involved with the new listing are not significant or have been catered for, before the assessment of the cash flows. This assumption needs to be reviewed and its accuracy assessed.

Reasons for the public listing

The main reason given for the public listing is to use the funds raised to eliminate the debt in the company. There are other reasons why a company may undertake a public listing. These include: gaining a higher reputation by being listed on a recognised stock exchange and therefore reducing the costs of contracting with stakeholders; being able to raise funds more easily in the future to undertake new projects; the listing will provide the current owners with a value for their equity stake; and the listing may enable the current owners to sell their equity stakes and gain from the value in the organisation.

Issuing shares at a discount

Issuing only 20% of the share capital to the public at the initial listing would make them minority shareholders effectively. As such, their ability to influence the decision-making process in the company would be severely curtailed, since even if all the new investors voted as a bloc against a decision, they would not be able to overturn it. The discounted share price would reflect the additional risk of investing in a company as a minority shareholder. In this case, the position of the unsecured bond holders is important. If the unsecured bond holders, holding between 10% and 12.6% of the share capital in an equity-for-debt swap, are included with the new investors, then the equity stake rises to 30%–32.6%. In such a case, shareholders, as a bloc, would have a significant influence on the company's decisions. The question that should be asked is whether the current unsecured bond holders are more closely aligned to the interests of the current owners or to the interests of the new investors.

The second reason for issuing shares at a discount is to ensure that they do all get sold and as a reward for the underwriters. Research suggests that, normally, for new listings, shares are issued at a discount and the price of such shares rises immediately after launch.

Conclusion

The report and the calculations in the appendices suggest a price range for the listing of between $4.51 and $5.86 per share, depending on whether or not the Bahari project is undertaken, the discount at which the shares are issued and the assumptions made. It is recommended that Mlima Co should consult its underwriters and potential investors about the possible price they would be willing to pay before making a final decision (known as book-building).

If 20 million shares are offered to the public for $4.51 each, this will result in total funds raised of just over $90 million. If the $80 million are spent in paying for the secured bond, just over $10 million liquid funds remain. Therefore, Mlima Co needs to consider whether issuing the shares at a discount would ensure sufficient liquid funds are available for it to continue its normal business. In addition to this, the Bahari investment may result in a change in the desired capital structure of the company and have an impact on the cost of capital. Finally, being listed will result in additional listing costs and annual costs related to additional reporting requirements.

These factors should be balanced against the benefits of undertaking the new listing before a final decision is made.

Report compiled by: XXX

Date: XXX

APPENDICES

Appendix 1: Mlima Co, cost of capital

Ziwa Co

MV debt = $1,700m × 1.05 = $1,785m MV equity = 200m × $7 = $1,400m

Ziwa Co, ungeared Ke

$Ke_g = Ke_u + (1 - t)(Ke_u - K_d) D/E$

$16.83\% = Ke_u + 0.75 × (Ke_u - 4.76\%) × 1,785/1,400$

$16.83\% + 4.55\% = 1.9563 × Ke_u$

$Ke_u = 10.93\%$ (say 11%)

Appendix 2: Mlima Co, estimate of value prior to Bahari project

Value based on future free cash flows

Historic mean sales revenue growth = $(389.1/344.7)^{1/2} - 1 = 0.625$ or 6.25%

Next four years annual growth rate of sales revenue = 120% of 6.25% = 7.5%

Thereafter 3.5% of cash flows per annum

Operating profit margin (approx) = 58.4/389.1 = 54.9/366.3 = 51.7/344.7 = 15%

Year (in $ millions)	1	2	3	4
Sales revenue	418.3	449.7	483.4	519.7
Operating profit	62.7	67.5	72.5	78.0
Less taxation (25%)	(15.7)	(16.9)	(18.1)	(19.5)
Less additional capital investment (30c per $1 change in sales revenue)	(8.8)	(9.4)	(10.1)	(10.9)
Free cash flows	38.2	41.2	44.3	47.6
PV of free cash flows (11%)	34.4	33.4	32.4	31.4

PV first four years $131.6m

PV after four years $(47.6 \times 1.035)/(0.11 - 0.035) \times 1.11^{-4}$ $432.7m

Value of company $564.3m

Appendix 3: Value of the Bahari project Base case present value

Year	Free Cash flows (in $ millions)	PV (11%) (in $ millions)
1	4.0	3.6
2	8.0	6.5
3	16.0	11.7
4	18.4	12.1
5	21.2	12.6
6 to 15	21.2	**74.0
Total		120.5

** The free cash flows in years 6 to 15 are an annuity for 10 years at 11%, then discounted back for five years: 21.2 × 5.889 × 0.593 = 74.0

PV of the tax shield and subsidy

Annuity factor (7%, 15 years) = 9.108

Annual tax shield benefit interest paid = 3% × $150m × 25% = $1.1m Subsidy benefit = 4% × $150m × (1 − 25%) = $4.5m PV of tax shield and subsidy benefit = 5.6 × 9.108 = $51.0m

Adjusted present value = $120.5m + $51.0m − $150.0m = $21.5m

Appendix 4: Estimated value of the unsecured bond

Assume a flat yield or yield to maturity of 7%

Annual coupon interest = $5.2m (13% × $40m)

10-year annuity at 7% = 7.024; Discount factor (10 years, 7%) = 0.508

Bond value = $5.2m × 7.024 + $40m × 0.508 = $56.8m

(b)   It is likely that Mlima Co's actions will be scrutinised more closely in the run up to the listing and once it has been listed. In both the situations, the company should consider the action it should take based on its ethical and accountability code. Most major corporations now publicise such codes of behaviour and would consult these in cases of ethical and/or accountability difficulties.

With the first situation concerning the relocation of the farmers, Mlima Co would consult its ethical code to judge how far its responsibility lay. It may take the view that the matter is between the farmers and the government, and it is not directly or indirectly responsible for the situation. In any case, it is likely that the mining rights will be assigned to another company, should Mlima Co decide to walk away from the deal. It is unlikely that, even if Mlima Co did not agree to the offer, the plight of the farmers would cease.

Instead, Mlima Co may decide to try to influence the government with respect to the farmers by urging the government to keep the community together and offer the farmers better land. Mlima Co may also decide to offer jobs and training to farmers who decide not to leave.

With the second situation concerning the Bahari president and Mlima Co's CEO, whilst it would make good business sense to forge strong relationships as a means of competitive advantage, Mlima Co should ensure that the negotiation was transparent and did not involve any bribery or illegal practice. If both the company and Bahari government can demonstrate that they acted in the best interests of the company and the country respectively, and individuals did not benefit as a result, then this should not be seen in a negative light.

Mlima Co needs to establish a clear strategy of how it would respond to public scrutiny of either issue. This may include actions such as demonstrating that it is acting according to its ethical code, pre-empting media scrutiny by releasing press statements, and using its influence to ensure the best and correct outcome in each case for the stakeholders concerned.

Tutorial note (from the examiner's model answer)

Credit will be given for alternative, relevant approaches to the calculations, comments and suggestions/ recommendations.

			Marks

ACCA marking scheme

			Marks
(a)	(i)	Explanation of Mlima Co's cost of capital based on Ziwa Co's ungeared cost of equity	3
		Ziwa Co, cost of ungeared equity	4
			7
	(ii)	Sales revenue growth rates	1
		Operating profit rate	1
		Estimate of free cash flows and PV of free cash flows for years 1 to 4	4
		PV of free cash flows after year 4	2
		Base case Bahari project value	2
		Annual tax shield benefit	1
		Annual subsidy benefit	1
		PV of the tax shield and subsidy benefits	1
		Value of the Bahari project	1
		Maximum	14
	(iii)	Calculation of unsecured bond value	2
		Comment	2
		Limitation	1
		Maximum	5
	(iv)	Comments on the range of values/prices with and without the project, and concluding statement	4–5
		Discussion of assumptions	3–4
		Explanation for additional reasons for listing	2–3
		Assessment of reasons for discounted share price	2–3
		Maximum	12
		Professional marks	
		Report format	1
		Structure and presentation of the report	3
		Maximum	4
(b)		Discussion of relocation of farmers	4–5
		Discussion of relationship between Bahari president and Mlima Co CEO	4–5
		Maximum	8
Total			**50**

16 NAHARA CO AND FUGAE CO (DEC 14)

Key answer tips

All the Section A questions are very time pressured, with lots of parts to complete in the time.

It is therefore critically important to attempt the easier parts of the question first and leave the more difficult parts until the end.

As part of your reading time, try to pick out the easier parts of the Section A question, so that you don't waste time trying to prioritise during the 3 hours of the exam.

(a) Risk diversification, especially into diverse business sectors, has often been stated as a reason for undertaking mergers and acquisitions (M&As). Like individuals holding well-diversified portfolios, a company with a number of subsidiaries in different sectors could reduce its exposure to unsystematic risk. Another possible benefit of diversification is sometimes argued to be a reduction in the volatility of cash flows, which may lead to a better credit rating and a lower cost of capital.

The argument against this states that since individual investors can undertake this level of risk diversification both quickly and cheaply themselves, there is little reason for companies to do so. Indeed, research suggests that markets do not reward this risk diversification.

Nevertheless, for Nahara Co, undertaking M&As may have beneficial outcomes, especially if the sovereign fund has its entire investment in the holding company and is not well-diversified itself. In such a situation unsystematic risk reduction can be beneficial. The case study does not state whether or not the sovereign funds are invested elsewhere and therefore a definitive conclusion cannot be reached.

If Nahara Co is able to identify undervalued companies and after purchasing the company can increase the value for the holding company overall, by increasing the value of the undervalued companies, then such M&As activity would have a beneficial impact on the funds invested. However, for this strategy to work, Nahara Co must:

(i) Possess a superior capability or knowledge in identifying bargain buys ahead of its competitor companies. To achieve this, it must have access to better information, which it can tap into quicker, and/or have superior analytical tools. Nahara Co should assess whether or not it does possess such capabilities, otherwise its claim is not valid.

(ii) Ensure that it has quick access to the necessary funds to pursue an undervalued acquisition. Even if Nahara Co possesses superior knowledge, it is unlikely that this will last for a long time before its competitors find out; therefore it needs to have the funds ready, to move quickly. Given that it has access to sovereign funds from a wealthy source, access to funds is probably not a problem.

(iii) Set a maximum ceiling for the price it is willing to pay and should not go over this amount, or the potential value created will be reduced.

If, in its assessment, Nahara Co is able to show that it meets all the above conditions, then the strategy of identifying and pursuing undervalued companies may be valid.

(b)   In a similar manner to the Competition and Markets Authority in the UK, the European Union (EU) will assess significant mergers and acquisitions' (M&As) impact on competition within a country's market. It will, for example, use tests such as worldwide turnover and European turnover of the group after the M&A. It may block the M&A, if it feels that the M&A will give the company monopolistic powers or enable it to carve out a dominant position in the market so as to negatively affect consumer choice and prices.

Sometimes the EU may ask for the company to sell some of its assets to reduce its dominant position rather than not allow an M&A to proceed. It would appear that this may be the case behind the EU's concern and the reason for its suggested action.

(b)   **Report to the Board of Directors, Avem Co**

Proposed acquisition of Fugae Co

This report evaluates whether or not it is beneficial for Avem Co to acquire Fugae Co. Initially the value of the two companies is determined separately and as a combined entity, to assess the additional value created from bringing the two companies together. Following this, the report considers how much Nahara Co and Avem Co will gain from the value created. The assumptions made to arrive at the additional value are also considered. The report concludes by considering whether or not the acquisition will be beneficial to Avem Co and to Nahara Co.

Appendix 1 shows that the additional value created from combining the two companies is approximately $451.5 million, of which $276.8 million will go to Nahara Co, as the owner of Fugae Co. This represents a premium of about 30% which is the minimum acceptable to Nahara Co. The balance of the additional value will go to Avem Co which is about $174.7 million, representing an increase in value of 1.46% [$174.7m/$12,000m].

Appendix 2 shows that accepting the project would increase Fugae Co's value as the expected net present value is positive. After taking into account Lumi Co's offer, the expected net present value is higher. Therefore, it would be beneficial for Fugae Co to take on the project and accept Lumi Co's offer, if the tourism industry does not grow as expected, as this will increase Fugae Co's value.

Assumptions

It is assumed that all the figures relating to synergy benefits, betas, growth rates, multipliers, risk adjusted cost of capital and the probabilities are accurate. There is considerable uncertainty surrounding the accuracy of these, and in addition to the probability analysis conducted in appendix 2 and the assessments of value conducted in appendix 1, a sensitivity analysis is probably needed to assess the impact of these uncertainties.

It is assumed that the rb model provides a reasonably good estimate of the growth rate, and that perpetuity is not an unreasonable assumption when assessing the value of Fugae Co.

It is assumed that the capital structure would not change substantially when the new project is taken on. Since the project is significantly smaller than the value of Fugae Co itself, this is not an unreasonable assumption.

When assessing the value of the project, the outcomes are given as occurring with discrete probabilities and the resulting cash flows from the outcomes are given with certainty. There may be more outcomes in practice than the ones given and financial impact of the outcomes may not be known with such certainty. The Black-Scholes Option Pricing model may provide an alternative and more accurate way of assessing the value of the project.

It is assumed that Fugae Co can rely on Lumi Co paying the $50m at the beginning of year two with certainty. Fugae Co may want to assess the reliability of Lumi Co's offer and whether formal contracts should be drawn up between the two companies. Furthermore, Lumi Co may be reluctant to pay the full amount of money once Fugae Co becomes a part of Avem Co.

Concluding comments

Although Nahara Co would gain more than Avem Co from the acquisition both in percentage terms and in monetary terms, both companies benefit from the acquisition. If Fugae Co were to take on the project, although it is value-neutral to the acquisition, Nahara Co could ask for an additional 30% of $12.3 million value to be transferred to it, which is about $3.7 million. Hence the return to Avem Co would reduce by a small amount, but not significantly.

As long as all the parties are satisfied that the value is reasonable despite the assumptions highlighted above, it would appear that the acquisition should proceed.

Report compiled by:

Date:

Appendices

Appendix 1: Additional value created from combining Avem Co and Fugae Co

Avem Co, current value = $7.5/share × 1,600 million shares = $12,000m

Avem Co, free cash flow to equity = $12,000 million/7.2 = $1,666.7m

The growth rate is calculated on the basis of the rb model.

Fugae Co, estimate of growth rate = 0.227 × 0.11 = 0.025 = 2.5%

Fugae Co, current value estimate = $76.5 million × 1.025/(0.11 − 0.025) = $922.5m

Combined company, estimated additional value created =

([$1,666.7m + $76.5m + $40m] × 7.5) − ($12,000m + $922.5m) = $451.5m

Gain to Nahara for selling Fugae Co, 30% × $922.5m = $276.8m

Avem Co will gain $174.7 million of the additional value created, $451.5m − $276.8m = $174.7m

Appendix 2: Value of project to Fugae Co

Appendix 2.1

Estimate of risk-adjusted cost of capital to be used to discount the project's cash flows

The project value is calculated based on its cash flows which are discounted at the project's risk adjusted cost of capital, to reflect the business risk of the project.

Reka Co's asset beta

Reka Co equity value = $4.50 × 80 million shares = $360m

Reka Co debt value = 1.05 × $340 million = $357m

Asset beta = 1.6 × $360m/($360m + $357m × 0.8) = 0.89

Project's asset beta (PAB)

0.89 = PAB × 0.15 + 0.80 × 0.85

PAB = 1.4

Fugae Co

MVe = $922.5m

MVd

Cost of debt = Risk free rate of return plus the credit spread

= 4% + 0.80% = 4.80%

Current value of a $100 bond: $5.4 × 1.048–1 + $5.4 × 1.048–2 + $5.4 × 1.048–3 + $105.4 × 1.048–4 = $102.14 per $100

MVd = 1.0214 × $380m = $388.1 m

Project's risk adjusted equity beta

1.4 × ($922.5m + $388.1m × 0.8)/$922.5m = 1.87

Project's risk adjusted cost of equity

4% + 1.87 × 6% = 15.2%

Project's risk adjusted cost of capital

(15.2% × $922.5m + 4.8% × 0.8 × $388.1m)/($922.5m + $388.1m) = 11.84%, say 12%

Appendix 2.2

Estimate of expected value of the project without the offer from Lumi Co

(All amounts in $, 000s)

Year	1	2	3	4
Cash flows	3,277.6	16,134.3	36,504.7	35,683.6
Discount factor for 12%	0.893	0.797	0.712	0.636
Present values	2,926.9	12,859.0	25,991.3	22,694.8

Probabilities are assigned to possible outcomes based on whether or not the tourism market will grow. The expected net present value (PV) is computed on this basis.

PV year 1: $2,926,900

50% of PV years 1 to 4: $32,236,000

PV years 2 to 4: $61,545,100

40% PV years 2 to 4: $24,618,040

Expected present value of cash flows = [0.75 × (2,926,900 + (0.8 × 61,545,100 + 0.2 × 24,618,040))] + [0.25 × 32,236,000]

= [0.75 × (2,926,900 + 54,159,688)] + [0.25 × 32,236,000] = 42,814,941 + 8,059,000 = $50,873,941

Expected NPV of project = $50,873,941 –- $42,000,000 = $8,873,941

Estimate of expected value of the project with the offer from Lumi Co

PV of $50m = $50,000,000 × 0.893 = $44,650,000

If the tourism industry does not grow as expected in the first year, then it is more beneficial for Fugae Co to exercise the offer made by Lumi Co, given that Lumi Co's offer of $44.65 million (PV of $50 million) is greater than the PV of the years two to four cash flows ($30.8 million approximately) for that outcome. This figure is then incorporated into the expected net present value calculations.

50% of year 1 PV: $1,463,450

Expected present value of project =

[0.75 × (2,926,900 + 54,159,688)] + [0.25 × (1,463,450 + 44,650,000)] = 42,814,941 + 11,528,363 = $54,343,304

Expected NPV of project = $54,343,304 — $42,000,000 = $12,343,304

(**Note:** Credit will be given for alternative, relevant approaches to the calculations, comments and suggestions/recommendations.)

				Marks
ACCA marking scheme				
(a)		Risk diversification		2–3
		Purchasing undervalued companies		4–5
			Maximum	7
(b)		1–2 marks per point	Maximum	4
(c)	(i)	Avem Co, current value		1
		Avem Co, free cash flows to equity		1
		Fugae Co, estimate of growth rate		2
		Fugae Co, current value estimate		2
		Combined company, estimated additional value created		2
		Gain to Nahara Co when selling Fugae Co		1
		Gain to Avem Co		1
			Maximum	10
	(ii)	Reka Co asset beta		2
		Project asset beta		1
		Fugae Co's market value of debt		2
		Project's risk adjusted equity beta		1
		Project's risk adjusted cost of equity		1
		Project's risk adjusted cost of capital		1
		Annual PVs of project		1
		Different outcomes PVs (year 1, years 2 to 4, 50% and 40%)		2
		Expected NPV of project before Lumi Co offer		3
		PV of Lumi Co offer		1
		Expected NPV of project with Lumi Co's offer		3
			Maximum	18
	(iii)	Presentation of benefits to each group of equity holders		
		With and without the project		2–3
		Assumptions made		3–4
		Concluding comments		1–2
			Maximum	7
		Note: Maximum 6 marks if no concluding comments given		
		Professional marks		
		Report format		1
		Structure and presentation of the report		3
			Maximum	4
Total				**50**

CORPORATE RECONSTRUCTION AND REORGANISATION

17   BBS STORES *Walk in the footsteps of a top tutor*

Key answer tips

Corporate reconstruction and weighted average cost of capital are commonly tested topics, but this question was very time pressured, with lots of parts to complete in the time.

Notice the efficient way which the answer has dealt with part (a) – laying out the original statement of financial position together with the necessary adjustments helped to show the impact of the unbundling clearly.

Report to Management

From: N Erd, Financial Consultant

(a)   **Impact of Property Unbundling on the Statement of Financial Position and the Reported Earnings per Share**

The unbundling of the buildings component entails a sale value of 50% of the land and buildings and 50% of the assets under construction to yield a sale value of $1,231 million. Under option 1 $360 million would be used to repay the outstanding medium-term loan notes and the balance as reinvestment within the business of $871 million. Option 2 would entail repayment of the loan and a share buyback. The value released would buy back $871 million/$4 = 217.75 million shares with a nominal value of $54.44 million and a charge to reserves of $817 million. The comparative balance sheets under each option are as follows:

Tutorial note

The examiner used the term "balance sheet" rather than "statement of financial position" throughout this question. The terms are interchangeable.

	As at year end 20X8 $m	Sale proceeds $m	Reinvestment option 1 $m	$m	Share buyback option 2 $m	$m	As at year end 20X7 $m
ASSETS							
Non-current assets							
Intangible assets	190			190		190	160
Property, plant and equipment	4,050	−1,231	871	3,690	−1,231	2,819	3,600
Other assets	500			500		500	530
	4,740			4,380		3,509	4,290
Current assets	840	1,231	−1,231	840		840	1,160
Total assets	5,580			5,220		4,349	5,450
EQUITY							
Called up share capital – equity	425			425	−54	371	420
Retained earnings	1,535			1,535	−817	718	980
Total equity	1,960			1,960		1,089	1,400
LIABILITIES							
Current liabilities	1,600			1,600		1,600	2,020
Non-current liabilities							
Borrowings and other financial liabilities	1,130		−360	770	−360	770	1,130
Other liabilities	890			890		890	900
	2,020			1,660		1,660	2,030
Total liabilities	3,620			3,260		3,260	4,050
Total equity and liabilities	5,580			5,220		4,349	5,450

The first option has the effect of reducing the company's book gearing from 36.6% (borrowing and other financial liabilities to total capital employed) to 28.2% with option 1 or increasing it to 41.4% with option 2. The net impact upon the earnings of the business is less straightforward. Under options 1 and 2 the company would benefit from a reduction in interest payable but would be required to pay an open market rent at 8% per annum on the property released. In addition, under option 1, the reduction in gearing would lead to a 30 basis points saving in interest on the variable component of the swap. Under option 1 the company would be able to earn a rate of return of 13% on the funds reinvested. The adjustment to the current earnings to show these effects is as follows:

Earnings for the year

	Current $m	Option 1 $m	Option 2 $m
Earnings for the year	670.00	670.00	670.00
add back interest saved (net of tax) $360 million × 6.2% × 0.65		14.51	14.51
reduction in credit spread on six-year debt $770 million × 0.003 × 0.65		1.50	
deduct additional property rent (net of tax) $1,231 × 8% × 0.65		−64.01	−64.01
add additional return on equity $871 million × 13% × 0.65			74.00
Revised earnings	670.00	696.00	620.50
Number of shares in issue	1,700	1,700	1,484
Revised EPS (c per share)	39.41	40.94	41.81

Given that the company has swapped out its variable rate liability there will be no change in the interest charge to earnings for the six-year debt from the current 5.5% per annum unless the lender has the ability to vary the variable rate on current borrowing for changes in credit rating. Because the fixed rate and the floating rate are the same at 6.2% (given the current credit spread is 70 basis points over LIBOR, or in addition to the swap rate of 5.5%) the nominal value of the company's debt is equal to its current market value.

(b) **Impact of unbundling on the firm's overall cost of finance**

Because the current firm is a combination of both retail and property it is necessary to estimate the asset beta for the retail business alone. Once this is achieved it is then straightforward to estimate the asset beta of a firm with a given element of property removed.

The current equity cost of capital is given as follows:

$E(r_e) = R_F + \beta_i \times ERP$

$E(r_e) = 5\% + 1.824 \times 3\% = 10.47\%$

The current weighted average cost of capital is:

$$WACC = \left[\frac{V_e}{V_e + V_d} \right] k_e + \left[\frac{V_d}{V_e + V_d} \right] k_d (1 - T)$$

$$WACC = \frac{6,800}{6,800 + 1,130} \times 10.47\% + \frac{1,130}{6,800 + 1,130} \times 6.2\% \times 0.65 = 9.56\%$$

To calculate the unbundled cost of equity capital we first ungear the current company beta as follows (assuming debt beta is zero):

$$\beta_a = \left[\frac{V_e}{(V_e + V_d(1 - T))} \beta_e \right]$$

so

$$\beta_a = \left[\frac{6,800}{(6,800 + 1,130(1 - 0.35))} 1.824 \right]$$

$= 1.646$

The retail asset beta can then be calculated from the weighted average of the component betas as:

$$\beta_a = \frac{V_{retail}}{V_{total}}\beta_{retail} + \frac{V_{property}}{V_{total}}\beta_{property}$$

$$1.646 = \frac{4,338}{6,800}\beta_{retail} + \frac{2,462}{6,800} \times 0.625$$

$$\beta_{retail} = \left[1.646 - \frac{2,462}{6,800} \times 0.625 \right] \times \frac{6,800}{4,338} = 2.225$$

However, the beta of the continuing firm will be a combination of this retail beta and the property beta of the remaining firm. On the assumption that the share price does not change under either option the cost of equity capital is estimated as follows:

Option 1

Value of the equity $= 425 \times 4 \times 4 = \$6,800$ million

Asset beta of reconstructed firm

$$\beta_a = \frac{V_{retail}}{V_{total}}\beta_{retail} + \frac{V_{property}}{V_{total}}\beta_{property}$$

$$\beta_a = \frac{5,569}{6,800} \times 2.225 + \frac{1,231}{6,800} \times 0.625 = 1.935$$

Equity beta of reconstructed firm

$$\beta_a = \left[\frac{V_e}{(V_e + V_d(1-T))}\beta_e \right]$$

So $1.935 = \left[\dfrac{6,800}{(6,800 + 770(1-0.35))}\beta_e \right]$

$$\beta_e = 2.0775$$

Cost of equity $= 5\% + 2.0775 \times 3\% = 11.23\%$

Option 2

Value of the equity $= 371 \times 4 \times 4 = \$5,936$ million

Asset beta of reconstructed firm

$$\beta_a = \frac{V_{retail}}{V_{total}}\beta_{retail} + \frac{V_{property}}{V_{total}}\beta_{property}$$

$$\beta_a = \frac{4,705}{5,936} \times 2.225 + \frac{1,231}{5,936} \times 0.625 = 1.893$$

Equity beta of reconstructed firm

$$\beta_a = \left[\frac{V_e}{(V_e + V_d(1-T))}\beta_e \right]$$

So $1.893 = \left[\dfrac{5,936}{(5,936 + 770(1-0.35))}\beta_e \right]$

$$\beta_e = 2.053$$

Cost of equity $= 5\% + 2.053 \times 3\% = 11.16\%$

$$\text{WACC(1)} = \frac{6,800}{(6,800 + 770)} \times 11.23\% + \frac{770}{(6,800 + 770)} \times 5.9\% \times 0.65 = 10.48\%$$

And

$$WACC(2) = \frac{5{,}936}{(5{,}936+770)} \times 11.16\% + \frac{770}{(5{,}936+770)} \times 6.2\% \times 0.65 = 10.34\%$$

Note that under option 1, the variable component of the swap would be reduced by 30 basis points. However, the market value of the debt would remain unchanged because given LIBOR and the fixed component of the swap are the same at 5.5%, the reduction in basis points will reduce the effective coupon and the yield to 5.9%.

Both options will significantly increase the cost of capital for the company from 9.56% to 10.48% in the case of option 1 and 10.34% in the case of option 2.

(c)   **The potential impact upon the value of the firm**

The value of the firm for a low geared business such as this is represented by the present value of the firm's future earnings discounted at the company's cost of capital. The ownership of property does not add value to the business providing that the company can enjoy a continuing and unencumbered use of the asset concerned.

On the assumption that an independent property company can be established and an arm's length rental agreement concluded then it is possible that the ownership of the property assets could be taken off balance sheet. However, the ease with which this can be done depends upon the local accounting regulations and accounting standards.

As it stands option 1 appears to increase the potential earnings more than currently or than option 2. However option 2 offers the highest EPS. With an unbundling exercise such as this it is difficult to predict with precision the likely impact upon the value of the firm. The removal of part of the firm's property portfolio will increase the equity beta but this will be offset by the reduction in the firm's gearing. Much also depends upon the ability of the business to generate a return of 13% on the reinvested proceeds of the property sale. If this is not achieved then a significant loss in shareholder value would result. For this reason the shareholders might prefer the lower risk option of a repurchase of their equity at 400c leaving the firm's EPS largely unchanged.

The analysis of the impact upon the firm's equity cost of capital assumes that the value of the firm's equity at 400c per share will remain unchanged. In practice that is unrealistic and a model of the firm's value would have to be constructed to test the full impact of either option on shareholder value. Given the problem is recursive in that the output value determines the estimation of the equity beta, which is also an input variable in the calculation, computer modelling would be required.

	ACCA marking scheme		
			Marks
(a)	Comparative statement of financial position under the two alternatives (2 each)		4
	Revision of earnings figure for each alternative and calculation of EPS (3 each)		6
	Discussion of the unbundling impact upon the statements of financial position and earnings		3
			___
		Maximum	13
(b)	Estimation of the current cost of equity		1
	Estimation of the current weighted average cost of capital		1
	Ungearing of current beta and estimation of retail beta		2
	Estimation of the cost of equity under each alternative		4
	Estimation of the WACC under each alternative		2
			___
		Maximum	10
(c)	Note on problems of taking property assets off balance sheet		2
	Difficulty of predicting net impact of unbundling on shareholder value		2
	Conclusion		2
			___
			6
(d)	Professional mark	Maximum	3
			___
Total			**32**
			___

Tutorial note (extract from the examiner's comments)

The techniques required to handle this question are straightforward although care was needed in working out the cost of capital and in particular the cost of equity capital if the unbundling proceeds.

Good candidates were able to make the necessary adjustments to the financial statements under either option effectively. However, the substantial majority were not able to do this and lost the opportunity to win a substantial proportion of the marks available.

Common errors in the question were:

- *Incorrect handling of the value released by unbundling and the necessary correction to both the called up share capital and the retained earnings account.*

- *Incorrect or missing calculations of the revised earnings figures taking into account the savings in interest, the impact of the revised property rent and the additional return generated by the new investment under option 1.*

- *Failure to recognise the need to calculate a retail beta for the unbundled business. The firm's current beta consists of both retail and a property beta. The calculation entails the estimation of the firm's current asset beta and the asset beta for the property sector. From this the unbundled asset beta can be estimated.*

In handling a question of this type it is important to work through the stages carefully spending some time on how the process of answering and presenting to the examiner can be simplified.

18   COEDEN CO (DEC 12)

Key answer tips

Weighted average cost of capital is a key syllabus area. Invariably, the calculation of cost of capital will involve degearing and/or regearing given beta factors and using the CAPM equation. It is vital that you have practised the calculations so that you are able to manipulate the beta factors quickly.

(a)   Before implementing the proposal

Cost of equity = 4% + 1.1 × 6% = 10.6%

Cost of debt = 4% + 0.9% = 4.9%

Market value of debt (MV$_d$):

Per $100: $5.2 × 1.049^{-1} + $5.2 × 1.049^{-2} + $105.2 × 1.049^{-3} = $100.82

Total value = $42,000,000 × $100.82/$100 = $42,344,400

Market value of equity (MV$_e$):

As share price is not given, use the free cash flow growth model to estimate this. The question states that the free cash flow to equity model provides a reasonable estimate of the current market value of the company.

Assumption 1: *Estimate growth rate using the rb model. The assumption here is that free cash flows to equity which are retained will be invested to yield at least at the rate of return required by the* company's *shareholders. This is the estimate of how much the free cash* flows *to equity will grow by each year.*

r = 10.6% and b = 0.4, therefore g is estimated at 10.6% × 0.4 = 4.24%

MV$_e$ = 2,600 × 1.0424/(0.106 – 0.0424) approximately = $42,614,000

The proportion of MV$_e$ to MV$_d$ is approximately 50:50

Therefore, cost of capital:

10.6% × 0.5 + 4.9% × 0.5 × 0.8 = 7.3%

After implementing the proposal

Coeden Co, asset beta estimate

1.1 × 0.5/(0.5 + 0.5 × 0.8) = 0.61

Asset beta, hotel services only

Assumption 2: *The question does not provide an asset beta for hotel services only, which is the approximate measure of Coeden* Co's *business risk once the properties are sold. Assume that Coeden* Co's *asset beta is a weighted average of the property companies'* average beta *and hotel services beta.*

Asset beta of hotel services only:

0.61 = Asset beta (hotel services) × 60% + 0.4 × 40% Asset beta (hotel services only) approximately = 0.75

Coeden Co, hotel services only, estimate of equity beta:

MV_e = $42,614,000 (Based on the assumption stated in the question)

MV_d = Per $100: $5.2 \times 1.046^{-1} + $5.2 \times 1.046^{-2} + 105.2×1.046^{-3} = $101.65

Total value = $12,600,000 \times $101.65/$100 = $12,807,900 say $12,808,000

0.75 = equity beta $\times$ 42,614/(42,614 + 12,808 $\times$ 0.8)

0.75 = equity beta $\times$ 0.806

Equity beta = 0.93

Coeden Co, hotel services only, weighted average cost of capital

Cost of equity = 4% + 0.93 $\times$ 6% = 9.6%

Cost of capital = 9.6% $\times$ 0.769 + 4.6% $\times$ 0.231 $\times$ 0.8 = 8.2%

Comment:

	Before proposal implementation	After proposal implementation
Cost of equity	10.6%	9.6%
WACC	7.3%	8.2%

Implementing the proposal would increase the asset beta of Coeden Co because the hotel services industry on its own has a higher business risk than a business which owns its own hotels as well. However, the equity beta and cost of equity both decrease because of the fall in the level of debt and the consequent reduction in the company's financial risk. The company's cost of capital increases because the lower debt level reduces the extent to which the weighted average cost of capital can be reduced due to the lower cost of debt. Hence the board of directors is not correct in assuming that the lower level of debt will reduce the company's cost of capital.

(b)   It is unlikely that the market value of equity would remain unchanged because of the change in the growth rate of free cash flows and sales revenue, and the change in the risk situation due to the changes in the business and financial risks of the new business.

In estimating the asset beta of Coeden Co as offering hotel services only, no account is taken of the changes in business risk due to renting rather than owning the hotels. A revised asset beta may need to be estimated due to changes in the business risk.

The market value of equity is used to estimate the equity beta and the cost of equity of the business after the implementation of the proposal. But the market value of equity is dependent on the cost of equity, which is, in turn, dependent on the equity beta. Therefore, neither the cost of equity nor the market value of equity is independent of each other and they both will change as a result of the change in business strategy.

(c)   **Demerger**

A demerger would involve the company splitting into two (or more) parts, with each part becoming a separate, independent company. The shareholders would then hold shares in each separate, independent company. Each company would most probably have its own separate management team. On the other hand, selling the hotel properties outright would be termed as a divestment, where a company would sell part of its assets.

Benefits

There are a number of possible benefits in pursuing a demerger option for Coeden Co and its shareholders. The management teams would be able to focus on creating value for each company separately, and create a unique financial structure that is suitable for each company. The full value of each company would become apparent as a result. Coeden Co's shareholders may have invested in the company specifically for its risk profile and selling the properties may imbalance their portfolios. With a demerger, the portfolio diversification remains unchanged. Communication may be stronger between the two management teams with a demerger. Since Coeden Co trades heavily on its brand name, the quality and maintenance of the hotel properties is critical, and good communication links will help ensure that these are safeguarded. However, responsibility for maintenance of the properties will need to be negotiated. Selling a lot of properties all at once may flood the market and lower the value that can be obtained for each hotel property.

Drawbacks

A number of possible drawbacks for Coeden Co and its shareholders may occur if it pursues the option to demerge. The demerger may be an expensive process to undertake and may result in a decline in the value of the companies overall. The bond holders may not agree to 70% of the long-term loans to be transferred to a property company and may ask for the terms of the loans to be re-negotiated. The new property company would need to raise the extra finance to pay the cash for the remaining property values. Coeden Co may not have the expertise amongst its management staff to manage a property company or to recruit an appropriate management team. Overall, the main drawbacks revolve around the additional costs that would probably need to be incurred if the demerger option is pursued.

[*Note:* **Credit will be given for alternative, valid points**]

	ACCA marking scheme		
			Marks
(a)	Prior to implementation of proposal		
	Cost of equity		1
	Cost of debt		1
	Market value of debt		2
	Market value of equity		3
	Cost of capital		1
	After implementing the proposal		
	Coeden Co's current asset beta		1
	Asset beta of hotel services business only		2
	Equity beta of hotel services business only		2
	Cost of equity		1
	Cost of capital		1
	Assumptions (1–2 marks per explained assumption, award marks for reasonable alternative assumptions not in the model answer)		2–3
	Comments		2–3
		Maximum	20
(b)	Discussion (1–2 marks per point)		5
(c)	Explanation of a demerger		2–3
	Benefits		2–3
	Drawbacks		2–3
		Maximum	8
Total			**33**

TREASURY AND ADVANCED RISK MANAGEMENT TECHNIQUES

19   SOMAX PLC

Key answer tips

It is important in this question NOT to focus on foreign exchange risk which is largely irrelevant as the loan can be arranged in the same currency in most domestic banking systems and the Euromarkets.

Tutorial note

The rates in this question might seem unusual, but you should answer the question on the basis of the data provided.

(a)   SFr260 million is approximately £110 million. This is a large sum to borrow from an individual bank. The largest domestic Swiss banks could handle individual loans of this size, but it is possible that the loan would be arranged through several Swiss banks, which spreads the default risk between them. Domestic banking systems are normally subject to more regulation and reserve requirements than the Euromarkets, leading to wider spreads between borrowing and lending rates. The cost of borrowing on domestic markets is often slightly more expensive than the Euromarkets, and may involve fixed or floating charges on corporate assets as security for loans. Few Euromarket loans require security. Domestic market loans may be either fixed or floating rate, but bank loans are more likely to be at a floating rate.

If Euromarkets are used the main choices are:

(i)   Eurocurrency loans from the international banking system.

(ii)   The issue of securities direct to the market by Somax.

A five year loan is quite long for the Eurocurrency market, which specialises in short to medium-term loans. Large loans can be raised quickly at little issue cost, often through investment syndicates of banks. However, medium-term to long-term international bank loans may be arranged by individual banks or syndicates of banks. Interest on these types of loan is normally floating rate, at SFr LIBOR plus a percentage dependent upon Somax's credit rating. Draw-down dates are often flexible, but commitment fees may be payable if the full amount of the loan is not drawn down immediately, and early redemption penalties are normal.

An argument in favour of using the banking system, whether domestic or international is that banks are specialists in analysing and monitoring debts. If large loans are agreed by banks this is a sign of good credit standing, and may facilitate access to cheaper funds on other capital markets.

Somax has a number of choices of issuing securities on the Euromarket. The Euronote market involves short to medium-term issue of paper such as Euro-commercial paper and Euro-medium term notes. Banks, for a fee, will arrange such issues and may underwrite their success.

Eurobonds (international bonds) are medium to long-term bonds sold in countries other than the country of the currency in which the issue is denominated. Both the eurobond and euronote market provide the opportunity to borrow either fixed or floating rate finance, depending upon which financial instrument is selected although most bond and note issues are at a fixed coupon. Some eurobonds may be convertible or have warrants attached which can offer attractions to both issuers and investors. A disadvantage of the eurobond market is that issue costs are higher than the eurocurrency market, and it takes longer to arrange a eurobond issue. In addition, only very large companies with a good credit rating are likely to issue bonds successfully in the European market. The main advantage of issuing bonds, notes or commercial paper on the euromarket is that funds may normally be raised at a lower interest cost than borrowing from the domestic or international banking system.

(b) The discount rate should be a weighted average cost of capital, which takes into account the systematic risk of the new investment.

Somax proposes to establish a new production plant in Switzerland. As this involves diversifying into a new industry, the company's existing equity beta is unlikely to reflect the systematic risk of the new investment. The project systematic risk may be estimated using the equity beta of the main Swiss competitor after allowing for differences in capital structure (financial risk) between the two companies.

Ungearing the equity beta of the Swiss competitor (using market values):

$$\beta a = \beta e \; \frac{E}{E + D(1-t)}$$

$$\beta a = 1.5 \; \frac{60}{60 + 40(1 - 0.33)} = 1.037$$

The asset beta must be re-geared to reflect the capital structure of Somax. Using market values:

			£m
Equity:	450 million shares at 376 pence		1,692.00
Debt:	Bank loans (210 – 75)		135.00
	14% bonds (£75 million × 1.195)		89.63
			————
			224.63
			————

$$\beta e = \beta a \; \frac{E + D(1-t)}{E}$$

$$\beta e = 1.037 \; \frac{1,692 + 224.63(1 - 0.33)}{1,692} = 1.129$$

Using CAPM, the cost of equity is:

$$Ke = R_F + (R_M - R_F)\, \beta e$$

$$Ke = 7.75\% + (14.5\% - 7.75\%)\, 1.129 = 15.37\%.$$

Somax is considering the use of two alternative forms of SFr floating rate financing which involved differing interest costs, varying from 5.75% to 6%. Issuing securities on the Euromarket would normally be slightly cheaper than borrowing directly from international banks. It is assumed that the 5.75% rate refers to Euromarket borrowing.

If the interest rate parity theorem holds, the likely UK interest rate can be calculated (using mid rate exchange rates) as:

$$2.2982 = 2.3273 \times \frac{1 + Swiss\ rate}{1 + UKrate}$$

With a Swiss interest rate of 5.75% – 6% per annum, this means a UK rate of approximately 8.25%–8.5% per annum.

Note that gearing levels are not expected to change. Therefore, the estimated weighted average cost of capital is:

$$15.37\% \times \frac{1,692}{1,692 + 224.63} + 8.25\%(1 - 0.33) \frac{224.63}{1,692 + 224.63}$$

= 14.24% or (14.22% using the 8.5% cost of debt)

(c) (i) The proposed swap is based on Somax issuing a five year sterling fixed rate bond. The cost of such a bond is not given, and must be estimated. The best estimate is provided by the yield to redemption of this existing fixed rate bond which has five years to maturity. The existing pre-tax yield to redemption is found by solving the following equation:

$$119.5 = \frac{14}{1 + Kd} + \frac{14}{(1 + Kd)^2} + \frac{14}{(1 + Kd)^3} + \frac{14}{(1 + Kd)^4} + \frac{14}{(1 + Kd)^5} + \frac{100}{(1 + Kd)^5}$$

Tutorial note

The redemption yield is found by trial and error. The coupon rate on the debt is 14%, but the market price is 19.5 above par. For a bond redeemable in five years, this is a large premium, showing that the redemption yield will be a lot lower than the coupon yield of 14%. As a starting point, we can try 14% – (19.5/4)% = about 10%.

By trial and error, using present value and annuity tables:

Year	Item	Cash flow	Discount factor at 10%	PV	Discount factor at 9%	PV
1 – 4	Interest	14.0	3.791	53.07	3.890	54.46
4	Redemption	100.0	0.621	62.10	0.650	65.00
				115.17		119.46
0	Market value	119.5	1.000	(119.50)		(119.50)
				(4.33)		(0.05)

The cost of the five year fixed rate bond is approximately 9%. Somax can borrow directly floating rate SFr at 5.75%, or 0.75% above SFr LIBOR. The Swiss company can borrow fixed rate sterling directly at 10.5%.

Swap transactions:

	Somax	Swiss company
	%	%
Actual borrowing	(9.0)	(SFr LIBOR + 1.5)
Swap payments		
Somax to Swiss company	(SFr LIBOR + 1.0)	SFr LIBOR + 1.0
Swiss company to Somax	9.5	(9.5)
Overall cost with the swap	(SFr LIBOR + 0.5)	(10.00)
Cost of direct borrowing	(SFr LIBOR + 0.75)	(10.50)
Gain compared with direct borrowing	0.25	0.50
Less bank fees	0.20	0.20
Overall gain	0.05	0.30

Note: Somax can borrow at a floating rate of 5.75%, and since LIBOR is currently 5%, this means that it can borrow at LIBOR + 0.75%.

The swap would benefit both parties, although most of the arbitrage gains are enjoyed by the bank and the Swiss company. The actual savings from the swap will slightly differ from the above figures as the SFr is strengthening relative to the pound. Any percentage receipts/payments in pounds will not be as large as the same percentage receipts/payments in Swiss francs. If the Swiss franc continues to strengthen, the overall gain to Somax could be eliminated.

(ii) The **benefits of swaps** include:

–   Access to markets in which it might be impossible to borrow directly because of an inadequate credit rating. This particularly relates to some fixed rate markets.

–   The opportunity to alter the proportion of debt on which fixed and floating rate interest is paid, without physically redeeming debt or issuing new debt.

–   Long-term hedges against both interest rate risk and currency risk. In this case Somax and the Swiss company are protected against currency risk for the full five years of the swap. The main benefit for the bank is the fees from the swap.

The **main risks of swaps** are:

–   Credit risk or default risk if the counterparty to the swaps default.

–   Position risk or market risk. This relates to the gain or loss from movements in interest rates and exchange rates relative to the position if the swap had not been undertaken.

– Spread risk. If a bank temporarily 'warehouses' a swap with two companies, spread risk exists as interest rates may change during this time lag. There may also be a mismatch in the size and desired duration of the swap between companies, which would expose banks to further risk and necessitate the bank arranging offsetting hedges.

20 LAMMER PLC *Walk in the footsteps of a top tutor*

Walkthrough question – key answer tips

Risk management questions like this one can be very time pressured, especially when you are not told which hedging methods to look at. It is important to adopt a systematic approach.

Part (a) is a very typical risk management question. The first job is to identify which transaction(s) will need to be hedged. Five transactions are presented here, but two of them are in sterling (the home currency) so they can immediately be ignored. Furthermore, the other three transactions are all in dollars and they all arise in five months' time, so they can be netted off. As a consequence, only one transaction (a net dollar payment of $1,150,000) needs covering. Had you not spotted this, you could have wasted a lot of time trying to cover all five transactions separately.

The next problem is to identify which hedging methods are available. Forward rates, futures prices and options prices are quoted explicitly, but notice also that you are given interest rates, so you will be able to set up a money market hedge too.

As you go through and present calculations on all these methods, make sure you keep explaining your methods too. The marking key shows that 6 of the 22 marks in Part (a) were awarded for discussion points.

Parts (b) and (c) between them account for one quarter of the total marks on the question. You must therefore make sure that you leave enough time to attempt them properly. Note that both parts are totally unrelated to the calculations in Part (a), so have a go at them even if you have struggled to finish Part (a).

Part (c) in particular contains some very easy marks, arguably the easiest marks on the whole question. If you want to be certain that you'll get the marks in Part (c), answer this part first, before you even start the more detailed work in the other parts of the question.

(a) Report on possible hedging strategies for the foreign exchange exposure in five months' time.

Only relevant net dollar exposures should be hedged. Net dollar imports in five months' time are $1,150,000. This is the amount to be hedged. The transactions in sterling are not exposed and should not be hedged. The exposure may be hedged using the forward foreign exchange market, a money market hedge, currency futures hedge or currency options hedge. A combination of these hedges is also possible, or alternatively a partial hedge may be selected that protects only part of the exposure.

Forward market hedge:

No five-month forward rate is given. The rate may be interpolated from the three-month and one-year rates for buying dollars.

The estimated five-month forward rate is:

$$1.9066 \times \frac{7}{9} + 1.8901 \times \frac{2}{9} = 1.9029$$

Hedging with a forward contact will fix the £ payment at:

$$\frac{\$1,150,000}{1.9029} = £604,341$$

Money market hedge:

In order to protect against any future strengthening of the dollar, Lammer could borrow £ now and convert £ into dollars to ensure that the company is not exposed if there are changes in the $/£ exchange rate.

Borrow £595,373 at 5.5% per annum for five months, total cost £609,017

Convert into dollars at the spot rate of $1.9156/£ to yield $1,140,496

Invest in the USA at 2.0% per annum to yield a total of $1,150,000, which will be used to make payment for the imports.

($1,140,496 × 1.008333 = $1,150,000)

A money market hedge is more expensive than the forward hedge.

Currency futures hedge:

The currency exposure is in five months' time. To protect against the risk of the dollar strengthening, December futures should be sold.

The basis is 1.9156 – 1.8986 = 1.7 cents. This relates to a futures contract maturing in seven months' time.

The expected basis in five months' time is $1.7 \times \frac{1}{7} \times 2 = 0.486$ cents

The expected lock-in futures rate may be estimated by:

1.8986 + 0.00486 = 1.9035

This is slightly more favourable than the forward market rate, but there are a number of possible disadvantages of using currency futures:

(i) Basis risk might exist. The actual basis at the close-out date in five months' time might be different from the expected basis of 0.486 cents.

(ii) Currency futures will involve either underhedging or overhedging as an exact number of contracts for the risk is not available.

$$\frac{\$1,150,000}{1.9035} = £604,150 \quad \frac{£604,150}{£62,500} = 9.67 \, \text{contracts}$$

(iii) Currency futures involve the upfront payment of a margin (security deposit). If daily losses are made on the futures contracts additional margin will need to be provided to keep the futures contracts open.

Currency options hedge:

As dollars need to be purchased, Lammer will need to buy December put options on £.

Exercise price	$	£	No. of contracts
1.8800	1,150,000	611,702	19.57
1.9000	1,150,000	605,263	19.37
1.9200	1,150,000	598,958	19.17

It is assumed that Lammer will underhedge using 19 contracts and will purchase the remaining dollars in the forward market (in reality it would probably wait and use the spot market in five months' time); 19 contracts is £593,750.

Exercise price	$	Premium $	Premium £ at spot	Underhedge $
1.8800	1,116,250	17,575	9,175	33,750
1.9000	1,128,125	25,769	13,452	21,875
1.9200	1,140,000	38,891	20,302	10,000

Worst-case outcomes if the options are exercised:

Exercise price	Basic cost (£)	Premium	Underhedged £ at forward	Total
1.8800	593,750	9,175	17,736	620,661
1.9000	593,750	13,452	11,496	618,698
1.9200	593,750	20,302	5,255	619,307

Tutorial note

This lengthy calculation has shown that the exercise price of 1.9000 is likely to be most attractive to Lammer (it has the lowest overall cost of £618,698. To reduce the amount of time spent on this calculation, you could have identified the cheapest exercise price right at the start as follows:

Exercise Price (A)	Premium($) (B)	(A)–(B)
1.8800	0.0296	1.8504
1.9000	0.0434	1.8566
1.9200	0.0655	1.8545

The (A)–(B) column shows the net amount of $ receivable, after paying the premium, for each £1 covered. The 1.9000 exercise price corresponds to the highest net $ receipt, so is the preferred option. Once you have identified the preferred exercise price, just present calculations for that one to save time

As is normal, the currency options worst-case outcomes are much more expensive than alternative hedges. However, if the dollar weakens relative to the pound, option contracts allow the company to purchase the required dollars in five months' time in the spot market and let the options lapse (or alternatively sell the options to take advantage of any remaining time value). In this situation the dollar would have to weaken to about 1.98/£ before the currency options became more favourable than the forward contract or futures hedge. This is possible, but unlikely, especially as the forward market expects the dollar to strengthen rather than weaken.

Forward contracts or futures contracts appear to be the best form of hedge.

(b)   Estimated effect on value:

	Exchange rate $/£	£ equivalent of $4.2m	£ difference to spot	DF (11%)	PV
Spot	1.9156	2,192,525	–	1	–
1 year	1.8581	2,260,374	67,849	0.901	61,132
2 years	1.8024	2,330,226	137,701	0.812	111,813
3 years	1.7483	2,402,334	209,809	0.731	153,370
4 years	1.6959	2,476,561	284,036	0.659	187,180
5 years	1.6450	2,553,191	360,666	0.593	213,875

                                                                              727,370

The strengthening of the dollar is expected to reduce the present value of cash flows, and, if the market is efficient, the market value of Lammer, by £727,370.

(c)   Economic exposure relates to the change in the value of a company as a result of unexpected changes in exchange rates.

Unless there are known contractual future cash flows it is difficult to hedge economic exposure using options, swaps, or other financial hedges, as the amount of the exposure is unknown.

Economic exposure is normally managed by internationally diversifying activities, and organising activities to allow flexibility to vary the location of production, the supply sources of raw materials and components, and international financing, in response to changes in exchange rates.

To some extent multinational companies may offset economic exposure by arranging natural hedges, for example by borrowing funds in the USA, and then servicing the interest payments and the repayment of principal on the borrowing with cash flows generated by subsidiaries in the USA.

Marketing strategies may also be used to offset the effects of economic exposure. For example, if UK products were to become relatively expensive in the USA due to a fall in the value of the dollar, a UK company might adopt an intensive marketing campaign to create a better brand or quality image for its products.

Tutorial note

To answer part (d) of this question, you need to be able to apply the formula for the standard deviation of returns of a two-asset portfolio, as a measurement of risk of the portfolio. This is given in the formula sheet for the examination. The most efficient portfolio will be the one that gives the highest return and the lowest risk. The expected return of a portfolio is simply the weighted average return of the two assets in the portfolio.

21 CASASOPHIA CO (JUN 11)

Key answer tips

This question covers the three most commonly tested currency hedging methods: forward contracts, futures and traded options. In any hedging question like this you should show how to set up the hedge and then demonstrate what the likely result of the hedge will be.

(a) The information provided enables Casasophia Co to hedge its US$ income using forward contracts, future contracts or option contracts.

Forward contracts

Since it is a dollar receipt, the 1.3623 rate will be used.

Locked in receipt = US$20,000,000/1.3623 = €14,681,054

The hedge fixes the rate at 1.3623 and is legally binding.

Futures Contracts

This hedging strategy needs to show a gain when the Dollar exchange rate depreciates against the Euro and the underlying market shows a loss. Hence, for a US$ receipt, the five-month futures contracts (two-month is too short for the required hedge period) need be bought, that is a long position needs to be adopted. It is assumed that the basis differential will narrow proportionally to the time expired. However, when the contract is closed out before expiry, this may not be the case due to basis risk, and a better or worse outcome may result.

Predicted futures rate = 1.3698 − (1/3 × (1.3698 − 1.3633)) = 1.3676 (when the five-month contract is closed out in four months' time)

Expected receipt = US$20,000,000/1.3676 = €14,624,159

Number of contracts to be bought = €14,624,159/€125,000 = 117 contracts

[OR: Futures lock-in rate may be estimated from the spot and five-month futures rate:

1.3698 − (1/5 × (1.3698 − 1.3618)) = 1.3682

US$20,000,000/1.3682 = €14,617,746

€14,617,746/€125,000 = 116.9 or 117 contracts (a slight over-hedge)]

This is worse than the forward rate. In addition to this, futures contracts require margin payments and are marked-to-market on a daily basis, although any gain is not realised until the contracts are closed out.

Like the forward contracts, futures contracts fix the rate and are legally binding.

Option Contracts

Options have an advantage over forwards and futures because the prices are not fixed and the option buyer can let the option lapse if the rates move favourably. Hence options have an unlimited upside but a limited downside. However, a premium is payable for this benefit.

Casasophia Co would purchase Euro call options to protect itself against a weakening Dollar to the Euro.

Exercise Price: $1.36/€1

€ receipts = 20,000,000/1.36 = 14,705,882 or 117.6 contracts

117 call options purchased

€ receipts = 117 × 125,000 = €14,625,000

Premium payable = 117 × 0.0280 × 125,000 = US$409,500

Premium in € = 409,500/1.3585 = €301,435

Amount not hedged = US$20,000,000 – (117 × €125,000 × 1.36) = US$110,000

Use forwards to hedge amount not hedged = US$110,000/1.3623 = €80,746

Total receipts = 14,625,000 – 301,435 + 80,746 = €14,404,311

Exercise Price: $1.38/€1

€ receipts = 20,000,000/1.38 = 14,492,754 or 115.9 contracts

115 call options purchased

€ receipts = 115 × 125,000 = €14,375,000

Premium payable = 115 × 0.0223 × 125,000 = US$320,563

Premium in € = 320,563/1.3585 = €235,968

Amount not hedged = US$20,000,000 – (115 × €125,000 × 1.38) = US$162,500

Use forwards to hedge amount not hedged = US$162,500/1.3623 = €119,284

Total receipts = 14,375,000 – 235,968 + 119,284 = €14,258,316

Both these hedges are significantly worse than the forward or futures contracts hedges. This is due to the high premiums payable to let the option lapse if the prices move in Casasophia Co's favour. With futures and forwards, Casasophia Co cannot take advantage of the Dollar strengthening against the Euro. However, this needs to be significant before the cost of the premium is covered.

Conclusion

It is recommended that Casasophia Co use the forward markets to hedge against the Dollar depreciating in four months time against the Euro in order to maximise receipts. However, Casasophia Co needs to be aware that forward contracts are not traded on a formal exchange and therefore default risk exists. And the exchange rate is fixed once the contract is agreed.

(b)   Amount expected from US$ receipts is €14,681,054 assuming that forward contracts used.

Invested for two months = €14,681,054 × (1 + (60/360 × 0.0180)) = €14,725,097 say €14,725,000 approximately.

Expected spot rate (E(s)) in 12 months (using purchasing power parity) =

E(s) = 116 × 1.097/1.012 = 125.7

Expected spot rate in 6 months

116 + (125.7 – 116)/2 = 120.9

Investment amount required = MShs 2,640,000,000/120.9 = €21.84m

Loan finance required = 21.84 − 14.73 = €7.11m

Casasophia Co will need to raise just over €7 million in loans in addition to the receipts from the USA to finance the project in Mazabia. This is on the assumption that the future spot rate follows the purchasing power parity conditions.

Tutorial note

Casasophia Co could also consider whether it may be more beneficial to transfer funds directly from the USA to Mazabia instead of converting them into Euros first. This would save transaction costs of converting first into Euros and then into MShs, and also the costs related to using the forward markets. The rates for investing the funds in the USA for two months and the exchange rate between US$ and MShs are not given, but if these were available a comparative analysis could be conducted. In these circumstances the amount of loan finance required would possibly be lower.

(c)   Calculate expected forward rates

Interest Rate Parity

Year	Forward rate [MShs/1€]
½ year	128 × 1.108/1.022 = 138.77
	128 + (138.77 − 128)/2 = 133.4
1.5 years	133.4 × 1.108/1.022 = 144.6
2.5 years	144.6 × 1.108/1.022 = 156.8
3.5 years	156.8 × 1.108/1.022 = 170.0

Present Value calculations (Present values in six months)

	Year 1	Year 2	Year 3	Total
Income (MShs, million)	1,500	1,500	1,500	
Income (€ million, based on forward rates)	10.37	9.57	8.82	
Discounted Income (€ million at 12%)	9.26	7.63	6.28	23.17

Net present value = €23.17m − €21.84m = €1.33m

The calculation of the forward rates based on the interest rate parity indicates that the MShs rates are depreciating against the Euro because the Mazabia base rates at 10.8% are higher than the European country's local base rates at 2.2%. However, even where the forward rates are fixed, based on interest rate parity, the project is worthwhile for Casasophia Co.

According to the purchasing power parity, future spot currency rates will change in proportion to the inflation level differentials between two countries. Hence if Mazabia's inflation level is higher than the European Union, its currency will depreciate against the Euro.

Given that the inflation level in Mazabia is expected to range from 5% to 15% over the next few years, there is uncertainty over the NPV of the project in Euros if the swap is not accepted. The swap fixes the future exchange rates, although Casasophia Co will lose out if the inflation rate is lower than 9.7%, since the future spot rate will depreciate by less than what is predicted by the forward rates. The situation will be opposite if the level of inflation is higher than 9.7%.

Casasophia Co will also need to consider the risk of default by the local bank. Casasophia Co may ask Mazabia's government to act as guarantor to reduce this risk. Overall, if such an agreement could be reached, it would probably be beneficial to agree to the swap to ensure a certain level of income.

Casasophia Co may also want to explore whether it is possible for the grant funding from the European Union being paid to it directly, to reduce its exposure to the likely depreciation of MShs.

ACCA marking scheme			
			Marks
(a)	Forward contract calculation		1
	Forward contract comment		1
	Futures contracts calculations		3
	Futures contracts comments		2–3
	Option contracts calculations		4
	Option contracts comments		2–3
	Conclusion		1
			___
		Maximum	15
			___
(b)	Income from US$ after six months		1
	Expected spot rate in six months		2
	Investment amount required		1
	Loan finance required		1
	Comments		1
			___
		Maximum	5
			___
(c)	Estimates of forward rates		3
	Estimates of present values and net present value in Euros		3
	Discussion		4–5
			___
		Maximum	10
			___
Total			**30**
			___

22   CMC CO (JUN 14)

Key answer tips

All the Section A questions are very time pressured, with lots of parts to complete in the time.

It is therefore critically important to attempt the easier parts of the question first and leave the more difficult parts until the end.

As part of your reading time, try to pick out the easier parts of the Section A question, so that you don't waste time trying to prioritise during the 3 hours of the exam.

(a)   The foreign exchange exposure of the dollar payment due in four months can be hedged using the following derivative products:

Forward rate offered by Pecunia Bank

Exchange-traded futures contracts; and

Exchange-traded options contracts

Using the forward rate

Payment in Swiss Francs = US$5,060,000/1.0677 = CHF4,739,159

Using futures contract

Since a dollar payment needs to be made in four months' time, CMC Co needs to hedge against Swiss Francs weakening.

Hence, the company should go short and the six-month futures contract is undertaken. It is assumed that the basis differential will narrow in proportion to time.

Predicted futures rate = 1.0647 + [(1.0659 – 1.0647) × 1/3] = 1.0651

[Alternatively, can predict futures rate based on spot rate: 1.0635 + [(1.0659 – 1.0635) × 4/6] = 1.0651]

Expected payment = US$5,060,000/1.0651 = CHF4,750,728

No. of contracts sold = CHF4,750,728/CHF125,000 = approx. 38 contracts

Using options contracts

Since a dollar payment needs to be made in four months' time, CMC Co needs to hedge against Swiss Francs weakening.

Hence, the company should purchase six-month put options.

Exercise price US$1.06/CHF1

Payment = US$5,060,000/1.06 = CHF4,773,585

Buy 4,773,585/125,000 = 38.19 put contracts, say 38 contracts

CHF payment = CHF4,750,000

Premium payable = 38 × 125,000 × 0.0216 = US$102,600

In CHF = 102,600/1.0635 = CHF96,474

Amount not hedged = US$5,060,000 – (38 × 125,000 × 1.06) = US$25,000

Use forward contracts to hedge this = US$25,000/1.0677 = CHF23,415

Total payment = CHF4,750,000 + CHF96,474 + CHF23,415 = CHF4,869,889

Exercise price US$1.07/CHF1

Payment = US$5,060,000/1.07 = CHF4,728,972

Buy 4,728,972/125,000 = 37.83 put contracts, say 38 contracts (but this is an over-hedge)

CHF payment = CHF4,750,000

Premium payable = 38 × 125,000 × 0.0263 = US$124,925

In CHF = 124,925/1.0635 = CHF117,466

Amount over-hedged = US$5,060,000 − (38 × 125,000 × 1.07) = US$22,500

Using forward contracts to show benefit of this = US$22,500/1.0677 = CHF21,073

Total payment = CHF4,750,000 + CHF117,466 − CHF21,073 = CHF4,846,393

Advice

Forward contracts minimise the payment and option contracts would maximise the payment, with the payment arising from the futures contracts in between these two. With the option contracts, the exercise price of US$1.07/CHF1 gives the lower cost. Although transaction costs are ignored, it should be noted that with exchange-traded futures contracts, margins are required and the contracts are marked-to-market daily.

It would therefore seem that the futures contracts and the option contract with an exercise price of US$1.06/CHF1 should be rejected. The choice between forward contracts and the 1.07 options depends on CMC Co's attitude to risk. The forward rate is binding, whereas option contracts give the company the choice to let the option contract lapse if the CHF strengthens against the US$. Observing the rates of inflation between the two countries and the exchange-traded derivatives this is likely to be the case, but it is not definite. Moreover, the option rates need to move in favour considerably before the option is beneficial to CMC Co, due to the high premium payable.

It would therefore seem that forward markets should be selected to minimise the amount of payment, but CMC Co should also bear in mind that the risk of default is higher with forward contracts compared with exchange-traded contracts.

(b)

	CMC Co	Counterparty	Interest rate differential
Fixed rate	2.2%	3.8%	1.6%
Floating rate	Yield rate + 0.4%	Yield rate + 0.8%	0.4%

CMC Co has a comparative advantage in borrowing at the fixed rate and the counterparty has a comparative advantage in borrowing at the floating rate. Total possible benefit before Pecunia Bank's fee is 1.2%, which if shared equally results in a benefit of 0.6% each, for both CMC Co and the counterparty.

	CMC Co	Counterparty
CMC Co borrows at	2.2%	
Counterparty borrows at		Yield rate + 0.8%
Advantage	60 basis points	60 basis points
Net result	Yield rate − 0.2%	3.2%

SWAP

Counterparty receives		Yield rate

CMC Co pays	Yield rate	
Counterparty pays		2.4%
CMC Co receives	2.4%	

After paying the 20 basis point fee, CMC Co will effectively pay interest at the yield curve rate and benefit by 40 basis points or 0.4%, and the counterparty will pay interest at 3.4% and benefit by 40 basis points or 0.4% as well.

[**Note:** Full marks will be given where the question is answered by estimating the arbitrage gain of 1.2% and deducting the fees of 0.4%, without constructing the above table.]

(c) Annuity factor, 4 years, 2% = 3.808

Equal annual amounts repayable per year = CHF60,000,000/3.808 = CHF15,756,303

Macaulay duration

15,756,303 × 0.980 × 1 year +

15,756,303 × 0.961 × 2 years +

15,756,303 × 0.942 × 3 years +

15,756,303 × 0.924 × 4 years)/60,000,000

= 2.47 years

Modified duration = 2.47/1.02 = 2.42 years

The equation linking modified duration (D), and the relationship between the change in interest rates (Δi) and change in price or value of a bond or loan (ΔP) is given as follows:

$\Delta P = [-D \times \Delta i \times P]$

(P is the current value of a loan or bond and is a constant)

The size of the modified duration will determine how much the value of a bond or loan will change when there is a change in interest rates. A higher modified duration means that the fluctuations in the value of a bond or loan will be greater, hence the value of 2.42 means that the value of the loan or bond will change by 2.42 times the change in interest rates multiplied by the original value of the bond or loan.

The relationship is only an approximation because duration assumes that the relationship between the change in interest rates and the corresponding change in the value of the bond or loan is linear. In fact, the relationship between interest rates and bond price is in the form of a curve which is convex to the origin (i.e. non-linear). Therefore duration can only provide a reasonable estimation of the change in the value of a bond or loan due to changes in interest rates, when those interest rate changes are small.

(d)   **MEMORANDUM**

From:

To: The Board of Directors, CMC Co

Date: xx/xx/xxxx

Subject: Discussion of the proposal to manage foreign exchange and interest rate exposures, and the proposal to move operations to four branches and consequential agency issues

This memo discusses the proposal of whether or not CMC Co should undertake the management of foreign exchange and interest rate exposure, and the agency issues resulting from the proposal to locate branches internationally and how these issues may be mitigated. Each proposal will be considered in turn.

(i)   **Proposal One: Management of foreign exchange and interest rate exposure**

The non-executive directors are correct if CMC Co is in a situation where markets are perfect and efficient, where information is freely available and where securities are priced correctly. In this circumstance, risk management or hedging would not add value and if shareholders hold well diversified portfolios, unsystematic risk will be largely eliminated. The position against hedging states that in such cases companies would not increase shareholder value by hedging or eliminating risk because there will be no further reduction in unsystematic risk. Furthermore, the cost of reducing any systematic risk will equal or be greater than the benefit derived from such risk reduction. Shareholders would not gain from risk management or hedging; in fact, if the costs exceed the benefits, then hedging may result in a reduction in shareholder value.

Risk management or hedging may result in increasing corporate (and therefore shareholder) value if market imperfections exist, and in these situations, reducing the volatility of a company's earnings will result in higher cash inflows. Proponents of hedging cite three main situations where reduction in volatility or risk may increase cash flows – in situations: where the rate of tax is increasing; where a firm could face significant financial distress costs due to high volatility in earnings; and where stable earnings increases certainty and the ability to plan for the future, thus resulting in stable investment policies by the firm.

Active hedging may also reduce agency costs. For example, unlike shareholders, managers and employees of the company may not hold diversified portfolios. Hedging allows the risks faced by managers and employees to be reduced. Additionally, hedging may allow managers to be less concerned about market movements which are not within their control and instead allow them to focus on business issues over which they can exercise control. This seems to be what the purchasing director is contending. On the other hand, the finance director seems to be more interested in increasing his personal benefits and not necessarily in increasing the value of CMC Co.

A consistent hedging strategy or policy may be used as a signalling tool to reduce the conflict of interest between bondholders and shareholders, and thus reduce restrictive covenants.

It is also suggested that until recently CMC Co had no intention of hedging and communicated this in its annual report. It is likely that shareholders will therefore have created their own risk management policies. A strategic change in the policy may have a negative impact on the shareholders and the clientele impact of this will need to be taken into account.

The case of whether to hedge or not is not clear cut and CMC Co should consider all the above factors and be clear about why it is intending to change its strategy before coming to a conclusion. Any intended change in policy should be communicated to the shareholders. Shareholders can also benefit from risk management because the risk profile of the company may change, resulting in a reduced cost of capital.

(ii) **Proposal Two: International branches, agency issues and their mitigation**

Principal–agent relationships can be observed within an organisation between different stakeholder groups. With the proposed branches located in different countries, the principal–agent relationship will be between the directors and senior management at CMC Co in Switzerland, and the managers of the individual branches. Agency issues can arise where the motivations of the branch managers, who are interested in the performance of their individual branches, diverge from the management at CMC Co headquarters, who are interested in the performance of the whole organisation.

These issues may arise because branch managers are not aware of, or appreciate the importance of, the key factors at corporate level. They may also arise because of differences in cultures and divergent backgrounds.

Mitigation mechanisms involve monitoring, compensation and communication policies. All of these mechanisms need to work in a complementary fashion in order to achieve goal congruence, much like the mechanisms in any principal–agent relationship.

Monitoring policies would involve ensuring that key aims and strategies are agreed between all parties before implementation, and results monitored to ensure adherence with the original agreements. Where there are differences, for example due to external factors, new targets need to be agreed. Where deviations are noticed, these should be communicated quickly.

Compensation packages should ensure that reward is based on achievement of organisational value and therefore there is every incentive for the branch managers to act in the best interests of the corporation as a whole.

Communication should be two-way, in that branch managers should be made fully aware of the organisational objectives, and any changes to these, and how the branch contributes to these, in order to ensure their acceptance of the objectives. Furthermore, the management at CMC Co headquarters should be fully aware of cultural and educational differences in the countries where the branches are to be set up and fully plan for how organisational objectives may nevertheless be achieved within these differences.

(**Note:** Credit will be given for alternative, relevant approaches to the calculations, comments and suggestions/recommendations).

	Marking scheme		*Marks*
(a)	Calculation of payment using the forward rate		1
	Going short on futures and purchasing put options		2
	Predicted futures rate based on basis reduction		1
	Futures: Expected payment and number of contracts		2
	Options calculation using either 1.06 or 1.07 rate		3
	Options calculation using the second rate (or explanation)		2
	Advice (1 to 2 marks per point)		4–5
		Max	15
(b)	Comparative advantage and recognition of benefit as a result		2
	Initial decision to borrow fixed by CMC Co and floating by counterparty		1
	Swap impact		2
	Net benefit after bank charges		1
			6
(c)	Calculation of annual annuity amount		1
	Calculation of Macaulay duration		2
	Calculation of modified duration		1
	Explanation		3
			7
(d)	(i) 2–3 marks per point	Max	9
	(ii) Discussion of the agency issues		3–4
	Discussion of mitigation strategies and policies		4–6
		Max	9
	Professional marks		
	Memorandum format		1
	Structure and presentation of the memorandum		3
			4
Total			**50**

ECONOMIC ENVIRONMENT FOR MULTINATIONALS

23   AVTO

Key answer tips

This question requires analysis of the viability of an overseas investment taking into account all relevant financial and non-financial effects, including possible blockage of remittances from the country.

Appraisal of the proposed investment in Terrania

The investment will be evaluated using both financial and non-financial criteria, including the possible political risk involved with investing in Terrania. However, international direct investment is sometimes undertaken for strategic reasons, which, at least in the short term, might outweigh financial considerations.

(a)   **Financial appraisal**

Projected cash flows:

		Terranian francs (million)				
Year	0	1	2	3	4	5
Sales (W2)		659	735	785	838	
Labour (W3)		228	262	288	317	
Local components (W4)		90	104	114	125	
German components (W5)		41	47	52	57	
Distribution (W6)		20	23	25	28	
Fixed costs (W6)		50	58	63	70	
Total costs		(429)	(494)	(542)	(597)	
Taxable cash flows		230	241	243	241	
Tax on cash flows at 20%		(46)	(48)	(49)	(48)	
Tax saved from depreciation (W7)		29	22	16	12	
Equipment	(580)				150	
Working capital (W8)	(170)	(34)	(31)	(23)	(26)	284
Remittable to the UK	(750)	179	184	187	329	284
Remittable to the UK (W9)	(20.35)	4.13	3.80	3.62	5.96	4.82
Additional 10% UK tax on Terranian cash flow (W10)		(0.20)	(0.27)	(0.31)	(0.33)	
	(20.35)	3.93	3.53	3.31	5.63	4.82
Discount factors at 15% (W11)	1.000	0.870	0.756	0.658	0.572	0.497
Present values	(20.35)	3.42	2.67	2.18	3.22	2.40

Net present value = (£6.46 million)

Workings

(W1) **Exchange rates**

Exchange rates are assumed to change in line with changes in inflation rates, in accordance with the purchasing power parity theory.

Year	0	1	2	3	4	5
Change factor		× (1.20/1.02)	× (1.15/1.03)	× (1.10/1.03)	× (1.10/1.03)	× (1.10/1.03)
T franc/£1	36.85	43.35	48.40	51.69	55.20	58.96
T franc/€1	23.32	27.44	30.63	32.71	34.94	

(W2) **Sales**

Year	1	2	3	4
Sales (units)	50,000	50,000	50,000	50,000
Sales price (€)	€480	€480	€480	€480
Revenue (€m)	24.0	24.0	24.0	24.0
Exchange rate (W1)	27.44	30.63	32.71	34.94
Revenue (T francs m)	659	735	785	838

(W3) **Labour**

Labour cost has been increased by a factor of 1.20 to reflect the use of 300 workers in order to gain use of the rent-free factory. The cost of 50 extra workers in Year 1 is (50/250) × (3,800 T francs × 50,000) = 38 million francs. The annual after-tax costing of renting the factory would be 75 million × (1 – 0.20) = 60 million francs. Avto would select the rent-free factory as the cost is lower.

The cost of 300 workers in Year 1 is (in T francs millions):

(3,800 × 50,000) + 38.0 = 228.

This will rise due to inflation by 15% in Year 2, 10% in Year 3 and 10% in Year 4.

(W4) **Local components**

Cost in Year 1 = 50,000 units × 1,800 T francs = 90 million T francs. This will rise with inflation by 15% in Year 2, 10% in Year 3 and 10% in Year 4.

(W5) **German components**

Cost in Year 1 = 50,000 units × €30 = €1,500,000. This cost will rise with inflation by 3% each year from Year 2 onwards.

Year	1	2	3	4
Cost (€000)	1,500	1,545	1,591	1,639
Exchange rate (W1)	27.44	30.63	32.71	34.94
Cost in T francs (m)	41	47	52	57

(W6) **Distribution costs, fixed costs and feasibility study costs**

The sales and distribution costs in Year 1 will be 50,000 × 400 T francs = 20 million T francs. These costs will rise with inflation, by 15% in Year 2, 10% in Year 3 and 10% in Year 4.

The fixed costs in Year 1 will be 50 million T francs. These costs will rise with inflation, by 15% in Year 2, 10% in Year 3 and 10% in Year 4.

The cost of the feasibility study is irrelevant, because it is a sunk cost.

(W7) **Tax saved from depreciation**

In T francs millions	Year 1	Year 2	Year 3	Year 4
Written down value at start of year	580	435	326	244
Tax-allowable depreciation (25%)	145	109	82	61
Tax saving (20%)	29	22	16	12

(W8) **Working capital**

Working capital is assumed to increase each year in line with inflation in Terrania, and to be released at the end of Year 5.

In TF millions	Year 0	Year 1	Year 2	Year 3	Year 4	Year 5
Working capital requirement	170	204	235	258	284	0
Cash flow in year	(170)	(34)	(31)	(23)	(26)	284

Tutorial note (on the working capital assumption)

The solution here gives the examiner's preferred approach to calculating the working capital cash flows. This assumes that working capital builds up into Year 4 and the investment in working capital is not recovered until Year 5. An alternative approach would be to assume that the working capital is recovered early in Year 5, i.e. at the end of Year 4 rather than at the end of Year 5. If you prefer this assumption, the cash flow in Year 4 would be +258 rather than –26, and there would be no cash flow at all in Year 5.

This alternative solution would have been fully acceptable, but the calculations of the cash flows and project NPV, and the analysis, would then be different.

(W9) **Funds remittable to the UK**

	Year 0	Year 1	Year 2	Year 3	Year 4	Year 5
In TF millions	(750)	179	184	187	329	284
Exchange rate (W1)	36.85	43.35	48.40	51.69	55.20	58.96
In £ millions	(20.35)	4.13	3.80	3.62	5.96	4.82

(W10) **Additional UK tax on Terranian cash flow**

Since a bilateral tax treaty exists between the UK and Terrania, and tax in Terrania is lower than tax in the UK by 10% (30% – 20%), an additional 10% taxation will be levied on Terranian cash flows in the UK.

In T francs millions	Year 1	Year 2	Year 3	Year 4
Taxable cash flows	230	241	243	241
Tax-allowable depreciation (25%)	145	109	82	61
Taxable in Terrania	85	132	161	180
Extra 10% tax	8.5	13.2	16.1	18.0
Exchange rate	43.35	48.40	51.69	55.20
Extra tax in £ millions	£0.20m	£0.27m	£0.31m	£0.33m

(W11) Discount rate, Terranian investment

Cost of capital = 4.5% + 1.5 (11.5 − 4.5)% = 15%.

(W12) Discount rate, UK investment

Cost of capital = 4.5% + 1.1 (11.5 − 4.5)% = 12.2%, say 12%.

(W13) Net cost of closure in Year 0

	£m
Closure costs	(35.0)
Tax saving (30%)	10.5
Proceeds from asset disposals	20.0
Net cash flow	(4.5)

(W14) Net cost of downsizing in Year 0

	£m
Closure costs	(20.0)
Tax saving (30%)	6.0
Proceeds from asset disposals	10.0
Net cash flow	(4.0)

Analysis

The expected NPV is: (£6.46) million. The expected investment in Terrania if viewed alone does not appear to be financially viable. However, the closure or downsizing of UK operations should also be considered.

Closure would have a Year 0 net cost, after tax, of at least £4.5 million (see W13). The cost could be more if the full existing market in the EU cannot be supplied from Terrania, and closure might have other adverse effects on the local community that have not been quantified, and on the government in terms of extra support for redundant workers and their families.

Downsizing would still have some of these effects, but would also offer the opportunity of selling to a larger market that could not otherwise have been supplied from Terrania alone. If the UK operation is downsized, the Year 0 net cost, after tax, of downsizing is £4 million (see W14). Expected annual net cash flows are (£4 million, less tax at 30%) £2.8 million at Year 0 values. Increasing these net cash flows by UK inflation, we can calculate a present value of the cash flows from downsizing, as follows:

In £ millions	Year 0	Year 1	Year 2	Year 3	Year 4
Cash flow	(4.0)	2.86	2.94	3.03	3.12
Discount factor at 12% (W12)	1.000	0.893	0.797	0.712	0.636
Present value of cash flow	(4.0)	2.55	2.34	2.16	1.98

Net present value = £5.03m

The total present value of cash flows from downsizing is £5.03 million over the four-year period. Downsizing results in a much more favourable outcome than total closure. If a period of longer than four years were considered, the expected present value from downsizing would be even larger.

Overall, the investment in Terrania plus downsizing does not appear to be financially viable, with an expected NPV of (£1.43) million (= £5.03m – £6.46m). However, one major problem with the cash flow estimates is the realisable value used for the Terranian assets in Year 4. If the Terranian investment is to continue beyond four years, which is implied in the information provided, then the present value of cash flows beyond four years should be considered, not the realisable value of assets. This present value is likely to be substantially higher. For example, even ignoring growth, the value of the operating cash flows (179 million Terranian francs in Year 4) for an additional 10 years at a discount rate of 15% would be TF 898 million (179 million × 5.019). This is much more than the TF 150 million estimated realisable value of assets used above in the DCF analysis.

(b) **Wider commercial considerations**

Aspects of the cash flows that would need to be investigated further before a decision was made include:

(i) What rent would be payable for the factory after Year 4?

(ii) How accurate are the forecasts of sales, costs, tax rates, etc? Sensitivity analysis or simulation analysis might be used to investigate the effect of changes in key cash flows.

(iii) Will the investment lead to other opportunities (future options)? If so, an attempt should be made to value such options.

(iii) The strategic importance of the investment to the company.

(iv) The political risk of Terrania. The fact that the country has had 12 changes of government in the last 10 years does not necessarily mean that there is substantial political risk. Countries such as Italy have also experienced frequent changes of government. However, the degree of international indebtedness and potential lack of support from the IMF could affect the future prospects of the country. It would be useful to know the ability of Terrania to service its debt, given the problems with the banana crop and competition from neighbouring countries.

(vi) The existence of better opportunities elsewhere. For example, would it be possible to produce the DVD players in neighbouring countries where labour costs are even lower?

(c) **The impact of blocked remittances**

Avto should investigate how likely are further restrictions on remittances from Terrania. If remittance restrictions are introduced, Avto could partially mitigate their effects by investing in the Terranian money market, but the effect of the restrictions would still reduce the present value of expected cash flows by approximately £1.83 million (see below) unless increased direct investment in Terrania was planned. Remittance restrictions might be avoided by increasing transfer prices paid by the foreign subsidiary to the parent company, or by trying to move cash out of Terrania by means of other forms of payment such as royalties, payment for patents, or management fees. It is likely that the Terranian government would try to prevent many of these measures being used.

If remittances were blocked for four years and the funds invested in the Terranian money market:

	Cash flow TF millions		*End of Year 4 value* TF millions
Year 1	179	(× 1.15 × 1.10 × 1.10)	249
Year 2	184	(× 1.10 × 1.10)	223
Year 3	187	(× 1.10)	206
Year 4	329		329
End-of-Year 4 remittable value			1,007
Expected exchange rate, end of Year 4			55.20
£m equivalent at end of Year 4			18.24
Discount factor at 15%			0.572
Present value			**10.43**

The present value of remittable funds (without additional UK tax) if no blockage exists is £12.26 million. The blockage would therefore reduce the expected present value of cash flows by approximately £1.83 million.

Any final decision regarding investment in Terrania must also take into account other non-financial factors such as the nature of the country's legal system, bureaucracy, efficiency of internal processes, cultural and religious differences, and local business practices and ethics.

24 OBERBERG AG

(a) (i) **Organic growth** is internal growth, achieved by expansion of existing business or investment in new projects. An advantage of organic growth is that any investment can be planned exactly to the needs of the organisation. A further advantage is that organic growth tends to be in a related area of business, thus overcoming the risks arising from diversification into non-core areas. (Diversification into non-core areas substantially increases the risk of failure.) Organic growth also avoids the payment of a considerable purchase premium over the existing market price that would often be required with growth through an acquisition. This premium is not always justified by expected savings/ synergies.

(ii) **Acquisitions** have the following potential advantages:

– Growth, market penetration, access to new markets or productive capacity may be achieved at a much quicker rate by buying existing operations.

– High start-up costs are avoided.

– Barriers to entry in an industry or country may be avoided.

– The acquisition may remove an actual or potential competitor from the market.

– The bidder acquires an instant market share, probable expertise of local markets, and an existing 'reputation' of the acquired company. In a foreign country with different language, culture, business practices and accounting, tax and legal systems, such expertise is essential.

– They may offer advantages that do not exist with organic growth. These include possible synergy, asset stripping, acquisition of skilled managers or labour, brands, patents and trademarks, acquisition of 'surplus' cash or tax losses.

The **relative risk of acquisitions and organic growth** is important. This is not always easy to quantify, but an acquisition in a foreign country would normally be less risky than an organic start-up in a foreign country, due to the lack of local knowledge, the lack of recognition in the local market, the non-existence of management control systems at a local level, and so on.

(b) **Report on the possible acquisition of Oberberg AG**

In financial terms, Oberberg should be purchased if the expected **adjusted present value (APV)** of the acquisition is positive, in other words if the present value of the incremental cash flows exceeds the price to be paid. However, it is important that the acquisition fits well with the strategic plans of Intergrand, and strategic issues or other non-financial considerations might outweigh the financial findings.

Discount rate for the operational free cash flows

The free cash flows of Oberberg should be discounted at a rate reflecting the risk of Oberberg. Assuming corporate debt to be virtually risk free, the ungeared ('asset') beta of Oberberg may be estimated using:

$$\beta_a = \left[\frac{V_e}{(V_e + V_d(1-T))} \beta_e \right]$$

V_e, the market value of equity is 150,000 shares × €300 per share = €45 million.

V_d, the market value of debt is (€18 million × 1.230) + €30 million = €52.14 million.

Beta asset = $1.4 \times \dfrac{45}{45 + 52.14(1 - 0.25)}$ = 0.749, say 0.75.

Using the capital asset pricing model, the cost of equity for Oberberg without gearing is therefore:

4% + 0.75 (11% − 4%) = 9.25%.

A cost of capital of 9% will therefore be used as the discount rate for operating cash flows.

Present value of the operational free cash flows

Based upon the data provided by Oberberg's managers, the expected operating cash flows of Oberberg are:

Year	20X3 Year 1 €m	20X4 Year 2 €m	20X5 Year 3 €m	20X6 Year 4 €m
Sales	38.2	41.2	44.0	49.0
Savings from synergies	–	2.0	2.0	2.0
	38.2	43.2	46.0	51.0
Labour	11.0	12.1	13.0	14.1
Materials	8.3	8.7	9.0	9.4
Overheads	3.2	3.2	3.3	3.4
Tax-allowable depreciation	6.3	5.8	5.6	5.2
	28.8	29.8	30.9	32.1

Taxable profit	9.4	13.4	15.1	18.9
Taxation in Germany (25%)	(2.4)	(3.4)	(3.8)	(4.7)
	7.0	10.0	11.3	14.2
Add back depreciation	6.3	5.8	5.6	5.2
Incremental operating working capital	(0.7)	(0.9)	(1.0)	(2.0)
Replacement investment	(4.2)	(4.2)	(4.2)	(4.2)
Operating free cash flows	8.4	10.7	11.7	13.2
Discount factor at 9%	0.917	0.842	0.772	0.708
Present value	7.7	9.0	9.0	9.3

Tutorial notes

(1)   The tax-allowable depreciation is first deducted in order to establish the taxable profits and the tax payable on those profits. The depreciation is then added back because it is not a cash flow. The operating cash flows are therefore profits after tax + depreciation.

(2)   To calculate the present value of the cash flows from Year 5 onwards, which grow by a constant annual percentage amount each year in perpetuity, we can use the dividend growth model formula, which is based on the same arithmetical concept.

Cash flows from 20X6 onwards in perpetuity

Cash flows after 20X6 (Year 5 onwards) are expected to grow at 2% per year. The Year 4 'present value' of these cash flows is:

$$\frac{€13.2m\,(1.02)}{(0.09-0.02)} = €192.3 \text{ million.}$$

Converting this Year 4 'present value' to a Year 0 value, we must discount at the Year 4 discount rate at 9%:

Present value of operational free cash flows from Year 5 in perpetuity = €192.3 million × 0.708 = €136.2 million.

The total present value of operating free cash flows is:

	€m
Year 1	7.7
Year 2	9.0
Year 3	9.0
Year 4	9.3
Years 5 onwards	136.2
	171.2

Present values of other relevant cash flows

Tutorial note

There will be other cash flows arising as a consequence of the decision, and we need to calculate the present value of these, using an appropriate discount rate. These are set out in the table below, and explained in the workings that follow.

	Workings	€ Million
Additional UK taxation	(W1)	(10.5)
Publicity benefit	(W2)	7.0
Lost exports	(W3)	(4.3)
Sale of assets	Assume year 0	8.0
Redundancy cost	Year 0	(5.0)
Investment for expansion	(W4)	(6.8)
Tax relief benefits from debt	(W5)	12.0
		———
Total		0.4
		———

Workings

(W1) **PV of extra taxation in the UK**

As the tax rate in the UK is 5% higher than in Germany, an extra tax liability would arise after acquisition. This extra tax is 5% of the taxable profits calculated earlier. A discount rate of 10%, the cost of Intergrand, will be used to calculate the present value of this tax cost.

Year	20X3	20X4	20X5	20X6
	Year 1	Year 2	Year 3	Year 4
	€m	€m	€m	€m
Taxable profit	9.4	13.4	15.1	18.9
Extra tax (5%)	(0.47)	(0.67)	(0.76)	(0.95)
Discount factor	0.909	0.826	0.751	0.683
Present value of extra tax	(0.43)	(0.55)	(0.57)	(0.65)

Extra tax after 20X6 (Year 5 onwards) is assumed to grow at 2% per year. Using the growth model to calculate the present value of cash flows in perpetuity, when there is a constant annual growth rate, the Year 4 'present value' of these cash flows is:

Based upon the present value to infinity, such cash flows are valued at

$$\frac{€0.95m\,(1.02)}{0.10 - 0.02} = €12.11 \text{ million.}$$

The Year 0 present value of this Year 4 value, discounting at 10%, is:

€12.11 million × 0.683 = €8.27 million.

The total present value of the extra tax payments is:

	€m
Year 1	(0.43)
Year 2	(0.55)
Year 3	(0.57)
Year 4	(0.65)
Years 5 onwards	(8.27)
	(10.47)

This is rounded in the summary table above to €10.5 million.

(W2) **PV of the benefit of extra publicity**

The benefit of extra publicity is €1 million per year, less tax relief (as the cost of advertising to Intergrand would have been net of tax relief). The tax rate is 30% (25% in Germany and 5% in the UK).

Using Intergrand's discount rate of 10%, the present value to infinity of this annual benefit is $\dfrac{€0.7m}{0.10}$ = **€7.0 million**.

(W3) **PV of lost export cash flows**

The investment should be charged with the lost export cash flows. After tax, these are £800,000 × 0.5 × (1 − 0.3) = £280,000 per year.

However, using purchasing power parity theory, sterling is expected to fall in value by $\dfrac{1.04}{1.02}$ = 1.0196 or 1.96% per year against the Euro.

Year	20X3	20X4	20X5	20X6
	Year 1	Year 2	Year 3	Year 4
Euro/£1 (÷ 0.1.0196 each year)	1.594	1.563	1.533	1.504
£280,000 in €	€446,320	€437,640	€429,240	€421,120
Discount factor at 10%	0.909	0.826	0.751	0.683
Present value in €	€405,705	€361,491	€322,359	€287,625

The Year 4 'present value' of the export losses after 20X6 (Year 5 onwards) is approximately $\dfrac{€421,120}{0.10}$ = €4,211,200.

This assumes a constant rate between the Euro and the pound sterling after 20X6, for example as a result of the UK joining the Eurozone.

The Year 0 present value of these export losses is €4,211,200 × 0.683 = €2,876,250.

The total expected PV of lost exports is:

	€
Year 1	405,705
Year 2	361,491
Year 3	322,359
Year 4	287,625
Years 5 onwards	2,876,250
	4,253,430

This will be rounded to €4.3 million.

(W4) **PV of investment for expansion**

The investment for expansion of €9 million in 20X5 (Year 3) is included in the evaluation because its effects have been included in the subsequent cash flows for 20X6 onwards.

The present value of this investment, using Intergrand's discount rate of 10%, is:

€9 million × 0.751 = **€6.8 million**.

(W5) **PV of tax relief from the use of debt**

The analysis has so far ignored the interest costs of Oberberg. This is because interest costs are reflected in the cost of capital/discount rate, not in the cash flows themselves, in DCF analysis. However, in this situation, Intergrand would be acquiring the tax relief on the interest costs of Oberberg's €48 million of debt, and the benefits of this tax relief should be included in the analysis.

Loans are assumed to be available to infinity, being re-financed as necessary. From the 20X2 proforma P&L account, medium- and long-term loans may be estimated to cost approximately 7.1% per year (3.4/48 × 100%).

The PV to infinity of tax relief at a cost of debt of 7.1% is:

$$\frac{€48m \times 0.071 \times 0.25}{0.071} = €12 \text{ million}.$$

This has been discounted at the cost of debt to reflect the risk of debt.

Tutorial note

As tax relief is allowed by the government and is almost certain, it might be argued that the discount rate should be the risk-free rate.

(W6) Cash spent on researching acquisition targets is a sunk cost, and therefore irrelevant to the decision.

The **expected adjusted present value (APV)** of the acquisition is:

	€m
Operating free cash flows	171.2
Other incremental cash flows	0.4
Total APV	**171.6**

However, in order to estimate the price to be paid for Oberberg's shares the value of any outstanding loans should be subtracted. For Oberberg these total €48 million.

The **maximum price to offer for Oberberg's shares** based on estimated cash flows to infinity is €171.6m – €48m = **€122.3 million**.

This is only slightly above the asking price of €115 million, and is subject to a **considerable margin of error**.

Factors that Intergrand should consider prior to making a final decision include:

(i) Cash flows to infinity are used. The present value of cash flows beyond 20X6 constitutes the majority of Oberberg's value. If a shorter time horizon were used, the present values would be much less.

(ii) The results are based on forecasts by the managers of Oberberg. The assumptions behind these forecasts need to be examined to assess the likely validity of the forecasts.

(iii) A single estimate of the APV is of limited value. Sensitivity analysis or simulation analysis should be undertaken to examine the impact of cash flows differing from those projected.

(iv) The data does not take into account any future embedded options that might arise from the purchase of Oberberg. Such options could increase the expected APV.

(v) The risk of the investment might be inaccurately estimated, and this risk could change over time.

(vi) Tax rates and tax allowance rules might alter.

(vii) Intergrand is a UK company that is primarily concerned with cash flows that are available in pounds sterling. If the Euro continues to appreciate in value, the economic value of the investment in sterling might increase, although economic exposure such as this is difficult to quantify. Additionally, it is not known whether or not the UK will join the Eurozone, and if so when this will occur.

(viii) There is no certainty that the lost exports can be diverted to an alternative market.

(ix) There is no information on the size of Intergrand, and how important the acquisition is relative to the total activities of Intergrand. If it is of major importance much more research needs to be undertaken into the proposed acquisition in terms of how integration would occur, including organisational structures, cultures and human resource policies.

(x) Do alternative investments exist that would be a better strategic fit for Intergrand, or have a higher expected NPV/APV?

(xi) Will the two organisations integrate successfully? Are there significant differences in organisational cultures?

(xii) Will key staff of Oberberg stay on after the acquisition?

(xiii) What will be the effect on morale within Oberberg of the redundancies and asset disposals?

(xiv) Would Intergrand need to make any additional investment in Oberberg?

Section 4

ANSWERS TO PRACTICE QUESTIONS – SECTION B

ROLE AND RESPONSIBILITY TOWARDS STAKEHOLDERS

25   TYR INC

Key answer tips

Dividend policy is often tested as a purely discursive topic. However, the examiner is always trying to find new ways of challenging students, so be prepared to incorporate calculations like the ones in this question if necessary.

(a)   Estimates of earnings and dividend per share, and their growth rates are shown below:

	Post-tax earnings per share (cents)	Growth (%)	Dividend per share (cents)	Growth (%)	Inflation (%)
20X1	47.9	–	19.2	–	
20X2	51.3	7.1	20.1	4.7	5
20X3	55.2	7.6	20.9	4.0	4
20X4	55.9	1.3	21.5	2.9	3
20X5	61.9	10.7	22.2	3.3	3
Average annual compound growth		6.6	3.7		

Notes:

1   Earnings per share 20X1 = 86.2/180 = 47.9 cents, and so on for other years.

2   Dividend per share 20X1 = 34.5/180 = 19.2 cents, and so on for other years.

3   Average annual growth in dividends per share = $4\sqrt{\dfrac{22.2}{19.2}} - 1$

= 1.037 − 1

= 0.037 or 3.7%

Current dividend policy

From the above data TYR appears to be following a policy of paying a constant dividend per share, adjusted for the current year's level of inflation.

Success of this policy

The only possible indication from the data of whether or not the dividend policy has been successful is the relative performance of TYR's share price in comparison to the market index. This, however, would rely upon the assumption that the choice of dividend policy influences the share price.

	Stock market all-share index	Growth (%)	Share price (cents)	Growth (%)
20X1	2895	–	360	–
20X2	3300	14.0	410	13.9
20X3	2845	(13.8)	345	(15.9)
20X4	2610	(8.3)	459	33.0
20X5	2305	(11.7)	448	(2.4)
Average annual compound (decline)/ growth		(5.5)		5.6

Notes:

4   Average annual change in all-share index = $\sqrt[4]{\dfrac{2{,}305}{2{,}895}} - 1$

   $= 0.945 - 1$

   $= -0.055$, or an average annual decline of 5.5%.

5   Average annual growth in TYR Inc share price = $\sqrt[4]{\dfrac{448}{360}} - 1$

   $= 1.056 - 1$

   $= 0.056$ or 5.6%.

TYR's share price has increased over the four-year period by an annual compound rate of 5.6%, much better than the average annual decline of 5.5% suffered by the all-share index. This does not prove that the dividend policy has been successful. The share price might be influenced by many other factors, especially the potential long-term cash flow expectations of the shareholders. Additionally, comparison with the all-share index does not measure the performance of TYR relative to companies in its own industry/sector.

(b)   **Additional information** might include:

(i)   Direct feedback from shareholders, especially institutional shareholders, stating whether or not they are happy with the current dividend policy.

(ii)   Full details of the registered shareholders, and size of holdings. TYR Inc might have a desired spread of shareholders, which could be influenced by the dividend policy adopted.

(iii)   Knowledge of the impact of taxation of dividends on shareholders' attitudes, and specifically on their preferences between dividends and capital gains.

(iv)   The amount of capital investment the company wishes to undertake. The use of retained earnings and other internally generated funds avoids issue costs and the information asymmetry problems of external financing. The level of dividends paid affects the amount of internal funds that are available for investment.

(v)   The impact of dividend payments on corporate liquidity.

(vi)   The signals provided by dividend payments about the future financial health of the company. For example, would the fact the dividend growth is lagging behind earnings growth be considered a positive or negative signal?

(c)   Using the Dividend Growth Model, market price $P_o = \dfrac{D_o(1+g)}{(r_e - g)}$

Using the average compound growth of 3.7%:

$$P_o = \frac{D_o(1-g)}{(r_e - g)} = \frac{22.2(1.037)}{0.11 - 0.037} = 315 cents$$

The actual share price at the end of 20X5 appears to be overvalued relative to the dividend growth model.

This does not prove that the actual market price is overvalued. The dividend growth model relies on restrictive assumptions, such as constant growth in dividends per share in perpetuity, which is unlikely to occur. There are also several factors that influence share prices that are not included within the model. Growth in earnings per share has increased more than growth in dividend per share, and it might be better to use the earnings growth rate in the model as this might more accurately reflect the financial health of the company.

(d)   **Bondholders** are concerned that payments of interest and repayments of principal should be made on time and without problems. The willingness of bondholders to provide funds to companies depends on the risks and returns that they face, including the companies' expected cash flows, assets (including available security on assets), and credit ratings for the bonds.

Shareholders, in theory, seek to maximise the value of their shares. This is not necessarily consistent with the interests of bondholders, nor the incentive to maximise the total value of the company (the value of equity plus debt). Shareholders seeking to maximise their wealth might take actions that are detrimental to bondholders. For example, shareholders (normally through their agents, the company's managers) might use the finance provide by bondholders to invest in very risky projects, which change the character of the risk that the bondholders face. If the risky projects are successful, then the rewards flow primarily to the shareholders. If the projects fail then much of the cost of failure will fall on the bondholders. If there are no constraints on shareholders, the shareholders might have a natural incentive to take such risks.

Management, acting on behalf of shareholders, might also reduce the wealth, and/or increase the risk of bondholders by:

(i)   selling off assets of the company

(ii)   paying large dividends

(iii)   borrowing additional funds that rank above existing bonds in terms of prior payment upon liquidation.

The incentive for shareholders to take on risks at bondholders' expense is especially strong when the company is in financial difficulties and in danger of failing. In such circumstances, the shareholders may believe that they have little to lose by undertaking risky projects. In the case of corporate failure, significant 'bankruptcy costs' normally exist. Direct costs of bankruptcy include receivers' and lawyers' fees, while indirect costs might include loss of cash flow prior to failure through loss of sales, worse credit terms, etc. When corporate failure occurs, most of the firm's value will be transferred to its debt holders who ultimately bear most of the bankruptcy costs.

26 FORTHMATE INC AND HERANDER INC

Key answer tips

Free cash flow and free cash flow to equity are two of the examiner's favourite subjects for exam questions. Make sure that you understand the definitions and the link between free cash flow to equity and dividend capacity.

Part (d) is not an excuse to write all you know about Forex management. You must consider the particular circumstances outlined and focus your answer accordingly. Ignore the lack of realism in the forecast inflation rates, and try to answer the question with technical accuracy.

(a)   **Forthmate**

	Payout ratio (%)	Dividends/FCFE (%)
20X1	20.0	42
20X2	20.1	37
20X3	20.0	−151
20X4	20.0	−250
20X5	19.9	78

Forthmate has adopted a policy of paying dividends that are a constant percentage of after-tax earnings. This is not normally recommended as it might lead to fluctuating levels of dividend per share (DPS) if earnings are volatile. If investors seek a minimum cash flow from dividend payments, wide fluctuations would not be welcome. In this case, however, there are only two small reductions in DPS over the period.

The payout ratio of 20% is also relatively low. This might be because investors have a preference for most of their income in the form of capital gains rather than dividends, as the tax treatment of capital gains is more favourable in some countries.

Herander

	Payout ratio (%)	Dividends/FCFE (%)
20X1	60.6	82
20X2	84.4	−118
20X3	56.3	50
20X4	50.7	119
20X5	63.9	167

Herander Inc appears to maintain a constant dividend per share, possibly increasing with inflation. Its payout ratio is much higher than that of Forthmate, perhaps to satisfy its own investment clientele.

Both companies act as if they believe that dividend policy is important to their investors, and potentially their share price, in contrast to the theories of Modigliani and Miller and others.

Both companies appear to relate their dividend policy to earnings. It might be better to link dividend policy to available cash flow.

(b)   Free cash flow to equity is the funds that remain after the company has undertaken all capital investment expenditure, any changes in non-cash working capital and debt issues and redemptions. It is effectively the amount left for investors after the company has met all other needs, and could be paid to shareholders as dividends.

A strategy of paying all of free cash flow as dividends might appear sensible, as the amount being paid is what the company can afford from its annual cash flow.

However, there may be reasons why a company might wish to pay dividends of less than the FCFE.

Payments of less than free cash flow may be because:

(i)   The company has a strategy of increasing cash reserves for a specific purpose, perhaps an acquisition

(ii)   Earnings and cash flows are volatile, and the cash is to be used to smooth out dividends

(iii)   There might be legal constraints such as covenants that prevent the return of cash to shareholders

(iv)   The company wishes to maintain a precautionary cash balance to meet unanticipated needs.

If the dividends to FCFE percentage are more than 100%, the company is paying out more than it can afford from annual cash flows and must be issuing new securities or reducing existing cash balances. It might do this to maintain an existing dividend per share, but as a result it will have to use relatively expensive external financing to meet its investment needs.

(c)   Herander Inc has paid dividends well in excess of its FCFE in the last two years, and has had more potential positive NPV projects than it has undertaken. An implication is that the high dividend payment might be constraining Herander's ability to undertake viable investments that would increase shareholder wealth. The company is likely to be losing value because of its dividend policy.

(d)   The order is not yet definite. If Forthmate Inc wishes to protect against foreign exchange risk at the tender stage, an over the counter option from a commercial bank is suggested. If the tender is not successful the option would not be exercised, and the total cost would be the option premium. An option to sell Kuwait dinar (buy a put option on dinar) could be taken for either:

(i)   the full 18-month period until payment is due

(ii)   the period until the result of the tender is known, and then a further hedge taken for the remainder of the period if the tender is successful. For a short maturity option during the tender period the premium would be low. The further hedge could be another option contract, or a money market hedge involving borrowing Kuwait dinar and converting to $ at the current spot rate. The sum to be borrowed, plus interest at 9% per year, would total the amount of the dinar receipts in 18 months' time. The funds converted to $ at spot would be immediately available in the USA.

Estimates of future exchange rates may be made using either the purchasing power parity theorem (PPP) or interest rate parity (IRP) theorem. Using the purchase price of $, the expected spot rate in 18 months is, according to PPP:

$$\text{Rate in 18 months} = S_o \times \left[\frac{(1+h_c)}{(1+h_b)}\right]^{18/12} = 3.3000 \times \left[\frac{(1.03)}{(1.09)}\right]^{18/12} = 3.0313$$

The $ will weaken against the dinar because of its higher inflation rate.

(This assumes that exchange rates are currently in equilibrium.)

Interest rate differentials between the $ and the dinar are 5% and 5.5% for borrowing and lending rates respectively. These could be used to estimate future spot rate, but evidence suggests that interest rate parity is not as accurate a predictor as purchasing power parity.

Forthmate Inc's normal price would be $350,000 × 1.25 = $437,500.

At spot (using the purchase price of $, because the company will sell its dinar income and buy $ in exchange) this suggests a tender price of 437,500 × 3.3000 = 1,443,750 dinars.

In order to make a competitive tender Forthmate Inc could use the expected spot rate in 18 months' time as the basis for the tender, giving a tender price of:

$350,000 × dinars 3.0313/$1 × 1.25 = 1,326,063 dinars.

Any tender lower than this would involve less than 25% mark-up.

If an option hedge is used, the tender price could be increased by the amount of the option premium. The recommended tender price is not less than 1,326,063 dinars, plus any option premium.

27 SATURN SYSTEMS *Walk in the footsteps of a top tutor*

Walkthrough question – key answer tips

Fully written questions can be daunting for students, but with a good exam technique it is relatively easy to score highly.

The key is to try to pick out as many key words or phrases from the question which you can use as sub-headings to structure your answer. For example, in part (a) of this question, the phrases 'regulatory issues', 'financial issues' and 'ethical issues' can be picked out quite easily. Effectively you have now converted a daunting looking 15 mark requirement into three separate requirements worth perhaps 5 marks each.

When writing your answer, assume that each well explained point you make will score 1 mark. Don't be too brief – to make sure you score a full mark per point, you need to state what the issue is, and briefly explain why it is important.

Tutorial note (extracted from the examiner's comments)

Regulatory regimes with respect to takeovers vary between different jurisdictions and in answering this question the examiners will wish to see evidence that candidates are either (a) aware of the regulations or codes within their own countries or (b) are familiar with the UK's City Code for Takeovers and Mergers.

Memorandum

To: John Moon

From: Conny Date

Potential Bid for Pluto Ltd

The remarks made at the dinner last night whilst general in nature and non-specific about this firm's intentions could be construed as an intention to bid for Pluto Ltd. Below are the principal regulatory, financial and ethical issues we currently face:

Regulatory issues

Most regulatory regimes around the world impose strict rules concerning the release of price sensitive information such as an intention to bid. Furthermore, as directors of a publicly quoted company we are obliged to take all reasonable care that any information we put into the public domain does not mislead investors. Within the UK for example, the City Code stresses the vital importance of absolute secrecy before any announcement is made. The Code places the burden of secrecy upon anybody in possession of confidential information, particularly where the information is price sensitive, and it stresses that they should conduct themselves so as to minimise the risk of any accidental disclosure.

When a target company is a particular subject of rumour, speculation or untoward movement in its share price, and where it is reasonable to assume that the source was the offeror, then the Code stipulates that an announcement of intention should be made.

An announcement that we do not intend to bid, or are withdrawing a bid, normally means that we are restricted from making another bid within a specified time period (normally six months) unless:

–   an offer to be made by us is recommended by the board of Pluto to its shareholders,

–   another offer is made by a third party,

–   a whitewash proposal is made by the board of Pluto or,

–   there is a significant change of circumstances such as the regulator is disposed to waive the requirement.

The underpinning requirement here is that in our public announcements we have a duty to be as clear as possible, not to be seen as creating a false market in the shares of Pluto Ltd and providing all shareholders (both our own and those of Pluto) with equal access to information about our intentions.

Financial issues

The comments made by you might not have been interpreted as significant by the market under different circumstances. However, the 15% price movement strongly suggests that the market now views Pluto as a target and Saturn as one of a number of potential predators. Evidence accumulated on the reaction of the market to information entering the public domain – the so called reaction studies of the semi-strong form of the Efficient Markets Hypothesis – confirms that the market has a powerful ability to anticipate announcements and it is no surprise that the market recognises the potential of the situation with respect to Pluto. The sudden price increase strongly suggests that we are now seen as potential bidders. The problems that we face are three fold: first, we are not yet in a position to announce a formal bid in that we have undertaken neither a due diligence study of Pluto nor have we undertaken a valuation of the company, second the price range over which we can negotiate has now been raised and third, if we withdraw we cannot make a further bid within six months.

The valuation of Pluto will not be straightforward. Our preliminary view is that although the company is part of our supply chain it may not carry our exposure to business risk. We have entered into preliminary discussions with our investment bankers about raising the necessary debt finance. The size of the acquisition means that it is most likely that we will alter both our exposure to business and financial risk. This means that the value of Pluto to us cannot be determined independently of a revaluation of our existing business on the presumption that the acquisition proceeds. The increase in the valuation of Saturn would determine the maximum that we should be willing to pay without impacting adversely upon our own shareholder value.

Ethical issues

One possibility is to deny that we are considering a bid for Pluto. The distinction we need to note here is whether our current investigations could be classed as 'strategic scanning' or we are actively considering this company as a bid target. The major difficulty we have is that Pluto is one of four companies discussed at the May board meeting as a potential target and although that discussion was very speculative investors will be aware that we have consistently sought growth through acquisition rather than organically. Given these circumstances and the commitment of this company to adopt the highest standards of ethical conduct with respect to transparency and the treatment of investors I recommend that we clarify our position.

Recommendation

I therefore recommend that following consultation with the regulator we make an announcement as follows:

Following recent speculation, the Board of Saturn Ltd confirms that it is considering a possible combination with Pluto Ltd. However, the Board has decided not to make an offer at this time. The Board reserves its right to make an offer or take any other action which might otherwise be restricted under the six month rule in the event of (a) an agreement from the Board of Pluto, (b) an announcement by any other party of a possible or actual offer, (c) a whitewash proposal from the board of Pluto Ltd or (d) significant change in circumstances.

Given this announcement we will still have the opportunity to develop a bid proposal and to enter into substantive negotiations with the board of Pluto. However, we will not be able to make a hostile bid in the absence of another company making a bid for Pluto.

	ACCA marking scheme	
		Marks
(a)	Identification of the problems created by Mr Moon's remarks	3
	Significance of the price reaction	3
	The firm's current position and identification of the holding option on the PR	4
	Ethical problems of insider information, fairness to stakeholders, avoidance of dissembling	5
		–––
		15
(b)	Issue of immediate press release	2
	Draft of statement reserving the company's position under six month rule	3
		–––
		5
		–––
Total		**20**
		–––

Tutorial note (extracted from the examiner's comments)

The many good answers to this question recognised the significance of the CEO's remarks and the weak position of the company both in terms of its state of preparation for an announcement and the regulatory implications of the remarks. A small minority of candidates did not recognise that there was a problem with the CEO's comments and spent considerable space discussing ways in which the bid might be defended.

Overall, many candidates performed well on this question providing well written and well argued answers. More attention to the wider implications, and particularly those relating to the ethical issues concerning the transparency and availability of price sensitive information, would have earned greater marks.

28 SOLAR SUPERMARKETS *Walk in the footsteps of a top tutor*

Key answer tips

This is a standard, fully written question. The 3 suggested heading of strategic, financial and ethical issues should have been entirely along the lines of what students were expecting.

The directors of Solar Supermarkets face a number of issues which may reflect a lack of understanding of the consequences:

(i)   The company's more hostile competitive environment with pressure on prices and costs;

(ii)   The need to offer management compensation that will provide an incentive to seek value adding business opportunities;

(iii)   The investor pressure to release the value in property assets with the implied concern that if they do not acquiesce a private equity team may well do the job for them; and

(iv)   The willingness of the firm to support the potential liabilities of a final salary pension scheme for its employees.

In reviewing these issues it is important to bear in mind the overarching duty of the directors which is to maximise the value of the firm and to act in its (i.e. the company's) best interests. Traditionally this concept of duty to the firm has been taken to mean the same as duty to existing shareholders. However, this is neither the legal nor arguably the moral duty of directors. The threat of a private equity acquisition may be real or it may simply be a ploy by institutional investors to liquidate a part of the value of the firm on the assumption that the firm will be able to operate just as effectively without owning its premises. Leaving aside the issue of whether such leases would be financial or operational, the investors do not appear to recognise that the market has valued the firm currently on the basis that its value generation is both retail and property driven. Disinvestment of the property portfolio will simply skew the risk of the business towards retail and given the increasing international competition in the sector this may result in the firm's value falling even if the firm manages to maintain its current levels of profitability and growth. As things stand the investors (and other stakeholders) in Solar Supermarkets benefit from its diversified value generation with the added benefit that management can focus on the difficult job of retailing and leave the property market to look after itself.

Disinvestment of the property portfolio could increase the risk of the business and in this context it is worth reviewing the share option proposal. Currently, senior management and directors are compensated by a mix of salary, perks and profit related bonuses. To this extent there is a degree of risk sharing between owners and managers. The problem with share options schemes is that they tend to increase the risk appetite of managers in that the holder is no longer so concerned about downside risk in the company's performance which is shifted to the writer (effectively the shareholders). However, to the extent that the firm is financed by debt, the shareholders in their turn hold a call option written by the lenders on the underlying assets of the firm and so the lenders are the ones who bear the ultimate risk. The combination of limited liability and equity options in the hands of directors may well create a wholly unacceptable appetite for risk and a willingness to take on new projects that they would otherwise have rejected.

Finally, the move to a money purchase pension scheme may be suggestive of a less than generous approach to the firm's future employees who, in the retail sector, tend to be poorly paid with incomes of shop floor workers close (in the UK and Europe) to the minimum hourly wage. It is safe to assume that the pension fund is principally designed for the various management grades within the firm. The move from a final salary scheme to a money purchase scheme brings benefits in terms of fund management and financing but passes risk to the beneficiaries of the fund particularly in terms of their exposure to future investment returns and annuity rates. The maintenance of the final salary scheme for existing staff will no doubt be welcomed by them but the firm should recognise that it may be more difficult to appoint staff of the same quality as currently at current rates of pay. In so far as the labour market is efficient we would anticipate wage rates to rise to compensate for the reduction of pension benefit and so the gains from this move may well be illusory.

From an ethical perspective, the directors are in the position of attempting to balance the interests of a range of different stakeholders as well as satisfying their own compensation requirements. It is clear that all four options involve the transfer of risk from one stakeholder group to another in ways which are not immediately obvious. The duties of directors in this case can be summarised as ones of transparency, effective communication and integrity in the choices that they make. It is important that the directors should not be seen as taking a more advantageous position with respect to other groups, without their consent, either in terms of the return they take or the risk they bear.

29 INTERNATIONAL ENTERPRISES   *Walk in the footsteps of a top tutor*

Key answer tips

Part (a) was a straightforward requirement asking for a cash flow forecast.

Part (b) focussed on EVA^{TM}, a key performance metric.

(a)   A short form cash flow statement is as follows

	$m
Operating profit	108.8
Add depreciation	28.0
	136.8
Add change in:	
Trade payables	1.1
Trade receivables	3.5
Inventories	0.5
Operating cash flow	141.9
Less interest	−2.3
Less taxation	−25.6
Free cash flow before reinvestment	114.0
CAPEX	−80.0
Dividends	−28.0
Financing	−10.0
Net cash change	−4.0

Tutorial note (extracted from the examiner's comments)

A more detailed analysis of operating cash flow is not required.

(b)   The necessary calculations for this report are as follows:

Cost of equity 20X7 using the capital asset pricing model

$E(R_e) = R_F + \beta_{i,m} \times ERP$

Tutorial note

The examiner regularly uses the abbreviation ERP to stand for 'equity risk premium', or $(r_m\text{-}r_f)$ in the CAPM equation.

$E(R_e) = 3\% + 1.4 \times 5\%$

$E(R_e) = 10\%$

The firm's market gearing ratio is:

Market gearing (20X7) = $\dfrac{45}{45+25\times4\times16.2}$ = 0.027

and the weighted average cost of capital is:

WACC (20X7) = $(1 - 0.027) \times 10\% + 0.027 \times 5\% \times 0.7 = 9.82\%$

On the basis of this the EVA for both years is:

EVA = NOPAT – WACC × Capital employed

Tutorial note

EVA is usually computed as NOPAT less (WACC × Opening Capital Employed). The official ACCA answer has used Closing Capital Employed in the EVA calculation here.

EVA (20X7) = $(102.3 \times 0.7) - 0.0982 \times (179.0 + 45) = \$49.6\,m$

Or 22.1% on capital employed and

EVA (20X8) = $108.8 \times 0.7 - 0.0982 \times (253.9 + 35) = \$47.79\,m$

Or 16.54% of the capital employed in the business

The return on capital employed (defined as profit before interest and tax over capital employed) is:

ROCE (20X7) = (102.3/224=) 45.7%

ROCE (20X8) = (108.8/288.9=) 37.7%

Report to Management

On the basis of the forecast for the next 12 months we estimate that profit before tax should rise from the current level of $102.3 million per annum to $108.8 million an increase of 6.16%. An estimate of the Economic Value Added for 20X7 and 20X8 (projected) shows a small decrease from $49.60 million to $47.79 million which is accounted for by an increase in the expected NOPAT figure from $71.61 million to $76.2 million offset by an increased capital charge incurred by the expected increase in the book value of capital employed and the increase in the firm's cost of capital.

Overall, the EVA return on capital employed is expected to fall from 22.1% to 16.54% and the EVA margin from 22.54% to 18.24%. This deterioration in the EVA figure is attributable to an increase to $36.1 million in the other operating costs of the business and an increase in the equity capital of the firm which on the current projections will not lead to a commensurate increase in the firm's value generation.

It is likely that the market will regard an outcome in line with our projections as a deterioration in the economic performance of the firm and this will inevitably have a negative impact upon both price of the firm's equity and the company's cost of capital. In order to surmount this difficulty the board should consider why the increased capital base of the firm (up by a projected 19.43%) is not being fully reflected in terms of increased revenue, profitability and value generation. Part of the explanation lies in the expected rate of increase of revenue which is expected to grow at a slower rate than the level of capital invested. However there is also an anticipated deterioration in margins (operating profit margin deteriorates from 39% to 37.7%) suggesting that further measures to control costs is necessary.

The underlying difficulty we face is the speed with which new capital is generating returns. This is largely governed by our actual reinvestment. Cash generation is well ahead of our planned rate of reinvestment and servicing of finance. In the medium term we need to review the use of this cash either in terms of new capital projects, acquisitions or repayment of capital.

30   KENGAI CO (DEC 11)

> **Key answer tips**
>
> This question shows how important it is to revise the whole syllabus in preparation for the exam. TBL reporting is a small topic in the syllabus but it was tested in detail here.

(a)   A triple bottom line (TBL) report provides a quantitative summary of a corporation's performance in terms of its economic or financial impact, its impact on environmental quality and its impact on social performance. The principle of TBL reporting is that a corporation's true performance must be measured in terms of a balance between economic (profits), environmental (planet) and social (people) factors; with no one factor growing at the expense of the others.

A corporation's sustainable development is about how these three factors can grow and be combined so that a corporation is building a reputation as being a good citizen. The contention is that a corporation that accommodates the pressures of all the three factors will enhance shareholder value by addressing the needs of its stakeholders.

Whereas TBL reporting is a quantitative summary of the corporation performance in the three factors over a previous time period, say a year, sustainable development tends to be forward looking and qualitative. Therefore TBL provides the measurement tool to assess a corporation's performance against its stated aims.

Each factor can be assessed or measured using a number of proxies. The economic impact can be measured by considering proxies such as operating profits, dependence on imports and the extent to which the local economy is supported by purchasing locally produced goods and services. Social impact can be measured by considering proxies such as working conditions, fair pay, using appropriate labour force (not child labour), ethical investments, and maintenance of appropriate food standards. Environmental impact can be measured by considering proxies such as ecological footprint, emissions to air, water and soil, use of energy and water, investments in renewable resources.

(b) An assessment by the management of a corporation's performance in the three factors – economic, environmental and social, that make up the TBL report will result in an improvement in the financial position, if long-term shareholder value is increased as a result of the report being produced. In this case, the benefits that accrue from the assessment and production of a TBL report must exceed the costs of undertaking the report. It is likely to be the case that the costs of producing the report are relatively easy to measure but the financial benefits may be more difficult to measure and may take place over a longer time period. Some examples of the ways in which Kengai Co may benefit financially are explained below.

Focusing on and reporting the company's environmental and social impact may build and enhance its reputation. Increasing reputation may increase the long-term revenue of Kengai Co. On the other hand, if Kengai Co does not follow (or even try to lead) its competitors in this area then the loss of reputation may damage its revenues stream and lower its corporate value.

Consideration and improvement of working standards and consulting employees as part of this process, when assessing social factors, may help in retaining and attracting high performing, high calibre employees. This will benefit Kengai Co in the long term because of increased employee motivation and performance. Employee involvement may also help reduce the costs related to the company's risk management activity and thus have a direct cost reduction impact.

Improvement of due diligence procedures as part of the economic factor assessment may help limit direct legal costs and indirect costs incurred in maintaining stakeholder relationships. Communication with stakeholders and thus improving the quality of reporting may result in improvements in governance procedures. This in turn would lead to a reduction of the costs related to risk management.

Assessing and improving the environmental factor impact in the TBL report may result in Kengai Co making efforts to reduce its carbon footprint by placing less reliance on exports and developing local expertise in producing the inputs it needs. This may reduce the risk of supplier related problems and alleviate problems related to possible inventory shortfalls. It may also improve Kengai Co's reputation, leading to long-term financial benefits.

Monitoring and reporting on the performance of employees and managers as part of the assessment of economic and social factors may help identify areas where work can be done more effectively and efficiently. It may help managers reconsider business processes and question areas where improvements can be made.

In all the above examples, the result of the assessment required in producing the TBL report and comparing the corporation's progress in relation to its aim of becoming a sustainable organisation will create opportunities which senior managers can develop into financial benefits. The extent to which these opportunities are successfully developed depends on the quality of assessment and the organisation's ability to enable change to happen.

Tutorial note (from the examiner's model answer)

This question can be answered in a variety of ways and the suggested answer is indicative. Credit will be given for reasonable answers considering alternatives or additions to the explanations and discussion given.

ACCA marking scheme		*Marks*
(a)	Explaining TBL and relation to sustainability	4–5
	Examples of proxies (up to 2 marks for proxies per TBL factor)	4–5
	Maximum	8
(b)	Discussion of long-term shareholder wealth maximisation and benefits exceeding costs	2
	2–3 marks per well-discussed example focusing on financial impact	8–9
	Maximum	10
Total		**18**

31   ENNEA CO (JUN 12)

Key answer tips

Notice how this model answer is presented in a very efficient way. The use of columns to show the current position and then the three proposals side by side makes it easy to identify the differences and similarities between the proposals.

(a)   **Forecast financial position**

Amounts in $000	*Current*	*Proposal 1*	*Proposal 2*	*Proposal 3*
Non-current assets	282,000	282,000	302,000	257,000
Current assets	66,000	64,720	67,720	63,682
Total assets	348,000	346,720	369,720	320,682

	Current	Proposal 1	Proposal 2	Proposal 3
Current liabilities	37,000	37,000	37,000	37,000
Non-current liabilities	140,000	160,000	160,000	113,000
Total liabilities	177,000	197,000	197,000	150,000
Share capital (40c/share)	48,000	45,500	48,000	48,000
Retained earnings	123,000	104,220	124,720	122,682
Total equity	171,000	149,720	172,720	170,682
Total liabilities and capital	348,000	346,720	369,720	320,682

Adjustments to forecast earnings

Amounts in $000	Current	Proposal 1	Proposal 2	Proposal 3
Initial profit after tax	26,000	26,000	26,000	26,000
Interest payable on additional borrowing ($20m × 6% × (1 − 0.2))		(960)	(960)	
Additional interest payable on extra coupon ($160m × 0.25% × (1 − 0.2))		(320)	(320)	
Interest saved on less borrowing ($27m × 6% × (1 − 0.2))				1,296
Interest saved on lower coupon ($113m × 0.15% × (1 − 0.2))				136
Return on additional investment ($20m × 15%)			3,000	
Return lost on less investment ($25m × 15%)				(3,750)
Profit on sale of non-current assets				2,000
Adjusted profit after tax	26,000	24,720	27,720	25,682

	Current	Proposal 1	Proposal 2	Proposal 3
Gearing % (non-current liabilities/equity)	81.9%	106.9%	92.6%	66.2%
Number of shares ('000)	120,000	113,750	120,000	120,000
Earnings per share (adjusted profit after tax/number of shares)	21.67c	21.73c	23.10c	21.40c

Note: Gearing defined as non-current liabilities/(non-current liabilities + equity) and/or using market value of equity is acceptable as well.

Tutorial note

Explanations are not required for the answer but are included to explain the approach taken.

Explanations of the financial position based on the three proposals

Proposal 1

Debt is increased by $20m and share capital reduced by the same amount as follows: from par value = $20m × 40c/320c = $2.5m; from retained earnings = $20m × 280c/320c = $17.5m.

Additional interest payable totalling $1,280,000 ($960,000 + $320,000) is taken off retained earnings due to reduction in profit after tax and taken off current assets because presumably it is paid from cash. Note that an alternative answer would be to add the additional interest payable to current liabilities.

Proposal 2

Debt and non-current assets are increased by $20m.

Additional interest payable as above, plus the additional investment of $20 million will generate a rate of return of 15%, which is $3,000,000 income. Net impact is $1,720,000 income which is added to retained earnings as an addition to profit after tax and added to current assets as a cash income (presumably).

Proposal 3

Net non-current assets are reduced by the $25 million, their value at disposal. Since they were sold for $27 million, this is how much the non-current liabilities are reduced by and the profit of $2 million is included in the retained earnings.

Interest saved totals $1,432,000 ($1,296,000 + $136,000). The reduction in investment of $25 million will lose $3,750,000, at a rate of return of 15%. Net impact is $2,318,000 loss which is subtracted from earnings as a reduction from profit after tax and deducted from current assets as a cash expense (presumably).

Discussion

Proposals 1 and 3 appear to produce opposite results to each other. Proposal 1 would lead to a small increase in the earnings per share (EPS) due to a reduction in the number of shares although profits would decrease by approximately 5%, due to the increase in the amount of interest payable as a result of increased borrowings. However, the level of gearing would increase substantially (by about 30%).

With proposal 3, although the overall profits would fall, because of the lost earnings due to downsizing being larger than the gain in interest saved and profit made on the sale of assets, this is less than proposal 1 (1.2%). Gearing would reduce substantially (19.2%).

Proposal 2 would give a significant boost in the EPS from 21.67c/share to 23.10c/share, which the other two proposals do not. This is mainly due to increase in earnings through extra investment. However, the amount of gearing would increase by more than 13%.

verall proposal 1 appears to be the least attractive option. The choice between proposals 2 and 3 would be between whether the company would prefer larger EPS or less gearing. This would depend on factors such as the capital structure of the competitors, the reaction of the equity market to the proposals, the implications of the change in the risk profile of the company and the resultant impact on the cost of capital. Ennea Co should also bear in mind that the above are estimates and the actual results will probably differ from the forecasts.

(**Note:** credit will be given for alternative relevant comments and suggestions)

(b)   Asset securitisation in this case would involve taking the future incomes from the leases that Ennea Co makes and converting them into assets. These assets are sold as bonds now and the future income from lease interest will be used to pay coupons on the bonds. Effectively Ennea Co foregoes the future lease income and receives money from sale of the assets today.

The income from the various leases would be aggregated and pooled, and new securities (bonds) issued based on these. The tangible benefit from securitisation occurs when the pooled assets are divided into tranches and tranches are credit rated. The higher rated tranches would carry less risk and have less return, compared to lower rated tranches. If default occurs, the income of the lower tranches is reduced first, before the impact of increasing defaults move to the higher rated tranches. This allows an asset of low liquidity to be converted into securities which carry higher liquidity.

Ennea Co would face a number of barriers in undertaking such a process. Securitisation is an expensive process due to management costs, legal fees and ongoing administrative costs. The value of assets that Ennea Co wants to sell is small and therefore these costs would take up a significant proportion of the income. High cost implications mean that securitisation is not feasible for small asset pools.

Normally asset pools would not offer the full value of the asset as securities. For example, only 90% of the asset value would be converted into securities, leaving the remaining 10% as a buffer against possible default. This method of credit enhancement would help to credit-rate the tranches at higher levels and help their marketability. However, Ennea Co would not be able to take advantage of the full asset value if it proceeds with the asset securitisation.

(**Note:** credit will be given for alternative relevant comments and suggestions)

ACCA marking scheme		
		Marks
(a)	Financial position calculations: proposal 1	3
	Financial position calculations: proposal 2	2
	Financial position calculations: proposal 3	3
	Adjustments to forecast earnings	
	Interest payable on additional borrowing and higher coupon	2
	Interest saved lower borrowing and lower coupon	1
	Return on additional investment	1
	Return lost on less investment and profit on sale of non-current assets	1
	Gearing and EPS calculations	2
	Discussion of the results of the proposals	2–3
	Discussion of the implications (e.g. risk, market reaction, etc.)	2–3
	Maximum	20
(b)	Explanation of the process	2–3
	Key barriers in undertaking the process	2–3
	Maximum	5
Total		**25**

32   LIMNI CO (JUN 13)

Key answer tips

This was a very wide-ranging question, covering risk management, dividend policy and financing. Use these three subheadings in your answer to make sure that you are addressing all the necessary issues.

(a)   As a high growth company, Limni Co probably requires the cash flows it generates annually for investing in new projects and has therefore not paid any dividends. This is a common practice amongst high-growth companies, many of which declare that they have no intention of paying any dividends. The shareholder clientele in such companies expects to be rewarded by growth in equity value as a result of the investment policy of the company.

Capital structure theory would suggest that because of the benefit of the tax shield on interest payments, companies should have a mix of equity and debt in their capital structure. Furthermore, the pecking order proposition would suggest that companies tend to use internally generated funds before going to markets to raise debt capital initially and finally equity capital. The agency effects of having to provide extra information to the markets and where one investor group benefits at the expense of another have been cited as the main deterrents to companies seeking external sources of finance. To a certain extent, this seems to be the case with Limni Co in using internal finance first, but the pecking order proposition seems to be contradicted in that it seeks to go straight to the equity market and undertake rights issues thereafter. Perhaps the explanation for this can be gained from looking at the balance of business and financial risk. Since Limni Co operates in a rapidly changing industry, it probably faces significant business risk and therefore cannot afford to undertake high financial risk, which a capital structure containing significant levels of debt would entail. This, together with agency costs related to restrictive covenants, may have determined Limni Co's financing policy.

Risk management theory suggests that managing the volatility of cash flows enables a company to plan its investment strategy better. Since Limni Co uses internally generated funds to finance its projects, it needs to be certain that funds will be available when needed for the future projects, and therefore managing its cash flows will enable this. Moreover, because Limni Co faces high business risk, managing the risk that the company's managers cannot control through their actions, may be even more necessary.

The change to making dividend payments or undertaking share buybacks will affect all three policies. The company's clientele may change and this may cause share price fluctuations. However, since the recommendation for the change is being led by the shareholders, significant share price fluctuations may not happen. Limni Co's financing policy may change because having reduced internal funds means it may have to access debt markets and therefore have to look at its balance between business and financial risk. The change to Limni Co's financial structure may result in a change in its risk management policy, because it may be necessary to manage interest rate risk as well.

(Note: Credit will be given for alternative relevant comments)

(b) In the case of company Theta, dividends are growing but not at a stable rate. In fact company Theta is paying out $0.40 in dividends for every $1 in earnings, and has a fixed dividend cover ratio of 2.50. This would be confusing for the shareholders, as they would not know how much dividend they would receive from year to year. Although profits have risen over the past five years, if profits do fall, company Theta may reduce dividends and therefore send the wrong signals to shareholders and investors. This may cause unnecessary fluctuations of the share price or result in a depressed share price.

In the case of company Omega, annual dividends are growing at a stable rate of approximately 5% per year, while the company's earnings are growing steadily at around 3% per year, resulting in an increasing payout ratio. Also a high proportion of earnings are paid out as dividends, increasing from 60% in 20W9 to almost 65% in 20X3. This would indicate a company operating in a mature industry, signalling that there are few new projects to invest in and therefore reducing the retention rate. Such an investment would be attractive to investors requiring high levels of dividend returns from their investments.

In the case of company Kappa, although a lower proportion of earnings is paid out as dividends (from about 20% in 20W9 to about 27% in 20X3), they are growing at a higher but stable rate of 29%–30% per year. The company's earnings are growing rapidly but erratically, ranging between 3% and 35% between 20W9 and 20X3. This probably indicates a growing company, possibly similar to Limni Co itself, where perhaps returns to investors having been coming from share price growth, but one where dividends are becoming more prominent. Such an investment would be attractive to investors requiring lower levels of dividend returns, but higher capital returns from their investments.

Due to company Theta's confusing dividend policy, which may lead to erratic dividend payouts and a depressed share price, Limni Co would probably not want to invest in that company. The choice between company Omega and company Kappa would depend on how Limni Co wants to receive its return from the investment, maybe taking into account factors such as taxation implications, and the period of time it wishes to invest for, in terms of when the returns from an investment will be maximised and when it will need the funds for future projects.

(Note: Credit will be given for alternative relevant comments)

(c) **Limni Co, current dividend capacity**

	$000
Profit before tax (23% × $600,000,000)	138,000
Tax (26% × $138,000,000)	(35,880)
Profit after tax	102,120
Add back depreciation (25% × $220,000,000)	55,000
Less investment in assets	(67,000)
Remittances from overseas subsidiaries	15,000
Additional tax on remittances (6% × $15,000,000)	(900)
Dividend capacity	104,220

Increase in dividend capacity = 10% × $104,220,000 = $10,422,000

Gross up for tax = $10,422,000/0.94 = $11,087,234

Percentage increase in remittances from overseas subsidiaries = 73.9% [$11,087,234/$15,000,000]

Dividend repatriations need to increase by 73.9% from Limni Co's international subsidiaries in order to increase the dividend capacity by 10%. Limni Co would need to consider whether or not it is feasible for its subsidiaries to increase their repatriations to such an extent, and the impact this will have on the motivation of the subsidiaries' managers and on the subsidiaries' ability to operate as normal.

(d)   The main benefit of a share buyback scheme to investors is that it helps to control transaction costs and manage tax liabilities. With the share buyback scheme, the shareholders can choose whether or not to sell their shares back to the company. In this way they can manage the amount of cash they receive. On the other hand, with dividend payments, and especially large special dividends, this choice is lost, and may result in a high tax bill. If the shareholder chooses to re-invest the funds, it will result in transaction costs. An added benefit is that, as the share capital is reduced, the earnings per share and the share price may increase. Finally, share buybacks are normally viewed as positive signals by markets and may result in an even higher share price.

(Note: Credit will be given for alternative relevant comments)

ACCA marking scheme			Marks
(a)	Discussion of dividend policy		1–2
	Discussion of financing policy		3–4
	Discussion of risk management policy		1–2
	Effect of dividends and share buybacks on the policies		2–3
		Maximum	8
(b)	2 marks per evaluation of each of the three companies		6
	Discussion of which company to invest in		2
		Maximum	8
(c)	Calculation of initial dividend capacity		3
	Calculation of new repatriation amount		2
	Comment		1–2
		Maximum	6
(d)	1 mark per relevant point		3
Total			**25**

33 KAMALA CO (DEC 14)

Key answer tips

Remember that EVA™ measures the amount of shareholder wealth generated in a period. Therefore, if possible, you should always try to adjust any given profit figures so that they show the cash impact. Hence in this question it was important to adjust for the economic value of depreciation.

(a)   **Advantages of EVA™**

The cost of capital indicates the minimum value which is required by the investors of a company and therefore any positive economic profit greater than the cost of capital times the capital employed should result in an increase in value for the investors. If the debt holders are paid a fixed return, then all the additional value created will go to the shareholders. EVA™ focuses on creating shareholder value.

Capital is needed for investment purposes to create value and EVA™ recognises this when it takes into account the capital employed.

EVA™ captures performance into a single figure, which if positive should increase shareholder value. Ratios on the other hand may require various different targets to be set.

EVA™ is based on the residual income value principle and therefore it is relatively easy to understand. An EVA™ trend would give an indication of how the company is creating value over a number of years.

Drawbacks of EVA™

EVA™ is an annual measure and therefore it is relatively easy to manipulate. Short-term projects with early redemption but low yields may be chosen to the detriment of longer term, high yield projects which may not show immediate high returns. Focusing on annual EVA™ figures may make the company's managers adopt a short-term attitude and this may be to the detriment of the company's long-term success. Paying attention to EVA™ trends instead may reduce or eliminate this drawback.

Furthermore, EVA™ is an absolute measure, making comparison between companies in different industrial sectors more difficult.

(b)   **EVA™ calculation: Kamala Co**

	30 November 2013 $m	30 November 2014 $m
Operating profit	819	1,098
Add: Depreciation	826	1,150
Less: Economic depreciation	(990)	(1,380)
Add: Non-cash expenses	150	170
Taxation excluding finance costs: 2013: 25% × $819m and 2014 25% × $1,098m	(205)	(275)
Economic profit	600	763

Capital employed: 2013: $1,484m + $2,226m;

2014: $2,184m + $2,577m + $616m	3,710	5,377
10% × capital employed	371	538
EVA™	229	225

(b) **Additional ratio trends: Kamala Co**

	2012	2013	2014	
Return on capital employed	19.2%	17.2%	16.7%	Operating profit/cap employed
Asset turnover	1.01	0.85	0.79	Sales revenue/cap employed
Current ratio	0.80	0.65	0.63	Current assets/current liabilities
Current ratio without bank overdraft (o/d)	0.80	0.92	0.93	(Current assets – bank o/d)/current liabilities
Gearing with bank o/d	40%	52%	60%	(NCL + bank o/d)/(equity + NCL + bank c/d)
Kamala Co PE ratio	11.0:1	12.3:1	13.0:1	Share price/earnings per share
Kamala Co dividend yield	2.7%	2.3%	1.9%	Dividend per share/share price

Activity trends

	Construction	Hospitals and biomedical
	%	%
Profit margin		
2012	19.0%	19.0%
2013	18.5%	23.4%
2014	18.9%	25.8%
Average annual growth: Sales revenue	23.0%	8.2%
Average annual growth: Operating profit	22.7%	26.3%

Share price and indices analysis

	%
Kamala Co: Average annual share price growth	26.2
Market index: Average annual growth	20.1
Industry index: Average annual growth	30.1

Evaluation

A number of ratios and the EVA™ figures support the CEO's assertions. The EVA™ shows that positive value is created in both years and these lend support to the increase in the share price, and this increase in the share price (26.2% annually over the last two years) has grown more rapidly than the market index (20.1% annually over the same period). There is a steady growth in the sales revenue, profit margin, earnings per share and dividend cover, together with significant investment in non-current assets, which seems to indicate a successful company. If the bank overdraft is not included, the current ratio has been improving as well.

On the other hand, there are a number of indicators which suggest that perhaps Kamala Co's investment strategy may be flawed. Even though the economic profit between 2013 and 2014 has increased, the EVA^{TM} in 2014 is less than the EVA^{TM} in 2013. This is because there has been a substantial investment in non-current assets. This is also evidenced by a decline in the asset turnover ratio. Less sales revenue is being generated for every $ invested, leading to a decline in the return on capital employed, even though there has been a small increase in the profit margin in the three-year period.

It may be that Kamala Co is making substantial investment now for deferred benefits in the future, but the markets do not seem to be convinced. In 2012, Kamala Co's price to earnings (PE) ratio was greater than the industry sector's average PE ratio (11.0 against 9.2), but by 2014 it was lower (13.0 against 15.3). The share price growth has also been lower at 26.2% on average annually, compared to the industry's index growth of 30.1% on average annually. Furthermore, the fall in dividend yield between 2012 and 2014 from 2.7% to 1.9% may not be viewed positively by equity holders, possibly leading to a less robust share price growth.

It seems that Kamala Co is making substantial investments in its construction activity (23% annual sales revenue growth) but significantly less in the hospitals and biomedical activity (8.2% annual sales revenue growth). However, the profit margin of the hospitals and biomedical research activity has grown faster, from 19% to 25.8%, compared to the construction activity, which has remained static at between 18.5% and 19%. The markets seemed to have viewed this in a less positive light, especially since the CEO stated that the company wanted to make further investment in an acquisition in the construction activity in 2015.

The financing strategy of Kamala Co is also problematic. There seems to be a higher reliance on debt as a finance source, with no fresh issues of equity between 2012 and 2014. Book value gearing has increased from 40% to 54% from 2012 to 2014. If the overdraft is added to gearing, based on the assumption that it is being used as a long-term source of finance, then the increase is even more pronounced, increasing from 40% to 60% in the same period. It seems that Kamala Co is continuing to carry on with this policy in the future as well, because it wants to acquire a new company using mostly debt finance, by issuing a new bond, with only a small rights issue. This may lead to an increase in financial risk, putting further pressure on the share price.

In conclusion, Kamala Co has been pursuing growth through debt finance. This may increase its financial risk but it is difficult to say for sure. If the industry's norm is to have higher debt levels, then the financial strategy may be acceptable. However, the investment strategy looks to be flawed. The company seems to be pursuing growth in the lower profit margin activity area. This may have led to the share price not increasing at the same rate as the industry sector as a whole. The investment strategy warrants a re-assessment.

(**Note:** credit will be given for alternative relevant comments for parts (a) and (c).)

	ACCA marking scheme		
			Marks
(a)	Advantages of EVA^{TM} (1–2 marks per point)		3–4
	Drawbacks of EVA^{TM} (1–2 marks per point)		2–3
			—
		Maximum	6
			—
(b)	For 2013 and 2014		
	Add depreciation and deduct economic depreciation to operating profit		1
	Adding back non-cash expenses		1
	Calculation of economic profit after tax		1
	EVA^{TM} calculations		2
			—
		Maximum	5
			—
(c)	Additional ratio trends (1 mark per key three-year ratio trend)		4–5
	Activity trends		2–3
	Analysis of the share price against market and industry indices		1–2
	Discussion of investment strategy including impact on share price, EVA^{TM} and PE ratios		3–4
	Discussion of financing strategy		1–2
	Other discussion points		1–2
	Concluding comments		1–2
			—
		Maximum	14
			—
	Note: Maximum 13 marks if no conclusion provided		
			—
Total			**25**
			—

ADVANCED INVESTMENT APPRAISAL

34   STRAYER PLC *Walk in the footsteps of a top tutor*

> ### Walkthrough question – key answer tips
>
> This is an excellent APV question, which covers all the examiner's favourite tricks in this syllabus area.
>
> Before you start by attempting the numbers in part (a), notice that the discussion in parts (b) and (c) is general bookwork which does not depend on the calculations. A good approach might be to do parts (b) and (c) first – as long as you label things clearly in your answer book, this will not cause a problem for the marker, but it will enable you to pick up the easy marks in the question.
>
> When you attempt the numbers, lay your answer out clearly so that the marker can understand your workings. APV is a topic which is easy to confuse!
>
> Start by identifying project cashflows – ignore any financing information for now. When you have picked up all the project cashflows (don't forget the tax impact), you need to discount them using an ungeared cost of equity. This is not given directly, but the method of degearing the industry equity beta and then using CAPM is extremely commonly tested, so make sure you are happy with that.
>
> Next, move on to the financing costs and benefits. The main benefit is the tax relief to be received on the debt interest, but don't forget to include the value of the subsidised loan too. In order to work out the present value of these costs and benefits, use the risk free rate (5.5%), or the pre-tax cost of debt (8%) as a discount rate. In theory, since APV was developed from the theories of Modigliani and Miller, the risk free rate and the pre-tax cost of debt should be one and the same thing, but if they aren't in a question, you will get credit for using either figure as a discount rate.

(a)   **Step 1: Base case NPV**

Assuming the risk of companies in the printing industry is similar to that of Strayer's new investment, the beta of the printing industry will be used to estimate the discount rate for the base case NPV.

Assuming that debt used in the printing industry is typically risk-free (i.e. has a beta of zero), then we can ungear the equity beta of the printing industry as follows:

$$\beta_a = \left[\frac{V_e}{(V_e + V_d(1-T))} \beta_e \right] = \left[\frac{50}{50 + 50(1-0.30)} \times 1.2 \right] = 0.706$$

Using the capital asset pricing model: $E(r_i) = R_f + \beta(E(r_m) - R_f)$

K_e ungeared = 5.5% + (12% − 5.5%) 0.706 = 10.09% or approximately 10%.

Annual after-tax cash flows = $5 million (1 − 0.3) = $3,500,000.

From annuity tables with a 10% discount rate:

			$
Present value of annual cash flows	3,500,000 × 6.145	=	21,507,500
Present value of the residual value	5,000,000 × 0.386	=	1,930,000
			23,437,500
Less initial investment			25,000,000
Base case NPV			(1,562,500)

Step 2: Financing side effects

Financing side effects relate to the tax shield on interest payments, the subsidised loan, and issue costs associated with external financing.

Tax relief:

- $5 million 8% loan.

  Interest payable is $400,000 per year, tax relief is $400,000 × 0.3 = $120,000 per year.

- $4 million subsidised loan.

  Interest is $240,000 per year, tax relief $72,000 per year.

- Total annual tax relief $192,000 per year. The present value of this tax relief, discounted at the risk-free rate of 5.5% per year, is: $192,000 × 7.541 = $1,447,872.

(The tax relief on interest payments allowed by government is assumed to be risk free. The mid-point between 5% and 6% in annuity tables is used. NB Discounting at a rate higher than the risk-free rate could be argued, especially if the company might be in a non-taxpaying position in some years.)

Subsidy:

- The company saves 2% per year on $4,000,000 equal to interest saved of $80,000

- After tax, this equates to $80,000 × (1 – 0.30) = $56,000.

- As this is a government subsidy, it is assumed to be risk free and will be discounted at 5.5% per year.

- Present value = $56,000 × 7.541 = $422,296.

Issue costs:

		$
Debt: $5 million × 1%	=	50,000
Equity: $10 million × 4%	=	400,000
		450,000

Step 3: APV = base case NPV + PV of financing side effects

	$
Base case NPV	(1,562,500)
PV of tax relief	1,447,872
PV of subsidy	422,296
Issue costs	(450,000)
APV	(142,332)

Based upon these estimates the project is not financially viable. The benefits of the finance are insufficient to outweigh the inherent problems with the proposed project.

(b)   Both APV and NPV are discounted cash flow techniques but differ in the way project finance is incorporated into the process. With NPV, finance is usually incorporated into the discount rate which is then applied to project-only (i.e. excluding finance) cash flows. The clearest example of this is when a project (or company) WACC is used to discount project cash flows.

APV involves a two stage process dealing with project and financing flows separately. Project cash flows are discounted at an ungeared cost of equity to calculate a base case NPV. Financing side effects are then discounted at an appropriate rate – usually the pre-tax risk free rate.

APV may be a better technique to use than NPV when:

(i)   There is a significant change in capital structure as a result of the investment.

(ii)   The investment involves complex tax payments and tax allowances, and/or has periods when taxation is not paid.

(iii)   Subsidised loans, grants or issue costs exist.

(iv)   Financing side effects exist (e.g. the subsidised loan), which require discounting at a different rate than that applied to the mainstream project.

(c)   **Islamic finance**

Islamic finance rests on the application of Islamic, or Shariah, law.

The main principles of Islamic finance are that:

- Wealth must be generated from legitimate trade and asset-based investment. The use of money for the purposes of making money is forbidden.

- Investment should also have a social and an ethical benefit to wider society beyond pure return.

- Risk should be shared.

- Harmful activities (such as gambling, alcohol and the sale of certain foods) should be avoided.

The raising of term loan debt finance as proposed by Strayer (where the lender would make a straight interest charge, irrespective of how the underlying assets fare) would violate the principle of sharing risk and of not using money for the purposes of making money. Under Islamic finance, the charging and receiving of interest (riba) is strictly prohibited. This is in stark contrast to more conventional, Western forms of finance.

One alternative form of finance would be Murabaha, a form of trade credit for asset acquisition. Here the provider of finance would buy the item and then sell it on to Strayer at a price that includes an agreed mark-up for profit. The mark-up is fixed in advance and cannot be increased and the payment is made by instalments.

Another form of finance would be Islamic bonds, known as sukuk. To be Shariah-compliant, the sukuk holders must have a proprietary interest in the assets which are being financed. The sukuk holders' return for providing finance is a share of the income generated by the assets. The key distinction between sukuk and murabaha is that sukuk holders have ownership of the cash flows but not the assets themselves.

35 TAMPEM INC

Key answer tips

Don't waste time by writing out all the cashflows in detail for the NPV and the APV calculations. Remember that (with the exception of financing issue costs) the cashflows are the same, but the discounting process is different: in NPV, use a WACC for discounting, but in APV, use a cost of equity for discounting then adjust for the impact of the financing separately.

(a)   The tax saving from capital allowances is:

Year	Written-down value	Capital allowance (25%)	Tax saving (30%)
1	4,400	1,100	330
2	3,300	825	248
3	2,475	619	186
4	1,856	464	139

NPV

					$000		
Year		*0*	*1*	*2*	*3*	*4*
Operating cash flows			1,250	1,400	1,600	1,800
Taxation (30%)			(375)	(420)	(480)	(540)
Tax saving			330	248	186	139
Investment cost		(5,400)				
Realisable value						1,500
		─────	─────	─────	─────	─────
Net cash flows		(5,400)	1,205	1,228	1,306	2,899
Discount factors @ 10%(W)			0.909	0.826	0.751	0.683
		─────	─────	─────	─────	─────
Present values		(5,400)	1,095	1,014	981	1,980
		─────	─────	─────	─────	─────

The expected NPV is $(330,000)

The investment does not appear to be financially viable.

Working: discount rate

The weighted average cost of capital is:

The investment K_e can be calculated using CAPM: $E(r_i) = R_f + \beta_i(E(r_m) - R_f)$

$K_e = 4\% + 1.5 \times (10\% - 4\%) = 13\%$

$$WACC = \left[\frac{V_e}{V_e + V_d}\right]k_e + \left[\frac{V_d}{V_e + V_d}\right]k_d(1-T)$$

$$= 13\% (0.6) + 8\% (1 - 0.3)(0.4) = 10.04\%$$

APV

Step 1: Base case NPV

The relevant cash flows for APV are the same as for the NPV, except for the issue costs, which are treated separately as a financing side effect.

					$000
Year	*0*	*1*	*2*	*3*	*4*
Net cash flows	(5,000)	1,205	1,228	1,306	2,899
Discount factors @ 9% (W)		0.917	0.842	0.772	0.708
Present values	(5,000)	1,105	1,034	1,008	2,052

Expected base case NPV is $199,000

Working: discount rate

The discount rate for the base case NPV is the ungeared cost of equity. Assuming corporate debt to be risk free (which is unlikely at 8%!)

$$\beta_a = \left[\frac{V_e}{(V_e + V_d(1-T))}\beta_e\right] = \left[\frac{2,700}{2,700 + 2,700(1-0.30)} \times 1.5\right] = 0.882$$

K_e ungeared $= 4\% + 0.882 \times (10\% - 4\%) = 9.29\%$. We shall round this to 9% for discounting.

Step 2: Financing side effects:

Annual tax saving on interest payments on $2.7 million debt

$2,700,000 \times 8\% \times 0.3 = \$64,800$

The present value of tax saving over four years discounted at the pre-tax cost of debt (8%) is: $64,800 \times 3.312 = \$214,618$

Step 3: APV

	$
Base case NPV	199,000
Tax savings	214,618
Issue costs	(400,000)
APV	13,618

The investment appears to be marginally viable based upon the APV method.

(b)   Manager A advocates the use of NPV, which is used by many companies worldwide. In an efficient market a positive NPV, in theory, should lead to a commensurate increase in the value of the company and share price. However, the use of the weighted average cost of capital (WACC) in NPV is only appropriate if there is no significant change in gearing as a result of the investment, the investment is marginal in size, and the operating risk of the company does not change. If WACC is estimated using the capital asset pricing model, it also relies upon the accuracy of this model, which has many unrealistic assumptions.

The adjusted present value model, advocated by manager B, treats the investment as being initially all equity financed and then directly adjusts for the present value of any cash flow effects associated with financing. As gearing is expected to change as a result of the investment, APV might be better suited to the evaluation of this investment. However, it is not always easy to identify all of the relevant financing side effects, or the discount rate that used be used on each of the financing side effects. APV also relies upon unrealistic assumptions with respect to ungearing beta and the existence of perpetual risk-free debt.

Both NPV and APV do not consider the potential value of real options (e.g. the abandonment option and the option to undertake further investments) that might exist as a result of undertaking the initial investment.

(c)   Ethics impact on many aspects of investment decisions. In theory companies seek to maximise shareholder wealth, often subject to constraining secondary objectives. Such secondary objectives include the welfare of the public. Companies are affected by ethical standards relating to:

- Health and safety. Employees and the public should be protected from danger, which includes working conditions, effective employment law and product safety.

- Environmental issues such as controlling pollution, protecting wildlife and the countryside. Fully satisfying these issues might be an expensive element in a capital investment.

- Bribes and other payments. Investment might proceed more quickly and efficiently if bribes, 'incentive payments', 'gifts' etc. are paid to officials. This is a difficult area, as gifts are part of the business culture in some countries. Even the ethics of political contributions is debatable.

- Corporate governance. Many examples exist of companies, e.g. Enron, where the results of investments and the true financial position have been hidden from shareholders and the public.

- Taxation. Companies may try to minimise their tax liability. Tax evasion is illegal, but there is an ethical question over the use of sophisticated tax avoidance measures, especially in developing countries.

- Wage levels. Should a company pay low wages to maximise shareholder wealth, especially in countries where the standard of living is very low?

- Individual manager's ethics. The ethics of individuals, including pursuing their own goals and self-interest (such as job security) rather than those of the organisation might influence the outcome of investment decisions.

There is inevitably some subjectivity as to what constitutes ethical behaviour, but there is little doubt that ethical issues are of increasing importance to companies. Acting in an ethically responsible way often has a direct detrimental impact upon expected cash flows and NPV. However, stakeholders, including shareholders, are increasingly expecting companies to act ethically. If they do not, then their share price might suffer as a result of adverse publicity and investors withdrawing their support.

The concept of ethical shareholder wealth creation is likely to become increasingly important in strategic financial management.

36 DIGUNDER

Key answer tips

In any Black Scholes question, start by writing out the five key input factors. This will ensure that you focus on picking out the key information from the question before you start using the formulae.

(a) Current price = Present Value of the Project = $28 million

Exercise price = capital expenditure = $24 million

Exercise date = 2 years (or 500 trading days)

Risk free rate = 5%

Volatility = 25%

Tutorial note (extracted from the examiner's comments)

The majority of candidates attempted this question and were able to specify all but one of the inputs to the Black and Scholes option pricing model. Nearly all were able to identify the exercise 'price' of the project – the capital investment – at $24 million, the volatility of the cash flows, the risk free rate and the time to exercise. Only a few candidates identified the present value of the project (net present value plus outlay) of $28 million as the value of the underlying investment asset.

Using the formula as specified:

$$d_1 = \frac{\ln\left(\frac{28}{24}\right) + \left(0.05 + 0.5 \times 0.25^2\right) \times 2}{0.25 \times \sqrt{2}} = 0.8956$$

$$d_2 = 0.8956 - 0.25 \times \sqrt{2} = 0.5421$$

The areas under the normal curves for these two values are $N(d_1) = 0.8147$ and $N(d_2) = 0.7061$.

Using the derived values for $N(d_1)$ and $N(d_2)$ the value of the call option on the value represented by this project is as follows:

$$c = 0.8147 \times 28 - 0.7061 \times 24 \times e^{-.05 \times 2} = \$7.48 \text{ million}$$

Tutorial note

Note that the value of $7.48m here is made up of an intrinsic value of $4m (the project's NPV) plus the time value of the option of $3.48m.

(b) **Digunder Ltd**

Housing Development at Newtown

This project has a net present value of $4 million on a capital expenditure of $24 million which whilst significant has a volatility estimate of 25% of the present value per annum. This volatility is brought about by uncertainties about Government's intentions with respect to the Bigcity–Newtown transport link and the consequential impact upon property values. Currently, the project presents substantial value at risk and there is a high likelihood that the project will not be value generating. To surmount this, an estimate is provided of the value of the option to delay construction for two years until the Government's transport plans will be made known.

The option to delay

The option to delay construction is particularly valuable in this case. It eliminates much of the downside risk that the project does not generate the cash flows expected and it gives us the ability to proceed at a point in time most favourable to us. The nature of the delay option is that it is more valuable the greater the volatility of the underlying cash flows and the greater the time period before we are required to exercise.

The valuation of the option to delay has been under taken using the Black and Scholes model which members have been briefed about with respect to fair value accounting practices under the International Financial Reporting Standards. The model has some limiting assumptions relating to the underlying nature of the cash flows and our ability to adjust our exposure to risk as time passes. In reality, the use of this type of modelling is more appropriate for financial securities that are actively traded. Our use of the model is an approximation of the value of the flexibility inherent in this project and although the model will not have the precision found in its security market applications it does indicate the order of magnitude of the real option available. A positive value of $7.48 million is suggested by the model underlying the considerable benefit in delay.

In interpreting this valuation it is important to note that the actual project present value at commencement could be significantly larger than currently estimated and will certainly not be less than zero (otherwise we will not exercise the option to build). The additional value reflects the fact that downside risk is eliminated by our ability to delay the decision to proceed.

On the basis of our valuation the option to delay commencement of the project should be taken and investment delayed until the Government's intention with respect to transport links becomes clearer. On this basis we would place a value of $7.48 million on the project including the delay option.

(c)   The Black and Scholes model makes a number of assumptions about the underlying nature of the pricing and return distributions which may not be valid with this type of project. More problematically it assumes that continuous adjustment of the hedged position is possible and that the option is European style. Where the option to delay can be exercised over any set period of time up to the exercise date the Black and Scholes model will cease to be accurate. For a call option, such as the option to delay, then the level of inaccuracy is likely to be quite low especially for options that are close to the money. Given that an option always has time value it will invariably be in the option holder's interest to wait until exercise date before exercising his or her option. However, in those situations where the level of accuracy is particularly important, or where it is suspected that the Black and Scholes assumptions do not hold, then the binomial option pricing approach is necessary.

ACCA marking scheme		
		Marks
(a)	Identification of inputs into BS model	4
	Calculation of d1 and d2	4
	Calculation of real option value	3
	Conclusion on the value of the option to delay	1
		———
		12
		———
(b)	Estimation of overall project value at $11.48 million	2
	Justification for the use of BS model	2
		———
		4
		———
(c)	Outline of the limitations of the BS model	2
	Identification of the American style real option in the given circumstances	1
	Note on the appropriate technique for solving the American style option	1
		———
		4
		———
Total		20
		———

37   KENAND CO

Key answer tips

In autumn 2011, the examiner wrote two articles for Student Accountant magazine about bonds, FRAs and swaps. The contents of the articles are tested in this question.

The contents of the articles were also tested in the December 2011 and June 2012 exams.

This shows how important it is to keep an eye on Student Accountant and to fully understand any articles presented there.

(a) (i) **AB Co bond value**

'Bid yield' = yield to maturity (YTM) = 6.2% i.e. the value of the bond should be the present value of the future receipts to an investor, discounted at 6.2%.

	Year 1	Year 2	Year 3	Year 4
Receipts (for a $100 nominal bond)	5	5	5	110+5
DF at 6.2%	$\dfrac{1}{1.062}$	$\dfrac{1}{1.062^2}$	$\dfrac{1}{1.062^3}$	$\dfrac{1}{1.062^4}$
PV	4.71	4.43	4.17	90.41

NPV (i.e. bond value, per $100 nominal) = $103.72

So with $1m, Kenand Co will be able to buy $1m/$103.72 = 9,641 bonds on the market.

XY Co bond value

These bonds have not yet been issued, so we need to compute the likely issue price based on the spot yield curve for an A rated company.

	1 year	2 year	3 year	4 year
Govt bond annual spot yield curve (%)	3.54	4.01	4.70	5.60
A rated credit spread (%)	0.26	0.39	0.50	0.60
Total = A rated company's annual spot yield curve (%)	3.80	4.40	5.20	6.20

XY Co's new 3 year bonds can be separated into three separate bonds with the following payment structures (for a $100 nominal bond):

	Year 1	Year 2	Year 3
Bond 1	4		
Bond 2		4	
Bond 3			104

The sum of the present values of these amounts (when each is discounted at the relevant rate from the A rated company's yield curve table above) is then the likely issue price of the bond.

i.e. issue price (bond value) =

$$\left(4 \times \frac{1}{1.0380}\right) + \left(4 \times \frac{1}{1.0440^2}\right) + \left(104 \times \frac{1}{1.0520^3}\right) = \$96.85$$

So with $1m, Kenand Co will be able to buy $1m/$96.85 = 10,325 bonds on issue.

(ii) To find the Macauley duration, we first need to calculate the yield to maturity (YTM), or gross redemption yield, of the bonds, which will be used to discount the cashflows to the investor.

YTM calculations

AB Co bonds

The bid yield of the bonds quoted in the question is the same as the bond's YTM. Therefore, 6.2% will be used to discount AB Co's bond cashflows.

XY Co bonds

The YTM is the IRR of the current bond value, the interest receipts and the redemption amount.

Tutorial note

The YTM will be very similar to the 5.20% rate calculated in part (a) above, which was the spot yield for a 3 year A rated bond. In the exam, using the 5.20% as a discount rate in the Macauley duration calculation would not be completely accurate, but it would save time.

	$	DF 4%	PV @ 4%	DF 6%	PV @ 6%
t_0	MV (96.85)	1	(96.85)	1	(96.85)
t_1-t_3	Interest 4	2.775	11.10	2.673	10.69
t_3	Redemption 100	0.889	88.90	0.840	84.00
			3.15		(2.16)

$$\text{So, IRR} = 4\% + \left[\left(\frac{3.15}{3.15+2.16}\right)(6\%-4\%)\right] = 5.19\%$$

Duration calculations

AB Co bonds

$$\text{PV of cashflows (years 1-4)} = \frac{5}{1.062} + \frac{5}{1.062^2} + \frac{5}{1.062^3} + \frac{115}{1.062^4}$$

=4.708 + 4.433 + 4.174 + 90.407

So Macauley duration=

[(4.708 × 1) + (4.433 × 2) + (4.174 × 3) + (90.407 × 4)]/103.72 = 3.74 years

XY Co bonds

$$\text{PV of cashflows (years 1–3)} = \frac{4}{1.0519} + \frac{4}{1.0519^2} + \frac{104}{1.0519^3}$$

=3.803 + 3.615 + 89.353

So Macauley duration=

[(3.803 × 1) + (3.615 × 2) + (89.353 × 3)]/96.85 = 2.88 years

Interpretation

Macauley duration is a measure of risk associated with a bond, or specifically a measure of the sensitivity of the bond value to changes in interest rates. Generally, the prices of shorter dated bonds are less sensitive to interest rate changes. This is proved by the Macauley duration calculations here, which show that AB Co's longer dated bonds have a higher duration, so the price of these bonds is more sensitive to interest changes.

Given that both companies have an A credit rating, it is perhaps initially surprising that there is such a large difference between the duration of the bonds. However, the greater risk attached to the longer dated bond is consistent with the spot yield and credit spreads information provided, which shows that the yield curve is upward sloping i.e. yields are higher on longer dated bonds in a particular risk class.

Tutorial note

There is a quicker way to derive the Macauley duration of the XY bonds, which avoids the need to first work out the YTM using the IRR method.

	Year 1	Year 2	Year 3
Receipts (for a $100 nominal bond)	4	4	104
DF at relevant spot yield rates	$\frac{1}{1.038}$	$\frac{1}{1.044^2}$	$\frac{1}{1.052^3}$
PV	3.854	3.670	89.328

So Macauley duration= [(3.854 × 1) + (3.670 × 2) + (89.328 × 3)]/96.85 = 2.88 years, as before.

(b) XY Co is an A rated company, so the annual spot yield curve for its bonds is:

1 year 3.54% + 0.26% = 3.80%

2 year 4.01% + 0.39% = 4.40%

3 year 4.70% + 0.50% = 5.20%

4 year 5.60% + 0.60% = 6.20%

(based on the spot yield for government bonds adjusted for the A rated company's credit spread – all information taken from the scenario of part (a)).

Therefore, the rate quoted on a 12 v 24 FRA will be $(1.0440^2/1.0380) - 1 = 5.00\%$.

Tutorial note 1

This calculation is explained as follows:

XY Co could borrow money for 2 years, without incurring interest rate risk, in two ways. It could issue a 2 year fixed rate bond and pay 4.40% per annum for each of the two years.

Alternatively it could issue a 1 year bond at 3.80%, redeem this and issue a 1 year bond again for the second year. In the latter case it could hedge the risk for the second year by using an FRA. The total interest cost has to be the same either way and therefore if R is the 12 v 24 FRA rate then:

$(1.0440^2) = (1.0380) \times (1+R)$

Tutorial note 2

Note that the forward rates on other FRAs could also be calculated as follows:

24 v 36 FRA	$(1.0520^3/1.0440^2) - 1 = 6.81\%$
36 v 48 FRA	$(1.0620^4/1.0520^3) - 1 = 9.26\%$

(c)   The bank will calculate the fixed interest rate to make sure that the present value of the fixed payments made by XY Co is equal to the present value of the variable payments made by the bank to XY Co when both are discounted at the spot yield.

Variable payments made by the bank to XY Co each year will be

$20m × expected interest rate for each year less 30 basis points.

In year 1 the expected interest rate is 3.80% (spot yield), so the expected payment will be $20m × (3.80% - 0.30%) = $0.7m.

In years 2–4 the expected interest rate is the forward rate calculated in part (b) above, hence the expected payments will be:

Year 2	$20m × (5.00% − 0.30%)	$0.94m
Year 3	$20m × (6.81% − 0.30%)	$1.302m
Year 4	$20m × (9.26% − 0.30%)	$1.792m

So, each year XY Co will pay a fixed amount (say X) to the bank in exchange for these variable amounts. In order for the present values of the fixed payments to be equal to the present values of the variable payments,

$$\frac{0.7}{1.0380}+\frac{0.94}{1.0440^2}+\frac{1.302}{1.0520^3}+\frac{1.792}{1.0620^4}=\frac{X}{1.0380}+\frac{X}{1.0440^2}+\frac{X}{1.0520^3}+\frac{X}{1.0620^4}$$

or, by simplifying the equation:

$$\frac{0.7}{1.0380}+\frac{0.94}{1.0440^2}+\frac{1.302}{1.0520^3}+\frac{1.792}{1.0620^4}=\left\|\frac{1}{1.0380}+\frac{1}{1.0440^2}+\frac{1}{1.0520^3}+\frac{1}{1.0620^4}\right\|X$$

so

4.064 = 3.526X

i.e. X = $1.153m

which (as a percentage of the $20m loan) is a rate of (1.153/20) = 5.77%.

Tutorial note

Whilst the present value of the fixed interest payments will equal the present value of the variable interest payments on the date that the swap is created, over time, as interest rates change, this will not be the case.

If, for example, interest rates, and the spot yields, rise, the present value of the fixed payments will fall (remember the higher the discount rate the lower the present value). This will not be the case with the variable payments because the payment itself will rise as the discount rate rises. This is why a swap will, in due course, become either a financial asset, or a financial liability.

38 FUBUKI CO

Key answer tips

APV is very commonly tested.

As long as you remember to use the ungeared cost of equity for discounting, the project appraisal is almost identical to a standard NPV question.

(a) **Base Case Net Present Value**

Fubuki Co: Project Evaluation

Base Case

Units Produced and sold				1,300	1,820	2,548	2,675
	$000 Unit price/cost	Inflation	Now	Year 1	Year 2	Year 3	Year 4
Sales revenue	2.5	3%		3,250	4,687	6,758	7,308
Direct costs	1.2	8%		1,560	2,359	3,566	4,044
Attributable fixed costs	1,000	5%		1,000	1,050	1,103	1,158
Profits				690	1,278	2,089	2,106
Working capital	15%		(488)	(215)	(311)	(82)	1,096
Taxation (W1)				(10)	(157)	(360)	(364)
Incremental cash flows							
Investment/sale			(14,000)				16,000
Net cash flows			(14,488)	465	810	1,647	18,838
Present Value (10%) (W2)			(14,488)	422	670	1,237	12,867
Base case NPV			708				

Workings

(W1)

Profits	690	1,278	2,089	2,106
Less: allowances	650	650	650	650
Taxable profits	40	628	1,439	1,456
Tax	10	157	360	364

(W2) Discount rate (Haizum's ungeared Ke)

$ke(g) = ke(u) + (1-t)(ke(u) - kd)Vd/Ve$

$Ve = 2.53 \times 15 = 37.95$

$Vd = 40 \times 0.9488 = 37.952$

Assume $Vd/Ve = 1$

$14 = ke(u) + 0.72 \times (ke(u) - 4.5) \times 1$

$14 = 1.72ke(u) - 3.24$

$ke(u) = 10.02$ assume 10%

Tutorial note

In calculating the ungeared cost of equity, this model answer has used the Modigliani and Miller formula from the formula sheet. The same answer could have been derived using the asset beta formula and the CAPM as follows:

CAPM: $E(r_i) = R_f + \beta_i(E(r_m) - R_f)$

So 14% = 4.5% + (β_i x4%)

Hence β_i=2.375 (this is the equity beta)

Therefore (since there is no debt beta in this question), the asset beta is:

$$2.375 \times \frac{1}{1+1(1-0.28)} = 1.381$$

Then CAPM can be used again to give the ungeared cost of equity as:

4.5% + (1.381 × 4) = 10.02%

The base case net present value is calculated as approximately $708,000. This is positive but marginal.

The following financing side effects apply

	$000
Issue costs 4/96 × $14,488	(604)

Tax Shield

Annual tax relief = (14,488 × 80% × 0.055 × 25%)

$$+ (14,488 × 20% × 0.075 × 25%)$$

$$= 159.4 + 54.3 = 213.7$$

	$000
213.7 × 3.588	766

Subsidy benefit

14,488 × 80% × 0.02 × 75% × 3.588	624
Total benefit of financing side effects	786
Adjusted present value (708 + 786)	1,494

The addition of the financing side effects gives an increased present value and probably the project would not be considered marginal. Once these are taken into account Fubuki Co would probably undertake the project.

Tutorial note (extracted from the examiner's comments)

In calculating the present values of the tax shield and subsidy benefits, the annuity factor used is based on 4.5% debt yield rate for four years. It could be argued that 7.5% may also be used as this reflects the normal borrowing/default risk of the company.

Full credit was given where this assumption was made to estimate the annuity factor.

(b)   The adjusted present value can be used where the impact of using debt financing is significant. Here the impact of each of financing side effects from debt is shown separately rather than being imputed into the weighted average cost of capital. The project is initially evaluated by only taking into account the business risk element of the new venture. This shows that although the project results in a positive net present value, it is fairly marginal and volatility in the input factors could turn the project. Sensitivity analysis can be used to examine the sensitivity of the factors. The financing side effects show that almost 110% value is added when the positive impact of the tax shields and subsidy benefits are taken into account even after the issue costs.

Assumptions (Credit given for alternative, valid assumptions)

1   Haizum Co's ungeared cost of equity is used because it is assumed that this represents the business risk attributable to the new line of business.

2   The ungeared cost of equity is calculated on the assumption that Modigliani and Miller's (MM) proposition 2 applies.

3   It is assumed that initial working capital requirement will form part of the funds borrowed but the subsequent requirements will be available from the funds generated from the project.

4   The feasibility study is ignored as a past cost.

5   It is assumed that the five-year debt yield is equivalent to the risk-free rate,

6   It is assumed that the annual reinvestment needed on plant and machinery is equivalent to the tax allowable depreciation.

7   It is assumed that all cash flows occur at the end of the year unless specified otherwise.

8   All amounts are given in $'000 to the nearest $'000. When calculating the units produced and sold, the nearest approximation for each year is taken.

Assumptions 4, 5, 6, 7 and 8 are standard assumptions made for a question of this nature. Assumptions 1, 2 and 3 warrant further discussion. Taking assumption 3 first, it is reasonable to assume that before the project starts, the company would need to borrow the initial working capital as it may not have access to the working capital needed. In subsequent years, the cash flows generated from the operation of the project may be sufficient to fund the extra working capital required. In the case of Fubuki Co, because of an expected rapid growth in sales in years 2 and 3, the working capital requirement remains high and the management need to assess how to make sufficient funds available.

Considering assumptions 1 and 2, the adjusted present values methodology assumes that MM proposition 2 applies and the equivalent ungeared cost of equity does not take into account the cost of financial distress. This may be an unreasonable assumption. The ungeared cost of equity is based on another company which is in a similar line of business to the new project, but it is not exactly the same. It can be difficult to determine an accurate ungeared cost of equity in practice. However, generally the discount rate (cost of funds) tends to be the least sensitive factor in investment appraisal and therefore some latitude can be allowed.

ACCA marking scheme		
		Marks
(a)	Sales revenue, direct costs and additional fixed costs	4
	Incremental working capital	1
	Taxation	2
	Estimation of Ke (ungeared)	2
	Net cash flows, present value and base case NPV	2
Total	Issue costs	1
	Calculation of tax shield impact	2
	Calculation of subsidy impact	1
	Adjusted present value and conclusion	2
		17
(b)	Discussion of using APV	2–3
	Assumption about Haizum as proxy and MM proposition 2	3–4
	Other assumptions	2–3
	Maximum	8
Total		**25**

39 INVESTMENT PROJECT REVIEW

Key answer tips

This is a clever way of testing investment appraisal. There are many errors in the original computation, but there are also some points which have been dealt with correctly.

List out the errors, to show the examiner clearly what adjustments need to be made, and then make any necessary adjustments to the given figures.

(a) The project cash flow contains a number of errors of principle which should be corrected. As the project cash flows are shown after tax, the corrections should be made net of tax by either adding back or deducting the change required.

- Interest has been deducted and should be added back as this finance charge is properly charged through the application of the discount rate.

- Depreciation should be added back as this is not a cash flow.

- The indirect cost charge should be added back as this does not appear to be a decision relevant cost.

- Infrastructure costs should be deducted as these have not been included in the original projection.

- Site clearance and reinstatement costs of $5 million have been included net of tax.

- The unclaimed capital allowance is calculated as follows:

	0	1	2	3	4	5	6
Capital investment	150.00	50.00					
Deduct FYA at 50%	−75.00	−25.00					
Deduct WDA at 25% of residual		−18.75	−20.31	−15.23	−11.43	−8.57	−6.43
Pool	75.00	81.25	60.94	45.71	34.28	25.71	19.28
Proceeds of sale							7.00
Unclaimed CA							12.28

This will generate a positive tax benefit in year six of $3·68 million at the tax rate of 30%.

The adjusted project cash flow and net present value calculation for this project are as follows:

	0	1	2	3	4	5	6
Project after tax cash flow	−127.50	−36.88	44.00	68.00	60.00	35.00	20.00
Add back net interest			2.80	2.80	2.80	2.80	2.80
Add back depreciation (net of tax)			2.80	2.80	2.80	2.80	2.80
Add back ABC charge (net of tax)			5.60	5.60	5.60	5.60	5.60
Less corporate infrastructure costs			−2.80	−2.80	−2.80	−2.80	−2.80
Estimate for site clearance							−3.50
Tax benefit of unrecovered capital allowances							3.68
Adjusted project cash flow	−127.50	−36.88	52.40	76.40	68.40	43.40	28.58
Discount factor	1.0000	0.9091	0.8264	0.7513	0.6830	0.6209	0.5645
Discounted cash flow at 10%	−127.50	−33.52	43.31	57.40	46.72	26.95	16.14
Net present value	29.48						

The sensitivity of the project to a 1% increase in capital expenditure is as follows:

Sensitivity to a $1 million increase in CAPEX at year 0

	0	1	2	3	4	5	6
Equipment purchase/written down value	1	0.50	0.37	0.28	0.21	0.16	0.12
FYA	−0.5						
WDA		−0.13	−0.09	−0.07	−0.05	−0.04	−0.03
Balance	0.5	0.37	0.28	0.21	0.16	0.12	0.09
Impact upon CAPEX	−1						
Tax saving due to WDA and FYA	0.15	0.039	0.028	0.021	0.015	0.012	0.009
Unrecovered allowance							0.027
Net impact	−0.85	0.039	0.028	0.021	0.015	0.012	0.036
Discount factor	1.0000	0.9091	0.8264	0.7513	0.6830	0.6209	0.5645
Discounted cash flow	−0.85	0.0355	0.0223	0.0158	0.0102	0.0075	0.0203
Net present value	−0.63						

Thus an increase in CAPEX by $1 million results in a loss of NPV of $0.63 million due to the benefit of the capital allowances available discounted over the life of the project.

(b)   The discounted payback is estimated as follows:

	0	1	2	3	4	5	6
Discounted cash flows from project	−127.50	−33.52	43.31	57.40	46.72	26.95	16.14
Cumulative discounted cash flow	−127.50	−161.02	−117.72	−60.32	−13.60	13.35	29.48
Payback (discounted)	4.50						

The duration of a project is the average number of years required to recover the present value of the project.

Duration	0	1	2	3	4	5	6
DCF at 10%			43.31	57.40	46.72	26.95	16.14
PV of return phase	190.52						
Proportion of present value in each year			0.2273	0.3013	0.2452	0.1415	0.0847
Weighted years			0.4546	0.9039	0.9809	0.7073	0.5082
Duration (= sum of the weighted years)	3.55						

Tutorial note

Duration is a relatively simple calculation once you have calculated NPV, so review this answer carefully.

Payback, discounted payback and duration are three techniques that measure the return to liquidity offered by a capital project. In theory, a firm that has ready access to the capital markets should not be concerned about the time taken to recapture the investment in a project. However, in practice managers prefer projects to appear to be successful as quickly as possible. Payback as a technique fails to take into account the time value of money and any cash flows beyond the project date. It is used by many firms as a coarse filter of projects and it has been suggested to be a proxy for the redeployment real option. Discounted payback does surmount the first difficulty but not the second in that it is still possible for projects with highly negative terminal cash flows to appear attractive because of their initial favourable cash flows. Conversely, discounted payback may lead a project to be discarded that has highly favourable cash flows after the payback date.

Duration measures either the average time to recover the initial investment (if discounted at the project's internal rate of return) of a project, or to recover the present value of the project if discounted at the cost of capital as is the case in this question. Duration captures both the time value of money and the whole of the cash flows of a project. It is also a measure which can be used across projects to indicate when the bulk of the project value will be captured. Its disadvantage is that it is more difficult to conceptualise than payback and may not be employed for that reason.

(c) **Report to Management Prepared by: D Obbin, ACCA**

Project acceptance and criteria for acceptability

I have reviewed the proposed capital investment and after making a number of adjustments have estimated that the project will increase the value of the firm by approximately $29.48 million. The project is highly sensitive to changes in the level of capital investment. Increases in immediate capital spending on this project will lead to a concomitant loss in the overall project value less the tax saving resulting from the increased capital allowances. However, given the size of the net present value of the project, it is unlikely that an adverse movement in this variable would lead to a significant reduction in the value of the firm.

The analysis of the payback on this project using discounted cash flows suggests that the value of the capital invested will be wholly recovered within four years of commencement. The bulk of the cash flow recovery occurs early within the life cycle of the project with an average recovery of the total present value occurring 3.55 years from commencement.

On the basis of the figures presented and the sensitivity analysis conducted, I recommend the Board approves this project for investment.

For many years the Board has used payback as one technique for evaluating investment projects. The Board has noted concerns that (i) the method chosen does not reflect the cost of finance either in the cash flows or in the discount rate applied and (ii) it fails to reflect cash flows beyond the payback date. Discounted payback surmounts the first but not the second difficulty. I would recommend that the Board considers the use of 'duration' which measures the time to recover either half the value invested in a project or, by alternative measurement, half the project net present value. Because this measure captures both the full value and the time value of a project it is recommended as a superior measure to either payback or discounted payback when comparing the time taken by different projects to recover the investment involved.

As part of its review process the Board has asked for sensitivities of the project to key variables. Sensitivity analysis demonstrates the likely gain or loss of project value as a result of small changes in the value of the variables chosen. Unfortunately, some variables such as, for example, price changes and the cost of finance, are highly correlated with one another and focusing upon the movement in a single variable may well ignore significant changes in another variable. To deal with this and given our background information about the volatility of input variables and their correlation, I would recommend that a simulation is conducted taking these component risks into account. Simulation works by randomly drawing a possible value for each variable on a repeated basis until a distribution of net present value outcomes can be established and the priority of each variable in determining the overall net present value obtained. Furthermore, the Board will be in a position to review the potential 'value at risk' in a given project.

I recommend that the Board reviews a simulation of project net present values in future and that this forms part of its continuing review process.

40   MMC (JUN 11)

Key answer tips

Before calculating the value of the real option, it is important to do a basic NPV calculation for the project, in order to identify the value of Pa for the Black-Scholes formula.

(a)   Net Present Value without the option to delay the decision

Year	Current	1	2	3	4	5	6
Cash flows ($)	–7m	–7m	–35m	25m	18m	10m	5m
PV (11%) ($)	–7m	–6.31m	–28.42m	18.28m	11.86m	5.93m	2.68m

Net Present Value = $(2.98 million)

On this basis the project would be rejected.

Value of option to delay the decision until the film is released and its popularity established. Black-Scholes Option Pricing model is used to value the call option.

Present value of project's positive cash flows discounted to current day:

$18.28m + $11.86m + $5.93m + $2.68m = $38.75m

Variables:

Current price (P_a) = $38.75m

Exercise price (P_e) = $35m

Exercise date = 2 years

Risk free rate = 3.5%

Volatility = 30%

$d_1 = [\ln(38.75/35) + (0.035 + 0.5 \times 0.30^2) \times 2]/(0.30 \times 2^{1/2}) = 0.6170$

$d_2 = 0.6170 - (0.30 \times 2^{1/2}) = 0.1927$

Using the Normal Distribution Table provided

$N(d_1) = 0.5 + 0.2291 + 0.7 \times (0.2324 - 0.2291) = 0.7314$

$N(d_2) = 0.5 + 0.0753 + 0.3 \times (0.0793 - 0.0753) = 0.5765$

Value of option to delay the decision = $38.75 \times 0.7314 - 35 \times 0.5765 \times e^{-0.035 \times 2}$ = 28.34 – 18.81 = $9.53m (positive value)

Hence by taking into account the option to delay the decision, the project should be accepted for investment.

(b)   The option to delay the decision has given MMC's managers the opportunity to monitor and respond to changing circumstances before committing to the project, such as a rise in popularity of this type of genre of films in the next two years or increased competition from similar new releases or a sustained marketing campaign launched by the film's producers before its launch. Although the project looks unattractive at present, it may not be the case if the film on which it is based is successful. The option pricing formula requires numerous assumptions to be made about the variables, the primary one being the assumption of volatility. It therefore does not provide a correct value but an indication of the value of the option to delay the decision. Hence it indicates that the management should consider the project further and not dismiss it, even though current conventional net present value is negative.

The option to delay the decision may not be the only option within the project. For example, the gaming platform that the company needs to develop for this game may have general programmes which may be used in future projects and MMC should take account of these. Or if the film is successful, it may lead to follow-on projects involving games based on film sequels.

(**Note:** credit will be given for alternative relevant comments)

ACCA marking scheme			Marks
(a)	Value of project without considering option to delay decision and conclusion		3
	Current price variable (P_a) for BSOP formula		1
	Additional cost (P_e) for BSOP formula		1
	Other variables for BSOP formula		1
	Calculation of $N(d_1)$		2
	Calculation of $N(d_2)$		2
	Value of the option to delay decision		1
	Conclusion		1
		Maximum	12
(b)	1 to 2 marks per well explained point		5
Total			**17**

41 TISA CO (JUN 12)

Key answer tips

Don't waste time here calculating IRR and MIRR for project Zeta. You are given the figures for Zeta to compare with your figures for Omega in part (b).

(a) Use Elfu Co's information to estimate the component project's asset beta. Then based on Tisa Co's capital structure, estimate the component project's equity beta and weighted average cost of capital. Assume that the beta of debt is zero.

Elfu Co MVe = $1.20 × 400m shares = $480m
Elfu Co MVd = $96m

Elfu Co portfolio asset beta =
1.40 × $480m/($480m + $96m × (1 − 0.25)) = 1.217
Elfu Co asset beta of other activities =
1.25 × $360m/($360m + $76.8m × (1 − 0.25)) = 1.078

1.217 = component asset beta × 0.25 + 1.078 × 0.75
Component asset beta = [1.217 − (1.078 × 0.75)]/0.25 = 1.634

Component equity beta based on Tisa Co capital structure =
1.634 × [($18m + $3.6m × 0.75)/$18m] = 1.879
Using CAPM, component Ke = 3.5% + 1.879 × 5.8% = 14.40%
Component WACC = (14.40% × $18m + 4.5% × $3.6m)/($18m + $3.6m) = 12.75%

(b) **Process Omega**

Year	0	1	2	3	4
Net cash flows ($000)	(3,800)	1,220	1,153	1,386	3,829
PV 12.75% ($000)	(3,800)	1,082	907	967	2,369
NPV ($000)	1,525				
PV 30%	(3,800)	938	682	631	1,341
NPV ($000)	(208)				

Internal rate of return is approximately 27.3%

Modified internal rate of return (MIRR) is approximately 22.7% ([$(5,325/3,800)^{1/4}$ × (1.1275)] – 1)

Alternatively:

MIRR can be calculated as follows:

Year	Cashflows ($000)	Multiplier	Re-invested amount ($000)
1	1,220	1.1275^3	1,749
2	1,153	1.1275^2	1,466
3	1,386	1.1275	1,563
4	3,829	1	3,829

Total re-invested amount ($000) = 8,607

MIRR = $(8,607/3,800)^{1/4}$ – 1 = 22.7%

The internal rate of return (IRR) assumes that positive cash flows in earlier years are reinvested at the IRR and therefore process Omega, which has higher initial cash flows when compared to process Zeta, gives a slightly higher IRR. The modified internal rate of return (MIRR) assumes that positive cash flows are reinvested at the cost of capital. This is a more reasonable assumption and produces a result consistent with the net present value. Hence, process Zeta should be adopted, although the difference is not significant.

[**Note:** Using 13% instead of 12.75% as the cost of capital is acceptable]

(c) 99% confidence level requires the value at risk (VAR) to be within 2.33 standard deviations from the mean, based on a single tail measure.

Annual VAR = 2.33 × $800,000 = $1,864,000

Five year VAR = $1,864,000 × $5^{1/2}$ approx. = $4,168,000

The figures mean that Elfu Co can be 99% confident that the cash flows will not fall by more than $1,864,000 in any one year and $4,168,000 in total over five years from the average returns. Therefore the company can be 99% certain that the returns will be $336,000 or more every year [$2,200,000 – $1,864,000]. And it can be 99% certain that the returns will be $6,832,000 or more in total over the five-year period [$11,000,000 – $4,168,000]. There is a 1% chance that the returns will be less than $336,000 each year or $6,832,000 over the five-year period.

ACCA marking scheme

			Marks
(a)	Reasoning behind cost of capital calculation		2
	Calculation of component asset beta		3
	Calculation of component equity beta, and Ke and WACC		3
			—
		Maximum	8
			—
(b)	Calculation of IRR for Process Omega		3
	Calculation of MIRR for Process Omega		1
	Recommendation and explanation of the recommendation		4
			—
		Maximum	8
			—
(c)	Annual and five-year VAR		2
	Explanation		2
			—
		Maximum	4
			—
Total			**20**
			—

42 ARBORE CO (DEC 12)

Key answer tips

This question shows how important it is to revise the whole syllabus in preparation for the exam. Capital rationing is a small topic in the syllabus but it was tested in detail here. You will never be expected to solve the capital rationing linear programming model, but it is important that you can interpret the results.

(a) **PDur05**

Annual sales revenue = $14 × 300,000 units = $4,200,000

Annual costs = $3,230,000

Annual cash flows = $970,000

Net present value of PDur05 =

($2,500,000) + ($1,200,000 × 1.11^{-1}) + ($1,400,000 × 1.11^{-2}) + $970,000 × 7.191 × 1.11^{-3}

= ($2,500,000) + ($1,081,000) + ($1,136,000) + $5,100,000

= $383,000

In order for the net present value to fall to nil, the PV of the project's annual cash flows needs to equal to: $2,500,000 + $1,081,000 + $1,136,000 = $4,717,000

Annual cash flows need to reduce to: $4,717,000/(7.191 × 1.11^{-3}) = $897,110

Sales revenue would reduce to: $897,110 + $3,230,000 = $4,127,110

Selling price would fall to: $4,127,110/300,000 units = $13.76

Percentage fall = ($14.00 − $13.76)/$14 × 100% = 1.7%

[**Note:** The estimate of the annual cash flows will differ if tables are used rather than a calculator. This is acceptable and will be allowed for when marking]

Comment: The net present value of the project is very sensitive to changes in the selling price of the product. A small fall in the selling price would reduce the net present value to nil or negative and make the project not worthwhile.

(b) A multi-period capital rationing model would use linear programming and is formulated as follows:

If:

$Y1$ = investment in project PDur01; $Y2$ = investment in project PDur02; $Y3$ = investment in project PDur03; $Y4$ investment in project PDur04; and $Y5$ = investment in project PDur05

Then the objective is to maximise

$464Y1 + 244Y2 + 352Y3 + 320Y4 + 383Y5$

Given the following constraints

Constraint year 1: $4,000Y1 + 800Y2 + 3,200Y3 + 3,900Y4 + 2,500Y5 \leq 9,000$

Constraint year 2: $1,100Y1 + 2,800Y2 + 3,562Y3 + 0Y4 + 1,200Y5$

$\leq 6,000$ Constraint year 3: $2,400Y1 + 3,200Y2 + 0Y3 + 200Y4 + 1,400Y5$

$\leq 5,000$

And where $Y1, Y2, Y3, Y4, Y5 \geq 0$

(c) **Category 1:** Total Final Value. This is the maximum net present value that can be earned within the three-year constraints of capital expenditure, by undertaking whole, part or none of the five projects. This amount is less than the total net present value of all five projects if there were no constraints.

Category 2: Adjustable Final Values. These are the proportions of projects undertaken within the constraints to maximise the net present value. In this case, all of project PDur05, 95.8% of project PDur01, 73.2% of project PDur03 and 40.7% of project PDur02 will be undertaken.

Category 3: Constraints utilised, slack. This indicates to what extent the constraint limits are used and whether any investment funds will remain unused. The figures indicate that, in order to achieve maximum net present value, all the funds in all three years are used up and no funds remain unused.

(d) (i) Normally, positive net present value projects should be accepted as they add to the value of the company by generating returns in excess of the required rate of return (the discount rate). However, in this case, Arbore Co seems to be employing soft capital rationing by setting internal limits on capital available for each department, possibly due to capital budget limits placed by the company on the amounts it wants to borrow or can borrow. In the latter case, the company faces limited access to capital from external sources, for example, because of restrictions in bank lending, costs related to the issue of new capital and lending to the company being perceived as too risky. This is known as hard capital rationing and can lead to soft capital rationing.

(ii) A capital investment monitoring system (CIMS) monitors how an investment project is progressing once it has been implemented. Initially the CIMS will set a plan and budget of how the project is to proceed. It sets milestones for what needs to be achieved and by when. It also considers the possible risks, both internal and external, which may affect the project. CIMS then ensures that the project is progressing according to the plan and budget. It also sets up contingency plans for dealing with the identified risks.

The benefits, to Arbore Co, of CIMS are that it tries to ensure, as much as possible, that the project meets what is expected of it in terms of revenues and expenses. Also that the project is completed on time and risk factors that are identified remain valid. A critical path of linked activities which make up the project will be identified. The departments undertaking the projects will be proactive, rather than reactive, towards the management of risk, and therefore possibly be able to reduce costs by having a better plan. CIMS can also be used as a communication device between managers charged with managing the project and the monitoring team. Finally CIMS would be able to re-assess and change the assumptions made of the project, if changes in the external environment warrant it.

	ACCA marking scheme		Marks
(a)	Calculation of project PDur05 net present value		2
	Calculation of percentage fall of selling price		3
	Comment		1
			—
		Maximum	6
			—
(b)	Formulation of objective function		1
	Formulation of constraints		2
			—
		Maximum	3
			—
(c)	Category 1		1
	Category 2		2
	Category 3		2
			—
		Maximum	5
			—
(d)	(i) Explaining the need for capital rationing		2
	(ii) Explanation of the features of a capital investment monitoring system		1–2
	Benefits of maintaining a capital investment monitoring system (1 mark per benefit)		2–3
			—
		Maximum	4
			—
Total			**20**
			—

43 BURUNG CO (JUN 14)

> 🔑
>
> **Key answer tips**
>
> This question presented the investment appraisal as part of the question, and asked for the necessary corrections to be made.
>
> This sort of question is an excellent test of whether you really understand the topic. A student with only a vague understanding of APV would have really struggled to pick out the subtle mistakes.

(a) **All figures are in $ million**

Year	0	1	2	3	4
Sales revenue (inflated, 8% p.a.)		24.87	42.69	61.81	36.92
Costs (inflated, 4% p.a.)		(14.37)	(23.75)	(33.12)	(19.05)
Incremental profit		10.50	18.94	28.69	17.87
Tax (W1)		(0.50)	(3.39)	(5.44)	(3.47)
Working capital (W2)	(4.97)	(3.57)	(3.82)	4.98	7.38
Investment/ sale of machinery	(38.00)				4.00
Cash flows	(42.97)	6.43	11.73	28.23	25.78
Discount factors (12%, (W3))	1	0.893	0.797	0.712	0.636
Present values	(42.97)	5.74	9.35	20.10	16.40

(W1) **All figures are in $ million**

Year	0	1	2	3	4
Incremental profit		10.50	18.94	28.69	17.87
Capital allowances		8.00	2.00	1.50	0.50
Taxable profit		2.50	16.94	27.19	17.37
Tax (20%)		0.50	3.39	5.44	3.47

(W2) **All figures are in $ million**

Year	0	1	2	3	4
Working capital (20% of sales revenue)		4.97	8.54	12.36	7.38
Working capital required/(released)	4.97	3.57	3.82	(4.98)	(7.38)

(W3) Lintu Co asset beta = 1.5 × $128m/($128m + $31.96m × 0.8) approx. = 1.25

All-equity financed discount rate = 2% + 1.25 × 8% = 12%

Financing side effects

	$000
Issue costs 2/98 × $42,970,000	(876.94)

Tax shield

Annual tax relief = ($42,970,000 × 60% × 0.015 × 20%)

+ ($42,970,000 × 40% × 0.04 × 20%)

= 77.35 + 137.50 = 214.85

The present value of the tax relief annuity = 214.85 × 3.63	779.91

Annual subsidy benefit

$42,970,000 × 60% × 0.025 × 80% = 515.64

The present value of the subsidy benefit annuity = 515.64 × 3.63	1,871.77
Total benefit of financing side effects	1,774.74

Financing the project entirely by debt would add just under $1.78 million to the value of the project, or approximately, an additional 20% to the all-equity financed project.

The adjusted present value (APV) of the project is just under $10.4 million and therefore it should be accepted.

Note: *In calculating the present values of the tax shield and subsidy benefits, the annuity factor used is based on 4% to reflect the normal borrowing/default risk of the company.*

Alternatively, 2% or 2.5% could be used depending on the assumptions made. Credit will be given where these are used to estimate the annuity factor, where the assumption is explained.

(b) **Corrections made to the original net present value**

The approach taken to exclude depreciation from the net present value computation is correct, but capital allowances need to be taken away from profit estimates before tax is calculated, reducing the profits on which tax is payable.

Interest is not normally included in the net present value calculations. Instead, it is normally imputed within the cost of capital or discount rate. In this case, it is included in the financing side effects.

Cash flows are inflated and the nominal rate based on Lintu Co's all-equity financed rate is used (see below). Where different cash flows are subject to different rates of inflation, applying a real rate to non-inflated amounts would not give an accurate answer.

The impact of the working capital requirement is included in the estimate as, although all the working capital is recovered at the end of the project, the flows of working capital are subject to different discount rates when their present values are calculated.

Approach taken

The value of the project is initially assessed considering only the business risk involved in undertaking the project. The discount rate used is based on Lintu Co's asset beta which measures only the business risk of that company. Since Lintu Co is in the same line of business as the project, it is deemed appropriate to use its discount rate, instead of 11% that Burung Co uses normally.

The impact of debt financing and the subsidy benefit are then considered. In this way, Burung Co can assess the value created from its investment activity and then the additional value created from the manner in which the project is financed.

Assumptions made

It is assumed that all figures used are accurate and any estimates made are reasonable. Burung Co may want to consider undertaking a sensitivity analysis to assess this.

It is assumed that the initial working capital required will form part of the funds borrowed but that the subsequent working capital requirements will be available from the funds generated by the project. The validity of this assumption needs to be assessed since the working capital requirements at the start of years 2 and 3 are substantial.

It is assumed that Lintu Co's asset beta and all-equity financed discount rate represent the business risk of the project. The validity of this assumption also needs to be assessed. For example, Lintu Co's entire business may not be similar to the project, and it may undertake other lines of business. In this case, the asset beta would need to be adjusted so that just the project's business risk is considered.

(**Note:** Credit will be given for alternative, relevant explanations.)

Marking scheme			Marks
(a)	Inflated incremental profit		2
	Taxation		2
	Working capital		2
	Estimate of discount rate		2
	Net present value		1
	Issue costs		1
	Tax shield benefit		2
	Subsidy benefit		1
	Adjusted present value and conclusion		2
			15
(b)	Corrections made		4–5
	Approach taken		2–3
	Assumptions made		3–4
		Max	10
Total			**25**

44   RIVIERE CO (DEC 14)

> **Key answer tips**
>
> Value at Risk is often perceived to be a tricky topic. Remember to multiply by the square root of 5 to extend your calculation from one year to five years.
>
> Don't worry if you find the mathematics involved in Value at Risk complex. There are plenty of easier, discursive marks in this question if you have a good exam technique.

(a)   A free trade area like the European Union (EU) aims to remove barriers to trade and allow freedom of movement of production resources such as capital and labour. The EU also has an overarching common legal structure across all member countries and tries to limit any discriminatory practice against companies operating in these countries. Furthermore, the EU erects common external barriers to trade against countries which are not member states.

Riviere Co may benefit from operating within the EU in a number of ways as it currently trades within it. It should find that it is able to compete on equal terms with rival companies within the EU. Companies outside the EU may find it difficult to enter the EU markets due to barriers to trade. A common legal structure should ensure that the standards of food quality and packaging apply equally across all the member countries. Due diligence of logistic networks used to transport the food may be easier to undertake because of common compliance requirements. Having access to capital and labour within the EU may make it easier for the company to set up branches inside the EU, if it wants to. The company may also be able to access any grants which are available to companies based within the EU.

(b)   **Project Drugi**

Internal rate of return (IRR)

10% NPV: €2,293,000 approximately

Year	Current	1	2	3	4	5
Cash flows (€000s)	(11,840)	1,230	1,680	4,350	10,240	2,200
Try 20%		0.833	0.694	0.579	0.482	0.402
	(11,840)	1,025	1,166	2,519	4,936	884

NPV = €(1,310,000)

IRR = 10% + 2,293/(2,293 + 1,310) × 10% approximately = 16.4%

Modified internal rate of return (MIRR)

Total PVs years 1 to 5 at 10% discount rate = €11,840,000 + €2,293,000 = €14,133,000

MIRR (using formula) = $[(14{,}133/11{,}840)^{1/5} \times 1.10] -- 1 = 14\%$

Alternatively:

Year	Cash flows	Multiplier	Re-invested amount
	(€000s)		(€000s)
1	1,230	1.14	1,801
2	1,680	1.13	2,236
3	4,350	1.12	5,264
4	10,240	1.11	11,264
5	2,200	1	2,200

Total re-invested amount approx. = €22,765,000

MIRR = $(€22,765,000/€11,840,000)^{1/5} - 1 = 14\%$

Value at risk (VAR)

Based on a single tail test:

A 95% confidence level requires the annual present value VAR to be within approximately 1.645 standard deviations from the mean.

A 90% confidence level requires annual present value VAR to be within approximately 1.282 standard deviations from the mean.

(**Note:** An approximation of standard deviations to two decimal places is acceptable.)

95%, five-year present value VAR = $\$400,000 \times 1.645 \times 5^{0.5}$ = approx. €1,471,000

90%, five-year present value VAR = $\$400,000 \times 1.282 \times 5^{0.5}$ = approx. €1,147,000

	Privi	Drugi
Net present value (10%)	€2,054,000	€2,293,000
Internal rate of return	17.6%	16.4%
Modified internal rate of return	13.4%	14.0%
VAR (over the project's life)		
95% confidence level	€1,103,500	€1,471,000
90% confidence level	€860,000	€1,147,000

The net present value and the modified internal rate of return both indicate that project Drugi would create more value for Riviere Co. However, the internal rate of return (IRR) for project Privi is higher. Where projects are mutually exclusive, the IRR can give an incorrect answer. This is because the IRR assumes that returns are re-invested at the internal rate of return, whereas net present value and the modified IRR assume that they are re-invested at the cost of capital (discount rate) which in this case is 10%. The cost of capital is a more realistic assumption as this is the minimum return required by investors in a company. Furthermore, the manner in which the cash flows occur will have a bearing on the IRR calculated. For example, with project Drugi, a high proportion of the cash flows occur in year four and these will be discounted by using the higher IRR compared to the cost of capital, thus reducing the value of the project faster. The IRR can give the incorrect answer in these circumstances. Therefore, based purely on cash flows, project Drugi should be accepted due to the higher net present value and modified IRR, as they give the theoretically correct answer of the value created.

The VAR provides an indication of the potential riskiness of a project. For example, if Riviere Co invests in project Drugi then it can be 95% confident that the present value will not fall by more than €1,471,000 over its life. Hence the project will still produce a positive net present value. However, there is a 5% chance that the loss could be greater than €1,471,000. With project Privi, the potential loss in value is smaller and therefore it is less risky. It should be noted that the VAR calculations indicate that the investments involve different risk. However, the cash flows are discounted at the same rate, which they should not be, since the risk differs between them.

Notwithstanding that, when risk is also taken into account, the choice between the projects is not clear cut and depends on Riviere Co's attitude to risk and return. Project Drugi gives the higher potential net present value but is riskier, whereas project Privi is less risky but gives a smaller net present value. This is before taking into account additional uncertainties such as trading in an area in which Riviere Co is not familiar. It is therefore recommended that Riviere Co should only proceed with project Drugi if it is willing to accept the higher risk and uncertainty.

(c)   **Possible legal risks**

There are a number of possible legal risks which Riviere Co may face, for example:

- The countries where the product is sold may have different legal regulations on food preparation, quality and packaging.

- The company needs to ensure that the production processes and the transportation of the frozen foods comply with these regulations. It also needs to ensure that the promotional material on the packaging complies with regulations in relation to what is acceptable in each country.

- The legal regulations may be more lax in countries outside the EU but Riviere Co needs to be aware that complying only with the minimum standards may impact its image negatively overall, even if they are acceptable in the countries concerned.

- There may be import quotas in the countries concerned or the governments may give favourable terms and conditions to local companies, which may make it difficult for Riviere Co to compete.

- The legal system in some countries may not recognise the trademarks or production patents which the company holds on its packaging and production processes. This may enable competitors to copy the food and the packaging.

- Different countries may have different regulations regarding product liability from poorly prepared and/or stored food which cause harm to consumers. For example, Riviere Co may use other companies to transport its food and different supermarkets may sell its food. It needs to be aware of the potential legal claims on it and its supplier should the food prove harmful to the customers.

Possible mitigation strategies

- Riviere Co needs to undertake sufficient research of the countries' current laws and regulations to ensure that it complies with the standards required. It may even want to ensure that it exceeds the required standards to ensure that it maintains its reputation.

- Riviere Co needs to ensure that it also keeps abreast of potential changes in the law. It may also want to ensure that it complies with best practice, even if it is not the law yet. Often current best practices become enshrined in future legislation.

- Riviere Co needs to investigate the extent to which it may face difficulty in overcoming quota restrictions, less favourable trading conditions and lack of trademark and patent protection. If necessary, these should be factored into the financial analysis. It could be that Riviere Co has already taken these into account.

- Strict contracts need to be set up between Riviere Co and any agents it uses to transport and sell the food. These could be followed up by regular checks to ensure that the standards required are maintained.

- All the above will add extra costs and if these have not been included in the financial analysis, they need to be. These extra costs may mean that the project is no longer viable.

(**Note:** Credit will be given for alternative, relevant discussion for parts (a) and (c).)

ACCA marking scheme			
			Marks
(a)	Discussion of the EU as a free trade area		2–3
	Discussion of the possible benefits to Riviere Co		2–3
		Maximum	5
(b)	Calculation of internal rate of return		2
	Calculation of modified internal rate of return		2
	Determining the two standard deviations (1.645 and 1.282)		1
	Calculations of the two value at risk figures		2
	Explanation of weakness of internal rate of return and why net present value and modified		
	internal rate of return are better		2–3
	Explanation of value at risk figures and what they indicate		2–3
	Recommendation		1–2
		Maximum	13
(c)	Discussion of possible legal risks		3–4
	Discussion of how these may be mitigated		3–4
		Maximum	7
Total			**25**

ACQUISITIONS AND MERGERS

45   DOUBLER INC *Walk in the footsteps of a top tutor*

> **Key answer tips**
>
> In a question like this with several parts, it is important to split your time allocation carefully between the different parts of the question. It would be easy to over-run on the early parts of this question and not to leave enough time for the relatively easy discursive final parts.

(a)   Doubler currently has 40 million ordinary shares, and Fader 30 million.

Earnings per share:

Doubler   *Fader*

$\dfrac{4.41}{40}$ = 11.025 cents $\dfrac{2.87}{30}$ = 9.567 cents

P/E ratios:

Doubler   *Fader*

$\dfrac{290}{11.025}$ = 26.30 $\dfrac{180}{9.567}$ = 18.81

(b)   A 2-for-3 share exchange will result in the issue of 30 million × 2/3 new shares, or 20 million shares, giving a total of 60 million shares.

	$ million
Current combined earnings after tax	7.28
Additional earnings from operating savings	0.75
	8.03

Ignoring the one-off redundancy payments the expected earnings per share is:

$\dfrac{8.03}{60}$ = 13.38 cents

Increasing earnings per share alone is not enough. The effect on the market value is the crucial factor. When a relatively high P/E company acquires a company with a lower P/E, the expected earnings per share will increase, but not necessarily the total market value of the companies.

(c) (i) The current combined value of the two companies is:

40m shares × 290 cents + 30m shares × 180 cents or $170 million.

If the market is efficient, ignoring any synergistic or other effects of the takeover, the post-acquisition P/E will be the weighted average (by earnings) of the current P/E ratios.

$$\frac{26.30 \times 4.41 + 18.81 \times 2.87}{7.28} = 23.35$$

The new EPS takes into account the operating savings.

Multiplying the P/E by the new EPS 23.35 × 13.38 = 312 cents × 60 million shares gives a market value of $187.2 million.

However, this ignores the impact of the redundancy costs, $700,000 after tax. When this is included the combined value of the companies is still expected to substantially increase.

(ii) Changes in expected cash flows as a result of the takeover are as follows:

PV of operating savings (to infinity)	$\dfrac{\$750,000}{0.12}$	$6,250,000
Redundancy costs, after tax relief		($700,000)
Net effect on NPV		$5,550,000

If the market is efficient the market value of the combined company should increase by $5,550,000 as a result of the expected increase in NPV, much less than the estimate using P/E based valuation.

(d) Both estimates are likely to be inaccurate. Many other factors are likely to affect the post-acquisition share price. For example:

(i) The effect of the acquisition on corporate growth rates.

(ii) There may be problems integrating the operations and workforce of the two companies.

(iii) Doubler's managers may be able to apply enhanced management skills to Fader's operations.

(iv) The effect of the change in risk and capital structure is not known.

With respect to the PE estimate:

(i) PE ratios use accounting data rather than cash flow data.

(ii) Accurate estimates of future earnings are very difficult, and earnings can rapidly change.

With respect to cash flows:

(i) The value of all expected cash flows pre and post-acquisition should be compared, not just the changes in a few cash flows. However, post-acquisition cash flows are very difficult to determine.

(ii) Cash flows savings of £750,000 per year forever are unrealistic.

(iii) The cost of capital of Doubler is likely to change as a result of the acquisition of Fader.

(e) **The implications of making a hostile bid**

The board should be clear about the strategic implications of making a hostile bid for a company rather than carrying out an aggressive investment programme of organic growth.

A hostile bid involves:

- A reduction in competition. The company may be buying a competitor who will no longer be competing against it and its competitive position should be improved.

- A much faster speed of growth. It is much quicker to buy an existing company with existing staff and existing contracts.

- Buying an under-performer. The challenge would be to tighten up the company and release its full potential.

- More expense than the organic alternative. A bidding company has to pay a premium to acquire a target company. However, there may be synergistic benefits from the merger that would make paying the premium worthwhile.

- Possible culture clash between ourselves and the target company managers and employees

- The use of cash resources to finance any cash alternative to the paper offer. If cash is tight, then the company should offer an unattractive cash alternative to try and persuade the target shareholders to accept paper rather than cash.

Organic growth involves:

- Less risk. Steady organic growth is a much safer option, where individual problems can be addressed as they arise, rather than having to deal with all the problems in an entire company from day one of ownership.

- Less damage to the stock price in the market. It is traditionally the case that the market will mark down the price of a bidding company's stock/shares on announcement of the bid, recognising the risk inherent in the deal and the fact that managers may concentrate on the deal rather than on running the existing business.

- More choice on precisely where to expand. Organic growth allows a company to choose more carefully the geographical areas and business areas that you wish to operate in.

(f) The regulation of takeovers usually includes the following factors:

- At the most important time in the company's life – when it is subject to a takeover bid – its directors should act in the best interest of their shareholders, and should disregard their personal interests.

- All shareholders must be treated equally

- Shareholders must be given all the relevant information to make an informed judgement.

- The board of the target company must not take action without the approval of shareholders, which could result in the offer being defeated.

- All information supplied to shareholders must be prepared to the highest standards of care and accuracy.

- The assumptions on which profit forecasts are based and the accounting polices used should be examined and reported on by accountants.

- An independent valuer should support valuations of assets

46 MERCURY TRAINING

Key answer tips

The solution strategy for part (a) of the question is to determine the proxy beta by weighting the individual asset betas and then gearing them to the level appropriate for Mercury Training Ltd. The required conversion formula is shown in the formula sheet. The equity and weighted average costs of capital are then straightforward.

(a) *Mercury's asset beta will be a weighted average of the asset betas for Financial Services (FS) and Jupiter as follows:*

Mercury's $\beta_a = (\frac{1}{3} \times FS\beta_a) + (\frac{2}{3} \times Jupiter\beta_a)$

Financial services

$$\beta_a = \frac{V_e}{V_e + V_d(1-T)} \times \beta_e = \frac{75}{75 + 25(1-0.40)} \times 0.9 = 0.75$$

Jupiter

$$\beta_a = \frac{V_e}{V_e + V_d(1-T)} \times \beta_e = \frac{88}{88 + 12(1-0.40)} \times 1.5 = 1.39$$

Therefore,

Mercury $\beta_a = \left(\frac{1}{3} \times 0.75\right) + \left(\frac{2}{3} \times 1.39\right) = 1.17$

Now, re-gearing this asset beta for Mercury's gearing level gives:

$$1.17 = \beta_e \times \frac{70}{70 + 30(1-0.40)}$$

$$\beta_e = 1.48$$

The equity and weighted average costs of capital are then as follows:

$r_e = RF + \beta\ i\ (Rm - RF)$

$r_e = 0.045 + 1.480 \times 0.035 = 9.68\%$

And

$$WACC = \frac{V_e}{V_e + V_d}\ k_e + \frac{V_d}{V_e + V_d}\ k_d(1-T)$$

so

WACC = [0.7 × 0.0968] + [0.3 × (0.045 + 0.025) × 0.60] = 8.04%

The equity cost of capital is used for valuing income flows (such as dividends or free cash flow to equity) which go directly to the equity investor. The weighted average cost of capital is for valuing flows attributable to the business entity such as project cash flows or NOPAT.

(b)   This part of the question requires advice on the likely range of prices.

At the low end the firm's net assets at fair value would be the realisable value of the equity between a willing buyer and seller. This is 650c per share which would represent the lower end of any negotiating range.

Using the dividend valuation model we estimate the share price at the upper end using the latest DPS of 25c/ per share and the cost of equity capital of 9.68%. Three potential growth rates present themselves: the historic earnings growth which at 12% is greater than the firm's equity cost of capital and is therefore not sustainable over the very long run, the anticipated growth rate of the two sectors weighted according to the firm's revenue from each (0.67 × 6% + 0.33 × 4% = 5.33%) and the rate implied from the firm's reinvestment:

$$g = br_e = \frac{(100 - 25))}{100} \times 0.0968 = 7.26\%$$

The value of the firm using the growth model and the higher of the two feasible growth rates is:

$$P_o = \frac{D_o(1+g)}{r_e - g}$$

$$P_o = \frac{25 \times (1.0726)}{(0.0968 - 0.0726)} = \$11.08 \, \text{per share}$$

In addition, the share price gives a spot estimate of the value of a dividend stream in the hands of a minority investor. If the option to float is taken then a share price of $11.08 could be achieved especially if a portion of the equity and effective control are retained. However, if a sale is made to a private equity investor then it may be appropriate to value the firm taking into account the benefits of control which can be substantial if the purchaser is able to generate significant synergistic benefits either in terms of revenue enhancement, cost efficiency or more favourable access to the capital market. Control premiums can be as much as 30–50% of the spot price of the equity. In this case an opening negotiation may start with a share price of $16.62.

(c)   **The Directors**

Mercury Training

The two principal sources of large-scale equity finance are either through a public listing on a recognised stock exchange or through the private equity market. The former represents the traditional approach for firms who have grown beyond a certain size and where the owners wish to release, in whole or in part, their equity stake within the firm, or where they wish to gain access to new, large scale equity finance. The procedure for gaining a public listing is lengthy and invariably requires professional sponsorship from a company that specialises in this type of work. Depending upon the jurisdiction there are three stages that may have to be fulfilled before a firm can raise capital on a stock exchange:

1   Formalise the company's status as a public limited company with rights to issue its shares to the public. In some jurisdictions this requires re-registration and in others it is implicit in the conferment of limited liability.

2   Seek regulatory approval for admission to a public list of companies who have met the basic criteria required for entry to a stock exchange (in the UK this process is under the jurisdiction of the Financial Services Authority).

3   Fulfil the requirements of the exchange concerned which may entail the publication of a prospectus which is an audited document containing, among other things, projections of future earnings and profitability.

The disadvantage of public listing is that a company will be exposed to stake building by other companies, regulatory oversight by the stock exchange and greater public scrutiny. Stock exchanges require that quoted companies comply with company law as a matter of course but also that they adhere to various codes of practice associated with good governance and takeovers. They must also comply with stock exchange rules with respect to the provision of information and dealing with shareholders.

Private equity finance is the name given to finance raised from investors organised through the mediation of a venture capital company or a private equity business. As the name suggests these investors do not operate through the formal equity market but they operate within the context of the wider capital market for high risk finance. Because of its position, PEF does not impose the same regulatory regime as the public market. Transaction costs tend to be lower and there is evidence to suggest that private equity finance offers companies the ability to restructure and take long term decisions which have adverse short term consequences. In some jurisdictions there are favourable tax advantages to private equity investors.

47   KODIAK COMPANY

Key answer tips

Business valuation is commonly tested, especially using the discounted cash flow method. Be careful to lay out your workings carefully. With lots of forecast figures to derive, it is easy to get in a muddle. A neat columnar format, with references to detailed workings, will ensure that you score well.

(a)   Given the details supplied, a forward forecast of the statement of profit or loss and of the statement of financial position is a precursor to the cash flow forecast. On the assumptions (as stated in the question but not reproduced here) the following projection is obtained (all figures in $000):

Projected statement of profit or loss

	Year 1	Year 2	Year 3
Revenue (9% growth)	5,450	5,941	6,475
Cost of sales (9% growth)	3,270	3,564	3,885
Gross Profit	2,180	2,377	2,590
Operating costs (W1)	2,012	2,159	2,317
Operating profit	168	218	273

Projected cash flows

Operating profit	168	218	273
Add depreciation (W2)	134	144	155
Less incremental working capital (W3)	(20)	(21)	(24)
Less taxation (W4)	(15)	(28)	(43)
Less interest	(74)	(74)	(74)
	193	239	287
Less investment in non-current assets (W2)	(79)	(95)	(114)
Free cash flow to equity	114	144	173

Workings

(W1) Operating costs

Variable costs (9% growth)	818	891	971
Fixed costs (6% growth)	1,060	1,124	1,191
Depreciation (W2)	134	144	155
Total operating costs	2,012	2,159	2,317

(W2) Non-current assets and depreciation

Non-current assets at beginning	1,266	1,345	1,440
Additions (20% growth)	79	95	114
Non-current assets	1,345	1,440	1,554
Depreciation (10%)	134	144	155

(W3) Working capital

Working capital (9% growth)	240	261	285
Incremental WC	240 – 220 = 20	261 – 240 = 21	285 – 261 = 24

Initial working capital equals net current assets less cash. Alternatively, the full 270 can be used as working capital as well. Credit will be given for either assumption.

(W4) Taxation

One year in arrears (30%)	15 (given)	$30\% \times (168 - 74)$	$30\% \cdot (218 - 74)$
		= 28	= 43

(b) Our estimate of the value of this business on a going concern basis assumes that cash will be generated and reinvestment made according to the above projection. The free cash flow after reinvestment which is potentially distributable and the terminal value of the business assuming a constant rate of reinvestment of 3% forward is as follows:

	0	1	2	3
Free cash flow after reinvestment		114	144	173
Terminal value				2,546
Required rate of return	10%			
Present value of cash flows (discounted at 10%)		104	119	2,043
Value of the firm	2,266			

The terminal value is calculated as follows:

$$Value_3 \frac{FCFE_3(1.03)}{R_e - 3\%}$$

$$Value_3(\$000)\frac{173 \times (1.03)}{10\% - 3\%} = 2,546$$

Where R_e is the required rate of return of 10% per annum.

The value of the firm, on the basis of the above projections, is $2,266,000.

(c) This valuation is based upon a number of assumptions which you should consider when reviewing this analysis. We have taken your judgement that 10% fairly reflects the market rate of return required for an investment of this type. This rate should compensate you for the business risk to which your firm is exposed. For an investment held within the context of a widely diversified portfolio the rate of return you should expect will only be conditioned by your exposure to market risk. However, in the context of a sole equity investment then the rate of return you may require could be more than that which would be available from the market for an investment of this type.

In generating our projections we have assumed the estimates are certain and that the firm is a going concern. In considering this investment further you may wish to explicitly consider the variability attaching to the underlying variables in the projection and the possible range of values that may result. Of particular importance is the assumption of a three-year forecast. In practice the period chosen does depend upon the nature of the business and in particular the uncertainties to which it is exposed.

Finally we have assumed a terminal value based upon future cash flows from year three forward growing at a compound rate of 3% into the indefinite future. The resulting value will be particularly sensitive to this figure and it may be that you may wish to consider a different rate depending upon what you regard as sustainable in the long term for a business of this type.

48   KILENC CO (JUN 12)

(a)   Kilenc Co needs to consider a number of risks and issues when making the decision about whether or not to set up a subsidiary company in Lanosia. It should then consider how these may be managed or controlled.

Tutorial note (from the examiner's model answer)

The following answer is indicative. Credit will be given for alternative suggestions of risks and issues, and their management or control.

Key Risks/Issues

Kilenc Co needs to assess the impact on its current exports to Lanosia and the nearby countries if the subsidiary is set up. Presumably, products are currently exported to these countries and if these exports stop, then there may be a negative impact on the employees and facilities currently employed in this area. Related to this may be the risk of loss of reputation if the move results in redundancies. Furthermore, Kilenc Co should consider how the subsidiary and its products would be seen in Lanosia and the nearby countries. For example, would the locally made products be perceived as being of comparative quality as the imported products?

The recession in Lanosia may have a negative impact on the market for the products. The cost of setting up the subsidiary company needs to be compared with the benefits from extra sales revenue and reduced costs. There is a risk that the perceived benefits may be less than predicted or the establishment of a subsidiary may create opportunities in the future once the country recovers from the recession.

Currently the government offers support for companies involved in the pharmaceutical industry. Kilenc Co may find it difficult to set up the subsidiary if it is viewed as impeding the development of the local industry by the government. For example, the government may impose restrictions or increase the taxes the subsidiary may have to pay. On the other hand, the subsidiary may be viewed as supporting the economy and the growth of the pharmaceutical industry, especially since 40% of the shares and 50% of the Board of Directors would be in local hands. The government may even offer the same support as it currently offers the other local companies.

Kilenc Co wants to finance the subsidiary through a mixture of equity and debt. The implications of raising equity finance are discussed in part (b) of the question. However, the risks surrounding debt finance needs further discussion. Raising debt finance in Lanosia would match the income generated in Lanosia with debt interest payments, but the company needs to consider whether or not it would be possible to borrow the money. Given that the government has had to finance the banks may mean that the availability of funds to borrow may be limited. Also interest rates are low at the moment but inflation is high, this may result in pressure on the government to raise interest rates in the future. The consequences of this may be that the borrowing costs increase for Kilenc Co.

The composition of the Board of Directors and the large proportion of the subsidiary's equity held by minority shareholders may create agency issues and risks. Kilenc Co may find that the subsidiary's Board may make decisions which are not in the interests of the parent company, or that the shareholders attempt to move the subsidiary in a direction which is not in the interests of the parent company. On the other hand, the subsidiary's Board may feel that the parent company is imposing too many restrictions on its ability to operate independently and the minority shareholders may feel that their interests are not being considered by the parent company.

Kilenc Co needs to consider the cultural issues when setting up a subsidiary in another country. These may range from cultural issues of different nationalities and doing business in the country to cultural issues within the organisation. Communication of how the company is organised and understanding of cultural issues is very important in this case. The balance between independent autonomy and central control needs to be established and agreed.

Risks such as foreign exchange exposure, product health and safety compliance, employee health and safety regulations and physical risks need to be considered and assessed. For example, foreign exchange exposures arising from exporting the products to nearby countries need to be assessed. The legal requirements around product health and safety and employee health and safety need to be understood and complied with. Risks of physical damage such as from floods or fires on the assets of the business need to be established.

Mitigating the Risks and Issues

A full analysis of the financial costs and benefits should be undertaken to establish the viability of setting up the subsidiary. Sensitivity and probability analysis should be undertaken to assess the impact and possibility of falling revenues and rising costs. Analysis of real options should be undertaken to establish the value of possible follow-on projects.

Effective marketing communication such as media advertising should be conducted on the products produced by the subsidiary to ensure that the customers' perceptions of the new products do not change. This could be supported by retaining the packaging of the products. Internal and external communication should explain the consequences of any negative impact of the move to Lanosia to minimise any reputational damage. Where possible, employees should be redeployed to other divisions, in order to minimise any negative disruption.

Negotiations with the Lanosian government should be undertaken regularly during the process of setting up the subsidiary to minimise any restrictions and to maximise any benefits such as favourable tax rates. Where necessary and possible, these may be augmented with appropriate insurance and legal advice. Continuing lobbying may also be necessary after the subsidiary has been established to reduce the possibility of new rules and regulations which may be detrimental to the subsidiary's business.

An economic analysis may be conducted on the likely movements in inflation and interest rates. Kilenc Co may also want to look into using fixed rate debt for its long-term financing needs, or use swaps to change from variable rates to fixed rates. The costs of such activity need to be taken into account.

Clear corporate governance mechanisms need to be negotiated and agreed on, to strike a balance between central control and subsidiary autonomy. The negotiations should involve the major parties and legal advice may be sought where necessary. These mechanisms should be clearly communicated to the major parties.

The subsidiary organisation should be set up to take account of cultural differences where possible. Induction sessions for employees and staff handbooks can be used to communicate the culture of the organisation and how to work within the organisation.

Foreign exchange exposure, health and safety regulation and risk of physical loss can be managed by a combination of hedging, insurance and legal advice.

(b) Dark pool trading systems allow share orders to be placed and matched without the traders' interests being declared publicly on the normal stock exchange. Therefore the price of these trades is determined anonymously and the trade is only declared publicly after it has been agreed. Large volume trades which use dark pool trading systems prevent signals reaching the markets in order to minimise large fluctuations in the share price or the markets moving against them.

The main argument put forward in support of dark pool trading systems is that by preventing large movements in the share price due to volume sales, the markets' artificial price volatility would be reduced and the markets maintain their efficiency. The contrary arguments suggest that in fact market efficiency is reduced by dark pool trading systems because such trades do not contribute to the price changes. Furthermore, because most of the individuals who use the markets to trade equity shares are not aware of the trade, transparency is reduced. This, in turn, reduces the liquidity in the markets and therefore may compromise their efficiency. The ultimate danger is that the lack of transparency and liquidity may result in an uncontrolled spread of risks similar to what led to the recent global financial crisis.

It is unlikely that the dark pool trading systems would have an impact on Kilenc Co's subsidiary company because the subsidiary's share price would be based on Kilenc Co's share price and would not be affected by the stock market in Lanosia. Market efficiency in general in Lanosia would probably be much more important.

ACCA marking scheme		
		Marks
(a)	Discussion of key risks or issues (2–3 marks for each)	8–10
	Suggestions for management or control of the risk or issue (1–2 marks each)	6–8
	Maximum	15
(b)	Explanation of dark pool trading systems	2–3
	Consequences and how these would affect Kilenc Co	2–3
	Maximum	5
Total		**20**

49 SIGRA CO (DEC 12 A)

Key answer tips

Different methods of payment (e.g. cash offer, share for share exchange) have been tested frequently in recent sittings. Valuation using P/E ratios is a critical starting point in this question.

(a) **Common reason why acquisitions are unsuccessful**

Lack of industrial or commercial fit

Failure can result from a takeover where the acquired entity turns out not to have the product range or industrial position that the acquirer anticipated.

Lack of goal congruence

This may apply not only to the acquired entity but, more dangerously, to the acquirer, whereby disputes over the treatment of the acquired entity might well take away the benefits of an otherwise excellent acquisition.

'Cheap' purchases

The 'turn around' costs of an acquisition purchased at what seems to be a bargain price may well turn out to be a high multiple of that price.

Paying too much

The fact that a high premium is paid for an acquisition does not necessarily mean that it will fail. Failure would result only if the price paid is beyond that which the acquirer considers acceptable to increase satisfactorily the long term wealth of its shareholders.

Failure to integrate effectively

An acquirer needs to have a workable and clear plan of the extent to which the acquired company is to be integrated. The plan must address such problems as differences in management styles, incompatibilities in data information systems, and continued opposition to the acquisition by some of the acquired entity's staff.

(b) Number of Sigra Co shares = 4,400,000/0.4 = 11,000,000 shares

Sigra Co earnings per share (EPS) = $4,950,000/11,000,000 shares = 45c/share

Sigra Co price to earnings (PE) ratio = $3.6/$0.45 = 8

Dentro PE ratio = 8 × 1.125 = 9

Dentro Co shares = $500,000/0.4 = 1,250,000 shares

Dentro Co EPS = $625,000/1,250,000 = 50c/share

Estimate of Dentro Co value per share = $0.5 × 9 = $4.50/share

Cash offer

Dentro share percentage gain under cash offer

$0.50/$4.50 × 100% = 11.1%

Share-for-share exchange

Equity value of Sigra Co = 11,000,000 × $3.60 =	$39,600,000
Equity value of Dentro Co = 1,250,000 × $4.50 =	$5,625,000
Synergy savings = 30% × $5,625,000 =	$1,688,000
Total equity value of combined company	$46,913,000
Number of shares for share-for-share exchange	
11,000,000 + [1,250,000 × 3/2] =	12,875,000
Expected share price of combined company	$3.644/share

Dentro share percentage gain under share-for-share offer

[($3.644 × 3 − $4.50 × 2)/2]/$4.50 × 100% = 21.5%

Bond offer

Rate of return

$$104 = \$6 \times (1 + r)^{-1} + \$6 \times (1 + r)^{-2} + \$106 \times (1 + r)^{-3}$$

If r is 5%, price is $102.72 If r is 4%, price is $105.55

r is approximately = 4% + (105.55 − 104)/(105.55 − 102.72) × 1% = 4.55%

Price of new bond =

$$\$2 \times 1.0455^{-1} + \$2 \times 1.0455^{-2} + \$102 \times 1.0455^{-3} = \$93.00$$

Value per share = $93.00/16 = $5.81/share

Dentro share percentage gain under bond offer

Bond offer: ($5.81 − $4.50)/$4.50 × 100% = 29.1%

Comments

An initial comparison is made between the cash and the share-for-share offers. Although the share-for-share exchange gives a higher return compared to the cash offer, Dentro Co's shareholders may prefer the cash offer as the gains in the share price are dependent on the synergy gains being achieved. However, purchase for cash may mean that the shareholders face an immediate tax burden. Sigra Co's shareholders would probably prefer the cash option because the premium would only take $625,000 of the synergy benefits ($0.50 × 1,250,000 shares), whereas a share-for-share exchange would result in approximately $1,209,000 of the synergy benefits being given to the Dentro Co shareholders (21.5% × $4.50 × 1,250,000 shares).

The bond offer provides an alternative which may be acceptable to both sets of shareholders. Dentro Co's shareholders receive the highest return for this and Sigra Co's shareholders may be pleased that a large proportion of the payment is deferred for three years. In present value terms, however, a very high proportion of the projected synergy benefits are given to Dentro Co's shareholders (29.1% × $4.50 × $1,250,000 = $1,637,000).

(c) The regulatory framework within the European Union, the EU takeovers directive, will be used to discuss the proposals. However it is acceptable for candidates to refer to other directives and discuss the proposals on that basis.

Proposal 1

With regards to the first proposal, the directive gives the bidder squeeze-out rights, where the bidder can force minority shareholders to sell their shares. However, the limits set for squeeze-out rights are generally high (UK: 90%; Belgium, France, Germany and the Netherlands: 95%; Ireland 80%). It is likely therefore that Sigra Co will need a very large proportion of Dentro Co's shareholders to agree to the acquisition before they can force the rest of Dentro Co's shareholders to sell their shares. Dentro Co's minority shareholders may also require Sigra Co to purchase their shares, known as sell-out rights.

Proposal 2

With regards to the second proposal, the principle of equal treatment in the directive requires that all shareholders should be treated equally. In general terms, the bidder must offer to minority shareholders the same terms as those offered to other shareholders. It could be argued here that the principle of equal treatment is contravened because later shareholders are not offered the extra 3 cents per share, even though the 30% is less than a majority shareholding. It is highly unlikely that Sigra Co will be allowed to offer these terms.

50 HAV CO (JUN 13)

Key answer tips

In many valuation questions you will also have to address discursive issues such as synergy. Make sure that you allocate your time carefully to enable you to attempt both the calculations and the discussion parts.

(a) An acquisition creates synergy benefits when the value of the combined entity is more than the sum of the two companies' values. Synergies can be separated into three types: revenue synergies which result in higher revenues for the combined entity, higher return on equity and a longer period when the company is able to maintain competitive advantage; cost synergies which result mainly from reducing duplication of functions and related costs, and from taking advantage of economies of scale; financial synergies which result from financing aspects such as the transfer of funds between group companies to where it can be utilised best, or from increasing debt capacity.

In this scenario, the following synergy benefits may arise from the two companies coming together. Financial synergies may be available because Strand Co does not have the funds to innovate new products. On the other hand, Hav Co has cash reserves available. It may be possible to identify and quantify this synergy based on the projects that can be undertaken after the acquisition, but would have been rejected before, and their corresponding net present value. Furthermore, as the company increases in size, the debt capacity of the combined company may increase, giving it additional access to finance. Finally, the acquisition may result in a decrease in the cost of capital of the combined company.

Cost synergies may arise from the larger company being able to negotiate better terms and lower costs from their suppliers. And there may be duplication of functional areas such as in research and development and head office which could be reduced and costs saved. These types of synergies are easier to identify and quantify but would be more short-lived. Therefore, if the markets are going to be positive about the acquisition, Hav Co will need to show where more long-term synergies are coming from as well as these.

Revenue synergies are perhaps where the greatest potential for growth comes from but are also more difficult to identify, quantify and enact. Good post-acquisition planning is essential for these synergies to be realised but they can be substantial and long-lasting. In this case, Hav Co's management can help market Strand Co's products more effectively by using their sales and marketing talents resulting in higher revenues and longer competitive advantage. Research and development activity can be combined to create new products using the technologies in place in both companies, and possibly bringing innovative products to market quicker. The services of the scientists from Strand Co will be retained to drive innovation forward, but these need to be nurtured with care since they had complete autonomy when they were the owners of Strand Co.

The main challenge in ensuring long-lasting benefits is not only ensuring accurate identification of potential synergies but putting into place integration processes and systems to gain full benefit from them. This is often the greater challenge for management, and, when poorly done, can result in failure to realise the full value of the acquisition. Hav Co needs to be aware of this and make adequate provision for it.

(Note: Credit will be given for alternative relevant comments and suggestions)

(b) **Maximum premium based on excess earnings method**

This method is similar to the EVA® method which measures excess return.

Average pre-tax earnings: (397 + 370 + 352)/3 = $373.0m

Average capital employed: [(882 + 210 − 209) + (838 + 208 − 180) + (801 + 198 − 140)]/3 = $869.3m

Excess annual value/annual premium = 373m − (20% × $869.3m) = $199.1m

After-tax annual premium = $199.1m × 0.8 = $159.3m

PV of annual premium (assume perpetuity) = $159.3m/0.07 = $2,275.7m

According to this method, the maximum premium payable is $2,275.7m in total.

Maximum premium based on price-to-earnings (PE) ratio method

Strand Co estimated PE ratio = 16.4 × 1.10 = 18.0

Strand Co profit after tax: $397m × 0.8 = $317.6m

Hav Co profit after tax = $1,980m × 0.8 =$1,584.0m

Hav Co, current value = $9.24 × 2,400 shares = $22,176.0m

Strand Co, current value = $317.6m × 18.0 = $5,716.8m

Combined company value = ($1,584m + $317.6m + $140.0m) × 14.5 = $29,603.2m

Maximum premium = $29,603.2m − ($22,176.0m + $5,716.8) = $1,710.4m

(c)   Strand Co, current value per share = $5,716.8m/1,200m shares = $4.76 per share

Maximum premium % based on PE ratio = $1,710.4m/$5,716.8m × 100% = 29.9%

Maximum premium % based on excess earnings = $2,275.7m/$5,716.8m × 100% = 39.8%

Cash offer: premium (%)

($5.72 – $4.76)/$4.76 × 100% = 20.2%

Cash and share offer: premium (%)

1 Hav Co share for 2 Strand Co shares

Hav Co share price = $9.24

Per Strand Co share = $4.62

Cash payment per share= $1.33

Total return = $1.33 + $4.62 = $5.95

Premium percentage = ($5.95 – $4.76)/$4.76 × 100% = 25.0%

Cash and bond offer: premium (%)

Each share has a nominal value of $0.25, therefore $5 is $5/$0.25 = 20 shares

Bond value = $100/20 shares = $5 per share

Cash payment = $1.25 per share

Total = $6.25 per share

Premium percentage = ($6.25 – $4.76)/$4.76 = 31.3%

On the basis of the calculations, the cash together with bond offer yields the highest return; in addition to the value calculated above, the bonds can be converted to 12 Hav Co shares, giving them a price per share of $8.33 ($100/12). This price is below Hav Co's current share price of $9.24, and therefore the conversion option is already in-the-money. It is probable that the share price will increase in the 10-year period and therefore the value of the convertible bond should increase. A bond also earns a small coupon interest of $3 per $100 a year. The 31.3% return is the closest to the maximum premium based on the excess earnings method and more than the maximum premium based on the PE ratio method. It would seem that this payment option transfers more value to the owners of Strand Co than the value created based on the PE ratio method.

However, with this option Strand Co shareholders only receive an initial cash payment of $1.25 per share compared to $1.33 per share and $5.72 per share for the other methods. This may make it the more attractive option for the Hav Co shareholders as well, and although their shareholding will be diluted most under this option, it will not happen for some time.

The cash and share offer gives a return in between the pure cash and the cash and bonds offers. Although the return is lower, Strand Co's shareholders become owners of Hav Co and have the option to sell their equity immediately. However, the share price may fall between now and when the payment for the acquisition is made. If this happens, then the return to Strand Co's shareholders will be lower.

The pure cash offer gives an immediate and definite return to Strand Co's shareholders, but is also the lowest offer and may also put a significant burden on Hav Co having to fund so much cash, possibly through increased debt.

It is likely that Strand Co's shareholder/managers, who will continue to work within Hav Co, will accept the mixed cash and bond offer. They, therefore, get to maximise their current return and also potentially gain when the bonds are converted into shares. Different impacts on shareholders' personal taxation situations due to the different payment methods might also influence the choice of method.

ACCA marking scheme			
			Marks
(a)	Distinguish between the different synergies		1–2
	Discuss possible financial synergy sources		2–3
	Discuss possible cost synergy sources		1–2
	Discuss possible revenue synergy sources		3–4
	Concluding comments		1–2
		Maximum	9
(b)	Average earnings and capital employed		1
	After-tax annual premium		1
	PV of premium (excess earnings method)		1
	Hav Co and Strand Co values		1
	Combined company value		1
	Value created/premium (PE method)		1
		Maximum	6
			6
(c)	Strand Co, value per share		1
	Cash offer premium (%)		1
	Cash and share offer premium (%)		2
	Cash and bond offer premium (%)		2
	Explanation and justification		4–5
		Maximum	10
Total			**25**

51 MAKONIS CO (DEC 13)

Key answer tips

Valuation using free cash flows is very commonly tested. However, the need to calculate a cost of capital for discounting here made this a very time-pressured question. Allocate time carefully to make sure that you leave enough time to attempt all parts of the question.

(a) **Combined company, cost of capital**

Asset beta

$(1.2 \times 480 + 0.9 \times 1,218)/(480 + 1,218) = 0.985$

Equity beta

$0.985 \times (60 + 40 \times 0.8)/60 = 1.51$

Cost of equity

$2\% + 1.51 \times 7\% = 12.57\%$

Cost of capital

$12.57\% \times 0.6 + 4.55\% \times 0.8 \times 0.4 = 9.00\%$

Combined company equity value

Years 1 to 4 ($ millions)

Year	1	2	3	4
Free cash flows before synergy (growing at 5%)	226.80	238.14	250.05	262.55
Synergies	20.00	20.00	20.00	20.00
Free cash flows	246.80	258.14	270.05	282.55
PV of free cash flows at 9%	226.42	217.27	208.53	200.17

Tutorial note

The present value (PV) figures are slightly different if discount table factors are used, instead of formulae. Full credit will be given if discount tables are used to calculate PV figures.

Total PV of cash flows (years 1 to 4) = $852.39 million

Total PV of cash flows (years 5 to perpetuity) = 262.55 × 1.0225/(0.09 — 0.0225) × 1.09–4 = $2,817.51 million

Total value to firm = $3,669.90 million

Value attributable to equity holders = $3,669.90 million × 0.6 = $2,201.94 million

Additional value created from the combined company = $2,201.94 million — ($1,218 million + $480 million) = $2,201.94 million — $1,698.00 million = $503.94 million (or 29.7%)

Although the equity beta and therefore the risk of the combined company is more than Makonis Co on its own, probably due to Nuvola Co's higher business risk (reflected by the higher asset beta), overall the benefits from growth in excess of the risk free rate and additional synergies have led to an increase in the value of combined company of just under 30% when compared to the individual companies' values.

However, a number of assumptions have been made in obtaining the valuation, for example:

- The assumption of growth of cash flows in perpetuity and whether this is realistic or not;

- Whether the calculation of the combined company's asset beta when based on the weighted average of market values is based on good evidence or not;

- It has been assumed that the figures such as growth rates, tax rates, free cash flows, risk free rate of return, risk premium, and so on are accurate and do not change in the future.

In all these circumstances, it may be appropriate to undertake sensitivity analysis to determine how changes in the variables would impact on the value of the combined company, and whether the large increase in value is justified.

(b)   Value of Nuvola equity = $2.40 × 200m shares = $480m

30% premium: 1.3 × $480m = $624m   50% premium: 1.5 × $480m = $720m

New number of shares = 210m + 1/2 × 200m = 310m

Loss in value per share of combined company, if 50% premium paid instead of 30% premium = ($720m — $624m)/310m shares = $0.31/share.

This represents a drop in value of approx. 5.3% on original value of a Makonis Co share ($0.31/$5.80).

(c)   The amount of cash required will increase substantially, by about $96 million, if Makonis Co agrees to the demands made by Nuvola Co's equity holders and pays the 50% premium. Makonis Co needs to determine how it is going to acquire the additional funds and the implications from this. For example, it could borrow the money required for the additional funds, but taking on more debt may affect the cost of capital and therefore the value of the company. It could raise the funds by issuing more equity shares, but this may not be viewed in a positive light by the current equity holders.

Makonis Co may decide to offer a higher proportion of its shares in the share-for-share exchange instead of paying cash for the additional premium. However, this will affect its equity holders and dilute their equity holding further. Even the current proposal to issue 100 million new shares will mean that Nuvola Co's equity holders will own just under 1/3 of the combined company and Makonis Co's shareholders would own just over 2/3 of the combined company.

Makonis Co should also consider what Nuvola Co's equity holders would prefer. They may prefer less cash and more equity due to their personal tax circumstances, but, in most cases, cash is preferred by the target firm's equity holders.

ACCA marking scheme		
		Marks
(a)	Market values of Makonis Co and Nuvola Co	1
	Combined company asset beta	1
	Combined company equity beta	1
	Combined company: cost of capital	1
	Combined company value: years 1 to 4	3
	Combined company value: years 5 to perpetuity	1
	Combined company value: value to equity holders and additional value	2
	Comment and discussion of assumptions	3–4
	Maximum	13
(b)	Payment if 30% premium paid	1
	Payment if 50% premium paid	1
	Estimate of impact on Makonis Co's equity holders	3
	Maximum	5
(c)	Additional amount payable if 50% premium paid instead of 30% premium	1
	Discussion of how Makonis Co would finance the additional premium	6
	Maximum	7
Total		**25**

52 VOGEL CO (JUN 14)

Key answer tips

This was a fairly typical question on acquisitions, with a good mix of calculations and discussion.

When asked to perform a valuation calculation, follow the clues in the question to decide which valuation method to use. In this case the given P/E ratios, costs of capital and growth rates meant that DCF and P/E methods should have been used.

(a)   Vogel Co may have switched from a strategy of organic growth to one of growth by acquisition, if it was of the opinion that such a change would result in increasing the value for the shareholders.

Acquiring a company to gain access to new products, markets, technologies and expertise may be quicker and less costly. Horizontal acquisitions may help Vogel Co eliminate key competitors and enable it to take advantage of economies of scale. Vertical acquisitions may help Vogel Co to secure the supply chain and maximise returns from its value chain.

Organic growth may take a long time, can be expensive and may result in little competitive advantage being established due to the time taken. Also organic growth, especially into a new area, would need managers to gain knowledge and expertise of an area or function, which they not currently familiar with. Furthermore, in a saturated market, there may be little opportunity for organic growth.

(**Note:** Credit will be given for alternative relevant comments.)

(b)   Vogel Co can take the following actions to reduce the risk that the acquisition of Tori Co fails to increase shareholder value.

Since Vogel Co has pursued an aggressive policy of acquisitions, it needs to determine whether or not this has been too aggressive and detailed assessments have been undertaken. Vogel Co should ensure that the valuation is based on reasonable input figures and that proper due diligence of the perceived benefits is undertaken prior to the offer being made. Often it is difficult to get an accurate picture of the target when looking at it from the outside. Vogel Co needs to ensure that it has sufficient data and information to enable a thorough and sufficient analysis to be undertaken.

The sources of synergy need to be properly assessed to ensure that they are achievable and what actions Vogel Co needs to undertake to ensure their achievement. This is especially so for the revenue-based synergies. An assessment of the impact of the acquisition on the risk of the combined company needs to be undertaken to ensure that the acquisition is not considered in isolation but as part of the whole company.

The Board of Directors of Vogel Co needs to ensure that there are good reasons to undertake the acquisition, and that the acquisition should result in an increase in value for the shareholders. Research studies into mergers and acquisitions have found that often companies are acquired not for the shareholders' benefit, but for the benefit or self-interest of the acquiring company's management. The non-executive directors should play a crucial role in ensuring that acquisitions are made to enhance the value for the shareholders. A post-completion audit may help to identify the reasons behind why so many of Vogel Co's acquisitions have failed to create value. Once these reasons have been identified, strategies need to be put in place to prevent their repetition in future acquisitions.

Procedures need to be established to ensure that the acquisition is not overpaid. Vogel Co should determine the maximum premium it is willing to pay and not go beyond that figure. Research indicates that often too much is paid to acquire a company and the resultant synergy benefits are not sufficient to cover the premium paid. Often this is the result of the management of the acquiring company wanting to complete the deal at any cost, because not completing the deal may be perceived as damaging to both their own, and their company's, reputation. The acquiring company's management may also want to show that the costs related to undertaking due diligence and initial negotiation have not been wasted. Vogel Co and its management need to guard against this and maybe formal procedures need to be established which allow managers to step back without loss of personal reputation.

Vogel Co needs to ensure that it has proper procedures in place to integrate the staff and systems of the target company effectively, and also to recognise that such integration takes time. Vogel Co may decide instead to give the target company a large degree of autonomy and thus make integration less necessary; however, this may result in a reduction in synergy benefits. Vogel Co should also have strategies which allow it sufficient flexibility when undertaking integration so that it is able to respond to changing circumstances or respond to inaccurate information prior to the acquisition. Vogel Co should also be mindful that its own and the acquired company's staff and management need to integrate and ensure a good working relationship between them.

(**Note:** The above answer covers more areas than would be needed to achieve full marks for the part. Credit will be given for alternative relevant comments.)

(c)   **Approach taken**

The maximum premium payable is equal to the maximum additional benefit created from the acquisition of Tori Co, with no increase in value for the shareholders of Vogel Co (although the shareholders of Vogel Co would probably not approve of the acquisition if they do not gain from it).

The additional benefit can be estimated as the sum of the cash gained (or lost) from selling the assets of Department C, spinning off Department B and integrating Department A, less the sum of the values of Vogel Co and Tori Co as separate companies.

Estimation

Cash gained from selling the assets of Department C = (20% × $98.2m) + (20% × $46.5m × 0.9) – ($20.2 + $3m) = $19.64m + $8.37m – $23.2m = $4.81m

Value created from spinning off Department B into Ndege Co

Free cash flow of Ndege Co	$ *million*
Current share of PBDIT (0.4 × $37.4m)	14.96
Less: attributable to Department C (10%)	(1.50)
Less: tax allowable depreciation (0.4 × 98.2 × 0.10)	(3.93)
Profits before tax	9.53
Tax (20%)	(1.91)
Free cash flows	7.62

Value of Ndege Co =

Present value of cash flow in year 1: $7.62m × 1.2 × 1.1^{-1} = $8.31m

Add: present value of cash flows from year 2 onwards:

($9.14m × 1.052)/(0.1 – 0.052) × 1.1^{-1} = $182.11m

Less: debt = $40m

Value to shareholders of Ndege Co = $150.42m

Vogel Co's current value = $3 × 380m = $1,140m

Vogel Co, profit after tax = $158.2m × 0.8 = $126.56m

Vogel Co, PE ratio before acquisition = $1,140.0m/$126.56m = 9.01 say 9

Vogel Co, PE ratio after acquisition = 9 × 1.15 = 10.35

Tori Co, PE ratio before acquisition = 9 × 1.25 = 11.25

Tori Co's current value = 11.25 × ($23.0 × 0.8) = $207.0m

Value created from combined company

($126.56m + 0.5 × $23.0m × 0.8 + $7m) × 10.35 = $1,477.57

Maximum premium = ($1,477.57m + $150.42m + $4.81m) – ($1,140m + $207.0m) = $285.80m

Assumptions

Based on the calculations given above, it is estimated that the value created will be 64.9% or $285.80m.

However, Vogel Co needs to assess whether the numbers it has used in the calculations and the assumptions it has made are reasonable. For example, Ndege Co's future cash flows seem to be growing without any additional investment in assets and Vogel Co needs to establish whether or not this is reasonable. It also needs to establish how the increase in its PE ratio was determined after acquisition. Perhaps sensitivity analysis would be useful to show the impact on value changes, if these figures are changed. Given its poor record in generating value previously, Vogel Co needs to pay particular attention to these figures.

	Marking scheme		
			Marks
(a)	1–2 marks per point	Max	4
(b)	2–3 marks per point	Max	7
(c)	Cash gained from sales of Department C assets		1
	Calculation of free cash flows for Ndege Co		2
	Calculation of present values of Ndege Co cash flows and value		2
	Vogel Co PE ratios before and after acquisition		2
	Tori Co PE ratio and value		1
	Value created from combining Department A with Vogel Co		1
	Maximum premium payable		1
	Approach taken		1–2
	Assumptions made		2–3
		Max	14
Total			**25**

CORPORATE RECONSTRUCTION AND REORGANISATION

53 REFLATOR INC

Key answer tips

In part (a) it is easier to discuss the advantages of MBOs by looking at the different stakeholders involved.

For part (c) you need to construct a statement of profit or loss for each year. The trickiest part is separating the interest and capital elements with the 'mortgage style' subordinated loan.

In part (d) look at the implications of the warrant scheme on ultimate shareholdings and control.

(a) The advantages of a buyout may be viewed from the perspectives of each of the parties involved.

The selling company may regard a buyout as preferable to the liquidation of a loss-making division. A buyout might result in a higher disposal price, and has the social effect of protecting jobs. Selling part of the organisation might allow the company to focus on its core competence.

The current managers, with their existing expertise of the markets, relationships with clients, etc., may have a better chance of successfully operating the company. They are also likely to be highly motivated through their significant equity holdings, and by the potential for large capital gains if the company succeeds.

A venture capitalist or other type of investor normally takes a high risk, in the hope of high returns mainly through capital gains. Most investors would seek some form of exit route for their investment after several years, possible through a listing on a stock market. In some countries investing in buyouts may offer tax advantages.

(b) Possible problems and pitfalls:

- Financing of the purchase – presenting a credible case to backers

- Compliance with the terms offered by financial backers, e.g. forfeit of some management control

- Determination of price and definition of what is to be purchased

- Loss of key employees, which may increase the risk of survival

- Cash flow forecasts – cash needs are often understated

- Industrial relations – in determining new staffing levels and wage rates

- Lack of expertise because the management team are incomplete.

(c) The increase in the value of equity may be estimated from the expected retained earnings over the four-year period. The maximum 15% dividend payment is assumed.

Year	0	1	2	3	4
Earnings before interest and tax		320,000	410,000	500,000	540,000
Interest 8.5%		170,000	170,000	170,000	170,000
Interest 9% loan[1]		27,000	23,411	19,499	15,236
Earnings before tax		123,000	216,589	310,501	354,764
Taxation (30%)		36,900	64,977	93,150	106,429
Earnings after tax		86,100	151,612	217,351	248,335
Dividend (15%)		12,915	22,742	32,603	37,250
Retained earnings		73,185	128,870	184,748	211,085
Book value of equity	800,000	873,185	1,002,055	1,186,803	1,397,888

Growth in the book value of equity from 800,000 to 1,397,888 over four years is a compound growth rate of 14.97%. This is considerably less than the 20% growth rate claimed by the managers.

It should be noted that this is a book value of equity. The market value of equity is much more relevant to a potential investor, and is likely to be very different from this book value.

Note:

[1]Interest on the 9% loan

The equal annual payment comprising interest and capital that is necessary to pay off a $300,000 loan over six years is:

$$\frac{300,000}{4.486} = \$66,875 \text{ (4.486 is the PV annuity factor for six years at 9\%)}$$

Year	Remaining value	Interest	Repayment of capital
1	300,000	27,000	39,875
2	260,125	23,411	43,464
3	216,661	19,499	47,376
4	169,285	15,236	51,639

(d) At the start of the buyout, the equity holding would be 1,000,000 shares by the managers, and 600,000 by the venture capital organisation. The initial warrant proposal would allow the venture capital organisation to purchase 300,000 new shares after four years, a total of 900,000. The revised suggestion would allow 450,000 new shares to be purchased, which would give majority ownership and control of the company to the venture capital organisation. This is likely to be unacceptable to the managers, unless they also will have further opportunities to increase their share ownership, for example through other forms of option.

(e) **Features of growth by acquisition versus organic growth**

The advantages of growth by acquisition or merger are:

- much quicker method of increasing market share than growing organically;

- if the two companies do not have perfectly correlated cash flows, combining them together will offer diversification opportunity and a reduction in the cost of capital. This should increase the value of the group and therefore increase shareholder wealth;

- buying out or merging with one's competitors reduces the competition faced in the market, thereby strengthening one's price-setting ability.

The disadvantages of growth by acquisition or merger are:

- acquisition is usually more expensive for the purchasing company. Research continually shows that in contested acquisitions it is the shareholders of the target company who gain the greatest share of the benefits arising;

- many acquisitions and mergers are planned in anticipation of generating synergistic cost savings, but in practice these synergies often fail to appear;

- there may be cultural clashes following the acquisition or merger between the two sets of employees. If skilled employees become demotivated and leave, then much of the skill set has been lost.

54 ALASKA SALVAGE

Key answer tips

The examiner is constantly trying to think of new ways to test the application of the Black-Scholes model. In previous exams, the application of the model to warrants had never been tested, so many students found this a very difficult question.

However, as with any Black-Scholes question, the key thing is to pick out the five key input factors at the start and to list them out. This will ensure that you are awarded all the available method marks even if you make an error with one or more of the input factors.

(a)   A warrant is an option attached to another financial instrument on issue which can be detached and negotiated independently of the underlying issue. Warrants are usually exercised over a longer term than traded options but can be valued in exactly the same way using the Black Scholes Option Pricing Model by inserting into the standard formula.

The calculation has been performed as follows:

$$c = 85N(d_1) - 90N(d_2)e^{-0.05 \times 5}$$

Where:

$$d_1 = \frac{\ln(85/90) + (0.05 + 0.5 \times 0.2^2) \times 5}{0.2 \times \sqrt{5}} = 0.6548$$

$$d_2 = d_1 - 0.2 \times \sqrt{5} = 0.2076$$

From normal tables we calculate the area under the normal curve represented by d_1 and d_2:

$$c = 85 \times 0.7437 - 90 \times 0.5822 \cdot e^{-0.05 \times 5} = 22.41$$

Given that each warrant represents an option on 100 equity shares the value of each warrant is $2,241.

The Black Scholes model makes a number of restrictive assumptions:

(1)   The warrant is a 'European' style option.

(2)   The share price follows a log-normal distribution and is continuously traded.

(3)   Unrestricted short selling of the underlying security is permitted.

(4)   There are no market frictions such as taxes or transaction costs.

(5)   No dividends are paid during the life of the warrant.

These assumptions are less realistic with a company such as Alaska Salvage than with a large enterprise with a full listing. It is unlikely, for example, that the company's shares will be actively traded or that the share market is efficient in its pricing of the equity.

(b)   The coupon rate is derived from the cash flow to the lender as follows:

(1)   Lay out the cash flow to the lender showing the value of the warrant as a benefit accruing immediately to the lender.

	0	1	2	3	4	5
Coupon	(10,000)	100 × c%	100 × c%	100 × c%	100 × c%	100 × c%
Repayment						10,000
Call value	2,241					
Cash flow to lender	(7,759)	100 × c%	100 × c%	100 × c%	100 × c%	10,000 + 100 × c%

(2)   Solve the following equation where c% is the coupon rate and A and V are the five-year annuity and discount factors at 13% respectively:

$$7{,}759 = 100 \times c\% \times A + 10{,}000 \times V$$

Therefore:

$$7{,}759 = 100 \times c\% \times 3.517 + 10{,}000 \times 0.543$$

By rearrangement:

$$c\% = \frac{7{,}759 - 10{,}000 \times 0.543}{100 \times 3.517}$$

Therefore a 6.62% coupon rate will give an effective rate of return on the investment to the lender of 13%.

(c)   Mezzanine debt such as this is one mechanism by which a small, high growth firm such as Alaska Salvage can raise debt finance where the risk of default is high and/or there is a low level of asset coverage for the loan. In this case raising a loan of $1.6 million would raise the market gearing of the firm from zero (assuming there is no current outstanding debt) to 13.6% (debt to total capitalisation). This increase in borrowing against what might be presumed to be specialised salvaging equipment and the forward cost of operation may not be attractive to the commercial banking sector and may need specialised venture finance. The issue of warrants gives the lender the opportunity to participate in the success of the venture but with a reasonable level of coupon assured. However, the disadvantage for the current equity investors is that the value of their investment will be reduced by the value of the warrants issued. The extent to which this will be worthwhile depends upon the value of the firm on the assumption that the project proceeds and is financed in the way described. This should ultimately decide the maximum value that they would be prepared to pay to finance the new project.

	ACCA marking scheme		
			Marks
(a)	Calculation of:		
	d_1		3.0
	d_2		1.0
	value of the warrant		2.0
	assumptions (one each to a maximum of 4)		4.0
			————
		Maximum	10.0
			————
(b)	Estimation of the coupon rate (2 marks for deducting option value from face value of warrant and 2 marks for calculation of coupon using annuity and discount factors)		4.0
			————
		Maximum	4.0
			————
(c)	Identification of mezzanine debt as a source of high risk finance		2.0
	Disadvantage for equity investors (reduction in equity value on exercise)		2.0
	Advantages: low coupon, additional equity participation		2.0
			————
		Maximum	6.0
			————
Total			**20**
			————

55 PROTEUS CO (DEC 11)

Key answer tips

In order to assess whether the debt/equity covenant will be breached, it is first necessary to forecast the debt level and the equity level over the next five years.

(a) Possible benefits of disposing Tyche Co through a management buy-out may include:

Management buy-out costs may be less for Proteus Co compared with other forms of disposal such as selling the assets of the company or selling the company to a third party.

It may be the quickest method in raising funds for Proteus Co compared to the other methods.

There would be less resistance from the managers and employees, making the process smoother and easier to accomplish.

Proteus Co may retain a better relationship and beneficial links with Tyche Co and may be able to purchase or sell goods and services to it, as seems to have happened with the management service.

It may be able to get a better price for the company. The current management and employees possibly have the best knowledge of the company and are able to make it successful. Therefore they may be willing to pay more for it.

It may increase Proteus Co's reputation among its internal stakeholders such as the management and employees. It may also increase its reputation with external stakeholders and the markets if it manages the disposal successfully and efficiently.

(**Note:** credit will be given for alternative relevant comments)

(b)   In order to calculate whether or not the covenant is breached every year, the proportion of debt to equity needs to be calculated each year. The debt will reduce by $3 million every year and the equity will increase by reserves every year. In order to calculate the increase in reserves every year, the forecast statements of profit or loss need to be determined.

Forecast statement of profit or loss ($000)

Year	1	2	3	4	5
Operating income before mgmt. fee (W1)	23,760	25,661	27,714	29,931	32,325
Management service fee	12,000	12,960	13,997	15,116	16,326
Interest payable (W2)	5,850	5,580	5,310	5,040	4,770
Profit before tax	5,910	7,121	8,407	9,775	11,229
Tax payable (25%)	1,478	1,780	2,102	2,444	2,807
Profit after tax	4,432	5,341	6,305	7,331	8,422
Dividend payable (25%)	1,108	1,335	1,576	1,833	2,106
Balance transferred to reserves	3,324	4,006	4,729	5,498	6,316

Book value of equity

Year	1	2	3	4	5
Opening equity	16,000	19,324	23,330	28,059	33,557
Reserves	3,324	4,006	4,729	5,498	6,316
Closing equity	19,324	23,330	28,059	33,557	39,873

Debt/Equity Computations

Year	1	2	3	4	5
Debt Outstanding at year end ($000's)	62,000	59,000	56,000	53,000	50,000
Equity value at year end	19,324	23,330	28,059	33,557	39,873
Debt/Equity	321%	253%	200%	158%	125%
Restrictive Condition	350%	250%	200%	150%	125%
Restriction Breached?	No	Yes	No	Yes	No

Workings

W1

Current operating profit before management service charge = $60,000,000 − ($12,000,000 + 22,000,000 + 4,000,000) = $22,000,000. This amount will grow by 8% every year.

W2

Year	1	2	3	4	5
Outstanding loan at the start of the year ($000's)	65,000	62,000	59,000	56,000	53,000
Interest ($000's)	5,850	5,580	5,310	5,040	4,770

(c)   **Implications**

Based on the calculations in part (b) above, the restrictive covenant is due to be breached in years two and four. In years three and five, it has just been met, and only in year one will Tyche Co be operating well within the conditions of the restrictive covenant. This raises two main issues: firstly, Tyche Co needs to establish how the bank will react to the conditions not being met and will it put Tyche Co's business in jeopardy? Secondly, because the conditions are nearly breached in years three and five, Tyche Co needs to determine the likelihood of the revenues and costs figures being achieved. A very small deviation from the figures may cause the conditions to be breached. Sensitivity analysis and other forms of risk analysis may need to be undertaken and provisions put into place to deal with unexpected breaches in the covenant.

Possible Actions

Tyche Co can consider the following possible actions in the years where it is likely that the covenant may be breached:

(i)   The directors may decide to award themselves and the other shareholders lower or no dividends. This would probably need to be negotiated and agreed.

(ii)   The directors may want to ask the venture capitalist to take a higher equity stake for more funds at the outset. Both parties would need to agree to this.

(iii) Tyche Co may want to try and negotiate less onerous terms with the bank or ask it for more flexibility when applying the restrictive covenant. Given that the restrictive covenant is not likely to be breached by a significant amount, the bank will probably not want to undertake legal proceedings to close Tyche Co and would probably be open to negotiations.

(iv)   Tyche Co may decide to pay off more of the loan each year from its cash reserves, if it has enough funds, in order to reduce the year-end outstanding debt.

(**Note:** only two actions needed)

ACCA marking scheme		
		Marks
(a)	1–2 marks for each point discussed	4
(b)	Calculations to get to profit before tax for the five years	3
	Calculations to get to the reserves figures for each year	2
	Calculation of the equity amount each year	1
	Calculation of debt to equity ratio for year and	
	Conclusion when the covenant is breached and when it is not	3
	Maximum	9
(c)	3 marks for discussion of implications	
	2 marks for actions Tyche Co may take	5
Total		**18**

56   DORIC CO (PILOT 2012)

Key answer tips

Many past exam questions on reconstruction have focussed on the difference from the stakeholders' point of view between liquidation and a given reconstruction scheme. Read the details of the reconstruction scheme carefully and follow the instructions exactly.

(a)   Possible benefits of disposing a division through a management buy-out may include:

Management buy-out costs may be less compared with other forms of disposal such as selling individual assets of the division or selling it to a third party.

It may be the quickest method in raising funds compared to the other methods.

There would be less resistance from the managers and employees making the process smoother and easier to accomplish than if both divisions were to be closed down.

It may offer a better price. The current management and employees possibly have the best knowledge of the division and are able to make it successful. Therefore they may be willing to pay more for it.

(**Note:** Credit will be given for alternative relevant benefits)

(b)   Close the company

	$m
Sale of all assets	210
Less redundancy and other costs	(54)
Net proceeds from sale of all assets	156
Total liabilities	280

The liability holders will receive $0.56 per $1 owing to them ($156m/$280m). Shareholders will receive nothing.

(c)

	$m
Value of selling fridges division (2/3 × 210)	140
Redundancy and other costs (2/3 × 54)	(36)
Funds available from sale of division	104
Amount of current and non-current liabilities	280
Amount of management buy-out funds needed to pay current and non-current liabilities (280 − 104)	176
Amount of management buy-out funds needed to pay shareholders	60
Investment needed for new venture	50
Total funds needed for management buy-out	286

Estimating value of new company after buy-out

	$m
Sales revenue	170
Costs	(120)
	———
Profits before depreciation	50
** Depreciation ((1/3 ×£100m + $50m) × 10%)	(8.3)
Tax (20%)	(7.8)
	———
** Cash flows before interest payment	33.9
	———

** It is assumed that the depreciation is available on the re-valued non-current assets plus the new investment. It is assumed that no additional investment in non-current assets or working capital is needed, even though cash flows are increasing.

Estimate of value based on perpetuity = $33.9 (1.035)/(0.11 − 0.035) = $467m

This is about 63% in excess of the funds invested in the new venture, and therefore the buy-out is probably beneficial. However, the amounts are all estimates and a small change in some variables like the growth rate or the cost of capital can have a large impact on the value. Also the assumption of cash flow growth in perpetuity may not be accurate. It is therefore advisable to undertake a sensitivity analysis.

(d) Potential buyers will need to be sought through open tender or through an intermediary. Depending upon the nature of the business being sold a single bidder may be sought or preparations made for an auction of the business. Doric Co's suppliers and distributors may be interested, as may be competitors in the same industry. High levels of discretion are required in the search process to protect the value of the business from adverse competitive action. Otherwise, an interested and dominant competitor may open a price war in order to force down prices and hence the value of the fridges division prior to a bid.

Once a potential buyer has been found, access should be given so that they can conduct their own due diligence. Up-to-date accounts should be made available and all legal documentation relating to assets to be transferred made available. Doric Co should undertake its own due diligence to check the ability of the potential purchaser to complete a transaction of this size. Before proceeding, it would be necessary to establish how the purchaser intends to finance the purchase, the timescale involved in their raising the necessary finance and any other issues that may impede a clean sale. Doric Co's legal team will need to assess any contractual issues on the sale, the transfer of employment rights, the transfer of intellectual property and any residual rights and responsibilities to Doric Co.

A sale price will be negotiated which is expected to maximise the return. The negotiation process should be conducted by professional negotiators who have been thoroughly briefed on the terms of the sale, the conditions attached and all of the legal requirements. The consideration for the sale, the deeds for the assignment of assets and terms for the transfer of staff and their accrued pension rights will also all be subject to agreement.

57   NUBO CO (DEC 13)

Key answer tips

Islamic finance came into the syllabus in 2013 and it was tested here for the first time. Make sure that you understand the different Islamic financing methods and how they differ from the more traditional financing options.

(a)   **Current and non-current liabilities = $387m + $95m = $482m**

Sale of assets of supermarkets division

Proportion of assets to supermarkets division

Non-current assets = 70% × $550m = $385m; Current assets = 70% × $122m = $85.4m

Sale of assets = $385m × 1.15 + $85.4m × 0.80 = $511.07m

Sale of supermarkets division as a going concern

Profit after tax attributable to the supermarkets division: $166m/2 = $83m

Estimate of value of supermarkets division based on the PE ratio of supermarket industry: $83 × 7 = $581m

Although both options generate sufficient funds to pay for the liabilities, the sale of the supermarkets division as a going concern would generate higher cash flows and the spare cash of $99m [$581m − $482m] can be used by Nubo Co for future investments. This is based on the assumption that the value based on the industries' PE ratios is accurate.

Proportion of assets remaining within Nubo Co 30% ×

($550m + $122m) = $201.6m

Add extra cash generated from the sale of $99m

Maximum debt capacity = $300.6m

Total additional funds available to Nubo Co for new investments = $300.6m + $99m = $399.6m

(b)   A demerger would involve splitting Nubo Co into two separate companies which would then operate independently of each other. The equity holders in Nubo Co would continue to have an equity stake in both companies.

Normally demergers are undertaken to ensure that each company's equity values are fair. For example, the value of the aircraft parts production division based on the PE ratio gives a value of $996m (12 × $83m) and the value of the supermarkets division as $581m. If the current company's value is less than the combined values of $1,577m, then a demerger may be beneficial. However, the management and shareholders of the new supermarkets company may not be keen to take over all the debt.

Nubo Co's equity holders may view the demerger more favourably than the sale of the supermarkets division. At present their equity investment is diversified between the aircraft parts production and supermarkets. If the supermarkets division is sold, then the level of their diversification may be affected. With the demerger, since the equity holders will retain an equity stake in both companies, the benefit of diversification is retained.

However, the extra $99m cash generated from the sale will be lost in the case of a demerger. Furthermore, if the new aircraft parts production company can only borrow 100% of its asset value, then its borrowing capacity and additional funds available to it for new investments will be limited to $201.6m instead of $399.6m.

(c) With a Mudaraba contract, the profits which Pilvi Co makes from the joint venture would be shared according to a pre-agreed arrangement when the contract is constructed between Pilvi Co and Ulap Bank. Losses, however, would be borne solely by Ulap Bank as the provider of the finance, although provisions can be made where losses can be written off against future profits. Ulap Bank would not be involved in the executive decision-making process. In effect, Ulap Bank's role in the relationship would be similar to an equity holder, holding a small number of shares in a large organisation.

With a Musharaka contract, the profits which Pilvi Co makes from the joint venture would still be shared according to a pre-agreed arrangement similar to a Mudaraba contract, but losses would also be shared according to the capital or other assets and services contributed by both the parties involved in the arrangement. Therefore a value could be put to the contribution-in-kind made by Pilvi Co and any losses would be shared by Ulap Bank and Pilvi Co accordingly. Within a Musharaka contract, Ulap Bank can also take the role of an active partner and participate in the executive decision-making process. In effect, the role adopted by Ulap Bank would be similar to that of a venture capitalist.

With the Mudaraba contract, Pilvi Co would essentially be an agent to Ulap Bank, and many of the agency issues facing corporations would apply to the arrangement, where Pilvi Co can maximise its own benefit at the expense of Ulap Bank. Pilvi Co may also have a propensity to undertake excessive risk because it is essentially holding a long call option with an unlimited upside and a limited downside.

Ulap Bank may prefer the Musharaka contract in this case, because it may be of the opinion that it needs to be involved with the project and monitor performance closely due to the inherent risk and uncertainty of the venture, and also to ensure that the revenues, expenditure and time schedules are maintained within initially agreed parameters. In this way, it may be able to monitor and control agency related issues more effectively and control Pilvi Co's risky actions and decisions. Being closely involved with the venture would change both Pilvi Co's and Ulap Bank's roles and make them more like stakeholders rather than principals and agents, with a more equitable distribution of power between the two parties.

Nubo Co's concerns would mainly revolve around whether it can work with Ulap Bank and the extra time and cost which would need to be incurred before the joint venture can start. If Pilvi Co had not approached Ulap Bank for funding, the relationship between Nubo Co and Pilvi Co would be less complex within the joint venture. Although difficulties may arise about percentage ownership and profit sharing, these may be resolved through negotiation and having tight specific contracts. The day-to-day running, management and decision-making process could be resolved through negotiation and consensus. Therefore having a third party involved in all aspects of the joint venture complicates matters.

Nubo Co may feel that it was not properly consulted about the arrangements between Pilvi Co and Ulap Bank, and Pilvi Co would need to discuss the involvement of Ulap Bank with Nubo Co and gets its agreement prior to formalising any arrangements. This is to ensure a high level of trust continues to exist between the parties, otherwise the venture may fail.

Nubo Co may want clear agreements on ownership and profit-sharing. They would want to ensure that the contract clearly distinguishes them as not being part of the Musharaka arrangement which exists between Pilvi Co and Ulap Bank. Hence negotiation and construction of the contracts may need more time and may become more expensive.

Nubo Co may have felt that it could work with Pilvi Co on a day-to-day basis and could resolve tough decisions in a reasonable manner. It may not feel the same about Ulap Bank initially. Clear parameters would need to be set up on how executive decision making will be conducted by the three parties. Therefore, the integration process of bringing a third partner into the joint venture needs to be handled with care and may take time and cost more money.

The above issues would indicate that the relationship between the three parties is closer to that of stakeholders, with different levels of power and influence, at different times, as opposed to a principal–agent relationship. This would create an environment which would need ongoing negotiation and a need for consensus, which may make the joint venture hard work. Additionally, it would possibly be more difficult and time consuming to accomplish the aims of the joint venture.

(Note: Credit will be given for alternative relevant comments and suggestions for parts (b) and (c) of the question)

ACCA marking scheme		
		Marks
(a) Sale of supermarkets division's assets		1
Sale of supermarkets division as going concern		1
Advice		2
Extra cash after liabilities are paid		1
Maximum debt which can be borrowed		1
Additional funds available to Nubo Co		1
	Maximum	7
(b) 1–2 marks per relevant point	Maximum	6
(c) Discussion of why Ulap Bank might prefer a Musharaka contract		6–7
Discussion of the key concerns of the joint venture relationship		5–6
	Maximum	12
Total		**25**

TREASURY AND ADVANCED RISK MANAGEMENT TECHNIQUES

58   BLACK-SCHOLES (AVT)

Key answer tips

Make sure you understand the written elements in this question – these are potentially very easy marks even for students who don't like the complexity of the calculations.

(a)   The existing bonus scheme, based on earnings per share, has the advantage that earnings per share are easily measured. However, this scheme suffers from the problems of all accounting-based measures in that it may be influenced by the accounting policies selected, and is not based on the economic cash flows of the company, which are likely to influence the share price. Maximisation of earnings per share is not the same as maximisation of share price and shareholder wealth.

The advantage of the share option scheme is that, in theory, it will motivate managers to improve the share price as they will directly benefit from this. This should achieve goal congruence with shareholders who are also seeking to maximise the share price. However, the extent to which their total remuneration is influenced by the incentive scheme may influence managers' decisions and their motivation to maximise share price. It is also debatable how much middle managers can directly influence the share price, and whether or not they are aware of which of their decisions will have the desired influence. A further problem of share option schemes is that share prices frequently move for reasons that are nothing to do with the actions of managers (e.g. lower interest rates will normally result in higher share prices). Ideally, managers should be rewarded for their contribution to share price increases, but this is very difficult to measure.

(b)   **Using the Black-Scholes model for European-style call options:**

A dividend payment is due during the option period. The share price, Ps, should therefore be reduced by the present value of this expected dividend. The dividend per share has remained constant for three years. It is assumed that it will be constant in the next year.

The present value of the dividend (discounted at the risk-free rate) is:

$$\frac{25}{1.06} = 23.58 \text{ cents}$$

The share price, Ps, is therefore estimated to be 610 – 23.58 = 586.42 cents.

Using the Black-Scholes model, the call price = $c = P_a N(d_1) - P_e N(d_2)e^{-rt}$

$$d_1 = \frac{\ln(P_a/P_e)+(r+0.5s^2)t}{s\sqrt{t}} = \frac{\ln(586.42/500)+(0.06+0.5(0.38)^2)(1)}{0.38\sqrt{1}}$$

= 0.7674. (Round this to 0.77.)

$d_2 = d_1 - s\sqrt{t} = 0.7674 - 0.38 = 0.3874$ (Round this to 0.39.)

The next step is to calculate $N(d_1)$ and $N(d_2)$. For 0.77 standard deviations, the probability is 0.2794. For 0.39 standard deviations, the probability is 0.1517. The values of d_1 and d_2 are both positive, so we add 0.5.

From normal distribution tables:

$N(d_1) = 0.5 + 0.2794 = 0.7794$

$N(d_2) = 0.5 + 0.1517 = 0.6517$

Inputting this data into the call option price formula $= c = P_a N(d_1) - P_e N(d_2)e^{-rt}$

$$\text{Call price} = 586.42(0.7794) - \frac{500(0.6517)}{e^{(0.06)(1)}}$$

$$= 457.06 - (325.85/1.062)$$

$$= 457.06 - 306.83 = 150.23 \text{ cents}$$

The expected option call price is 150.23 cents per share, giving a current option value of 5,000 × 150.23 cents = $7,511.

Tutorial note

Your answer may differ slightly due to rounding differences in the calculations.

Conclusion

The options are currently in the money and are likely to be attractive to managers as they have an expected value in excess of the bonuses that are currently paid. However, the risk to managers of the two schemes differs and this might influence managerial preferences, depending upon individual managers' attitudes to risk. The Black-Scholes model assumes that the volatility of the share price over the past year will continue for the coming year. This is very unlikely. A different volatility will greatly influence the value of the option at the expiry date.

(c) (1) AVT Inc should not agree to grant the manager put options. The holder of a put option, which allows a share to be sold at a fixed price, would benefit its holder more the further the price of the share fell below the exercise price of the option. As far as the options are concerned it would be in the manager's interest to take decisions that reduced the company's share price, rather than increase it!

  (2) The put option price may be found from the put-call parity equation.

$$p = c - P_a + P_e e^{-rt}$$

e^{-rt} = 1/1.062 (calculated earlier in this solution)

p = 150.23 − 586.42 + 500/1.062

= 34.62 cents

The manager is incorrect. Put options are not more valuable than call options in this situation.

59   UNIGLOW

(a)   Option prices in the basic Black-Scholes model relating to European options are determined by the following five factors:

(i)   The spot price of the underlying security

(ii)   The exercise price of the option

(iii)   The time until expiry of the option

(iv)   The risk of the option, as normally measured by the historic volatility of the return on the underlying security

(v)   The risk-free rate of interest within the economy

A decrease in the value of each of these factors will have the following effect:

(i)   *The spot price.* As the spot price falls the call option will become less valuable as the exercise of the option will result in the purchase of a security of lower value than previously.

(ii)   *The exercise price.* The lower the exercise price, the greater the value of a call option as there is more potential for profit upon exercising the option.

(iii)   *The time until expiry of the option.* A reduction in the time to expiry of the option will reduce the value of the option, as the time value element of the option price is reduced.

(iv)   *The risk of the option.* A reduction in risk will reduce the value of a call option. This is because the decrease in variance reduces the chance that the security price will lie within the tail of the distribution (i.e. above the exercise price) of the share price when the option expires.

(v)   *The risk-free rate.* A reduction in the risk-free rate will decrease the value of the call option because the money saved by purchasing the call option rather than the underlying security is reduced. If an option is purchased the cash saved could be invested at the risk-free rate. A reduction in the risk-free rate makes purchasing the call option relatively unattractive and reduces the option price.

(b)   **Delta** measures the change in the option price (premium) as the value of the underlying share moves by 1%.

$$Delta = \frac{change\ in\ the\ price\ of\ the\ option}{change\ in\ the\ price\ of\ the\ underlying\ share}$$

It is measured by N(d1) in the Black-Scholes option pricing model.

As the share price falls, delta falls towards zero. Delta may be used to construct a risk-free hedge position, whereby overall wealth will not change with small changes in share price.

Theta measures the change in the option price as the time to expiry increases. The longer the time to expiry of an option, the greater its value. Theta may be used to estimate by how much the value of an option will fall as time to expiry shortens.

Vega measures the change in option price as a result of a 1% change in the share price volatility or variance. As volatility increases, the value of both call and put options increases.

All three are of use to treasury managers when hedging their investments. As their values approach zero the hedged position will become unaffected by changes in these variables (share price, time to expiry and share price volatility).

(c) (i) N(d1) is required in order to determine the delta hedge.

$$d1 = \frac{1n(200/220) + 0.06(0.25)}{0.5\sqrt{0.25}} + 0.5(0.5)\sqrt{0.25}$$

$$= \frac{-0.09531 + 0.015}{0.25} + 0.125$$

$$= -0.32124 + 0.125$$

$$= -0.19624$$

From normal distribution tables:

$$N(d1) = 0.5 - 0.0778 = 0.4222$$

$$Delta = 0.4222$$

Tutorial note

The formula for d1 is given in the formula sheet in the examination, but you need to understand what the variables in the formula are, and how to do the calculation. It starts with the natural logarithm (ln) of (200/220), i.e. the share price divided by the exercise price for the call option. You need a calculator to work out natural logarithms, and ln (200/220) = ln 0.909091 = − 0.09531. Check all the other items in the formula carefully. Remember that T, the time to expiry, is three months = 0.25 years.

You should be able to calculate that d1 = − 0.19624. From the standard normal distribution table, 0.19624 standard deviations is above the 0.19 value (0.0753) but below the 0.20 value (0.0793). Interpolating, we get a value for 1.19624 of: [0.0753 + (624/1000) (0.0793 − 0.0753)] = 0.0778. This is the figure in the answer above.

d1 is less than 0, so subtract 0.0778 from 0.5.

In order to protect against a fall in Uniglow's share price, the easiest hedge would be to write (sell) options on Uniglow's shares. A delta of 0.4222 means that the relevant hedge ratio is:

$$\frac{1}{0.4222} = 2.368$$

In other words, a delta hedge would involve writing 2.368 options for every 1 share in the portfolio.

To hedge 100,000 shares (when option contracts are for 1,000 shares each):

$$\frac{100,000 \times 2.368}{1,000} = 237 \text{ options on Uniglow's shares need to be written.}$$

(ii) A hedge such is this is only valid for a **small change** in the underlying share price. As the share price alters the option delta will alter and the hedge will need to be periodically rebalanced.

---

60 MJY PLC

Key answer tips

Part (a) is a tricky question on hedging. It is vital that you approach this in a logical, systematic manner. First eliminate intra-group cash flows to estimate the foreign currency risk exposure of group. Next examine the possible use of forward contracts. Finally look at the options.

You need to contrast the options with the forward contracts to hedge the £:$ exposure. To do this, you must calculate the worst-case scenario cost in sterling of obtaining the dollars with the options, taking into account the premium (given in cents so convert at the spot rate) and the need to convert surplus dollars back into sterling at the forward rate.

(a) From a group perspective a sensible hedging strategy would be to net off as many offsetting currency receipts and payments as possible, and to only hedge the relevant net amounts.

As MJY is a UK-based multinational, the payments and receipts in pounds are not exposed to currency risk and should be ignored.

All $ and € receipts and payments within the group and with third party companies are relevant when estimating the group currency exposure. In the case of intragroup trade, a receipt for one company is a payment for another.

From a group view, relevant $ receipts are: 90 + 50 + 40 + 20 + 30 = 230

$ payments are: 170 + 120 + 50 = 340

$110,000 net payments need to be hedged

€ receipts are: 75 + 85 + 72 + 20 + 52 + 35 = 339

€ payments are: 72 + 35+ 50 + 20 + 65 = 242

€97,000 net receipts need to be hedged

Forward market hedges:

Buy $3 months forward: $\dfrac{\$110{,}000}{1.7835} = £61{,}676$

Sell €3 months forward: $\dfrac{\$97{,}000}{1.4390} = £67{,}408$

Currency options:

It is now 31 December. The time of the transactions is 31 March. As the February options will have expired, May options should be used. Pounds need to be sold to purchase dollars, therefore MJY will need to purchase put options. The dollar payment is $110,000, which is the equivalent of approximately one £62,500 option contract.

Option hedge

Strike price	$ if exercised	Premium ($)	Premium (£) – at spot 1.7982	Overhedge ($)	Overhedge (£) – at spot 1.7861
1.80	112,500	3,338	1,856	2,500	1,400
1.78	111,250	2,625	1,460	1,250	700

Worst-case outcomes using currency options:

1.80:62,500 + 1,856 – 1,400 = £62,956

1.78:62,500 + 1,460 – 700 = £63,260

These are both much worse than the forward hedge, but if the dollar was to weaken to more than the relevant strike price, the option could be lapsed, and the necessary $110,000 purchased in the spot market at a more favourable exchange rate.

For a relatively small hedge of this nature, a multinational company would probably use a forward contract as it involves less administrative time and costs, and fixes the payment of £61,676.

(b) There is no inconsistency between the views of Warren Buffett and the views of many corporate treasurers. Derivatives such as future contracts, swaps and options enable the holder to manage the risk associated with an underlying position. Thus they can be used to reduce the risk of a position (e.g. if you are due to receive a certain amount of foreign currency on a known date in the future, you can sell it forward and thus fix the amount of the receipt in your own home currency to eliminate the currency risk) or to speculate to increase the risk of a position (e.g. you can buy a financial futures contract for trading purposes, hoping that you can sell it in the future for more than you paid for it). Buffett is concerned about speculators who buy derivatives for trading purposes with no underlying need for them. Corporate treasurers see the value in using derivatives to hedge their risk away, thus reducing their overall risk exposure.

Let us consider Buffett's views in more detail. He has been a long-term investor in the US stock market. As an investor, he would like relevant and reliable financial information on the companies that he is thinking of investing in. In the past, the financial accounting for derivatives has been inadequate throughout the world. Favouring the historical cost convention meant that derivatives were stated at cost in the SOFP, with any profit or loss only being recognised when the derivative was sold. However the initial cost of a derivative is small or even zero, while its market value at a SOFP date might be large. It is in this sense that Buffett is correct in having described derivatives as a 'time-bomb', waiting for their profit or loss to be recognised in the future, at a time to be decided by the company holding the speculative position. However, this problem has now been mitigated somewhat by improved standards on financial accounting for derivatives. International Standard IAS 39 (and its US equivalent FAS 133 and UK equivalent FRS 26) now requires all derivatives to be measured at their fair values in each SOFP. This certainly improves the relevance of the SOFP, but the volatility of derivative values means that the description of a 'time-bomb' is still appropriate. Things can go wrong very quickly with derivatives, so the fact that they were measured at fair value in the previous SOFP is of little comfort to the investor who has seen his company suddenly lose a huge sum of money through losing control (e.g. Procter and Gamble lost $150m in 1994 when speculating on the spread between the German mark and the US dollar).

The opposite view is generally held by corporate treasurers who see derivatives as a means of reducing risk, whether currency risk, interest rate risk or other market risk. Many treasury departments are set up as cost centres and instructed not to engage in speculation. One often sees the statement in companies' Annual Reports that the company does not engage in speculation with derivative instruments. The situation is less clear-cut where the treasury is set up as a profit centre which may choose to take speculative positions within established limits. It is often in these circumstances that the distinction between hedging and speculation becomes blurred in the department's pursuit of profits, and once again the time-bomb can blow up with devastating consequences.

61   COLLAR HEDGE

Key answer tips

A collar is a combination of a call and a put option. A trial and error approach is needed here to find which combination will achieve the company's stated objective of receiving more than £6,750,000.

(a)   Interest rate caps and collars are available as over the counter (OTC) transactions with a bank, or may be devised using market-based interest rate options (options on interest rate futures). They may be used to hedge current or expected interest receipts or payments.

An **interest rate cap** is a series of call options on a notional amount of principal, exercisable at regular intervals over the term to expiry of the cap. The effect of a cap is to place an upper limit on the interest rate to be paid, and is therefore useful to a borrower of funds who will be paying interest at a future date. By purchasing a cap, a borrower will limit the net interest paid to the agreed cap strike price (less any premium paid for the cap). OTC caps are available for periods of up to ten years and can thus protect against long-term interest rate movements. As with all options, if interest rates were to move in a favourable direction, the buyer of the cap could let the option lapse and take advantage of the more favourable rates in the spot market.

The main disadvantage of options is the premium cost. An **interest rate collar** option reduces the premium cost by limiting the possible benefits of favourable interest rate movements. A collar involves the simultaneous purchase and sale of options, or in the case of OTC collars the equivalent to this. The premium paid for the purchase of one option would be partly or wholly offset by the premium received from the sale of another option. A borrower using an OTC collar would in effect buy a cap at one strike price, to secure a maximum interest cost, and sell a floor at a lower strike rate, which sets a minimum interest cost. The effective interest cost would be somewhere between the exercise price for the floor and the exercise price for the cap. The premium cost would be the cost of the cap less the selling price of the floor. A zero cost collar is a collar for which the cost of the cap is offset exactly by the sales value of the floor.

(b)   (i)   For the company to earn interest of £6,750,000, it would need to earn an annualised interest rate, after premium costs of $\frac{£6,750,000}{£400,000,000} \times \frac{12}{5} = 4.05\%$.

The collar needs to produce a minimum of more than 4.05% including premium costs, allowing for the fact that the company can invest at 0.25% below LIBOR.

As Troder plc is investing, a lending collar will be required. To create a lending collar with options on interest rate futures, the company will simultaneously buy a floor and sell a cap. (***Tutorial note:*** A borrower would buy a cap and sell a floor, but an investor should buy a floor and sell a cap.)

- *Buying a floor.* To buy a floor, the company should buy a call option on interest rate futures (giving it the right to buy futures). The call option will increase in value if interest rates fall. This will set the floor, or minimum interest rate.

- *Selling a cap.* The cap is created by selling put options. This sets the maximum interest. If interest rates rise, the market price of the option (and the underlying futures) will fall. The buyer will exercise the option (or the options position will be closed at a loss). As a result, the company would forego any higher interest rate than the put option exercise price.

- *Premium.* The overall cost of the collar will be the call option premium paid less the put option premium received.

In order to achieve a return of more than 4.05% (£6,750,000), a collar needs to be arranged with the call strike price higher than the put strike price (in order to set the maximum interest that can be received).

Alternatives are:

Call strike price	Put strike price	Minimum interest rate secured by call	Less call cost	Plus put receipt	Minimum LIBOR rate secured
95750	95500	4.25%	(0.165)%	0.170%	4.255%
95750	95250	4.25%	(0.165)%	0.085%	4.170%
95500	95250	4.50%	(0.280)%	0.085%	4.305%

Call strike price	Put strike price	Minimum LIBOR rate secured	Invest at LIBOR minus 0.25% Minimum net yield
95750	95500	4.255%	4.005%
95750	95250	4.170%	3.920%
95500	95250	4.305%	4.055%

Note: The maximum net yield obtainable from the collar hedge is determined by the put option exercise price. It can be calculated as the minimum net yield, as shown in the table above, plus the difference between the put option interest rate and the call option interest rate.

Of the alternatives considered above, only the purchase of a call at 95500 and sale of a put at 95250 will result in a minimum return of £6,750,000. The actual minimum return (ignoring any possible remaining time value that might increase the return) is:

£400,000,000 × $^5/_{12}$ × 4.055% = £6,758,333.

However, there is a possibility that the net yield will be 0.25% higher (the difference between the call option and put option rates), in which case the return would be £400,000,000 × $^5/_{12}$ × 4.305% = £7,175,000.

Tutorial note

If a collar is set with the same put and call price the return will be:

Strike price	Interest rate	Less call cost	Plus put receipt	Less 0.25%	Investment return
95250	4.75%	(0.445)%	0.085%	(0.250)%	4.140%
95500	4.50%	(0.280)%	0.170%	(0.250)%	4.140%
95750	4.25%	(0.165)%	0.305%	(0.250)%	4.140%

This would achieve the required 4.05%, but would not allow Troder to take advantage of any favourable movement in interest rates.

(ii)   The maximum return would occur if market interest rates are at least 4.75% and the call option were allowed to lapse. The put option would be exercised by its buyer and the maximum overall return would be:

Call option strike price	Interest rate (call not exercised)	Less call cost	Plus put receipt	Less 0.25%	Investment return
95500	4.75%	(0.280)%	0.085%	(0.250)%	4.305%

This would yield:

£400,000,000 × $^5/_{12}$ × 4.305% = £7,175,000.

(c)   The objectives of integrated reporting include:

- To improve the quality of information available to providers of financial capital to enable a more efficient and productive allocation of capital

- To provide a more cohesive and efficient approach to corporate reporting that draws on different reporting strands and communicates the full range of factors that materially affect the ability of an organisation to create value over time

- To enhance accountability and stewardship for the broad base of capitals (financial, manufactured, intellectual, human, social and relationship, and natural) and promote understanding of their interdependencies

- To support integrated thinking, decision making and actions that focus on the creation of value over the short, medium and long term.

62   INTEREST RATE HEDGES   *Walk in the footsteps of a top tutor*

Walkthrough question – key answer tips

This is a technical, but routine, question on interest rate hedging.

First, you should allocate time carefully between the five different requirements. There is a lot to do here, so it is critical not to spend too long on any part of the question.

Notice that the final two parts (d and e) are written questions which are independent of the earlier calculations. It would be advisable to do these parts first, to get the easy marks

With regard to the calculations, try to separate the FRA and the futures information so that you don't muddle things up.

Before you start trying to set up the hedges, identify the transaction carefully first. If you mistakenly interpret the transaction the wrong way round (it is a deposit here) you will lose marks for setting up the hedges incorrectly.

(a)   The company is worried about a fall in interest rates during the next five months. It will need a long futures hedge, with December futures purchased at 96.60. If interest rates fall, the futures price will rise and the contracts may be closed out at a higher price to partially offset the cash market interest rate fall. For a risk of £7.1 million to protect a four-month period the company will need to buy:

$$\frac{£7,100,000}{£500,000} \times \frac{4}{3} = 18.93, \text{ or 19 contracts, a slight over hedge.}$$

Basis is futures rate less spot rate, or 96.60 – 96.00 = 0.60% (the current LIBOR of 4% is equivalent to a futures price of 96.00).

The time to expiry of the December futures contract is seven months. Remaining time at the close-out date (five months' time) is two months.

The expected basis for two months is $0.60\% \times \frac{2}{7} = 0.171\%$

The expected LIBOR lock-in rate is 96.60 – 0.171 = 96.429 or 3.571%

The company will invest in commercial paper at LIBOR + 0.60%. The overall expected lock-in rate is 4.171%.

(b)   The relevant FRA rate is 5 v 9. The company would sell the FRA to a bank to fix the interest rate at 3.45%. This is a lower rate than the expected futures LIBOR lock-in rate of 3.571%.

(c)   **Cash market:**

Expected receipts from the investment on 1 November: $£7.1m \times 4.1\% \times \frac{4}{12} =$ £97,033 (4.1% is LIBOR of 3.5% + 0.6%)

Futures market:

1 June: Buy 19 December contracts at 96.60

1 November: Sell 19 December contracts at 96.671 (spot of 96.50 plus expected remaining basis of 0.171).

Profit from futures is 7.1 basis points × £12.50 × 19 = £1,686

Overall receipts are £97,033 + £1,686 = £98,719

(NB $\dfrac{£98,719}{£7,100,000} \times \dfrac{12}{4} = 4.171\%$, the expected lock-in rate).

FRA:

The FRA fixed rate is 3.45%. Actual LIBOR is 3.5%. The company will therefore have to make a payment to the bank.

This will be: $£7.1m\,(3.50\% - 3.45\%) \times \dfrac{4}{12} \times \dfrac{1}{1+(3.5\%\times 4/12)}$ or £1,169.65

This will be deducted from the actual receipts of £97,033 (estimated above) to give a net £95,863, a return of 4.05%. (NB This is the FRA rate of 3.45 plus the 0.6% over LIBOR from the commercial paper.)

(d)　The futures market outcome might differ because:

(i)　The hedge is not exact; 19 contracts is a slight over hedge.

Basis risk might exist. The basis at the futures close-out date might differ from the expected basis of 0.171.

Commercial paper interest rates might not move exactly with LIBOR rates.

(ii)　Any gains or losses on futures contracts would be taken/payable daily when the futures contracts are marked to market. The interest effect of such receipts or payments is ignored in the calculations.

(iii)　The above analysis ignores transactions costs.

(e)　An FRA could be described as a single-period interest rate swap. In an interest rate swap, two parties agree to exchange 'interest' payments on an underlying notional principal amount. With a coupon swap, one party might pay LIBOR and receive a fixed rate (the swap rate), and the other party will pay the fixed rate and receive LIBOR.

There are some differences between a swap and an FRA.

(i)　A swap is a long-term agreement, whereas an FRA is an agreement over a shorter period of time. (However, a company can arrange to buy or sell a strip of FRAs covering a period up to about two years.)

(ii)　With a swap, the interest payment dates for the two parties do not have to coincide.

(iii)　With a swap, the settlement of payments is usually at the end of the notional interest periods, rather than at the beginning.

63 POLYTOT PLC

Key answer tips

For an open-ended question like this in part (a), where you are asked to discuss the alternative forms of hedge but you are not specifically told which hedging methods to discuss, start by establishing what information is presented in the question. For example, in this question you are not given any interest rates, so a money market hedge cannot be used.

(a)   Possible currency hedges are a forward market hedge, currency futures hedge or currency options hedge.

Forward market hedge

The forward market hedge locks into a known exchange rate at the time the payment by the customer is made. It is a legally binding obligation.

A forward rate is required for four months' time. This may be estimated by interpolating between the three-month and one-year forward rates.

$1.5362 - 1.5140 = 0.0222 \times 1/9 = 0.0025$

The four-month rate is $1.5362 - 0.0025 = 1.5337$

$1.5398 - 1.5178 = 0.220 \times 1/9 = 0.0024$

The four-month rate is $1.5398 - 0.0024 = 1.5374$

60% of the receipts will be in $US, i.e. the equivalent to 405m pesos.

At the official rate $\dfrac{P405m}{98.20} = \$4,124,236$

Selling $ forward, $\dfrac{\$4,124,236}{1.5374} = £2,682,605$

The balance of 270m pesos will be converted at 115% of the official rate

$\dfrac{270}{179.745} = £1,502,128$

Total expected receipts are £4,184,733.

Futures hedge

A futures hedge locks the transaction into an expected exchange rate. In this case December futures will need to be bought as the September contract will have expired by the date of the payment, 1 November.

Basis on the December contract is $1.5510 - 1.5275$, or 2.35 cents. The expected basis on 1 November is 2/6 (the remaining period of the futures contract) × 2.35 cents, or 0.78 cents. The expected lock-in futures price, no matter what happens to actual spot rates, is $1.5275 + 0.0078 = \$1.5353$.

This is slightly better than the forward market rate.

However, basis on 1 November when the futures contract would be closed out (by buying an identical contract) might not be 0.78 cents, due to the existence of basis risk. A better or worse outcome than the expected lock-in rate is possible. The hedge is for $4,124,236.

This will require $\dfrac{4,124,236}{1.5353}$ = £2,686,274 or 42.98 £62,500 contracts.

43 contracts would be needed, a slight overhedge.

Futures contracts also require the payment of margin, a security deposit. Profit on futures contracts through favourable currency movement may be taken daily, but any losses will result in daily variation margin calls in order to keep the hedge open. The futures contract looks to offer a slightly better rate than the forward contract, but will involve more risks. The company must choose whether or not the expected extra return would compensate for these risks.

Currency options hedge

Currency options offer an advantage over both forwards and futures in that they not only protect against downside risk, they also allow the buyer of the option to take advantage of favourable currency movements by allowing the option to lapse. The price of this extra benefit is the option premium.

Given that the dollar is strengthening against the pound in the forward market, the currency option rates do not look very favourable. As Polytot wishes to exchange dollars for pounds, it will need to purchase December call options. Probably only the 1.5250 and 1.550 strike prices would be considered, as the other rates are far less favourable than the forward market.

Strike price	$ receipts	£ equivalent	Number of contracts	Number used
1.5250	4,124,236	2,704,417	86.54	86 (or 87)
1.5500	4,124,236	2,660,797	85.13	85

86 contracts is $4,098,438 at 1.5250, leaving $25,798 over which could be sold forward at $1.5374/£ to yield £16,780.

85 contracts is $4,117,188 at 1.550, leaving $7,048 over which could be sold forward to yield £4,584.

Strike price	Premium ($)	Premium	£ receipts	£ over	Worst-case outcome
		(£ at spot)			
1.5250	90,031	(58,179)	2,687,500	16,780	2,646,101
1.5500	59,766	(38,621)	2,656,250	14,584	2,622,213

These outcomes are much worse than the forward or futures hedges, but if the dollar was to strengthen further, the options could be lapsed and the pounds purchased in November in the spot market. For example, in order for the 1.5250 option to become better than the forward market hedge the dollar would have to strengthen at least to approximately 1.5250 – (1.5250 – 1.5374 + 0.0335) or 1.5039/£.

The recommended hedge is either the forward market (unless Polytot is happy with the extra risks of futures), or currency options at a probable strike price of 1.5250.

(b)   The proposed countertrade needs to be compared with the 40% of expected receipts that are at 15% less than the official rate. Three million kilos at 50–60 pence per kilo gives receipts of between £1.5 and £1.8 million. This compares with £1,502,128 from the foreign exchange transaction. The price for the strawberries would need to be in excess of 50 pence per kilo. Other factors that would need to be considered in any countertrade include:

(i)   How reliable is the supplier of the strawberries? Are they of suitable quality and could such a large quantity be supplied?

(ii)   Strawberries are perishable and require specialised transportation. Who is responsible for the costs of transportation, insurance etc?

(iii)   What additional administrative/organisational expense will the countertrade involve?

(iv)   What are the tax implications of a countertrade in strawberries?

64   ARNBROOK PLC

Key answer tips

Some students make the error in this question of constructing the swap in detail. This is not necessary to answer all requirements.

In part (a) ensure that you consider the bank's perspective as well as Arnbrook's. Similarly, in part (b) ensure you consider all three parties.

In part (c) an alternative approach to calculating discount rates after 6 months is to incorporate both the 5.7% and 6.2% rates. For example, the discount rate for 2 years = $1/(1.057^{0.5} \times 1.062^{1.5})$.

(a)   The risks faced by Arnbrook and the bank include:

(i)   Default risk by the counterparty to the swap. If the counterparty is a bank this risk will normally be very small. A bank would face larger counterparty default risk, especially from counterparties such as the BBB company with a relatively low credit rating.

(ii)   Market or position risk. This is the risk that market interest rate will change such that the company undertaking the swap would have been better off, with hindsight, if it had not undertaken the swap.

(iii)   Banks often undertake a 'warehousing' function in swap transactions. The size and/or maturity of the transactions desired by each counterparty to the bank often do not match. In such cases, the bank faces gap or mismatch risk, which it will normally hedge in the futures or other markets.

(b)

	Fixed rate	*Floating rate*
Arnbrook	6.25%	LIBOR + 0.75%
BBB company	7.25%	LIBOR + 1.25%
	———	———
Difference	1.00%	0.50%

There is a potential 0.50% arbitrage saving from undertaking the swap.

On a £50 million swap this is £250,000 per year.

Arnbrook would require 60% of any saving, or £150,000 annually. The BBB company would receive £100,000 annually.

The bank would charge each party £120,000 per year. After tax, this is a cost of £84,000 each. This would leave a net saving of £16,000 for the BBB-rated counterparty company.

The swap is potentially beneficial to all parties, but the counterparty company might press for a larger saving than £16,000.

(c) Arnbrook will pay floating rate interest as a result of the swap. If Arnbrook receives 60% of the arbitrage savings, it will save 0.5% (0.60) on its interest rates relative to borrowing directly in the floating-rate market, and effectively pay LIBOR + 0.45%, or 5.70% at current interest rates. If LIBOR moves to 5.75% in six months' time, Arnbrook will then pay 6.20% floating rate interest for the remaining period of the swap.

Interest savings in each six-month period are £50 million × 0.30% × 0.5 = £75,000

If the money market is efficient, the relevant discount rate will be the prevailing interest rate paid by Arnbrook.

Period:	Savings £	Discount factor	Present value (£)
0–6 months	75,000	0.972 (5.7%)	72,900
6 months–1 year	75,000	0.942 (6.2%)	70,650
1 year–18 months	75,000	0.913 (6.2%)	68,475
18 months–2 years	75,000	0.887 (6.2%)	66,525
2 years–30 months	75,000	0.860 (6.2%)	64,500
30 months–3 years	75,000	0.835 (6.2%)	62,625
Total present values			405,675

The interest rate swap is estimated to produce interest rate savings with a present value of £405,675 relative to borrowing floating rate directly. The swap would be beneficial, and, with hindsight, would result in lower interest costs than would have been available by borrowing at 6.25% in the fixed-rate market.

(d) In practice, most swaps are arranged through banks that run a 'swaps book'. There are several advantages in dealing with a bank rather than directly with another company.

1   In dealing with a bank, there is no problem about finding a swaps counterparty with an equal and opposite swapping requirement. The bank will arrange a swap to meet the specific requirements of each individual customer, as to amount and duration of the swap.

2   In dealing with a bank, the credit risk is that the bank might default, whereas in dealing directly with another company, the credit risk is that the other company might default. Banks are usually a much lower credit risk than corporates.

3   Banks are specialists in swaps, and are able to provide standard legal swaps agreements. The operation of the swap is likely to be administratively more straightforward.

The significant drawback to using a bank is that the bank will want to make a profit from its operations. In practice, it will generally do this by charging different swap rates for fixed rate payments and fixed rate receipts on different swaps.

(e) One central principle of Islamic finance is that making money out of money is not acceptable, i.e. interest is prohibited. A mudaraba contract, in Islamic finance, is a partnership between one party that brings finance or capital into the contract and another party that brings business expertise and personal effort into the contract. The first party is called the owner of capital, while the second party is called the agent, who runs or manages the business. The mudaraba contract specifies how profit from the business is shared proportionately between the two parties. Any loss, however, is borne by the owner of capital, and not by the agent managing the business. It can therefore be seen that three key characteristics of a mudaraba contract are that no interest is paid, that profits are shared, and that losses are not shared.

If Arnbrook were to decide to seek Islamic finance for the planned expansion and if the company were to enter into a murdaraba contract, the company would therefore be entering into a partnership as an agent, managing the business and sharing profits with the Islamic bank that provided the finance and which was acting as the owner of capital. The Islamic bank would not interfere in the management of the business and this is what would be expected if Arnbrook were to finance the business expansion using debt such as a bank loan. However, while interest on debt is likely to be at a fixed rate, the murdaraba contract would require a sharing of profit in the agreed proportions.

65 ASTEROID SYSTEMS *Walk in the footsteps of a top tutor*

Key answer tips

Although the calculations in this question test the money market hedge in a different way from previous questions, the discursive parts are very standard and straightforward. Make sure you leave enough time to attempt all parts of the question.

Currency hedging

The objective is to fix (Euro/SFr) currency exchange rates for two months for an expected remittance of SFr 2.4299 million. This is achieved with a money market hedge for the two month exposure.

(a) **Hedging the two month Swiss franc exposure**

Forward contracts in the money market are the most straightforward way of eliminating transaction risk. The exposure to movements in the Swiss Franc can be eliminated by entering into a forward contract to purchase the currency at Euro SFr 1.6199 (see note 1). Alternatively, given access to fixed rate finance in the Swiss market a reverse money market hedge can be established by borrowing in SFr and depositing in Euros. Given that the interest rates can be locked in this would offer a better forward rate at two months at any borrowing rate less than SFr LIBOR + 7 (note 2).

Supporting notes

Note (1)

The current expectation of remittances is based upon an estimate of the two month forward rate of (1.6223 + 1.6176)/2 = 1.6199 for the Swiss Franc.

Swiss Francs = 1.6199 × 1.5m = SFr 2.4299 million in two months using the forward rate above.

Note (2)

The money market hedge is based upon interest rate parity and using the IRP formula we can calculate the maximum rate of interest that can be borne for the money market hedge to be worthwhile.

The technique for a reverse money market hedge is identical to that for a conventional hedge except that the counter currency is borrowed in the foreign market, converted at spot and deposited in the domestic market. However, for a money market hedge to work, the company must be able to secure short term money market finance in both the base and the counter currency area. With the SFr exposure it is possible to borrow at fixed in the Swiss market. Using the no arbitrage condition of the interest rate parity formula we can determine the maximum rate of interest the company should agree in creating a money market hedge. The interest rate in the base currency to use is the best rate for depositing in the Euro market:

$$1.6199 = 1.6242 \times \frac{\left(1 + i_c \times \dfrac{2}{12}\right)}{\left(1 + 0.03725 \times \dfrac{2}{12}\right)}$$

$i_c = 2.13\%$

If the company can borrow at less than spot Swiss 2.13% in the Swiss market then the money market hedge will be preferred to a forward sale of SFr 1.5 million.

Tutorial note

An alternative to this Interest Rate Parity calculation would have been to set up the Money Market Hedge from first principles, and to derive the Swiss borrowing rate of 2.13% as the balancing figure which makes the Swiss receipt equivalent to €1.5m in 2 months.

(b) The relative advantages and disadvantages of the use of a money market hedge versus exchange traded derivatives A money market hedge is a mechanism for the delivery of foreign currency, at a future date, at a specified rate without recourse to the forward FOREX market. If a company is able to achieve preferential access to the short term money markets in the base and counter currency zones then it can be a cost effective substitute for a forward agreement. However, it is difficult to reverse quickly and is cumbersome to establish as it requires borrowing/lending agreements to be established denominated in the two currencies.

Exchange traded derivatives such as futures and foreign exchange options offer a rapid way of creating a hedge and are easily closed out. For example, currency futures are normally closed out and the profit/loss on the derivative position used to offset the gain or loss in the underlying. The fixed contract sizes for exchange traded products mean that it is often impossible to achieve a perfect hedge and some gain or loss on the unhedged element of the underlying or the derivative will be carried. Also, given that exchange traded derivatives are priced in a separate market to the underlying there may be discrepancies in the movements of each and the observed delta may not equal one. This basis risk is minimised by choosing short maturity derivatives but cannot be completely eliminated unless maturity coincides exactly with the end of the exposure. Furthermore less than perfectly hedged positions require disclosure under IFRS 39. Although rapid to establish, currency hedging using the derivatives market may also involve significant cash flows in meeting and maintaining the margin requirements of the exchange. Unlike futures, currency options will entail the payment of a premium which may be an expensive way of eliminating the risk of an adverse currency movement.

With relatively small amounts, the OTC market represents the most convenient means of locking in exchange rates. Where cross border flows are common and business is well diversified across different currency areas then currency hedging is of questionable benefit. Where, as in this case, relatively infrequent flows occur then the simplest solution is to engage in the forward market for hedging risk. The use of a money market hedge as described may generate a more favourable forward rate than direct recourse to the forex market. However the administrative and management costs in setting up the necessary loans and deposits are a significant consideration.

(c) The only risk which will impact on a firm's cost of capital is that risk which is priced in either the equity or the debt markets. Considering these two markets in turn:

Currency risk forms part of a firm's exposure to market risk and will impact on a firm's cost of capital through its beta value and, as a result, its equity cost of capital. The extent to which this is significant depends on the exposed volume of currency transactions conducted in a given period, the average duration of the exposure and the correlation of the currency with the market. If a given currency has the same correlation with the market as the company, removing currency risk will have no impact on the firm's overall exposure to market risk and as a result no impact on the firm's cost of capital. The greater the difference in the relative correlations the higher the potential improvement in shareholder value from hedging.

The impact on the cost of debt is more complex. The most significant impact is through the firm's exposure to default risk. If currency transactions are significant and the foreign currency is highly correlated with the domestic currency then the impact is unlikely to be significant and the gains from hedging modest. Where the degree of correlation is low or indeed negative then eliminating currency risk may significantly alter the firm's default risk. However, unlike market risk default risk is related to the overall volatility of a firm's underlying value and its ability to finance its debt. The elimination of currency risk is therefore likely to have at least some impact on the volatility of the firm's cash flows and therefore its cost of capital.

	ACCA marking scheme	
		Marks
(a)	Calculation of forward rates	4
	Calculation of minimum rate at LIBOR + 7 through reverse money market hedge	5
	Conclusion	1
		——
		10
(b)	Advantages and disadvantages of OTC versus ET derivatives	
	Basis risk	2
	Under/over hedging	1
	Counterparty risk	1
	Flexibility	1
	Margin	1
		——
		6
(c)	Impact upon the cost of equity capital	2
	Impact upon cost of debt capital	2
		——
		4
		——
Total		**20**
		——

Tutorial note (extracted from the examiner's comments)

This was not a popular question and only a minority of candidates who attempted it were able to identify the money market requirements and the procedure for setting up a hedge of this type.

Common sources of error with this question were:

(i)   *Incorrect estimation of the appropriate forward rate*

(ii)   *Being unable to use the money market hedge in a situation where there is a remittance as opposed to a commitment in the foreign currency concerned.*

(iii)   *Not recognising the role of the interest rate parity relationship in determining the minimum acceptable rate for borrowing.*

(iv)   *Not appreciating the significance of the correlation between the domestic and the counter currency in determining the potential gains from hedging.*

66   PHOBOS CO *Walk in the footsteps of a top tutor*

> **Key answer tips**
>
> This is a very standard question on Interest Rate hedging.
>
> Identify the transaction first, to ensure you get your hedges the right way round, and lay out all your workings clearly.

(a)   (i)   Step (1) Calculate the current interest:

Current interest = (LIBOR + 50) × exposure time × principal

Current interest = $6.50\% \times \dfrac{4}{12} \times £30,000,000 = £650,000$

Step (2) Select the shortest available future with maturity following the commencement of exposure and choose the appropriate hedging strategy.

Sell March with an open of 93.8 and a settlement of 93.88.

> **Tutorial note**
>
> *When the Open and Settlement prices are both quoted, it is the Settlement price which is relevant as the price at which we initially buy or sell the futures contracts.*

Step (3) Calculate the number of contracts:

$$\text{Contracts} = \frac{\text{principal}}{\text{contract size}} \times \frac{\text{Exposure period}}{\text{Contract period}}$$

$$\text{Contracts} = \frac{£30,000,000}{£500,000} \times \frac{4}{3} = 80$$

Step (4) Calculate the basis:

Basis = spot price − futures price = 94.00 − 93.88 = 12 basis points or 'ticks'

Assuming linear convergence then movement between closure and maturity is four ticks given the contracts will have one month to run.

Step (5) Estimate close-out price if interest rates (a) increase by 100 basis points (b) decrease by 100 basis points.

(a)   Close out will be 93.00 − 0.04 = 92.96

(b)   Close out will be 95.00 − 0.04 = 94.96

Step (6) Calculate gain and/or loss in the futures market and the equivalent cost:

Interest rate at close out	7.00%	5.00%
Current open price	93.88	93.88
Futures price at close out	92.96	94.96
Ticks	92	−108
On 80 contracts at £12.50 per tick	92,000	−108,000
Cost of loan in spot market	750,000	550,000
Less profit/(loss) on futures	92,000	−108,000
Net cost of loan	658,000	658,000
Annual equivalent	6.58%	6.58%

(ii) Traded options allow the management of this type of risk, but the hedge carries a premium. Given the current LIBOR of 6% and an exposure commencing in March the end of March puts at 94,000 are best suited for this type of exposure. A put option allows the holder, at exercise, the right to short the futures at the stated price. These options are exercised (or sold back to the market) if the March futures rate is less than the stated exercise price.

Step (1) Choose the most effective option strategy to minimise basis risk from the point of exposure to contract exercise date on the underlying and to minimise time value.

March puts on three month futures at 94.000

Step (2) Calculate the required numbers of contracts:

The calculation as for futures = 80 contracts

Step (3) Calculate premium payable:

Premium = 80 × 16.8 × £12.50 = £16,800

Step (4) Calculate basis on the underlying (as before) = 4 ticks

Step (5) Test outcomes against expected movements in interest rates:

Interest rate at close out	7.00%	5.00%
Futures price at close out	92.96	94.96
Exercise price	94.00	94.00
Option payoff	104.00	0
Position payoff on 80 contracts at £12.50 per tick	104,000	0
Cost of loan in spot market	750,000	550,000
Less option payoff	−104,000	0
Less premium	16,800	16,800
Net cost of loan	662,800	566,800
Annual equivalent	6.63%	5.67%
Expected payoff assuming equal likelihoods	6.15%	

In this calculation we have ignored the time value of the option at close out but have assumed that it will only be the intrinsic value. With one month before close out with the volatilities implied in this example the time value of the in-the-money options could be significant and should be calculated.

At 6.63% the effective cost is just above the required threshold of 6.6% but with an expected payoff of 6.15% (given equal likelihoods of a rise or a fall in interest rates). Given the absence of a time value estimate on close out, and the possibility of capturing the benefit of a fall in rates, the use of options should be the preferred alternative.

(b) Derivatives offer an opportunity for a firm to vary its exposure to interest rate risk at a given rate of interest on the underlying principal (hedging) or to decrease the rate of interest on its principal at an increased level of risk exposure. For hedging purposes derivatives permit the management of exposure either for the long term (swaps) or for the short term (Forward Rate Agreements (FRAs), Interest Rate Futures (IRFs), Interest Rate Options (IROs) and hybrids). With forward and futures contracts, the mechanism of hedging is the same in that an offsetting position is struck such that both parties forego the possibility of upside in order to eliminate the risk of downside in the underlying rate movements. Where the option to benefit from favourable rate movements is required or in situations where there is uncertainty whether a hedge will be required, then an IRO may be the more appropriate but higher cost alternative. Such hedging can be more or less efficient depending upon the ability to set up perfectly matched exposures with zero default risk. Matching depends upon the nature of the contract. With OTC agreements the efficiency of the match may be perfect but the risk of default remains. With traded derivatives, the efficiency of the match may be less than perfect either through size effects or because of the lack of a perfect match on the underlying (for example the use of a LIBOR derivative against an underlying reference rate which is not LIBOR). There will also be basis risk where the maturity of the derivative does not coincide exactly with the underlying exposure.

Where a company forms a view that future spot rates will be lower than those specified by the forward yield curve they may decide to alter their exposure to interest rate risk in order to capture the benefit of the reduced rate. This can be achieved through the use of IROs. Alternatively, leveraged swap or leveraged FRA positions can be taken to avoid the upfront cost of an IRO. For example, taking multiples of the variable leg of a swap (i.e. agreeing to swap fixed for variable) where a higher than market fixed rate is swapped for 'n' multiples of the variable rate. However, as a number of cases have demonstrated it may be very difficult with these types of arrangement to gauge the degree of risk exposure and to ensure that they are effectively managed by the firm. In the 1990s a number of companies in the US and elsewhere took leveraged positions, without recognising the degree of their exposure and took losses that threatened the survival of the firm.

ACCA marking scheme		
		Marks
(a)	Calculate current interest rate	1
	Identification of appropriate future and hedge strategy	1
	Calculation of number of contracts	3
(i)	Calculation of basis for IRF 2 Calculate gain or loss on alternative closeouts	2
(ii)	Identification of most appropriate option strategy	1
	Calculate premium payable	1
	Calculate loan cost under alternative payoffs	2
	Estimate expected payoff given equal likelihoods	1
	Maximum	14
(b)	Discussion of the use of derivatives for interest rate risk management	
	Problems of making an efficient match	1
	Hedge efficiency issues	1
	Default and basis risk	1
	Use of derivatives to reduce interest rate	
	Leveraged swaps and FRAs	2
	Dangers of leveraging	1
	Maximum	6
Total		**20**

67 MULTIDROP

Key answer tips

There are a number of ways this problem can be handled. Two methods are shown here, the first uses a transactions matrix ('tabular approach') and the second is a route minimisation algorithm ('diagrammatic approach').

(a) Companies that trade with different currencies will be exposed to the risk that exchange rate changes impact the value of their transactions. This can happen for one-off transactions (transaction risk) or on a long-term basis (economic risk).

The impact of exchange rate changes can impact either positively or negatively, but the key issue is that any uncertainty created by currency risk can reduce the attractiveness of the company to its investors and potential investors. Investors don't like nasty surprises, so they prefer companies to hedge against risks to reduce the potential variability of returns.

Hence, companies that effectively manage their exposure to currency risk are more likely to be appealing to investors, so there could be a positive impact on shareholder wealth if a company can reduce the risk created by exchange rate movements.

(b)   **Determination of the currency transfers required**

Given that all balances are to be cleared through the European office, proceed as follows.

Convert all indebtedness between parties to Euros using the specified exchange rates:

	million	€ million
US$	6.40	4.67
S$	16.00	7.75
US$	5.40	3.94
Euros	8.20	8.20
US$	5.00	3.65
Rm	25.00	5.01
£	2.20	2.34
S$	4.00	1.94
Rm	8.30	1.66

Transactions Matrix

		Europe	US	Owed to Malaysia	Singapore	UK	Owed by
	Europe		4.67	1.66			6.33
	US	8.20					8.20
Owed by	Malaysia		3.94			2.34	6.28
	Singapore	7.75	3.65	5.01			16.41
	UK				1.94		1.94
	Owed to	15.95	12.26	6.67	1.94	2.34	
	Owed by	6.33	8.20	6.28	16.41	1.94	
	Net	9.62	4.06	0.39	−14.47	0.40	

(All amounts are in € million)

Multidrop (Europe) pays the US, UK and Malaysian business €4.06 million, €0.40 million, and €0.39 million respectively, and receives from Singapore €14.47 million. The net income is €9.62 million to Multidrop (Europe).

Route Minimisation Algorithm

Step 1: Network of Indebtedness

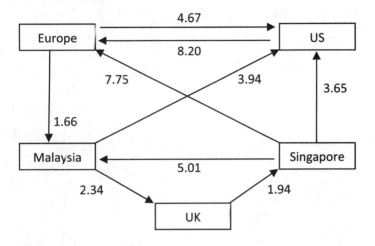

Step 2: Resolve any bilaterals

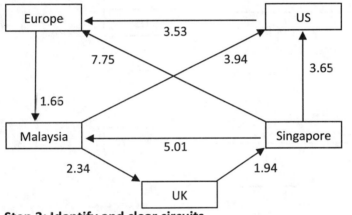

Step 3: Identify and clear circuits

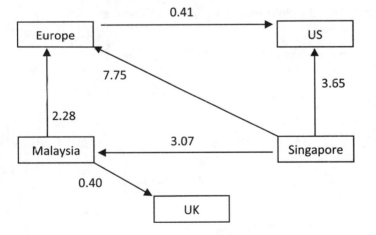

Step 4: Identify and clear cross indebtedness

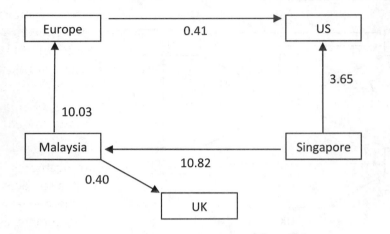

And also:

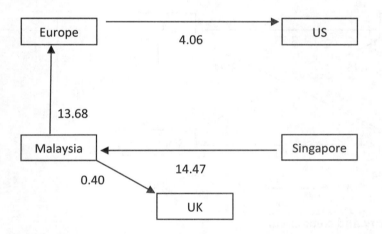

Step 5: Finally resolve all indebtedness in favour of Europe

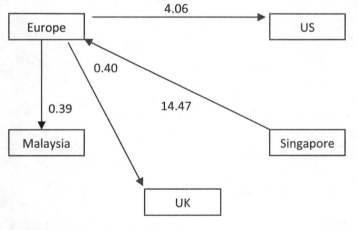

(All amounts are in € million)

(c) **Netting Arrangements with the global business and trading partners**

Netting is a mechanism whereby mutual indebtedness between group members or between group members and other parties can be reduced. The advantages of such an arrangement is that the number of currency transactions can be minimised, saving transaction costs and focusing the transaction risk onto a smaller set of transactions that can be more effectively hedged. It may also be the case, if exchange controls are in place limiting currency flows across borders, that balances can be offset, minimising overall exposure. Where group transactions occur with other companies the benefit of netting is that the exposure is limited to the net amount reducing hedging costs and counterparty risk.

The disadvantages: some jurisdictions do not allow netting arrangements, and there may be taxation and other cross border issues to resolve. It also relies upon all liabilities being accepted – and this is particularly important where external parties are involved. There will be costs in establishing the netting agreement and where third parties are involved this may lead to re-invoicing or, in some cases, re-contracting.

ACCA marking scheme		
		Marks
(a)	1 mark per sensible point	Max 5
	Maximum	5
(b)	EITHER: Using Transactions Matrix Method	
	Set principal as European business	1
	Conversion to Euros	3
	Initial amounts owed and owing	2
	Totals owed and owing	2
	Net amounts owed	2
	Conclusion: Payments and receipts to Multidrop (Europe)	2
	Maximum	12
	OR: Using Route Minimisation Algorithm Method	1
	Set principal as European business	
	Conversion to Euros	3
	Step 1: Network of Indebtedness	2
	Steps 2 and 3: Resolve bilaterals and resolve circuits	2
	Steps 4 and 5: Clear cross Indebtedness and resolve in favour of Multidrop (Europe)	2
	Conclusion: Payments and receipts to Multidrop (Europe)	2
	Maximum	12
(c)	Minimisation of number of transactions	1–2
	Minimisation of cost of transacting	1–2
	Avoidance of exchange controls	1–2
	Minimisation of hedging costs	1–2
	Limiting exposure to net	1–2
	Taxation issues	1–2
	Acceptance of liability	1–2
	Re-invoicing and re-contracting	1–2
	Maximum	8
Total		25

68   PONDHILLS

(a)   Translation exposure exists because of the need for multinational companies to periodically consolidate the financial statements of overseas subsidiaries with those of the parent company in order to present the financial details and to assess the performance of the entire group. In order to achieve consolidation the subsidiaries™ accounts need to be translated from a foreign currency basis into the currency of the parent company. Translation is not a physical exchange of currencies; it is the change in the monetary expression of the subsidiaries™ activities from one currency to another.

There are several methodologies for translating financial statements. Governments or professional accounting standards bodies will normally specify the preferred or required method(s). Depending on the method used the resulting foreign exchange gain or loss on translation will significantly differ. Translation exposure does not directly measure the cash flow implications of exchange rate changes, or the effect of such changes on the value of a multinational. Because of this many multinational companies do not hedge against translation exposure. However, if the exposure is expected to result in a significant reported loss, which the company believes might, in an inefficient market, have a detrimental effect on share price, some hedging might be undertaken.

Economic exposure results from the fact that a company's economic value will change as a result of changes in foreign exchange rates. It is often categorised into two forms:

(i)   **Transaction exposure**, which focuses on the short-term impact on cash flow, for example through foreign trade activities. Many multinationals hedge against the potential cash flow loss of transaction exposure through forward markets, currency options etc.

(ii)   **Real operating exposure**, which considers the longer term effects on cash flow and NPV after the effect of inflation has been removed.

Economic exposure refers to unexpected changes in exchange rates. As economic exposure has a direct effect on the value of the firm it is important for multinationals to try to manage such exposure. However, as the size and nature of the exposure is unknown it is difficult to hedge against international diversification of sales, production, raw material sources and financing is suggested as this will provide more flexibility to respond to adverse unexpected change in exchange rates.

(b)   (i)   **Translation exposure**

Analysis is required of the possible foreign exchange exposure of Pondhills Inc the parent company from the operations of its African subsidiary.

The current/closing rate method translates all EXPOSED assets and liabilities at the exchange rate prevailing at the year end. However, from the viewpoint of Pondhills Inc, not all of Ponda SA's assets and liabilities are exposed, as sales are denominated in US dollars, and some payables are payable in sterling. As no change is expected between the dollar and sterling exchange rates, the exposure to Pondhills Inc is only from assets and liabilities that are denominated in dinars.

Current exchange rate is 246.3 dinars/US$1. If a 15% devaluation occurs this will move to 246.3 × 1.15 = 283.2 dinars/US$1.

	Million dinars	Exposed	In US$ at current rate	In US$ post devaluation
Non-current assets	510	Yes	2.071	1.801
Current assets:				
Cash	86	Yes	0.349	0.304
Receivables	410	No	1.665	1.665
Inventory	380	Yes	1.543	1.342
Total current assets	876		3.557	3.311
Short-term payables	(296)	50%	(1.202)	(1.124)
Long–term loans	(500)	Yes	(2.030)	(1.766)
Net assets	590		2.396	2.222
Shareholder's equity	590		2.396	2.222

The balance sheet exposure is (510 + 86 + 380) – ((50% of 296) + 500) or 328 million dinars.

The expected loss on translation exposure:

Exposure in dinars: 328 million	In US$ million
At current exchange rate	1.332
At post-devaluation exchange rate	1.158
Expected loss on translation	0.174

This is the change in shareholders' equity shown in the table above, $US2.396m – $2.222m = $0.174 million.

(ii) Economic exposure measures the cash flow effects of a change in exchange rates. The data below shows the change over a full year with a 15% devaluation of the dinar.

	million			
	Current dinars	Post devaluation dinars	Current dollars	Post devaluation dollars
Revenue (all US$)	2,300	2,645	9.338	9.338
COGS and operating expenses:				
Local (dinars)	966	966	3.922	3.411
Overseas (sterling)	644	741	2.615	2.615
Interest (dinars)	60	60	0.244	0.212
Net cash flows	630	878	2.557	3.100

There is an initial annualised gain in cash flow for Pondhills Inc of US$543,000 ($3.100m – $2.557m), resulting from the devaluation of the dinar.

(c) Unlike the translation exposure estimate where a loss was forecast, the expected impact on economic exposure results in an exposure gain. Translation exposure does not measure the effect of exchange changes on cash flows. Unless a reported translation loss is expected to have a detrimental effect on Pondhills Inc's share price, (which it should not if the market is efficient), no hedging against translation exposure is recommended.

In the light of the expected economic exposure gain there is no need to hedge against the possible devaluation, although it might be advisable to pay any hard currency liabilities to third parties (e.g. sterling creditors) and to reduce dinar cash levels before any devaluation occurred.

69 CURRENCY SWAPS

Key answer tips

There are some very easy marks in the discussion parts of this question. Make sure that you leave time to answer the written parts as well as the calculations.

(a) **Advantages of currency swaps include:**

(i) They allow companies to undertake foreign currency hedging, often for longer periods than is possible with forwards.

(ii) They are usually cheaper than long-term forwards, where such products exist.

(iii) Finance may be obtained at a cheaper rate than would be possible by borrowing directly in the relevant market. This occurs by taking advantage of arbitrage if a company has a relative funding advantage in one country.

(iv) They may provide access to finance in currencies that could not be borrowed directly, e.g. due to government restrictions, or lack of a credit rating in the overseas market.

(v) Currency swaps offer the opportunity to restructure the company's debt profile without physically redeeming debt or issuing new debt.

(vi) Currency swaps might be used to avoid a country's exchange control restrictions.

Potential problems include:

(i) If the swap is directly with a corporate counterparty the potential default risk of the counterparty must be considered. Swaps arranged with a bank as the direct counterparty tend to be much less risky.

(ii) Political or sovereign risk; the possibility that a government will introduce restrictions that interfere with the performance of the swap.

(iii) Basis risk. With a floating to floating swap, basis risk might exist if the two floating rates are not pegged to the same index.

(iv) Exchange rate risk. The swap may result in a worse outcome than would have occurred if no swap had been arranged.

(b)   (i)   Interest rate differentials:

	Fixed rate	Floating rate
Galeplus	6.25%	PIBOR + 2%
Counterparty	8.30%	PIBOR + 1.5%
	(2.05%)	0.5%

The overall arbitrage opportunity from using a currency swap is 2.55% per year. Bank fees are 0.75% per year, leaving 1.8%; 75% of 1.8% is 1.35%. That would be the benefit per year to Galeplus in terms of interest saving from using a currency swap.

(ii)   Assuming inflation rates in Perdia are between 15% and 50% per year, the best and worst case exchange rates are:

	Rubbits/£	
	Best case	Worst case
Spot	85.40	85.40
Year 1	98.21	128.10
Year 2	112.94	192.15
Year 3	129.88	288.23

Cash flows (million rubbits)

Year	0	1	2	3
Purchase cost	(2,000)			
Fees		40	40	40
Sale price				4,000
	(2,000)	40	40	4,040
Discount factors (15%)	1	0.870	0.756	0.658
Present values	(2,000)	34.8	30.24	2,658.32

With a currency swap, 2,000 million of the Year 3 cash flows will be at the current spot rate of 85.40 rubbits/£, with the remainder at the end of Year 3 spot rate.

Discounted cash flows (£ million)

Worst-case rates	(23.42)	0.27	0.16	20.07
Estimated NPV	(£2.92 million)			
Best-case rates	(23.42)	0.35	0.27	25.75
Estimated NPV	£2.95 million			

The financial viability of the investment depends upon exchange rate movements. The greater the depreciation in the value of the rubbit relative to the pound, the worse the outcome of the investment. This is due to the Year 3 price of the telecommunications centre remaining constant no matter what the exchange rate is at the time.

These estimates assume that exchange rates remain in the above range. In reality they could be better or worse. Additionally, non-financial factors such as political risk would influence the decision. For example, given the government's current cash flow position, how likely is the payment of 4,000 million rubbits to be made in three years' time? Other factors such as taxation in the UK would also need to be considered.

Unless there are strong strategic reasons for buying the centre, for example possible future cash flow benefits beyond Year 3, the investment is not recommended. In order for the investment to take place a better hedge against currency risk would need to be found, or the price to be received in Year 3 renegotiated to reflect the impact of adverse exchange rate changes.

70 FNDC PLC

(a) Short-term interest rate futures (STIRs) allow a company to hedge an interest rate risk by attempting to create a gain on the futures market to offset a potential loss in the underlying cash market. The futures hedge is expected to protect interest rates at the expected futures price at the time the futures contracts mature or are closed out. However, hedges will rarely be perfect because:

   (i)   The size of the risk might not correspond to an exact number of futures contracts; the risk might need to be underhedged or overhedged.

   (ii) Basis risk might exist, which means that the futures price at the close-out date might be different to that expected.

   (iii) The futures contract is based on LIBOR or equivalent. The underlying risk might be based upon a short-term interest rate instrument with different characteristics to LIBOR.

Futures also involve an up-front margin payment, and payments of variation margin if prices move in an adverse direction. They are highly standardised and have a limited number of expiry dates.

Market-traded options on futures share many of the characteristics of the underlying futures contracts. The major differences are that the option contracts involve the payment of an option premium, which is payable whether or not the option is exercised. Additionally, options have the advantage of allowing the buyer to take advantage of favourable movements in interest rates, while still protecting against adverse movements. Options also offer a wider choice of the level of interest rate that may be used to protect against adverse movements.

(b) **Futures hedge**

The period at risk is two months commencing in five months' time, on 1 May. The June futures contract will be used as it has the first maturity date after the period of risk commences. Futures will be sold in order to make a profit if interest rates rise.

As the period at risk is two months, the number of contracts required is:

$$\frac{£45,000,000}{£500,000} \times \frac{2}{3} = 60$$

Sixty June contracts will be sold.

LIBOR is currently 4%, or the equivalent to a futures price of 96.00

The basis is $95.55 - 96.00 = -0.45$

There are seven months until the futures contract matures. If there is a linear fall in basis (no basis risk) then the expected basis in five months' time when the futures contracts are closed out is:

$$-0.45 \times \frac{2}{7} = -0.13$$

The expected lock-in rate for the futures contract is 95.55 + 0.13 = 95.68 or 4.32%.

FNDC borrows at LIBOR plus 1.25%, therefore the expected lock in interest rate is 5.57%, or £417,750, no matter what rate LIBOR moves to.

Calculations of cash market and futures market profits/losses are not essential, but would be as follows:

0.5% increase in interest rates:

Cash market:

Actual borrowing cost in five months' time

$$(4.5\% + 1.25\%) \times £45,000,000 \times \frac{2}{12} = £431,250$$

Futures market:

1 December sell 60 June contracts at 95.55

1 May buy 60 contracts at the expected futures price of 95.37 (100 – 4.5% – 0.13)

Futures profit is 0.18 or 18 ticks.

18 × 60 × £12.50 = £13,500

The net interest cost is £431,250 – £13,500 = £417,750

$$\frac{£417,750}{£45,000,000} \times \frac{12}{2} = 5.57\%$$

0.5% decrease in interest rates:

Cash market:

Actual borrowing cost in five months' time

$$(3.5\% + 1.25\%) \times £45,000,000 \times \frac{2}{12} = £356,250$$

Futures market:

1 December sell 60 June contracts at 95.55

1 May buy 60 contracts at 96.37 (100 – 3.5% – 0.13)

Futures loss is 0.82 or 82 ticks.

82 × 60 × £12.50 = £61,500

The total interest cost is £356,250 + £61,500 = £417,750 or 5.57%

Interest rate options

Options to sell futures are required, hence June put options will be purchased.

Only three possible exercise prices exist.

Exercise price	Option premium
9,500	45,000,000 × 0.015% × 2/12 = 1,125
9,550	45,000,000 × 0.165% × 2/12 = 12,375
9,600	45,000,000 × 0.710% × 2/12 = 53,250

If interest rates increase by 0.5%, leading to an expected futures price of 95.37 at the close-out date of 1 May.

Exercise price	Exercise option	Profit from exercising options
9,500	No	
9,550	Yes	(95.50 − 95.37) ÷ 0.005 × 60 × £6.25 = £9,750
9,600	Yes	(96.00 − 95.37) ÷ 0.005 × 60 × £6.25 = £47,250

Overall cost if options are used:

	Market borrowing cost	+ Option premium	− Option profit	Total
9,500	431,250	1,125	–	432,375
9,550	431,250	12,375	9,750	433,875
9,600	431,250	53,250	47,250	437,250

As expected, all are worse than the expected cost of £417,750 using futures.

If interest rates were to fall by 0.5%, the expected futures close-out price is 96.37

Exercise price	Exercise option
9,500	No
9,550	No
9,600	No

In all cases the option will be allowed to lapse, or sold for any remaining time value.

Overall cost if options are used:

	Market borrowing cost	+ Option premium	Total
9,500	356,250	1,125	357,375
9,550	356,250	12,375	368,625
9,600	356,250	53,250	409,500

All of these outcomes are much better than the futures hedge, but would rely on interest rates falling rather than rising. This is not expected to happen by 'the market'. The 9500 exercise price is probably the most attractive of the option contracts as it is relatively low cost and gives a very favourable outcome if interest rates fall. However, it is still £14,625 more expensive than the futures hedge if interest rates rise.

(c) A maximum interest rate to the company of 5.75% implies a LIBOR rate of 4.5%, or 9550. A minimum rate of 5.25% implies LIBOR of 4.0% or 9600.

The collar hedge would be to buy 60 June 9550 put option contracts and to sell 60 June 9600 call option contracts.

The net premium payable would be 0.165 − 0.070 = 0.095, or a cost of:

£45,000,000 × 0.095% × 2/12 = £7,125

If interest rates increase by 0.5%, the 9550 put option will be exercised.

Market borrowing cost	+	*net option premium*	–	*option profit*	=	*Total*
£431,250		£7,125		£9,750		£428,625

If interest falls by 0.5%, the put option will not be exercised, but there will be a loss on the call option as it will be exercised by its buyer.

Market borrowing cost (4.75%) = £356,250

Loss on call option is: (96.00 – 96.37) × 2 × 100 × 60 × 6.25 = £27,750

Total cost is £356,250 + £27,750 + £7,125 = £391,125

The collar hedge saves premium cost and might be attractive to FNDC, although the worst-case outcome is still much more expensive than the futures hedge.

71 LEVANTE CO (DEC 11)

Key answer tips

This question (from the December 2011 exam) tested the contents of an article written by the examiner and published in the September 2011 issue of Student Accountant magazine. It is common for the examiner to test topics covered in recent articles, so keep an eye out for any new articles published.

(a) Spot yield rates applicable to Levante Co (based on A credit rating)

1 year	3.85%
2 year	4.46%
3 year	5.07%
4 year	5.80%
5 year	6.12%

Bond value based on A rating =

$\$4 \times 1.0385^{-1} + \$4 \times 1.0446^{-2} + \$104 \times 1.0507^{-3} = \$97.18$ per $100

Current price based on AA rating = $98.71

Fall in value = (97.18 – 98.71)/98.71 × 100% = 1.55%

(b) Spot rates applicable to Levante Co (based on A credit rating) [from above]

1 year	3.85%
2 year	4.46%
3 year	5.07%
4 year	5.80%
5 year	6.12%

(i)   Value of 5% coupon bond

$\$5 \times 1.0385^{-1} + \$5 \times 1.0446^{-2} + \$5 \times 1.0507^{-3} + \$5 \times 1.0580^{-4} + \$105 \times 1.0612^{-5}$
$= \$95.72$

Hence the bond will need to be issued at a discount if only a 5% coupon is offered.

(ii)   New coupon rate for bond valued at $100 by the markets

Since the 5% coupon bond is only valued at $95.72, a higher coupon needs to be offered. This coupon amount can be calculated by finding the yield to maturity of the 5% coupon bond discounted at the above yield curve. This yield to maturity will be the coupon amount for the new bond such that its face value will be $100.

Therefore, if the yield to maturity is denoted by YTM then

$\$5 \times (1 + YTM)^{-1} + \$5 \times (1 + YTM)^{-2} + \$5 \times (1 + YTM)^{-3} + \$5 \times (1 + YTM)^{-4} + \$105 \times (1 + YTM)^{-5} = \$95.72$

Solve by trial and error, assume YTM is 5.5%. This gives the bond value as $97.86.

Assume YTM is 6%; this gives the bond value as $95.78, which is close enough to $95.72

$\$5 \times (1.06)^{-1} + \$5 \times (1.06)^{-2} + \$5 \times (1.06)^{-3} + \$5 \times (1.06)^{-4} + \$105 \times (1.06)^{-5} = \$95.78$

Hence if the coupon payment is 6% or $6 per $100 bond unit then the bond market value will equal the par value at $100.

$\$6 \times (1.06)^{-1} + \$6 \times (1.06)^{-2} + \$6 \times (1.06)^{-3} + \$6 \times (1.06)^{-4} + \$106 \times (1.06)^{-5} = \$100$

Alternatively:

Take R as the coupon rate, such that:

$(R \times 1.0385^{-1}) + (R \times 1.0446^{-2}) + (R \times 1.0507^{-3}) + (R \times 1.0580^{-4}) + (R \times 1.0612^{-5}) + (100 \times 1.0612{-}5) = \$100$

4.2826R + 74.30 = $100

R = 6% or $6 per $100

Advice:

If only a 5% coupon is offered, the bonds will have to be issued at just under a 4.3% discount. To raise the full $150 million, if the bonds are issued at a 4.3% discount, then 1,567,398 $100 bond units need to be issued, as opposed to 1,500,000. This is an extra 67,398 bond units for which Levante Co will need to pay an extra $6,739,800 when the bonds are redeemed in five years.

On the other hand, paying a higher coupon every year of 6% instead of 5% will mean that an extra $1,500,000 is needed for each of the next five years.

If the directors feel that the drain in resources of $1,500,000 every year is substantial and that the project's profits will cover the extra $6,739,800 in five years' time, then they should issue the bond at a discount and at a lower coupon rate. On the other hand, if the directors feel that they would like to spread the amount payable then they should opt for the higher coupon alternative.

(c)   Industry risk measures the resilience of the company's industrial sector to changes in the economy. In order to measure or assess this, the following factors could be used:

Impact of economic changes on the industry in terms of how successfully the firms in the industry operate under differing economic outcomes;

How cyclical the industry is and how large the peaks and troughs are;

How the demand shifts in the industry as the economy changes.

Earnings protection measures how well the company will be able to maintain or protect its earnings in changing circumstances. In order to assess this, the following factors could be used:

Differing range of sources of earnings growth;

Diversity of customer base;

Profit margins and return on capital.

Financial flexibility measures how easily the company is able to raise the finance it needs to pursue its investment goals. In order to assess this, the following factors could be used:

Evaluation of plans for financing needs and range of alternatives available;

Relationships with finance providers, e.g. banks;

Operating restrictions that currently exist as debt covenants.

Evaluation of the company's management considers how well the managers are managing and planning for the future of the company. In order to assess this, the following factors could be used:

The company's planning and control policies, and its financial strategies;

Management succession planning;

The qualifications and experience of the managers;

Performance in achieving financial and non-financial targets.

(**Note:** credit will be given for alternative relevant comments and suggestions)

ACCA marking scheme		
		Marks
(a) Calculation of company specific yield curve		1
Calculation bond value based on credit rating of A		1
Calculation of percentage fall in the value of the bond		1
		–––
	Maximum	3
		–––
(b) Calculation of bond value based on 5% coupon		1
Calculation of new coupon rate		4
Advice on which type of bond to issue		2–3
		–––
	Maximum	7
		–––
(c) For each of the four criteria –		
2 marks for explanation and suggestion of factors		8
		–––
Total		18
		–––

72 SEMBILAN CO (JUN 12)

Key answer tips

This question (from the June 2012 exam) tested the contents of an article written by the examiner and published in the November 2011 issue of Student Accountant magazine. It is common for the examiner to test topics covered in recent articles, so keep an eye out for any new articles published.

(a) Gross amounts of annual interest receivable by Sembilan Co from Ratus Bank based on year 1 spot rate and years 2, 3 and 4 forward rates:

Year 1 $0.025 \times \$320m = \$8m$

Year 2 $0.037 \times \$320m = \$11.84m$

Year 3 $0.043 \times \$320m = \$13.76m$

Year 4 $0.047 \times \$320m = \$15.04m$

Gross amount of annual interest payable by Sembilan Co to Ratus Bank: 3.76¼% × $320m = $12.04m

At the start of the swap, Sembilan Co will expect to receive or (pay) the following net amounts at the end of each of the next four years:

Year 1: $8m – $12.04m = $(4.04m) payment

Year 2: $11.84m – $12.04m = $(0.20m) payment

Year 3: $13.76m – $12.04m = $1.72m receipt

Year 4: $15.04m – $12.04m = $3m receipt

Tutorial note

At the commencement of the swap contract the net present value of the net annual flows, discounted at the yield curve rates, is zero.

The reason the equivalent fixed rate of 3.76¼% is less than the 3.8% four-year yield curve rate, is because the 3.8% rate reflects the zero-coupon rate with only one payment made in year four. Here the bond pays coupons at different time periods when the yield curve rates are lower. Therefore the fixed rate is lower.

(b) After taking the swap, Sembilan Co's net effect is as follows:

	% Impact	Yield Interest 3%	Yield Interest 4%
Borrow at yield interest + 60bp	(Yield+0.6)%	$(11.52m)	$(14.72m)
Receive yield	Yield	$9.6m	$12.8m
Pay fixed 3.76¼%	(3.76¼)%	$(12.04m)	$(12.04m)
Fee 20bp	(0.2)%	$(0.64m)	$(0.64m)
Net Cost	(4.56¼)%	$(14.6m)	$(14.6m)

The receipt and payment based on the yield curve cancels out interest rate fluctuations, fixing the rate at 3.76¼% + 0.6% + 0.2% = 4.56¼%

(c) Reducing the amount of debt by issuing equity and using the cash raised from this to reduce the amount borrowed changes the capital structure of a company and Sembilan Co needs to consider all the possible implications of this.

As the proportion of debt increases in a company's financial structure, the level of financial distress increases and with it the associated costs. Companies with high levels of financial distress would find it more costly to contract with their stakeholders. For example, they may have to pay higher wages to attract the right calibre of employees, give customers longer credit periods or larger discounts, and may have to accept supplies on more onerous terms. Furthermore, restrictive covenants may make it more difficult to borrow funds (debt and equity) for future projects. On the other hand, because interest is payable before tax, larger amounts of debt will give companies greater taxation benefits, known as the tax shield. Presumably, Sembilan Co has judged the balance between the levels of equity and debt finance, such that the positive and negative effects of gearing result in minimising the required rate of return and maximising the value of the company.

By replacing debt with equity the balance may no longer be optimal and therefore the value of Sembilan Co may not be maximised. However, reducing the amount of debt would result in a higher credit rating for the company and reduce the scale of restrictive covenants. Having greater equity would also increase the company's debt capacity. This may enable the company to raise additional finance and undertake future profitable projects more easily. Less financial distress may also reduce the costs of contracting with stakeholders.

The process of changing the financial structure can be expensive. Sembilan Co needs to determine the costs associated with early redemption of debt. The contractual clauses of the bond should indicate the level and amount of early redemption penalties. Issuing new equity can be expensive especially if the shares are offered to new shareholders, such as costs associated with underwriting the issue and communicating or negotiating the share price. Even raising funds by issuing rights can be expensive.

As well as this, Sembilan Co needs to determine the extent to which the current shareholders will be able to take up the rights and the amount of discount that needs to be given on the rights issue to ensure 100% take up. The impact on the current share price from the issue of rights needs to be considered as well. Studies on rights issues seem to indicate that the markets view the issue of rights as a positive signal and the share price does not reduce to the expected theoretical ex-rights price. However, this is mainly because the markets expect the funds raised to be used on new, profitable projects. Using funds to reduce the debt amount may not be viewed so positively.

Sembilan Co may also have to provide information and justification to the market because both the existing shareholders and any new shareholders will need to be assured that the company is not benefiting one group at the expense of the other. If sufficient information is not provided then either shareholder group may discount the share price due to information asymmetry. However, providing too much information may reduce the competitive position of the company.

(**Note:** credit will be given for alternative relevant comments and suggestions)

ACCA marking scheme

		Marks
(a)	Gross amount receivable by Sembilan Co	1
	Gross amounts payable by Sembilan Co	1
	Net amounts receivable or payable every year	2
	Explanation of why fixed rate is less than the four-year yield curve rate	2
	Maximum	6
(b)	Demonstration of impact of interest rate changes	4
	Explanation and conclusion	1
	Maximum	5
(c)	1–2 marks per relevant discussion point Maximum	9
Total		**20**

73 LIGNUM CO (DEC 12 A)

Key answer tips

Currency risk is most commonly tested in the context of transaction risk. However, this question also covered economic risk and translation risk. Make sure that you understand all three types of risk and how they can be managed.

Report to the Treasury Division, Lignum Co

Discussion and recommendations for managing the foreign exchange exposure

The report discusses and makes recommendations on how the treasury division may manage the foreign exchange exposure it faces under three unrelated circumstances or cases.

The appendices to the report show the detailed calculations to support the discussion around case one (see appendix I) and around case two (see appendix II).

Foreign exchange exposures

With case one, Lignum Co faces a possible exposure due to the receipt it is expecting in four months in a foreign currency, and the possibility that the exchange rates may move against it between now and in four months time. This is known as transactions exposure. With case two, the exposure is in the form of translation exposure, where a subsidiary's assets are being translated from the subsidiary's local currency into Euro. The local currency is facing an imminent depreciation of 20%. Finally in the third case, the present value of future sales of a locally produced and sold good is being eroded because of overseas products being sold for a relatively cheaper price. The case seems to indicate that because the US$ has depreciated against the Euro, it is possible to sell the goods at the same dollar price but at a lower Euro price. This is known as economic exposure.

Hedging strategies

Case one

Transactions exposure, as faced by Lignum Co in situation one, lasts for a short while and is easier to manage by means of derivative products or more conventional means. Here Lignum Co has access to two derivative products: an OTC forward rate and OTC option. Using the forward rate gives a higher return of €963,988, compared to options where the return is €936,715 (see appendix I). However, with the forward rate, Lignum Co is locked into a fixed rate (ZP145.23 per €1) whether the foreign exchange rates move in its favour or against it. With the options, the company has a choice and if the rate moves in its favour, that is if the Zupeso appreciates against the Euro, then the option can be allowed to lapse. Lignum Co needs to decide whether it is happy receiving €963,988, no matter what happens to the exchange rate over the four months or whether it is happy to receive at least €936,715 if the ZP weakens against the €, but with a possibility of higher gains if the Zupeso strengthens.

Lignum Co should also explore alternative strategies to derivative hedging. For example, money markets, leading and lagging, and maintaining a Zupeso account may be possibilities. If information on the investment rate in Zupesos could be obtained, then a money market hedge could be considered. Maintaining a Zupeso account may enable Lignum Co to offset any natural hedges and only convert currency periodically to minimise transaction costs.

Case two

Hedging translation risk may not be necessary if the stock market in which Lignum Co's shares are traded is efficient. Translation of currency is an accounting entry where subsidiary accounts are incorporated into the group accounts. No physical cash flows in or out of the company. In such cases, spending money to hedge such risk means that the group loses money overall, reducing the cash flows attributable to shareholders. However, translation losses may be viewed negatively by the equity holders and may impact some analytical trends and ratios negatively. In these circumstances, Lignum Co may decide to hedge the risk.

The most efficient way to hedge translation exposure is to match the assets and liabilities. In Namel Co's case the assets are more exposed to the Maram Ringit compared to the liabilities, hence the weakening of the Maram Ringit from MR35 per €1 to MR42 per €1 would make the assets lose more (accounting) value than the liabilities by €1,018,000 (see appendix II). If the exposure for the assets and liabilities were matched more closely, for example by converting non-current liabilities from loans in Euro to loans in MR, translation exposure would be reduced.

Case three

Economic exposure, which is not part of transactions exposure, is long-term in nature and therefore more difficult to manage. There are for example, few derivatives which are offered over a long period, with the possible exception of swaps. A further issue is that economic exposure may cause a substantial negative impact to a company's cash flows and value over the long period of time. In this situation, if the US$ continues to remain weak against the Euro, then Lignum Co will find it difficult to maintain a sustained advantage against its American competitor. A strategic, long-term viewpoint needs to be undertaken to manage risk of this nature, such as locating production in countries with favourable exchange rates and cheaper raw material and labour inputs or setting up a subsidiary company in the USA to create a natural hedge for the majority of the US$ cash flows.

In conclusion, the report examined, discussed and made recommendations on managing foreign exchange exposure in each of the three cases.

Report compiled by: XXX

Date: XXX

APPENDICES

Appendix I: Financial impact of derivative products offered by Medes Bank (case one)

Using forward rate

Forward rate = 142 × (1 + (0.085 + 0.0025)/3)/(1 + (0.022 − 0.0030)/3) = 145.23

Income in Euro fixed at ZP145.23 = ZP140,000,000/145.23 = €963,988

Using OTC options

Purchase call options to cover for the ZP rate depreciating

Gross income from option = ZP140,000,000/142 = €985,915

Cost

€985,915 × ZP7 = ZP6,901,405

In € = ZP6,901,405/142 = €48,601

€48,601 × (1 + 0.037/3) = €49,200

(Use borrowing rate on the assumption that extra funds to pay costs need to borrowed initially; investing rate can be used if that is the stated preference)

Net income = €985,915 − €49,200 = €936,715

Appendix II: Financial impact of the devaluation of the Maram Ringit (case two)

MR devalued rate = MR35 × 1.20 = MR42 per €1

	MR 000	Exposed?	€000 at current rate MR35 per €1	€000 at devalued rate MR42 per €1
Non-current assets	179,574	Yes	5,131	4,276
Current assets	146,622	60%	2,514	2,095
Non-current liabilities	(132,237)	20%	(756)	(630)
Current liabilities	(91,171)	30%	(781)	(651)
Share capital and reserves	102,788		6,108	5,090

Translation loss = €6,108,000 − €5,090,000 = €1,018,000

	ACCA marking scheme			
				Marks
(a)	**Requirement (i)**			
	1 mark per exposure explained			3
	Requirement (ii)			
	Calculation of forward rate			1
	Calculation of income using the forward rate			1
	Calculation of cash flows using option contracts			3
	Discussion of relative merits of forwards and options			2–3
	Discussion of alternative hedging possibilities and conclusion			1–2
				———
			Maximum	9
				———
	Requirement (iii)			
	Calculation of devalued rate			1
	Calculation of translation loss			3
	Discussion of whether risk of translation loss should be managed			2–3
	Discussion of how risk of translation loss should be managed			1–2
				———
			Maximum	8
				———
	Requirement (iv)			
	1 mark per point			3
	Professional Marks			
	Structure and presentation of report			2
				———
Total				25
				———

74 ALECTO CO (PILOT 2012)

Key answer tips

In any interest rate hedging question, be prepared to comment on the advantages and disadvantages of setting up a collar. This question also covers the calculations on the two most commonly tested hedging methods (futures and traded options) in a very typical way.

(a) The main advantage of using a collar instead of options to hedge interest rate risk is lower cost. A collar involves the simultaneous purchase and sale of both call and put options at different exercise prices. The option purchased has a higher premium when compared to the premium of the option sold, but the lower premium income will reduce the higher premium payable. With a normal uncovered option, the full premium is payable.

However, the main disadvantage is that, whereas with a hedge using options the buyer can get full benefit of any upside movement in the price of the underlying asset, with a collar hedge the benefit of the upside movement is limited or capped as well.

(b) **Using Futures**

Need to hedge against a rise in interest rates, therefore go short in the futures market. Alecto Co needs June contracts as the loan will be required on 1 May.

No. of contracts needed = €22,000,000/€1,000,000 × 5 months/3 months = 36.67 say 37 contracts.

Basis

Current price (on 1/1) – futures price = total basis

(100 – 3.3) – 96.16 = 0.54 Unexpired basis = 2/6 × 0.54 = 0.18

If interest rates increase by 0.5% to 3.8%

Cost of borrowing funds = 4.6% × 5/12 × €22,000,000 =€421,667   Expected futures price = 100 – 3.8 – 0.18 = 96.02

Gain on the futures market = (9,616 – 9,602) × €25 × 37 = €12,950 Net cost = €408,717

Effective interest rate = 408,717/22,000,000 × 12/5 = 4.46%

If interest rates decrease by 0.5% to 2.8%

Cost of borrowing funds = 3.6% × 5/12 × €22,000,000 =€330,000   Expected futures price = 100 – 2.8 – 0.18 = 97.02

Loss on the futures market = (9,616 – 9,702) × €25 × 37 = €79,550 Net cost = €409,550

Effective interest rate = 409,550/22,000,000 × 12/5 = 4.47%

(**Note:** Net cost should be the same. Difference is due to rounding the number of contracts)

Using Options on Futures

Need to hedge against a rise in interest rates, therefore buy put options. As before, Alecto Co needs 37 June put option contracts (€22,000,000/€1,000,000 × 5 months/ 3 months).

If interest rates increase by 0.5% to 3.8%

Exercise Price	96.00	96.50
Futures Price	96.02	96.02
Exercise ?	No	Yes
Gain in basis points	0	48
Underlying cost of borrowing (from above)	€421,667	€421,667
Gain on options (0 and €25 × 48 × 37)	€0	€44,400
Premium		
16˙3 × €25 × 37	€15,078	
58˙1 × €25 × 37		€53,743
Net cost	€436,745	€431,010
Effective interest rate	4.76%	4.70%

If interest rates decrease by 0.5% to 2.8%

Exercise Price	96.00	96.50
Futures Price	97.02	97.02
Exercise ?	No	No
Gain in basis points	0	0
Underlying cost of borrowing (from above)	€330,000	€330,000
Gain on options	€0	€0
Premium		
16.3 × €25 × 37	€15,078	
58.1 × €25 × 37		€53,743
Net cost	€345,078	€383,743
Effective interest rate	3.76%	4.19%

Using a collar

Buy June put at 96.00 for 0.163 and sell June call at 96.50 for 0.090.

Premium payable = 0.073

If interest rates increase by 0.5% to 3.8%

	Buy put	Sell Call
Exercise Price	96.00	96.5
Futures Price	96.02	96.02
Exercise ?	No	No
Underlying cost of borrowing (from above)	€421,667	
Premium		
7.3 × €25 × 37	€6,753	
Net cost	€428,420	
Effective interest rate	4.67%	

If interest rates decrease by 0.5% to 2.8%

	Buy put	Sell Call
Exercise Price	96.00	96.50
Futures Price	97.02	97.02
Exercise ?	No	Yes
Underlying cost of borrowing (from above)	€330,000	
Premium		
7.3 × €25 × 37	€6,753	
Loss on exercise (52 × €25 × 37)	€48,100	
Net cost	€384,853	
Effective interest rate	4.20%	

Hedging using the interest rate futures market fixes the rate at 4.47%, whereas with options on futures or a collar hedge, the net cost changes. If interest rates fall in the future then a hedge using options gives the most favourable rate. However, if interest rates increase then a hedge using futures gives the lowest interest payment cost and hedging with options give the highest cost, with the cost of the collar hedge being in between the two. If Alecto Co's aim is to fix its interest rate whatever happens to future rates then the preferred instrument would be futures.

This recommendation is made without considering margin and other transactional costs, and basis risk, which is discussed below. These need to be taken into account before a final decision is made.

(*Note:* credit will be given for alternative approaches to the calculations in part (b))

(c) Basis risk occurs when the basis does not diminish at a constant rate. In this case, if a futures contract is held until it matures then there is no basis risk because at maturity the derivative price will equal the underlying asset's price. However, if a contract is closed out before maturity (here the June futures contracts will be closed two months prior to expiry) there is no guarantee that the price of the futures contract will equal the predicted price based on basis at that date. For example, in part (b) above, the predicted futures price in four months assumes that the basis remaining is 0.18, but it could be more or less. Therefore the actual price of the futures contract could be more or less.

This creates a problem in that the effective interest rate for the futures contract above may not be fixed at 4.47%, but may vary and therefore the amount of interest that Alecto Co pays may not be fixed or predictable. On the other hand, it could be argued that the basis risk will probably be smaller than the risk exposure to interest rates without hedging and therefore, although some risk will exist, its impact will be smaller.

ACCA marking scheme			
			Marks
(a)	Discussion of the main advantage		2
	Discussion of the main disadvantage		2
			——
		Maximum	4
			——
(b)	Recommendation to go short if futures are used and purchase puts if options are used		1
	Calculation of number of contracts and remaining basis		2
	Futures contracts calculations		4
	Options contracts calculations		4
	Collar approach and calculations		4
	Supporting comments and conclusion		2–3
			——
		Maximum	17
			——
(c)	Explanation of basis risk		2–3
	Effect of basis risk on recommendation made		2–3
			——
		Maximum	4
			——
Total			**25**
			——

75   GNT CO (PILOT 2012)

Key answer tips

Historically, duration has been more commonly tested in the context of project appraisal, but note that it can also be usefully applied to bonds, to assess the risk associated with different bonds.

(a)   In order to calculate the duration of the two bonds, the present value of the annual cash flows and the price or value at which the bonds are trading at need to be determined. To determine the present value of the annual cash flows, they need to be discounted by the gross redemption yield (i).

Gross Redemption Yield

Try 5%

$60 \times 1.05{-}1 + 60 \times 1.05{-}2 + 60 \times 1.05{-}3 + 60 \times 1.05{-}4 + 1{,}060 \times 1.05{-}5 =$

$60 \times 4.3295 + 1{,}000 \times 0.7835 = 1{,}043.27$

Try 4%

$60 \times 4.4518 + 1{,}000 \times 0.8219 = 1{,}089.01$

$i = 4 + [(1{,}089.01 - 1{,}079.68)/(1{,}089.01 - 1{,}043.27)] = 4.2\%$

Bond 1 (PV of cash flows)

$60 \times 1.042^{-1} + 60 \times 1.042^{-2} + 60 \times 1.042^{-3} + 60 \times 1.042^{-4} + 1{,}060 \times 1.042^{-5}$

PV of cash flows (years 1 to 5) = 57.58 + 55.26 + 53.03 + 50.90 + 862.91 = 1,079.68

Market price = $1,079.68

Duration = [57.58 × 1 + 55.26 × 2 + 53.03 × 3 + 50.90 × 4 + 862.91 × 5]/1,079.68 = 4.49 years

Bond 2 (PV of Coupons and Bond Price)

Price = $40 \times 1.042^{-1} + 40 \times 1.042^{-2} + 40 \times 1.042^{-3} + 40 \times 1.042^{-4} + 1{,}040 \times 1.042^{-5}$

PV of cash flows (years 1 to 5) = 38.39 + 36.84 + 35.36 + 33.93 + 846.63 = 991.15

Market Price = $991.15

Duration = [38.39 × 1 + 36.84 × 2 + 35.36 × 3 + 33.93 × 4 + 846.63 × 5]/991.15 = 4.63 years

(b)   The sensitivity of bond prices to changes in interest rates is dependent on their redemption dates. Bonds which are due to be redeemed at a later date are more price-sensitive to interest rate changes, and therefore are riskier.

Duration measures the average time it takes for a bond to pay its coupons and principal and therefore measures the redemption period of a bond. It recognises that bonds which pay higher coupons effectively mature 'sooner' compared to bonds which pay lower coupons, even if the redemption dates of the bonds are the same. This is because a higher proportion of the higher coupon bonds' income is received sooner. Therefore these bonds are less sensitive to interest rate changes and will have a lower duration.

Duration can be used to assess the change in the value of a bond when interest rates change using the following formula: $\Delta P = [-D \times \Delta i \times P][1 + i]$, where P is the price of the bond, D is the duration and i is the redemption yield.

However, duration is only useful in assessing small changes in interest rates because of convexity. As interest rates increase, the price of a bond decreases and vice versa, but this decrease is not proportional for coupon paying bonds, the relationship is non-linear. In fact, the relationship between the changes in bond value to changes in interest rates is in the shape of a convex curve to origin, see below.

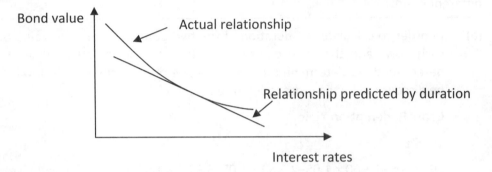

Duration, on the other hand, assumes that the relationship between changes in interest rates and the resultant bond is linear. Therefore duration will predict a lower price than the actual price and for large changes in interest rates this difference can be significant.

Duration can only be applied to measure the approximate change in a bond price due to interest changes, only if changes in interest rates do not lead to a change in the shape of the yield curve. This is because it is an average measure based on the gross redemption yield (yield to maturity). However, if the shape of the yield curve changes, duration can no longer be used to assess the change in bond value due to interest rate changes.

(**Note:** Credit will be given for alternative benefits/limitations of duration)

(c) Industry risk measures the resilience of the company's industrial sector to changes in the economy. In order to measure or assess this, the following factors could be used:

–   Impact of economic changes on the industry in terms how successfully the firms in the industry operate under differing economic outcomes;

–   How cyclical the industry is and how large the peaks and troughs are;

–   How the demand shifts in the industry as the economy changes.

Earnings protection measures how well the company will be able to maintain or protect its earnings in changing circumstances. In order to assess this, the following factors could be used:

–   Differing range of sources of earnings growth;

–   Diversity of customer base;

–   Profit margins and return on capital.

Financial flexibility measures how easily the company is able to raise the finance it needs to pursue its investment goals. In order to assess this, the following factors could be used:

– Evaluation of plans for financing needs and range of alternatives available;

– Relationships with finance providers, e.g. banks;

– Operating restrictions that currently exist in the form of debt covenants.

Evaluation of the company's management considers how well the managers are managing and planning for the future of the company. In order to assess this, the following factors could be used:

– The company's planning and control policies, and its financial strategies;

– Management succession planning;

– The qualifications and experience of the managers;

– Performance in achieving financial and non-financial targets.

76   KENDURI CO (JUN 13)

(a)   Only the transactions resulting in cash flows between Kenduri Co and Lakama Co are considered for hedging. Other transactions are not considered.

Net flow in US$: US$4.5m payment – US$2.1m receipt = US$2.4m payment

Hedge the US$ exposure using the forward market, the money market and options.

Forward market

US$ hedge: 2,400,000/1.5996 = £1,500,375 payment

Money market

US$ hedge

Invest in US$: 2,400,000/(1 + 0.031/4) = US$2,381,543 Convert into £ at spot: US$2,381,543/1.5938 = £1,494,255 Borrow in £: £1,494,255 × (1 + 0.040/4) = £1,509,198

(*Note:* **Full credit will be given to candidates who use the investing rate of 2.8% instead of the borrowing rate of 4%, where this approach has been explained and justified)**

The forward market is preferred due to lower payment costs.

Options

Kenduri Co would purchase Sterling three-month put options to protect itself against a strengthening US$ to £.

Exercise price: $1.60/£1

£ payment = 2,400,000/1.60 = 1,500,000 or 24 contracts

24 put options purchased

Premium payable = 24 × 0.0208 × 62,500 = US$31,200

Premium in £ = 31,200/1.5938 = £19,576

Total payments = £1,500,000 + £19,576 = £1,519,576

Exercise price: $1.62/£1

£ payment = 2,400,000/1·62 = 1,481,481 or 23·7 contracts

23 put options purchased

£ payment = 23 × 62,500 = £1,437,500

Premium payable = 23 × 0·0342 × 62,500 = US$49,163

Premium in £ = 49,163/1.5938 = £30,846

Amount not hedged = US$2,400,000 − (23 × 62,500 × 1.62) = US$71,250

Use forwards to hedge amount not hedged = US$71,250/1.5996 = £44,542

Total payments = 1,437,500 + 30,846 + 44,542 = £1,512,888

Both these hedges are worse than the hedge using forward or money markets. This is due to the premiums payable to let the option lapse if the prices move in Kenduri Co's favour. Options have an advantage over forwards and money markets because the prices are not fixed and the option buyer can let the option lapse if the rates move favourably. Hence options have an unlimited upside but a limited downside. With forwards and money markets, Kenduri Co cannot take advantage of the US$ weakening against the £.

Conclusion

The forward market minimises the payment and is therefore recommended over the money market. However, options give Kenduri Co the choice of an unlimited upside, although the cost is higher. Therefore the choice between the forward market and the option market depends on the risk preference of the company.

(b)   Based on spot mid-rates: US$1·5950/£1; CAD1·5700/£1; JPY132·75/£1 **In £000**

				Payments from		
		UK	USA	Canada	Japan	Total
Receipts to	UK		1,316.6	2,165.6		3,482.2
	USA	2,821.3		940.4	877.7	4,639.4
	Canada	700.6			2,038.2	2,738.8
	Japan		2,410.5			2,410.5
Total payments		3,521.9	3,727.1	3,106.0	2,915.9	
Total receipts		3,482.2	4,639.4	2,738.8	2,410.5	
Net receipt/(payment)		(39.7)	912.3	(367.2)	(505.4)	

Each of Kenduri Co, Jaia Co and Gochiso Co will make payments of £ equivalent to the amount given above to Lakama Co.

Multilateral netting involves minimising the number of transactions taking place through each country's banks. This would limit the fees that these banks would receive for undertaking the transactions and therefore governments who do not allow multilateral netting want to maximise the fees their local banks receive. On the other hand, some countries allow multilateral netting in the belief that this would make companies more willing to operate from those countries and any banking fees lost would be more than compensated by the extra business these companies and their subsidiaries bring into the country.

(c) Gamma measures the rate of change of the delta of an option. Deltas range from near 0 for a long call option which is deep out-of-money, where the price of the option is insensitive to changes in the price of an underlying asset, to near 1 for a long call option which is deep in-the-money, where the price of the option moves in line and largely to the same extent as the price of the underlying asset. When the long call option is at-the-money, the delta is 0.5 but also changes rapidly. Hence, the gamma is highest for a long call option which is at-the-money. The gamma is also higher when the option is closer to expiry. It would seem, therefore, that the option is probably trading near at-the-money and has a relatively short time period before it expires.

ACCA marking scheme			
			Marks
(a)	Calculation of net US$ amount		1
	Calculation of forward market US$ amount		1
	Calculation of US$ money market amount		2
	Calculation of one put option amount (1.60 or 1.62)		3
	Calculation of the second put option amount or if the preferred exercise price choice is explained		2
	Advice and recommendation		3–4
		Maximum	12
(b)	Mid spot rates calculation		1
	Calculation of the £ equivalent amounts of US$, CAD and JPY		4
	Calculation of the net receipt/payment		2
	Explanation of government reaction to multilateral hedging		3
		Maximum	10
(c)	1 mark per relevant point		
		Maximum	3
Total			25

77 AWAN CO (DEC 13)

Key answer tips

This was a very typical question on interest rate hedging. With any hedging question, make sure that you identify the transaction correctly at the start. In this question, you were asked to hedge the interest receipts on a deposit (rather than the more commonly tested interest payments on a borrowing).

(a)   **Using forward rate agreements (FRAs)**

FRA rate 4.82% (3–7), since the investment will take place in three months' time for a period of four months.

If interest rates increase by 0.9% to 4.99%

Investment return = 4.79% × 4/12 × $48,000,000 =	$766,400
Payment to Voblaka bank = (4.99% – 4.82%) × $48,000,000 × 4/12 =	$(27,200)
Net receipt =	$739,200
Effective annual interest rate = 739,200/48,000,000 × 12/4 =	4.62%

If interest rates decrease by 0.9% to 3.19%

Investment return = 2.99% × 4/12 × $48,000,000 =	$478,400
Receipt from Voblaka Bank = (4.82% –- 3.19%) × $48,000,000 × 4/12 =	$260,800
Net receipt =	$739,200
Effective annual interest rate (as above)	4.62%

Using futures

Need to hedge against a fall in interest rates, therefore go long in the futures market. Awan Co needs March contracts as the investment will be made on 1 February.

No. of contracts needed = $48,000,000/$2,000,000 × 4 months/3 months = 32 contracts.

Basis

Current price (on 1/11) – futures price = total basis

(100 – 4.09) –- 94.76 = 1.15

Unexpired basis = 2/5 × 1.15 = 0.46

If interest rates increase by 0.9% to 4.99%

Investment return (from above) =	$766,400
Expected futures price = 100 – 4.99 – 0.46 = 94.55	
Loss on the futures market = (0.9455 – 0.9476) × $2,000,000 × 3/12 × 32 =	$(33,600)
Net return =	$732,800
Effective annual interest rate = $732,800/$48,000,000 × 12/4 =	4.58%
If interest rates decrease by 0.9% to 3.19%	
Investment return (from above) =	$478,400
Expected futures price = 100 – 3.19 –- 0.46 = 96.35	
Gain on the futures market = (0.9635 –- 0.9476) × $2,000,000 × 3/12 × 32 =	$254,400
Net return =	$732,800
Effective annual interest rate (as above) =	4.58%

Using options on futures

Need to hedge against a fall in interest rates, therefore buy call options. As before, Awan Co needs 32 March call option contracts ($48,000,000/$2,000,000 × 4 months/3 months).

If interest rates increase by 0.9% to 4.99%

Exercise price	94.50	95.00
Futures price	94.55	94.55
Exercise ?	Yes	No
Gain in basis points	5	0
Underlying investment return (from above)	$766,400	$766,400
Gain on options (0.0005 × 2,000,000 × 3/12 × 32, 0)	$8,000	$0
Premium		
0.00432 × $2,000,000 × 3/12 × 32	$(69,120)	
0.00121 × $2,000,000 × 3/12 × 32		$(19,360)
Net return	$705,280	$747,040
Effective interest rate	4.41%	4.67%

If interest rates decrease by 0.9% to 3.19%

Exercise price	94.50	95.00
Futures price	96.35	96.35
Exercise ?	Yes	Yes
Gain in basis points	185	135
Underlying investment return (from above)	$478,400	$478,400
Gain on options		
(0.0185 × 2,000,000 × 3/12 × 32)	$296,000	
(0.0135 × 2,000,000 × 3/12 × 32)		$216,000
Premium		
As above	$(69,120)	
As above		$(19,360)
Net return	$705,280	$675,040
Effective interest rate	4.41%	4.22%

Discussion

The FRA offer from Voblaka Bank gives a slightly higher return compared to the futures market; however, Awan Co faces a credit risk with over-the-counter products like the FRA, where Voblaka Bank may default on any money owing to Awan Co if interest rates should fall. The March call option at the exercise price of 94.50 seems to fix the rate of return at 4.41%, which is lower than the return on the futures market and should therefore be rejected. The March call option at the exercise price of 95.00 gives a higher return compared to the FRA and the futures if interest rates increase, but does not perform as well if the interest rates fall. If Awan Co takes the view that it is more important to be protected against a likely fall in interest rates, then that option should also be rejected. The choice between the FRA and the futures depends on Awan Co's attitude to risk and return, the FRA gives a small, higher return, but carries a credit risk. If the view is that the credit risk is small and it is unlikely that Voblaka Bank will default on its obligation, then the FRA should be chosen as the hedge instrument.

(b) The delta value measures the extent to which the value of a derivative instrument, such as an option, changes as the value of its underlying asset changes. For example, a delta of 0.8 would mean that a company would need to purchase 1.25 option contracts (1/0.8) to hedge against a rise in price of an underlying asset of that contract size, known as the hedge ratio. This is because the delta indicates that when the underlying asset increases in value by $1, the value of the equivalent option contract will increase by only $0.80.

The option delta is equal to $N(d_1)$ from the Black-Scholes Option Pricing (BSOP) formula. This means that the delta is constantly changing when the volatility or time to expiry change. Therefore even when the delta and hedge ratio are used to determine the number of option contracts needed, this number needs to be updated periodically to reflect the new delta.

ACCA marking scheme		Marks
(a) Calculation of impact of FRA for interest rate increase and decrease		2
Decision to go long on futures		1
Selection of March futures and options		1
Unexpired basis calculation		1
Impact of interest rates increase/decrease with futures		3
Decision to buy call options		1
Impact of interest rates increase/decrease with options		5
Discussion (up to 2 marks available for general explanation of the products' features)		5–6
	Maximum	19
(b) 1–2 marks per well explained point	Maximum	6
Total		25

78 FAOILEAN CO (JUN 14)

Key answer tips

Option pricing has often been tested in the P4 exam, but this question was unusual in that it covered just the discursive aspects and no calculations.

This emphasises how important it is to be able to understand the topics in detail at this level, rather than just be able to manipulate the numbers.

(a) With conventional investment decisions, it is assumed that once a decision is made, it has to be taken immediately and carried to its conclusion. These decisions are normally made through conventional assessments using methods such as net present value. Assessing projects through option pricing may aid the investment decision making process.

Where there is uncertainty with regard to the investment decision and where a company has flexibility in its decision making, valuing projects using options can be particularly useful. For example, situations may exist where a company does not have to make a decision on a now-or-never basis, or where it can abandon a decision, which has been made, at some future point, or where it has an opportunity for further expansion as a result of the original decision. In such situations, using option pricing formulae, which incorporate the uncertainty surrounding a project and the time before a decision has to be made, can determine a value attached to this flexibility. This value can be added to the conventional net present value computation to give a more accurate assessment of the project's value.

In the situation which Faoilean Co is considering, the initial exploration rights may give it the opportunity to delay the decision of whether to undertake the extraction of oil and gas to a later date. In that time, using previous knowledge and experience, it can estimate the quantity of oil and gas which is present more accurately. It can also use its knowledge to assess the variability of the likely quantity. Faoilean Co may be able to negotiate a longer time scale with the government of Ireland for undertaking the initial exploration, before it needs to make a final decision on whether and how much to extract.

Furthermore, Faoilean Co can explore the possibilities of it exiting the extraction project, once started, if it is proving not to be beneficial, or if world prices of oil and gas have moved against it. It could, for example, negotiate a get-out clause which gives it the right to sell the project back to the government at a later date at a pre-agreed price. Alternatively, it could build facilities in such a way that it can redeploy them to other activities, or scale the production up or down more easily and at less cost. These options give the company the opportunity to step out of a project at a future date, if uncertainties today become negative outcomes in the future.

Finally, Faoilean Co can explore whether or not applying for the rights to undertake this exploration project could give it priority in terms of future projects, perhaps due to the new knowledge or technologies it builds during the current project. These opportunities would allow it to gain competitive advantage over rivals, which, in turn, could provide it with greater opportunities in the future, but which are uncertain at present.

Faoilean Co can incorporate these uncertainties and the time before the various decisions need to be made into the option formulae to determine the additional value of the project, on top of the initial net present value calculation.

The option price formula used with investment decisions is based on the Black-Scholes Option Pricing (BSOP) model. The BSOP model makes a number of assumptions as follows:

- The underlying asset operates in perfect markets and therefore the movement of market prices cannot be predicted.
- The BSOP model uses the risk-free rate of interest. It is assumed that this is known and remains constant, which may not be the case where the time it takes for the option to expire may be long.
- The BSOP model assumes that volatility can be assessed and stays constant throughout the life of the project; again with long-term projects these assumptions may not be valid.
- The BSOP model assumes that the underlying asset can be traded freely. This is probably not accurate where the underlying asset is an investment project.

These assumptions mean that the value based around the BSOP model is indicative and not definitive.

(**Note:** Credit will be given for alternative relevant comments.)

(b) Equity can be regarded as purchasing a call option by the equity holders on the value of a company, because they will possess a residual claim on the assets of the company. In this case, the face value of debt is equivalent to the exercise price, and the repayment term of debt as the time to expiry of the option.

If at expiry, the value of the company is greater than the face value of debt, then the option is in-the-money, otherwise if the value of the firm is less than the face value of debt, then the option is out-of-money and equity is worthless.

For example, say V is the market value of the assets in a company, E is the market value of equity, and F is the face value of debt, then...

If at expiry $V > F$ (option is in-the-money), then the option has intrinsic value to the equity holders and $E = V - F$.

Otherwise if $F > V$ (option is out-of-money), then the option has no intrinsic value and no value for the equity holders, and $E = 0$.

Prior to expiry of the debt, the call option (value to holders of equity) will also have a time value attached to it. The BSOP model can be used to assess the value of the option to the equity holders, the value of equity, which can consist of both time value and intrinsic value if the option is in-the-money, or just time value if the option is out-of-money.

Within the BSOP model, $N(d_1)$, the delta value, shows how the value of equity changes when the value of the company's assets change. $N(d_2)$ depicts the probability that the call option will be in-the-money (i.e. have intrinsic value for the equity holders).

Debt can be regarded as the debt holders writing a put option on the company's assets, where the premium is the receipt of interest when it falls due and the capital redemption. If $N(d_2)$ depicts the probability that the call option is in-the-money, then $1 - N(d_2)$ depicts the probability of default.

Therefore the BSOP model and options are useful in determining the value of equity and default risk.

Option pricing can be used to explain why companies facing severe financial distress can still have positive equity values. A company facing severe financial distress would presumably be one where the equity holders' call option is well out-of-money and therefore has no intrinsic value. However, as long as the debt on the option is not at expiry, then that call option will still have a time value attached to it. Therefore, the positive equity value reflects the time value of the option, even where the option is out-of-money, and this will diminish as the debt comes closer to expiry. The time value indicates that even though the option is currently out-of-money, there is a possibility that due to the volatility of asset values, by the time the debt reaches maturity, the company will no longer face financial distress and will be able to meet its debt obligations.

(**Note:** Credit will be given for alternative relevant comments.)

(c) According to the BSOP model, the value of an option is dependent on five variables: the value of the underlying asset, the exercise price, the risk-free rate of interest, the implied volatility of the underlying asset, and the time to expiry of the option. These five variables are input into the BSOP formula, in order to compute the value of a call option (the value of an equivalent put option can be computed by the BSOP model and put-call parity relationship). The different risk factors determine the impact on the option value of the changes in the five variables.

The 'vega' determines the sensitivity of an option's value to a change in the implied volatility of the underlying asset. Implied volatility is what the market is implying the volatility of the underlying asset will be in the future, based on the price changes in an option. The option price may change independently of whether or not the underlying asset's value changes, due to new information being presented to the markets. Implied volatility is the result of this independent movement in the option's value, and this determines the 'vega'. The 'vega' only impacts the time value of an option and as the 'vega' increases, so will the value of the option.

(**Note:** Credit will be given for alternative relevant comments.)

	Marking scheme		Marks
(a)	Discussion of the idea of using options in making the project investment decision		7–8
	Explanation of the assumptions		3–4
		Max	11
(b)	Discussion of using options to value equity		4–5
	Discussion of using options to assess default risk		2–3
	Discussion of financial distress and time value of an option		2–3
		Max	9
(c)	Explanation of why option values are determined by different risk factors		2–3
	Explanation of what determines 'vega'		2–3
		Max	5
Total			**25**

79 KESHI CO (DEC 14)

Key answer tips

More than half the marks in the marking scheme for this question are for the discussion points rather than the calculations. Unfortunately, many students in the real exam focussed on the numbers exclusively so were unable to score a pass mark.

Always make sure that you attempt all parts of all questions in order to maximise your chances of passing the exam.

(a)   **Using traded options**

Need to hedge against a rise in interest rates, therefore buy put options.

Keshi Co needs 42 March put option contracts ($18,000,000/$1,000,000 × 7 months/ 3 months).

Expected futures price on 1 February if interest rates increase by 0.5% = 100 – (3.8 + 0.5) – 0.22 = 95.48

Expected futures price on 1 February if interest rates decrease by 0.5% =

100 – (3.8 – 0.5) – 0.22 = 96.48

If interest rates increase by 0.5% to 4.3%

Exercise price	95.50	96.00
Futures price	95.48	95.48
Exercise?	Yes	Yes
Gain in basis points	2	52
Underlying cost of borrowing		
4.7% × 7/12 × $18,000,000	$493,500	$493,500
Gain on options		
0.0002 × $1,000,000 × 3/12 × 42	$2,100	
0.0052 × $1,000,000 × 3/12 × 42		$54,600
Premium		
0.00662 × $1,000,000 × 3/12 × 42	$69,510	
0.00902 × $1,000,000 × 3/12 × 42		$94,710
Net cost	$560,910	$533,610
Effective interest rate	5.34%	5.08%

If interest rates decrease by 0.5% to 3.3%

Exercise price	95.50	96.00
Futures price	96.48	96.48
Exercise?	No	No
Gain in basis points	0	0
Underlying cost of borrowing		
3.7% × 7/12 × $18,000,000	$388,500	$388,500
Gain on options	$0	$0
Premium	$69,510	$94,710
Net cost	$458,010	$483,210
Effective interest rate	4.36%	4.60%

Using swaps

	Keshi Co	Rozu Bank offer	Basis differential
Fixed rate	5.5%	4.6%	0.9%
Floating rate	LIBOR + 0.4%	LIBOR + 0.3%	0.1%

Prior to the swap, Keshi will borrow at LIBOR + 0.4% and swaps this rate to a fixed rate. Total possible benefit is 0.8% before Rozu Bank's charges.

Keshi Co borrows at	LIBOR + 0.4%
From swap Keshi Co receives	LIBOR
Keshi Co gets 70% of the benefit	
Advantage (70% × 0.8 − 0.10)	0.46%
Keshi Co's effective borrowing rate (after swap)	5.04%

Alternatively (Swap)

From swap Keshi Co receives	LIBOR
Keshi Co pays	4.54%
Effective borrowing rate (as above)	4.54% + 0.4% + 0.10% = 5.04%

Discussion and recommendation

Under each choice the interest rate cost to Keshi Co will be as follows:

	Doing nothing	95.50 option	96.00 option	Swap
If rates increase by 0.5%	4.7% floating; 5.5% fixed	5.34%	5.08%	5.04%
If rates decrease by 0.5%	3.7% floating; 5.5% fixed	4.36%	4.60%	5.04%

Borrowing at the floating rate and undertaking a swap effectively fixes the rate of interest at 5.04% for the loan, which is significantly lower than the market fixed rate of 5.5%.

On the other hand, doing nothing and borrowing at the floating rate minimises the interest rate at 4.7%, against the next best choice which is the swap at 5.04% if interest rates increase by 0.5%. And should interest rates decrease by 0.5%, then doing nothing and borrowing at a floating rate of 3.7% minimises cost, compared to the next best choice which is the 95.50 option.

On the face of it, doing nothing and borrowing at a floating rate seems to be the better choice if interest rates increase or decrease by a small amount, but if interest rates increase substantially then this choice will no longer result in the lowest cost.

The swap minimises the variability of the borrowing rates, while doing nothing and borrowing at a floating rate maximises the variability. If Keshi Co wants to eliminate the risk of interest rate fluctuations completely, then it should borrow at the floating rate and swap it into a fixed rate.

(b) Free cash flows and therefore shareholder value are increased when corporate costs are reduced and/or income increased. Therefore, consideration should be given to how the centralised treasury department may reduce costs and increase income.

The centralised treasury department should be able to evaluate the financing requirements of Keshi Co's group as a whole and it may be able to negotiate better rates when borrowing in bulk. The department could operate as an internal bank and undertake matching of funds. Therefore it could transfer funds from subsidiaries which have spare cash resources to ones which need them, and thus avoid going into the costly external market to raise funds. The department may be able to undertake multilateral internal netting and thereby reduce costs related to hedging activity. Experts and resources within one location could reduce duplication costs.

The concentration of experts and resources within one central department may result in a more effective decision-making environment and higher quality risk monitoring and control. Further, having access to the Keshi Co group's entire cash funds may give the company access to larger and more diverse investment markets. These factors could result in increasing the company's cash inflows, as long as the benefits from such activity outweigh the costs.

Decentralising Keshi Co's treasury function to its subsidiary companies may be beneficial in several ways. Each subsidiary company may be better placed to take local regulations, custom and practice into consideration. An example of custom and practice is the case of Suisen Co's need to use Salam contracts instead of conventional derivative products which the centralised treasury department may use as a matter of course.

Giving subsidiary companies more autonomy on how they undertake their own fund management may result in increased motivation and effort from the subsidiary's senior management and thereby increase future income. Subsidiary companies which have access to their own funds may be able to respond to opportunities quicker and establish competitive advantage more effectively.

(c)   Islamic principles stipulate the need to avoid uncertainty and speculation. In the case of Salam contracts, payment for the commodity is made at the start of the contract. The buyer and seller of the commodity know the price, the quality and the quantity of the commodity and the date of future delivery with certainty. Therefore, uncertainty and speculation are avoided.

On the other hand, futures contracts are marked-to-market daily and this could lead to uncertainty in the amounts received and paid every day. Furthermore, standardised futures contracts have fixed expiry dates and pre-determined contract sizes. This may mean that the underlying position is not hedged or covered completely, leading to limited speculative positions even where the futures contracts are used entirely for hedging purposes. Finally, only a few commodity futures contracts are offered to cover a range of different quality grades for a commodity, and therefore price movement of the futures market may not be completely in line with the price movement in the underlying asset.

(**Note:** Credit will be given for alternative, relevant discussion for parts (b) and (c))

ACCA marking scheme		
		Marks
(a)	Buy put options and number of contracts	1
	Futures prices if interest rates increase or decrease	1
	Option contracts calculations: either exercise price	3
	Option contract calculations: second exercise price (or justification for calculations of just one exercise price)	2
	Swap: Keshi Co initially borrows at the floating rate and resulting advantage	2
	Swap impact	2
	Effective borrowing rate	1
	Discussion and recommendation	3–4
	Maximum	15
(b)	Discussion of why a centralised treasury department may increase value	3–4
	Discussion of reasons for decentralisation	2–3
	Maximum	6
(c)	1–2 marks per point Maximum	4
Total		**25**

ECONOMIC ENVIRONMENT FOR MULTINATIONALS

80   DEPUTY CHIEF FINANCIAL OFFICER *Walk in the footsteps of a top tutor*

Key answer tips

Ethical issues are often tested in the P4 exam. Part (iv) contained some specific detail which would have been beyond the knowledge of all but the most widely read students, but there were plenty of easy marks elsewhere.

To: Chief Financial Officer

From: Deputy Financial Officer

Four issues of concern

The four issues you have raised with me touch upon our ethical and commercial responsibilities

(i)   The payment of a commission to an official in any country can be justified if it was in recognition of a service performed that (a) she or he was legitimately entitled to perform for payment, (b) that the payment was duly authorised within this company and (c) a service was received for which the payment was fair and reasonable. Clearly, such a payment should not have been made if it contravened the ruling law in either this or the official's country. Given this, a payment for consultancy, legal or lobbying services to an independent consultant would be legitimate. However, given that the individual concerned was an official of the agency concerned then the payment should not have been authorised. As the payment was for a substantial amount the matter should be taken up with the company's chief executive officer with a view to an internal investigation being mounted. Disciplinary action should be considered when a more detailed understanding of the circumstances is known. It may also be appropriate to raise this with the health department in the government of the country concerned with a view to full public disclosure of the facts once the situation has been clarified.

(ii)   The actions of the agent in using price sensitive information for personal gain would be classed as insider dealing irrespective of whether the transactions took place on the shares, or on options on the shares of our company. Much depends on what could be established in the circumstances. Did the agent know that the licensing agreement would be forthcoming or was it a speculative trade on the anticipation that it would be granted? If it were the former then it would be classed as insider trading. The more difficult issue relates to speculative trading in that if the attempt to gain the licence was in the public domain then the dealing would not be an issue. If however, the agent was only aware of the possibility through his or her relationship with this company then it would be insider dealing.

(iii)   This problem raises a number of issues. First, hedging is not an efficient means of reducing translation risk. Translation risk arises because of the conversion of assets and liabilities held in dollars into the domestic currency for accounting purposes. Translation risk will impact upon the residual earnings of the business but does not impact upon the firm's cash flow as no transaction has occurred. There would appear to be an absence of risk management policy in this area and even though a senior member of the treasury team has been making the trades, policy of this type should be set at board level through a risk management committee. Second, substantial trades of this type should be authorised and again, it would appear, that there is an absence of policy in this area. Disciplinary action against the treasury manager concerned would only be appropriate if trading of this type lay outside his or her role description or if there was an explicit policy in place requiring authorisation for trades of greater than a given size. In deciding what action to take, making a gain or a loss is irrelevant. Third the current position suggests a $1.25 million loss is likely against a dollar position of $12.5 million. This may not be material from the point of view of the company's overall financial position but the potential for further loss on an uncovered position such as this should be immediately reversed by shortening the contract concerned. If the loss is deemed material then a brief statement to shareholders should be made specifying the magnitude of the loss and the action taken.

(iv) This problem appears to be an abuse of copyright and as such is against the WTO's Trade Related Aspects of Intellectual Property Rights 'TRIPS' agreement. However, to gain protection under TRIPS we have to make sure that we have made supply available of the drugs concerned. If a member country takes the view that we have abused our patent position then they can issue a 'compulsory licence' which would allow a competitor to produce the product under licence. At the Doha ministerial conference in 2001 it was agreed that TRIPS should not prevent a country adopting measures for the protection of its population's health. In this case it would appear that the dispute is one of piracy and gaining protection through the local courts. Whilst this could in principle be resolved through the WTO and the dispute resolution procedure, this may be an issue which would be most satisfactorily resolved through intergovernmental mediation. Any bilateral concession would need to be multilateralised through the WTO in light of the member's most favoured-nation obligations. It would be worthwhile attempting to discover exactly why the government concerned has blocked access to the courts to ensure that there are no public health policy issues involved and from there attempting to secure the involvement of our own government in helping to resolve the issue.

ACCA marking scheme	
	Marks
Essay	
Discussion of problems of paying commission, principles, ethics and recommendation	5
Discussion of scope of insider trading and application to agents and options markets	5
Discussion of relevance of hedging, authority for trading and action to be taken	5
Advice on position with respect to abuse of patent with reference to TRIPS	5
Total	**20**

81   MOOSE CO

Key answer tips

The examiner has stated his intention to make the P4 exam a contemporary test of current real world issues. This question is a good example of how real world issues in financial management can be tested.

(a)   The credit crunch has led to an unwillingness by the banks to lend, particularly to one another, resulting in a drain in the liquidity across the capital markets. Interest rates are now low as central banks attempt to stimulate their economies. The business of banks is to earn profits by borrowing short and lending long and they are still willing to lend to high class corporate customers. And probably at competitive interest rates. The banks will be concerned about the following:

The risk of default: although there has been a slackening of demand for the company's product our relatively high credit rating would still make us an attractive prospect for lenders. They will need to undertake a credit risk assessment which will include a thorough examination of our asset strength, existing capitalisation, operating strength and income gearing. An important measure will be the firm's current cash flow/debt obligations ratio.

Recovery: the assessment of our asset strength will form a part of their assessment of the potential recoverability of the debt in the event of default.

(b)   Syndication is where a group of banks combine with one bank taking the lead in the arrangement. Syndication allows banks to offer much larger loans in combination than would be feasible singly, and given the range of banks involved can tailor loans (perhaps across different currencies) to more exactly match our requirements. The management of the syndicate lies with the arranging bank but the effective cost will be somewhat higher than with a conventional loan but usually much lower than the cost of raising the necessary finance through a bond issue.

A bond issue is where the debt is securitised and floated onto the capital market normally with a fixed interest coupon and a set redemption date. Initial set up costs can be high especially if the issue is underwritten. A loan of the size envisaged is towards the low end of what would normally be raised through this means. Some bond issues can be syndicated in that a number of borrowers of similar risk are combined by the investment bank chosen to manage the issue.

The advantage of syndication is that it reduces the costs of issue. However, it may be that the best offer would entail accepting a variable rate based on LIBOR which would have to be swapped out if we wished to minimise interest rate risk.

(c)   In assessing this capital investment we have to make some assumptions about the immediate future in terms of the general economic conditions and to what extent we have a delay option on the project concerned. Where there is a positive delay option then from a financial perspective the best advice may be to delay investment dependent on the likely actions by the competitors and how markets for the product develop. Where there are significant competitive reasons for proceeding we should only proceed if the net present value of the project is worthwhile. Given the magnitudes of the uncertainties involved at this stage of the economic cycle the decision to proceed should only be made when we are sure that we have estimated the potential magnitude of the risks and taken them into account in our analysis.

Examiner's note: For all parts to this question, credit will be given for alternative and relevant points.

ACCA marking scheme		Marks
The mark ranges reflect the flexibility the examiners use in assessing this question. The following points are indicative only:		
(a) Importance of asset strength and default assessment		3–4
Other relevant comments		3–4
Maximum		7.0
(b) Loan syndication as a means of spreading load and risk		1–2
Flexibility of syndication and possibility of cross-border finance		2–3
Cost of loan syndication versus bond issues		1–2
Flexibility of bonds in terms of repayment and size of issue		1–2
Maximum		7.0
(c) Note on the significance of the real option to delay and the factors that might influence that decision. And other relevant points such as strategic and operational benefits of not delaying. up to 6		6.0
Maximum		6.0
Total		**20**

82   LAMRI CO

Key answer tips

When asked to calculate dividend capacity, you should try to estimate the amount of cash that the company will generate, after paying any operating expenses and interest, and investing in assets. This is commonly known as the free cash flow to equity.

(a)   **Dividend Capacity Prior to TE Proposal Implementation**

	$000
Operating profit (30% × $80,000,000)	24,000
Less interest (8% × $35,000,000)	(2,800)
Less taxation (28% × (24,000 – 2,800))	(5,936)
Less investment in working capital (15% × (20/120 × 80,000))	(2,000)
Less investment in additional non-current assets (25% × (20/120 × 80,000))	(3,333)
Less investment in project	(4,500)
Cash flows from domestic operations	5,431
Cash flows from overseas subsidiary dividend remittances (W1)	3,159
Additional tax payable on Magnolia profits (6% × 5,400)	(324)
Dividend capacity	8,266

Dividend Capacity After TE Proposal Implementation

Cash flows from domestic operations (as above)	5,431
Cash flows from overseas subsidiaries dividend remittances (W2)	2,718
Additional tax payable on Magnolia profits (6% × 3,120)	(187)
Dividend capacity	7,962
Estimate of actual dividend for coming year	
(7,500 × 1.08)	8,100

Note: The impact of depreciation is neutral, as this amount will be spent to retain assets at their current productive capability.

Workings

(W1) **Prior to Implementation of TE Proposal**

	$000	$000
	Strymon	*Magnolia*
Sales revenue	5,700	15,000
Cost		
Variable	(3,600)	(2,400)
Fixed	(2,100)	(1,500)
Transfer		(5,700)
Profit before tax	Nil	5,400
Tax	Nil	1,188
Profit after tax	Nil	4,212
Remitted	Nil	3,159
Retained	Nil	1,053

(W2) **After Implementation of TE Proposal**

	$000	$000
	Strymon	*Magnolia*
Sales revenue	7,980	15,000
Cost		
Variable	(3,600)	(2,400)
Fixed	(2,100)	(1,500)
Transfer		(7,980)
Profit before tax	2,280	3,120
Tax (42%, 22%)	958	686
Profit after tax	1,322	2,434
Remitted (75% × 1,322 × 90%)	892	
Remitted		1,826
Retained	331	608
Total remitted	2,718	

(b) Lamri's dividend capacity before implementing TE's proposal ($8,266,000) is more than the dividend required for next year ($8,100,000). If the recommendation from TE is implemented as policy for next year then there is a possibility that Lamri will not have sufficient dividend capacity to make the required dividend payments. It requires $8,100,000 but will have $7,962,000 available. The reason is due to the additional tax that will be paid in the country in which Strymon operates, for which credit cannot be obtained. Effectively 14% additional tax and 10% withholding tax will be paid. Some of this amount is recovered because lower additional tax is paid on Magnolia's profits but not enough.

The difference between what is required and available is small and possible ways of making up the shortfall are as follows. Lamri could lower its growth rate in dividends to approximately 6.2% (7962/7500 − 1 × 100%) and have enough capacity to make the payment. However, if the reasons for the lower growth rate are not explained to the shareholders and accepted by them, the share price may fall.

An alternative could be to borrow the small amount needed possibly through increased overdraft facilities. However, Lamri may not want to increase its borrowings and may be reluctant to take this option. In addition to this, there is a possibility that because of the change of policy this shortfall may occur more often than just one off, and Lamri may not want to increase borrowing regularly.

Lamri may consider postponing the project or part of the project, if that option were available. However, this must be considered in the context of the business. From the question narrative, the suggestion is that Lamri have a number of projects in the pipeline for the future. The option to delay may not be possible or feasible.

Perhaps the most obvious way to get the extra funds required is to ask the subsidiary companies (most probably Strymon) to remit a higher proportion of their profits as dividends. In the past Strymon did not make profits and none were retained hence there may be a case for a higher level of remittance from there. However, this may have a negative impact on the possible benefits, especially manager morale.

(Note: credit will be given for alternative relevant suggestions)

ACCA marking scheme		
		Marks
(a)	Calculation of operating profit, interest and domestic tax	3
	Calculation of investments in working capital and non-current assets (including correct treatment of depreciation)	3
	Calculation of dividend remittance before new policy implementation	2
	Calculation of additional tax payable on Magnolia profits before new policy implementation	1
	Calculation of dividend remittance after new policy implementation	3
	Calculation of additional tax payable on Magnolia profits after new policy implementation	1
	Dividend capacity	1
		———
		14
(b)	Concluding comments and explanation of reason	2
	Possible actions (1 mark per suggestion)	2
		———
		6
		———
Total		**20**
		———

EMERGING ISSUES IN FINANCE AND FINANCIAL MANAGEMENT

83 GOSLO MOTOR CORPORATION

Key answer tips

The examiner has stated his intention to make the P4 exam a contemporary test of current real world issues. This question is a good example of how real world issues in financial management can be tested.

The calculations in part (a) appear to be complex at first glance, but they are in fact quite simple when you read the detail in the question carefully.

Don't be thrown by the calculations. With good exam technique you should be able to score a pass mark on this sort of question by performing well in the written parts.

(a)   In order to estimate the returns an annual cash account should be created showing the cash flow receivable from the pool of assets and the cash payments against the various liabilities created by the securitisation process. In this securitisation a degree of leverage has been introduced by the swap giving a return of 19.05% to the holders of the subordinate certificates but carrying a high degree of risk.

Cash flow receivable	$ million	Cash flow payable		$ million
$200 million × 10.5%	21.00	A-rated bonds	LIBOR	2.13
Less service charge	0.24	$152 million at 1.4%		
		B-rated bonds		
		$19 million at 11%		2.09
		SWAP		
		Receive LIBOR	−LIBOR	
		Pay 8.5% on $152m		12.92
	———			———
	20.76			17.14
	———			———
		Balance to the subordinated certificates		3.62

The return to the holders of the certificates is $3.62 million on $19 million or 19.05%. A reduction of 1% in the cash flow receivable brings about a fall in the annual receivable to $20.79 million, reducing the balance available for the subordinated certificates to $3.41 million. A reduction of 1% in the cash flow receivable, results in a fall of 5.80% ([3.62 – 3.41]/3.62) in revenue of the subordinated certificates.

(b)   A securitisation of this type is a common method of refinancing in a large business. After the securitisation of mortgages, car loan securitisation is the most important source of refinancing in the US and in Europe. Structured finance arrangements such as this are also used in a variety of other industries from banking to entertainment. The process of credit enhancement is the process whereby a relatively high risk cash flow (car loans) can be converted into a range of collateralised loan obligations satisfying the varying risk appetites of different investors. In the securitisation process a rating agency would normally advise on the structure of the liabilities created such that the AAA tranche will attract investors such as banks and other financial institutions who demand a low level of risk exposure. This reduction in risk for the senior and intermediate level notes is balanced by a significant transfer of risk to the subordinated certificate holders. Tranching the issue rather than creating a single issue of an asset backed security is the most important mechanism for credit enhancement.

Other approaches can entail insuring the risk of the issue through the use of credit default swaps or by transferring a greater asset pool than is securitised (over collateralisation).

(c) There are a number of risks inherent in the securitisation process faced by the investor:

Correlation risk: it is often assumed that defaults on the asset side of the securitisation process are uncorrelated. However, if a degree of positive correlation is present (such as defaulting car loans and repossessions) being positively associated with rising unemployment) then this can create higher than anticipated volatility in the receivables.

Timing and liquidity risk: the question only refers to average returns which presumably consist of a mixture of repayments, interest and possibly the anticipated recovery from repossessions. Modelling the cash flow 'waterfall' is a difficult issue where the timing of the cash receipts is crucial in fulfilling the commitments to the various tranches.

Default and collateral risk: the success of the securitisation will be dependent upon the assessment of the quality of the loans made to car purchasers. Dealers selling cars are responsible for the primary credit assessment and tight controls are necessary for ensuring that the loans are properly negotiated. Risk arises both in terms of default but also in the value of the vehicle on repossession.

From GoSlo's perspective the risks attaching to the process are more straightforward and to a certain extent depend on the motivation for the securitisation. If it is simply to refinance activity then the risk is that the issues will be undersubscribed. If it is also to remove the assets from the SOFP then much will depend on whether loans of this type can be transferred to a special purpose vehicle such that full legal ownership passes.

> **Examiner's note:** This final paragraph is not required to answer part (c), but has been included for tutorial purposes.

ACCA marking scheme		
		Marks
(a)	Calculation of expected return from pool (inc service charge and over-collateralisation)	2
	Impact of swap on A-tranche	2
	Calculation of annual cash flows payable on interest for tranches A-rated and B-rated	2
	Estimation of return to subordinated certificates	1
	Impact of marginal change and calculation of sensitivity	3
		———
	Maximum	10
(b)	Explanation and purpose of securitisation	1–2
	Methods of credit enhancement:	
	Tranching	
	Ratings agency involvement	
	Over-collateralisation	
	Others	2–3
		———
	Maximum	4
(c)	Correlation risk	2–3
	Timing and liquidity risk	1–2
	Collateral risk	2–3
	(Credit will be given for alternative, relevant points) Maximum	6
		———
Total		**20**
		———

84 JJJ CO

Key answer tips

The examiner often sets questions to test that students have an awareness of real world financial management issues (such as the Eurozone debt crisis here).

As well as studying your text book to prepare for the P4 exam, you should regularly read a good quality business newspaper to keep up to date with current issues.

(a) **Eurozone debt crisis**

In the early to mid 2000s, financial regulations had been relaxed by most European governments and Europe saw a period of sustained growth. The European Central Bank set a single interest rate for all the countries within the Eurozone, so many of the countries found that they had access to cheaper funds than they had been used to before the introduction of the single currency. Consequently, debt levels for many of the Eurozone countries rose to levels which would have been unthinkable before the creation of the Eurozone.

In the late 2000s, when the sub prime mortgage crisis in the US started the 'credit crunch', many of the world's economies slipped into recession and began to find it difficult to repay their high levels of debt.

Countries such as the United Kingdom (not a member of the Eurozone) were able to use techniques such as quantitative easing to protect their own economies and to reduce the risk of default. However, because of the common monetary policy, single interest rate and the inflexibility of the exchange rate within the Eurozone, such techniques were not available to the individual Eurozone countries. Also, some countries (like Greece) had relatively short maturity dates on their bonds, making the problem more short term in nature.

Consequently, some of the individual Eurozone member states (such as Ireland, Portugal and Greece) could not afford to repay their debts had to be 'bailed out' by the European Union and the International Monetary Fund.

Financial contagion

Financial contagion refers to the spread of economic and financial problems from one country to another. Within the Eurozone, barriers to trade, investment and capital flows have been reduced or eliminated, so the resultant 'single market' economy is more susceptible to contagion.

Financial contagion potentially worsens the impact of the Eurozone debt crisis. If financial problems in one country directly lead to similar problems in several others it accentuates the debt servicing difficulties. During the last few years, the credit-worthiness of some of the stronger Eurozone economies (e.g. Germany, France) has been compromised by them having to bail out the weaker economies (e.g. Ireland, Greece).

This can be seen in the scenario here. The downgrade of France's credit rating is probably more a reflection on the problems within the Eurozone as a whole rather than a specific reflection on France's ability to settle its own debts.

(b)   The credit rating agencies assign a credit rating to corporate and government bonds after making an assessment of the credit risk of the entity which issued the bonds. Credit risk is the risk that the entity which issued the bonds will not be able to meet its obligations to pay the interest and/or redeem the bonds.

The credit rating agencies have traditionally assessed credit risk by analysing a company's financial statements with 'accounting based credit-scoring methods'. These methods can be used to try to predict whether a company is creditworthy, or whether it is likely to fail. However, such accounting based prediction methods are often criticised for being too simplistic.

Hence, more sophisticated methods, known as 'structural models' have been developed in recent years. These models use statistical methods (such as normal distribution theory) to analyse the riskiness of a firm's assets and cash generation, and to calculate the likelihood of a firm defaulting on its interest and/or capital repayments.

Once the level of credit risk has been determined, a credit rating is awarded to the entity. According to the S&P system, an AAA rated entity has virtually no credit risk. Riskier entities are assigned credit ratings by S&P according to the following categories, where a lower rating is associated with a higher level of risk.

AA+   ⎫
AA
AA–   ⎬ Investment grade ratings
A+
A
BBB   ⎭

BB   ⎫
B
CCC   ⎬ Non-investment grade (junk bond) ratings
CC
C   ⎭

(c)   The first shareholder comment questions why the interest receipts on the bonds have not changed, even though yields on debt have risen. The shareholder seems to think that the yield is the same as the interest receipts. This is not the case.

Coupon rate

The interest receipts to an investor are determined by the coupon rate on a bond, which is fixed at the time the bond is issued. In this case, the French bonds are 4.5% coupon bonds and the Belgian bonds are 3.5% coupon bonds, which means that this percentage of nominal value will be paid out each year to the bond holder. It should therefore not be surprising that the interest receipts have stayed constant.

With this in mind, it is now clear that there is no scope for JJJ Co to do what the third shareholder suggests i.e. to demand that the French government increases its interest payments.

Yield

The yield on a bond is the required return to an investor. This is linked directly to the credit rating of the bond.

In general, a more risky bond will have a higher yield (as the table from the S&P website shows) because investors who perceive more risk will demand higher returns. However, as identified above, the yield is not the same as the coupon rate paid out on a bond.

In fact the yield is defined as being the internal rate of return (IRR) of the bond's market value, the interest paid and the redemption amount. Thus if yield changes but interest payments and redemption amount are fixed, the only possible consequence is that the market value of the bond will fluctuate until the situation returns to an equilibrium position. The relationship between yield on a bond and its market value is an inverse one i.e. as yield rises, market value of the bond falls.

Impact on JJJ Co

In this case, the downgrade of the French government bonds from an AAA to an AA+ rating means that the yield on JJJ Co's 5 year bonds will rise from 3.95% to 4.15% (numbers taken from the S&P spot yields table). However, the coupon rate of 4.5% cannot change, so the impact on JJJ Co is that the market value of its investment will fall.

It is not clear whether JJJ Co intends to try to sell the bonds (in which case it will have to accept a lower value) or whether it intends to keep them until maturity (in which case it will face a slightly higher risk of default).

The credit rating of the Belgian bonds has been left at the same level, so seemingly S&P believes that the risk of these bonds is unchanged. Therefore the yield on the Belgian government bonds, and the bonds' market value, will be unchanged.

Comparison of French and Belgian coupon rates and yields

The second shareholder comment again shows a lack of understanding that yields and coupon rates are not the same thing. This issue has been explained above.

However, the second comment also tries to compare coupon rates and yields on the different bonds. From the information in the table on the S&P website, we can see that the Belgian bonds (3 year, AA rated) will have a yield of 4.11% while the French bonds (5 year AA+ rated) will have a yield of 4.15%. The second shareholder is concerned that this looks illogical – he suggests that surely the less risky French government bonds should have a lower yield?

Once again, the shareholder's comment shows a lack of understanding of the whole picture. As part of understanding yields on bonds, it is important to understand the expectation of an 'upward sloping yield curve'. This means that bonds with a longer period of maturity require a higher interest rate as compensation for risk. This can once again be seen by looking at the table from the S&P website – across each row in the table (so for bonds of the same risk class) the yields increase as the time to maturity increases.

Therefore, it is not valid to compare yields on bonds of different risk classes and with different terms, because doing so may throw up anomalies like this, where the better rated bond actually has a higher yield.

85 STROM CO (DEC 12 A)

> **Key answer tips**
>
> The examiner often sets questions to test that students have an awareness of real world financial management issues (such as the IMF and the banking/debt crisis here).
>
> As well as studying your text book to prepare for the P4 exam, you should regularly read a good quality business newspaper to keep up to date with current issues.
>
> Note that the examiner's model answer was accompanied by the following statement: 'The following answer is indicative. Credit will be given for alternative, valid points.'

(a) The role of the IMF is to oversee the global financial systems, in particular to stabilise international exchange rates, help countries to achieve balance of payments and facilitate in the country's development through influencing the economic policies of the country in question. Where necessary, it offers temporary loans, from member states' deposits, to countries facing severe financial and economic difficulties. These temporary loans are often offered with different levels of conditions or austerity measures.

The IMF believes that in order to regain control of the balance of payments, the country should take action to reduce the level of demand for goods and services. To achieve this, the IMF often requires countries to adopt strict austerity measures such as reducing public spending and increased taxation, as conditions of the loan.

It believes these conditions will help control the inflationary pressures on the economy, and reduce the demand for goods and services. As a result, this will help the country to move away from a position of a trade deficit and achieve control of its balance of payments.

However, these deflationary pressures may cause standards of living to fall and unemployment to rise. The IMF regards these as short-term hardships necessary to help countries sort out their balance of payment difficulties and international debt problems. The IMF has faced a number of criticisms for the conditions it has imposed, including the accusation that its policies impact more negatively on people with lower or mid-range incomes, hinder long-term development and growth, and possibly result in a continuous downward spiral of economic activity.

Strom Co trades throughout Europe and economic activity in these countries has been curtailed in the last few years due, initially, to the banking crisis, and then due to the austerity measures that governments have adopted. For retailers, this could pose two possible problems. First, with limited growth and higher taxes, people would have less money to spend. Secondly, increasing levels of unemployment would also limit disposable incomes. It is possible that customers may have curtailed their expenditure on clothes and clothing accessories in order to meet other needs.

Some companies may have to spend proportionally more on marketing and possibly offer more discounts and other customer incentives in order to stay competitive and to maintain market share. This additional cost would hit their profit levels negatively. From the details in the question, it is evident that in 2011 profits have reduced by more than the fall in sales revenue. This could be due to Strom Co being forced to spend more on activities such as marketing or it could be because it has found it difficult to reduce its cost base. More analysis is needed to determine the exact cause.

It seems that Strom Co is trying to address the problem of declining profitability by trimming its costs. In circumstances where sales revenues are declining, and it is not possible to stabilise or increase these, then cost structures may need to be altered in order to make reasonable profits.

(b)   The low-price clothing retailers might have benefited from the austerity measures because of a switch by customers from mid-price clothes to low-price clothes. If, due to the austerity measures, people have less money to spend, and if, as stated above, austerity measures impact the mid-income and low-income earners more negatively, then it is possible that their buying preferences change from mid-price to low-price clothes. This would be especially true if there is limited brand loyalty and customers perceive that the low-price items are of a similar quality or provide a better value-for-money.

On the other hand, it is possible that brand loyalty is more significant with high-price clothes, making switching to mid-price clothes difficult. Customers who buy these clothes may prefer not to switch and would rather spend less elsewhere. It is also possible that the austerity measures did not affect the population who buy high-price clothes to the same extent as other groups of the population. Or it may be that this population group is more resilient to the austerity measures imposed by the government, especially if the assertion is true that the IMF conditions affect people who are in the low or mid income categories more than the people in the high income category.

(c)   The obvious risk in reducing resources allocated to the quality control functions would be that some inspections would be reduced. This may result in defective goods being sold. The costs related to processing returns of defective goods may outweigh the savings made. Reduction in monitoring the working conditions of employees of the clothing suppliers may encourage them to retain their questionable employment practices. This may compromise the company's ethical stance and standards.

The less obvious, but more significant, risk is the impact that unethical labour practices and working conditions may have on the reputation of the company and its products. Potentially, lower quality and defective clothes could seriously harm the company's reputation and result in lower sales revenue over a long period of time. Once damaged, such reputation would be hard to rebuild. The damage in reputation of the company regarding its ethical stance could also be potentially disastrous. Different stakeholder groups could react in negative ways, for example, customers may switch their custom, investors may sell their shares and the press may run negative campaigns against the company. The consequences of such damage could be long term and sometimes permanent.

Strom Co will need to review where and how resources are allocated in order to decrease or minimise the detrimental impact of a reduction in the quality control costs. For example, savings could be made by eliminating duplicated quality control processes or eliminating processes that are not necessary. Strom Co should also evaluate whether alternative, less resource intensive processes and procedures can be implemented without compromising the quality control and monitoring of working conditions. Experts should be used to undertake the assessment. Critical processes and procedures should be retained even if they require significant resources. The risk of making errors in the assessment should be evaluated and discussed at a senior level to ensure that Strom Co is comfortable with undertaking the likely risk.

(d)   Money laundering is a process in which assets obtained or generated by criminal activity are moved or concealed to obscure their link with the crime.

Terrorist activities are sometimes funded from the proceeds of illegal activities, and perpetrators must find ways to launder the funds in order to use them without drawing the attention of authorities.

The international community has made the fight against money laundering and terrorist financing a priority.

International efforts to combat money laundering have resulted in:

- the establishment of an international task force on money laundering

- the issue of specific recommendations to be adopted by nation states

- the enactment of legislation by many countries on matters covering:

    – the criminal justice system and law enforcement

    – the financial system and its regulation

    – international cooperation.

ACCA marking scheme		
		Marks
(a) Explanation of the role and aims of the IMF		5–6
Reasons for austerity measures affecting Strom Co negatively		4–5
		——
	Maximum	10
		——
(b) Suggestion(s) for not affecting low-price retailers		2
Suggestion(s) for not affecting high-price retailers		2
		——
	Maximum	4
		——
(c) Discussion of the risks		3–4
Reduction of the detrimental impact		2–3
		——
	Maximum	6
		——
(d) Definition of money laundering		1-2
Explanation of steps taken		3-4
		——
	Maximum	5
		——
Total		**20**
		——

86 INTEGRATED REPORTING

Key answer tips

Integrated reporting is a new syllabus area, so make sure you are aware of the different concepts and terms and keep an eye open for relevant articles for further guidance on how it may be examined.

(a)   In its simplest form, integrated reporting can be understood as the merging of the sustainability report and the financial report into a single 'narrative', as described by the Marketing Director.

However, the International Integrated Reporting Council (IIRC) does not use the word 'sustainability' in its definition of the concept.

According to the IIRC's 'International <IR> Framework,' an integrated report is 'a concise communication about how an organization's strategy, governance, performance and prospects, in the context of its external environment, lead to the creation of value over the short, medium and long term.'

The key emphasis of this definition is the idea of sustainable **value creation**, which makes the report and the processes underpinning it far more valuable than simply a compliance or reporting exercise.

Furthermore, this framework is intended as **guidance** for all businesses producing integrated reports, rather than compliance with a set of rules.

(b)   The <IR> Framework recognizes the importance of looking at financial and sustainability performance in an integrated way - one that emphasizes the relationships between what it identifies as the 'six capitals':

Financial capital

This is what we traditionally think of as 'capital' - e.g. shares, bonds or banknotes. It enables the other types of Capital described below to be owned and traded.

Manufactured capital

This form of capital can be described as comprising of material goods, or fixed assets which contribute to the production process rather than being the output itself – e.g. tools, machines and buildings.

Intellectual capital

This form of capital can be described as the value of a company or organisation's employee knowledge, business training and any proprietary information that may provide the company with a competitive advantage.

Human capital

This can be described as consisting of people's health, knowledge, skills and motivation. All these things are needed for productive work.

Social capital

This can be described as being concerned with the institutions that help maintain and develop human capital in partnership with others; e.g. Families, communities, businesses, trade unions, schools, and voluntary organisations.

Natural capital

This can be described as any stock or flow of energy and material within the environment that produces goods and services. It includes resources of a renewable and non-renewable materials e.g. Land, water, energy and those factors that absorb, neutralise or recycle wastes and processes – e.g. climate regulation, climate change, CO_2 emissions.

The fundamental assumption of the <IR> Framework is that each of these types of capital—whether internal or external to the business, tangible or intangible—represents a potential source of value that must be managed for the long run in order to deliver sustainable value creation.

(c)   The objectives for integrated reporting include:

- To improve the quality of information available to providers of financial capital to enable a more efficient and productive allocation of capital
- To provide a more cohesive and efficient approach to corporate reporting that draws on different reporting strands and communicates the full range of factors that materially affect the ability of an organisation to create value over time
- To enhance accountability and stewardship for the broad base of capitals (financial, manufactured, intellectual, human, social and relationship, and natural) and promote understanding of their interdependencies
- To support integrated thinking, decision making and actions that focus on the creation of value over the short, medium and long term.

(d)   As well as external reporting to a range of stakeholders, the principles of <IR> can be extended to performance management systems. This is sometimes referred to as 'internal integrated reporting'.

An emphasis on these types of capital could result in more focussed performance management in the following ways:

- KPIs can be set up for each of the six capitals, ensuring that each of the drivers of sustainable value creation are monitored, controlled and developed.

- These can be developed further to show how the KPIs connect with different capitals, interact with, and impact each other.

- The interaction and inter-connectedness of these indicators should then be reflected in greater integration and cooperation between different functions and operations within the firm.

- This should result in greater transparency of internal communications allowing departments to appreciate better the wider implications of their activities.

- Together this should result in better decision making and value creation over the longer term.